Measuring African Development

The chief economist for the World Bank's Africa region, Shanta Devarajan, delivered a devastating assessment of the capacity of African states to measure development in his 2013 article "Africa's Statistical Tragedy". Is there a "statistical tragedy" unfolding in Africa now? If so, it becomes important to examine the roots of the problem as far as the provision of statistics in poor economies is concerned. This book, on measuring African development in the past and in the present, draws on the historical experience of colonial French West Africa, Ghana, Sudan, Mauritania and Tanzania and the more contemporary experiences of Ethiopia and the Democratic Republic of Congo. The authors each reflect on the changing ways statistics represent African economies and how they are used to govern them.

This book was published as a special issue of the *Canadian Journal of Development Studies*.

Morten Jerven is associate professor at Simon Fraser University. He is an economic historian, publishing widely on patterns of African economic development including a recent book, *Poor Numbers: How We Are Misled by African Development Statistics and What to Do About It.*

Measuring African Development

Past and Present

Edited by
Morten Jerven

Routledge
Taylor & Francis Group
LONDON AND NEW YORK

First published 2015 by Routledge

2 Park Square, Milton Park, Abingdon, Oxon OX14 4RN
711 Third Avenue, New York, NY 10017, USA

Routledge is an imprint of the Taylor & Francis Group, an informa business

First issued in paperback 2017

British Library Cataloguing in Publication Data
A catalogue record for this book is available from the British Library

ISBN 13: 978-1-138-84211-3 (hbk)
ISBN 13: 978-1-138-05665-7 (pbk)

Typeset in Times New Roman
by RefineCatch Limited, Bungay, Suffolk

Publisher's Note
The publisher accepts responsibility for any inconsistencies that may have
arisen during the conversion of this book from journal articles to book chapters,
namely the possible inclusion of journal terminology.

Disclaimer
Every effort has been made to contact copyright holders for their permission to
reprint material in this book. The publishers would be grateful to hear from any
copyright holder who is not here acknowledged and will undertake to rectify
any errors or omissions in future editions of this book.

Contents

CONTENTS

Citation Information

The chapters in this book were originally published in the *Canadian Journal of Development Studies* volume 35, issue 1 (March 2014). When citing this material, please use the original page numbering for each article, as follows:

Chapter 1
Measuring African development: past and present. Introduction
Morten Jerven
Canadian Journal of Development Studies volume 35, issue 1 (March 2014) pp. 1–8

Chapter 2
An uneven statistical topography: the political economy of household budget surveys in late colonial Ghana, 1951–1957
Gerardo Serra
Canadian Journal of Development Studies volume 35, issue 1 (March 2014) pp. 9–27

Chapter 3
Des revenus nationaux pour l'Afrique? La mesure du développement en Afrique occidentale française dans les années 1950
Vincent Bonnecase
Canadian Journal of Development Studies volume 35, issue 1 (March 2014) pp. 28–43

Chapter 4
Measuring the Sudanese economy: a focus on national growth rates and regional inequality, 1959–1964
Alden Young
Canadian Journal of Development Studies volume 35, issue 1 (March 2014) pp. 44–60

Chapter 5
The bureaucratic performance of development in colonial and post-colonial Tanzania
Felicitas Becker
Canadian Journal of Development Studies volume 35, issue 1 (March 2014) pp. 61–76

Chapter 6
Economic calculations, instability and (in)formalisation of the state in Mauritania, 2003–2011
Boris Samuel
Canadian Journal of Development Studies volume 35, issue 1 (March 2014) pp. 77–96

Chapter 7

Reliable, challenging or misleading? A qualitative account of the most recent national surveys and country statistics in the DRC
Wim Marivoet and Tom De Herdt
Canadian Journal of Development Studies volume 35, issue 1 (March 2014) pp. 97–119

Chapter 8

The use, abuse and omertà on the "noise" in the data: African democratisation, development and growth
Dwayne Woods
Canadian Journal of Development Studies volume 35, issue 1 (March 2014) pp. 120–135

Chapter 9

Measuring development progress in Africa: the denominator problem
Roy Carr-Hill
Canadian Journal of Development Studies volume 35, issue 1 (March 2014) pp. 136–154

Chapter 10

Monitoring performance or performing monitoring? Exploring the power and political dynamics underlying monitoring the MDG for rural water in Ethiopia
Katharina Welle
Canadian Journal of Development Studies volume 35, issue 1 (March 2014) pp. 155–169

Chapter 11

How to do (and how not to do) fieldwork on Fair Trade and rural poverty
Christopher Cramer, Deborah Johnston, Bernd Mueller, Carlos Oya and John Sender
Canadian Journal of Development Studies volume 35, issue 1 (March 2014) pp. 170–185

Chapter 12

Collecting high frequency panel data in Africa using mobile phone interviews
Johannes Hoogeveen, Kevin Croke, Andrew Dabalen, Gabriel Demombynes and Marcelo Giugale
Canadian Journal of Development Studies volume 35, issue 1 (March 2014) pp. 186–207

Please direct any queries you may have about the citations to
clsuk.permissions@cengage.com

Measuring African development: past and present. Introduction

Morten Jerven

School for International Studies, Simon Fraser University, Vancouver, British Columbia, Canada

ABSTRACT The chief economist for the World Bank's Africa region, Shanta Devarajan, delivered a devastating assessment of the capacity of African states to measure development in his 2013 article "Africa's Statistical Tragedy". Is there a "statistical tragedy" unfolding in Africa now? If so then examining the roots of the problem of provision of statistics in poor economies is certainly of great importance. This Special Issue on measuring African development in the past and in the present draws on the historical experience of colonial French West Africa, Ghana, Sudan, Mauritania and Tanzania and the more contemporary experiences of Ethiopia and the Democratic Republic of Congo. The authors each reflect on the changing ways statistics represent African economies and how they are used to govern them.

RÉSUMÉ Dans son article de 2013 intitulé « Africa's Statistical Tragedy », Shanta Devarajan, économiste en chef de la région Afrique à la Banque Mondiale, faisait une évaluation désastreuse de la capacité des états africains à mesurer le développement. Y a-t-il actuellement une « tragédie statistique » en Afrique? Si oui, il est assurément important d'examiner les causes du problème dans les pays pauvres. Ce numéro spécial sur la mesure du développement africain, hier et aujourd'hui, se penche sur l'histoire de l'expérience de l'Afrique-Occidentale française, du Ghana, du Soudan, de la Mauritanie et de la Tanzanie, ainsi que sur la situation plus contemporaine en Éthiopie et en République démocratique du Congo. Les auteurs réfléchissent sur l'évolution de la manière dont les statistiques représentent les économies africaines et dont elles sont utilisées pour gouverner.

Recently Shanta Devarajan, chief economist for the World Bank's Africa region, delivered a devastating assessment of the capacity of African states to evaluate development in his article "Africa's Statistical Tragedy" (Devarajan 2013). His assessment falls in line with the literature that since the 1980s has offered a generally dismal view of African states and their capacity for economic development. In recent literature, African states have often been described as either incapable of or uninterested in development (see van de Walle 2001; Bayart 2000; Bates 2008). However, the actual capacities of African states to measure, plan and target development have not been fully historicised or contextualised.

This collection of essays contributes to an analysis of measuring development in the African context by putting the role of planning and measurement in African development into historical perspective. In the context of the current renewed emphasis on developmental states in Africa (Mkandawire 2001; Kelsall 2013) and increased demands for targeted development, such as in the Millennium Development Goals (Black and White 2004), a fuller understanding of the role of data and measurement in the pursuit of progress is essential. Planning techniques and statistical tools, during colonialism, after independence and until this current day, have been and still are crucial for designing and implementing development policies and assessing the economic performance of African countries.

This Special Issue on measuring African development in the past and in the present draws on the historical experience of colonial French West Africa, Ghana, Sudan, Mauritania and Tanzania and the more contemporary experiences of Ethiopia and the Democratic Republic of Congo. The authors each reflect on the changing ways statistics represent African economies and govern them. If a "statistical tragedy" is unfolding in Africa now (Devarajan 2013) and has been doing so over the past decades (Jerven 2013a, 2013b),[1] then examining the roots of the problem of provision of statistics in poor economies is certainly of great importance.

I would suggest that the issue of measurement is best approached using interdisciplinary methods. Because numerical "facts" are products, and because they are embedded in the social and political structure of the time and place where they were made, the task of interpretation falls within the purview of many disciplines. These statistics are observations; they are approximations and best guesses. That means that the basic critical skills of a good social scientist are needed. One needs to ask the following questions: How good is the observation? Who made the observation? Under what conditions was the observation made? And while the statement that numbers need to be engaged critically applies universally, the matter is particularly pressing when evaluating African economic development.

This Special Issue includes contributions by economic historians, historians, economists, sociologists and political scientists and, like many contemporary development studies, draws upon the theoretical foundations of anthropology and philosophy rather than relying narrowly on the tools available to the classically trained statistician. The contributions assess the economic, political and cultural implications of planning and statistics across the twentieth century and into the twenty-first century in Africa. In doing so, they shed some much-needed light on some of the basic questions in measurement and development. An historical analysis of planning and statistics in Africa is an important step in building a bridge between area studies and other disciplines such as economics and economic history; even more to the point, these historical experiences have a bearing on contemporary development policy.

This Special Issue sheds light on both measurement and comparative state development capacity in sub-Saharan Africa. The central questions posed in these essays are about how and to what extent African states formulated and evaluated development in the twentieth century. The articles address the general knowledge problem in African economic and social development and help us understand what exactly we can learn from development statistics. They investigate the fundamental problems of appropriate categories and techniques of measurement and thus offer important questions about emerging development agendas, such as what type of development should be targeted in Africa and elsewhere in the post-Millennium Development Goals era (Jerven 2013c).

Why Africa?

Why a particular focus on Africa? Is the provision of statistics more constrained in Africa than elsewhere? There are a priori reasons to believe this is indeed the case. The paucity of data and uneven recordkeeping has been a particular challenge for historians of African statistics (Jerven 2011a). In the colonial period, when data and good records were available they often were produced by travelers or other observers; toward the end of the nineteenth century, colonial administrators became the main generators of economic data. At independence, not only most state borders but also basic ways of counting and organising economic knowledge were inherited from colonial times (Tilley 2011). This tradeoff, or even sometimes conflict, between the need for global standards and the local applicability of such standards continues today (Jerven 2011b). Numbers are important for knowledge, but they are also important for governance.

There are reasons to expect that poorer economies will have lower-quality statistics. A poorer economy will have relatively fewer available financial resources to support the functions of an official statistics office. Furthermore, the quality, the availability and therefore the cost of collecting statistics depends on the record keeping of individuals and companies. In poorer countries, individuals and enterprises are less likely to be officially registered and to keep formal records of their economic activities.

Additional characteristics that justify a special regional focus pertain specifically to African states. Economic historians have emphasised that African polities were typically land abundant but labour scarce (Austin 2008). This has implications for a state's property rights regime, how labour is organised and for state formation. Land has typically not been subject to private property rights, and therefore states have not collected taxes on land holdings. Where land has been relatively scarce, private property rights have developed (Berry 2002), but presently, private land titling secured by states remains the exception on the continent. Similarly, less formal labour markets have affected the recording of statistics about wages and employment. The institutions that control these important factors of economic progress are an indicator of the power and legitimacy of the state. Political science scholars have established a link between historically low population densities and the contemporary weakness of African states (Herbst 2000). Historians have used the concept of the "gatekeeper state" to characterise how colonial and postcolonial African states have adapted to their inability to control access to land (Cooper 2002). Unable to collect taxes on land, income or production, states settled for collecting taxes at ports by levying duties on exports and imports.

It is not easy to gauge exactly how the statistical capacity of contemporary African states measures up to the capacity of states in other regions of the world, but the closest thing to a comparative metric is provided by the Bulletin Board on Statistical Capacity developed by the Development Data Group at the World Bank (World Bank 2011). They compile the Statistical Capacity Indicator, which ranks countries from 0 to 100, on the statistical methodology, the source data and the periodicity and timeliness of the official statistics each country provides. African countries score below the world average in statistical capacity. For 2012, the average overall score for 53 African countries considered was 59, while the average of the whole sample of the countries was 66. The metric covers only the countries to which the International Bank for Reconstruction and Development (IBRD) or International Development Association (IDA) lend. Aside from the West Bank and Gaza, which scored 0 for overall statistical capacity in the years 2005 through 2008, African countries received the minimum overall score for the years 2004 to 2012. There are also high-scoring countries on the continent (Egypt, Morocco, South Africa, Malawi and Ethiopia), and some countries have shown slow improvement over the decade (including Mozambique and Uganda). But others have shown a steady decline (Cote d'Ivoire, Senegal). The relative ranking average for the African continent was 59 out of 100. In comparison, Latin American countries averaged 77 out of 100, countries in Europe and Central Asia that receive IDA and IBRD assistance averaged 68 out of 100, and countries in East Asia and the Pacific averaged 70 out of 100. The quality of metadata on the reliability of statistics can be as poor as the statistics themselves (Jerven 2013d), but it does at least confirm the underlying problem of the poor capacity of states to measure and monitor development in the African region.

Why the history of measurement matters

States do not collect statistics just because they are curious. The statistics they collect reflect their interests. The roots of the word "statistics" lie in the Latin word *statisticus*, which means "of state affairs". The term as used today refers to data collected by states about economic or social conditions. Thus, looking at the record of how states have measured themselves provides a direct view of how it is to be "seeing like a state", as James Scott (1998) put it.

For example, although colonial administrations collected meticulous statistics about trade, they did so only for areas the colonial state controlled and saw as important. The validity of the statistics they collected could be interpreted as varying with the power or legitimacy of the state and/or the agency acting on its behalf. The ability to collect information and the ability to collect taxes are closely related, and the form and extent of monitoring and intervention states have undertaken have varied over time and across space (Jerven 2013a).

History matters for economic development. The papers in this Special Issue underline how the history of measurement matters and suggest that the bureaucratic record of states provide insight into the political economy of states and thus give a good indication of how states changed over the twentieth century.

Although it is not possible to obtain facts directly on living standards, poverty or progress from an analysis of the statistical record, that record will give a clear indication of the state of knowledge in development. It is also possible to draw insights based on what was counted and how it was counted. A comparison may be made to the history of maps of Africa made by Europeans. The earliest maps of the continent offered surprising and fantastic details about the interior, whereas maps drawn in the early years of European exploration were filled with blank spaces in the areas representing unknown territories and focused largely on waterways and navigable routes (Rogers 2012). At the end of the nineteenth century, maps were drawn with straight lines, reflecting the geopolitical agreements made at the Berlin Conference in 1884 (Green 2012). The maps tell you more about the intellectual mindset of those who drew the maps than they do about the physical geography of Africa.

The statistical record can yield similar insights. This is not just a matter of history; the mindsets of statisticians translate into policy. In the "least developed economies", and most of these are on the African continent, numbers do more than inform politics; they sometimes circumvent political debate altogether – as embodied in the phrase "evidence based policy". The policy circle is often depoliticised and is dominated by technocrats, donors and representatives of international organisations who may abort, change or initiate policies based on weak statistics. Such decisions include rankings of countries as low or middle income or assessments of policies as successes or failures. In contemporary debates on development, there are calls for a "data revolution" to inform future development policy. Such calls must be based on an understanding that how progress is measured and defined affects states and development debates and is crucial for understanding future trajectories of development in African and beyond. A failure to understand how evidence is generated may result in "policy based evidence" instead of "evidence based policy".

Organisation of the Special Issue

In this Special Issue we are first taken to the Gold Coast, the former British colony that makes up the territory that is contemporary Ghana. Here, the Office of the Government Statistician was instituted in 1948. Gerardo Serra analyses the 1950s, when household budget surveys emerged as an important statistical tool. Borrowing a term from Catherine Boone (2003), who has shown that the interaction of rulers with local conditions resulted in an "uneven institutional topography" in Ghana, Senegal and Cote d'Ivoire, Serra suggests that the wide variations Boone identified in the institutions of the nation-state were reflected in the ways planners designed household budgets in different parts of the Gold Coast, resulting in what Serra calls an "uneven statistical topography". He particularly emphasises the uneven geographical sampling in household surveys.

Vincent Bonnecase investigates national accounting in colonial French West Africa. There, the national accounting tool was developed in the interwar years. The account starts in 1953, when the Finance Directorate of French West Africa began to perform the calculation of national income. Bonnecase emphasises that not only were these figures highly unreliable, they also reflected political priorities rather than economic realities.

Alden Young focuses on the decolonisation moment in Sudan and the implementation and use of national accounting in the first ten year development plan in the independent nation (1961/1962–1970/1971). He pays particular attention to how the bureaucracy and its practices, particularly planning, served to structure elite conflict and bargaining and argues that policymaking and bureaucracy in postcolonial Africa cannot be dismissed as a purely decorative performance. Young contends that the language used by bureaucrats to discuss and analyse economic development in turn determined which demands on the state were deemed legitimate. He also notes that national income accounting heightened Sudanese planners' awareness of income inequality between their nation and other states but decreased their awareness of regional inequality within Sudan.

Felicitas Becker adds another perspective on development planning as a bureaucratic performance in her study of agricultural policies in colonial and postcolonial Tanzania. The fallacy of grand development plans in this region has been well illustrated in studies of the groundnut scheme in the colonial period (Hogendorn and Scott 1981) and of villagisation in the 1970s (Hyden 1981). Becker analyses recurring and changing approaches in small-scale projects that have targeted a specific crop, cassava root, in southeast Tanzania since the 1920s. She argues that the best way to make sense of the disparity between official documents and development realities is to think of the documents as political rhetoric. In Becker's view, these official documents on development projects are not the technocratic assessments and evaluations they purport to be. But neither are they dominated by the looming presence of a forceful state. They are better understood as expressions of bureaucrats seeking to legitimise their activities.

Boris Samuel takes us to Mauritania and shows how the mismatch between reported numbers and real economic data can happen. He documents the crisis that the authorities in Mauritania experienced in 2004, when the new governor of the Central Bank of Mauritania flew to Washington DC and had to admit that previous macroeconomic data had been falsified and that crucial indicators such as holdings of foreign reserves had been misreported. Samuel's analysis of the use of macroeconomic calculation in Mauritania from 2003 to 2010 shows that in contrast to what most theories of neopatrimonial or failed states would suggest, the use of statistics in Mauritania is not a case of inability or neglect. Rather, technical competence is part of the legitimate repertoire that can be used politically on the domestic and international scene.

Wim Marivoet and Tom De Herdt study what we really know about the Democratic Republic of Congo (DRC) and offer a qualitative interpretation of the national information architecture there from 1970 to 2010. The authors display the arbitrariness of GDP estimates in the DRC, which they describes as the "dubious outcome of an obscure estimation process", in an analysis that coheres well with other assessments of statistics in the DRC and in other African economies (MacGaffey 1991; Jerven 2013a). Marivoet and De Herdt extend the analysis to microlevel and survey data and show why survey information is particularly challenging to use because of problems with sampling. All sampling designs in the DRC rely on the 1984 census, which was poorly processed. The authors conclude that the problem is not always the quality of primary data itself; rather, it is limitations in access to data and fragmented metadata. They suggest that scholars and analysts should not dismiss such numbers altogether but should instead pay attention to the many warning signs that go with them.

Dwayne Woods offers a study of how scholars, particularly those who are interested in analysing correlates of economic growth and political variables, approach the data problem. He argues that overwhelming evidence suggests that most data on sub-Saharan Africa is "noisy" and that it follows that scholars should always take this fact into account. However, his review of recent important work shows that most scholars do not take data quality into account and instead make very brave causal assertions based on data that we know to be very weak and sometimes biased. Woods concludes that this is a major constraint in the generation of knowledge about the politics of African economic development.

Roy Carr-Hill offers an evaluation of the evidence in the denominator. When we make statements about per capita trends, such as measures of economic progress (economic growth) or any other indicator, we rely on a total population estimate. In order to get this information we need a population census. Carr-Hill reminds us that, in contrast, surveys that are used to assess progress toward development goals are based increasingly on household surveys. By design, these surveys omit the homeless, those in institutions, and mobile, nomadic or pastoralist populations. Moreover, in practice, household surveys typically underrepresent those in fragile, disjointed households, slum populations and those living in areas that pose security risks. Carr-Hill concludes that, because of these factors, existing measures of progress toward the Millennium Development Goals are positively biased.

Katherina Welle takes us to Ethiopia and studies how politics entered the measurement of progress toward one very important development target: access to clean water. Her research on monitoring the water supply in rural Ethiopia shows that different measurement methods yielded very different results: by one method, only a quarter of users had access to water in Ethiopia's southern region; by another, more than half had access. Welle explores how power and political dynamics are inherent in the monitoring of sector performance.

Christopher Cramer, Deborah Johnston, Bernd Mueller, Carlos Oya and John Sender present a study of a different issue in Ethiopia. They report on an attempt to deal with some of the problems in the methodological foundations of many rural socioeconomic studies, especially those that study the impact of fair trade. Many studies suffer from lack of clarity about research site selection, and ill-considered sampling methods are often compounded by ideological blind spots. Some studies have missed crucial dynamics and have neglected some of the poorest residents because of poor survey design. Their study shows that updating household lists using GPS technology and making an effort to record the presence of short-term residents gives a different and more balanced picture of the impacts of fair trade.

Johannes Hoogeveen, Kevin Croke, Andrew Dabalen, Gabriel Demombynes and Marcelo Giugale also emphasise some of the opportunities that come with new technology in measurement. They report on results from a pilot project that used mobile phones to collect high-frequency panel data on poverty and development. These data may yield different and timelier data than other, more time-consuming, surveys. The main constraints are attrition among respondents and the problem of reaching the poorest of the poor. Their study points to the importance of thinking of innovative methods that can use new technologies to collect data that capture change and progress in a way that is suitable for poorer economies.

Implications for policy and further study

The state of the scholarly literature today, particularly in African studies and international development but also more generally in the social sciences, is deeply and doubly unsatisfactory. To date it has either neglected the issue of data quality and accepted national statistical data at face value or dismissed the data as unreliable and therefore irrelevant. The articles in this Special Issue often point to the fact that numbers are powerful elements of political debate; they can inform or they can misinform. In the "least developed economies", policymakers may make key decisions about economic development based on very unreliable statistics.

More research is needed on how African states represent and measure their economies and economic progress. Although these numbers are shaped by global standards, they are ultimately determined by local conditions. These articles show how this process has an effect on the value of statistical information and how it affects policy formulation and implementation. It is hoped that this historical and political inquiry into the construction of development indicators is a step toward a more precise assessment of what is known about economic development in Africa and beyond. On this basis it should be possible to build a more balanced appraisal of the role of states in economic development.

This Special Issue is an encouragement to further scholarship. Histories of development are written with these numbers; decisions are made because of them. Scholars who already are critical of how numbers are used in both scholarship and policy should use their critical skills to engage further with the numbers. Numbers should and will continue to be important for the study and practice of development. Decisions about what to measure, who to count and by whose authority the final number is selected do matter. I hope this Special Issue leaves us better equipped to take on the task of taking part in these decisions and in debates on measurement.

Acknowledgements

I am first of all extremely grateful for all the contributing authors to this Special Issue, and to all the external reviewers who commented on papers. I have received excellent advice and editorial assistance from Thanh Lam, Martha Snodgrass and John Harriss at the *Canadian Journal of Development Studies*. The papers were presented at the Centre for African Studies Annual International Conference, University of Edinburgh, June 2012, African Studies Association UK, Leeds, 6–8 September 2012, and finally at the conference on African Economic Development: Measuring Success and Failure, Vancouver, 18–20 April 2013. I am grateful to organisers and participants at all these events.

The conference that was held in Vancouver Canada, 18–20 April 2013, was supported by Simon Fraser University (with funding from the School for International Studies, the Dean of Faculty of Arts and Social Sciences, Vice President Academic and Vice President Research); Social Sciences and Humanities Research Council, International Development Research Center, the African Economic History Network, the African Development Bank and the Global Venture Fund.

Biographical note

Morten Jerven is associate professor at Simon Fraser University in Vancouver, Canada. He is an economic historian, has published widely on patterns of African economic development including a recent book, *Poor Numbers: How We Are Misled by African Development Statistics and What to Do About It*, published by Cornell University Press in 2013. Jerven's second book, *Economic Growth and Measurement Reconsidered in Botswana, Kenya, Tanzania, and Zambia, 1965–1995*, will be published by Oxford University Press in 2014.

Note

1. Or, as one observer suggests, a statistical renaissance is currently taking place (Kiregyera 2013).

References

Austin, Gareth. 2008. "Resources, Techniques and Strategies South of the Sahara: Revising the Factor Endowments Perspective on African Economic Development, 1500–2000." *Economic History Review* 61 (3): 587–624.

Bates, R. H. 2008. *When Things Fell Apart.* Cambridge: Cambridge University Press.

Bayart, Jean-François. 2000. "Africa in the World: A History of Extraversion." *African Affairs* 99 (395): 217–267.

Berry, Sara. 2002. "Debating the Land Question in Africa." *Comparative Studies in Society and History* 44 (4): 638–668.

Black, Richard, and White, Howard, eds. 2004. *Targeting Development: Critical Perspectives on the Millennium Development Goals.* New York: Routledge.

Boone, Catherine. 2003. *Political Topographies of the African State: Territorial Authority and Institutional Choice.* Cambridge: Cambridge University Press.

Cooper, Frederick. 2002. *Africa since 1940: The Past of the Present.* New York: Cambridge University Press.

Devarajan, Shantayanan. 2013. "Africa's Statistical Tragedy." *Review of Income and Wealth* 59 (S1): S9–S15.

Green, Elliot. 2012. "On the Size and Shape of African States." *International Studies Quarterly* 56: 229–244.

Herbst, Jeffrey I. 2000. *States and Power in Africa: Comparative Lessons in Authority and Control.* Princeton, NJ: Princeton University Press.

Hogendorn, J. S., and Scott, K. M. 1981. "The East African Groundnut Scheme: Lessons of a Large-Scale Agricultural Failure." *African Economic History* 10: 81–115.

Hyden, Goran. 1981. *Beyond Ujamaa in Tanzania: Underdevelopment and an Uncaptured Peasantry.* Berkeley: University of California Press.

Jerven, Morten. 2011a. "A Clash of Disciplines? Economists and Historians Approaching the African Past." *Economic History of Developing Regions* 26 (2): 111–124.

Jerven, Morten. 2011b. "Users and Producers of African Income: Measuring the Progress of African Economies." *African Affairs* 110 (439): 169–190.

Jerven, Morten. 2013a. *Poor Numbers: How We Are Misled by African Development Statistics and What to Do About It.* Ithaca, NY: Cornell University Press.

Jerven, Morten. 2013b. "Comparability of GDP Estimates in Sub-Saharan Africa: The Effects of Revisions in Sources and Methods since Structural Adjustment." *Review of Income and Wealth* 59 (S1): S16–S36.

Jerven, Morten. 2013c. "What Kind of Data Revolution Do We Need?" *Post2015.org*, November 5. Accessed December 10, 2013. http://post2015.org/2013/11/05/new-blog-series-what-kind-of-data-revolution-do-we-need-for-post-2015/

Jerven, Morten. 2013d. "Why We Need to Invest in African Development Statistics: From a Diagnosis of Africa's Statistical Tragedy towards a Statistical Renaissance." *African Arguments*, September 26. Accessed December 10, 2013. http://africanarguments.org/2013/09/26/why-we-need-to-invest-in-african-development-statistics-from-a-diagnosis-of-africas-statistical-tragedy-towards-a-statistical-renaissance-by-morten-jerven/

Kelsall, Tim. 2013. *Business, Politics and the State in Africa: Challenging the Orthodoxies on Growth and Transformation.* London: Zed Books.

Kiregyera, Ben. 2013. "The Dawning of a Statistical Renaissance in Africa." Paper presented at the conference African Economic Development: Measuring Success and Failure, Simon Fraser University, Vancouver, April 18–20.

MacGaffey, Janet. 1991. *The Real Economy of Zaire: The Contribution of Smuggling & Other Unofficial Activities to National Wealth.* Philadelphia: University of Pennsylvania Press.

Mkandawire, Thandika. 2001. "Thinking about Developmental States in Africa." *Cambridge Journal of Economics* 25: 289–314.

Rogers, Simon. 2012. "Africa Mapped: How Europe Drew a Continent." *Datablog*, October 2. Accessed December 10, 2013. http://www.theguardian.com/news/datablog/gallery/2012/oct/02/africa-maps-history#/?picture=397029248&index=1

Scott, James C. 1998. *Seeing Like a State: How Certain Schemes to Improve the Human Condition Have Failed.* New Haven, CT: Yale University Press.

Tilley, Helen. 2011. *Africa as a Living Laboratory: Empire, Development, and the Problem of Scientific Knowledge, 1870–1950.* Chicago: University of Chicago Press.

Van de Walle, N. 2001. *African Economies and the Politics of Permanent Crisis, 1979–1999.* Cambridge: Cambridge University Press.

World Bank. 2011. "Bulletin Board on Statistical Capacity." Accessed December 10, 2013. http://go.worldbank.org/LP2D32CR70

An uneven statistical topography: the political economy of household budget surveys in late colonial Ghana, 1951–1957

Gerardo Serra

Department of Economic History, London School of Economics and Political Science, London, UK

ABSTRACT   This paper reconstructs the history of household budget surveys in late colonial Ghana. It is argued that the household budgets institutionalised an "uneven statistical topography". This unevenness comprises a spatial and a conceptual dimension. The former refers to the choice of the sampling locations, closely mirroring the uneven will of the state to exercise control over different parts of the country. The latter refers to the fact that household budget surveys incorporated different cognitive tools and served different aims depending on what the government envisaged as its political and economic agenda in the surveyed areas.

RÉSUMÉ   Cette recherche s'intéresse à l'histoire des enquêtes portant sur le budget des ménages à la fin de la période coloniale au Ghana. Elle affirme que les budgets des ménages ont institutionnalisé une « topographie statistique irrégulière », qui comprend une dimension spatiale et une dimension conceptuelle. La dimension spatiale porte sur le choix des endroits étudiés, qui reflétait la volonté de l'État de contrôler certaines régions du pays. La dimension conceptuelle fait référence au fait que les variables et la façon de les mesurer différaient d'une enquête à l'autre selon les objectifs poursuivis par l'agenda politique et économique du gouvernement dans les régions où les enquêtes étaient menées.

Introduction

The literature on the role of the state in African economic development is extremely rich, cutting across disciplines and comprising many contrasting positions.[1] Yet, what is usually missing from these discussions is an understanding of the cognitive basis upon which African policymakers decided to (or not to) act. As argued some time ago by Friedrich von Hayek, the problem faced by policymakers in their attempt to construct a "rational economic order" is not simply one of allocation of scarce resources; it is rather "a problem of the utilisation of knowledge not given to anyone in its totality" (Hayek 1945, 520).

There is little doubt that, historically, the collection and dissemination of statistics emerged as the privileged way for the state to aggregate otherwise dispersed information in order to reach informed policy decisions.[2]

Although historians of statistics have gone as far as to identify in specific historical moments a "co-construction of state and statistics" (Desrosières 2003, 560), still very little is known about this co-evolution in the African context.[3] This paper contributes to fill this gap by looking at the construction of statistics in colonial Ghana (Gold Coast)[4] in the phase of decolonisation, ending with the achievement of independence from Britain in 1957. As rightly lamented by Toyin Falola (1996, xx) in his study of Nigerian colonial planning, historians of decolonisation have paid much attention to "the more dramatic issues of constitution-making, political party formation, emergence of the first generation of leaders" and, more generally, have focused on "the politics of decolonisation". Admittedly historical research on decolonisation has become much more inclusive in recent years, dealing with issues as different as sexuality, sport and culture,[5] yet little has changed with reference to such "unfashionable" topics as economic planning and statistics.

The departure point of this work is the assumption that statistics are not necessarily the "neutral reflection" of social and economic reality; rather they "are produced by particular social actors in an effort to make sense of the complex and unmanageable reality that surrounds them" (Tooze 2001, 3). However, rather than understanding the construction of statistical knowledge as a by-product of the aesthetics of high modernism (Scott 1998), or as part of a Foucauldian discourse (Ferguson 1994), this paper is closer to what might be labelled a "political economy of statistics" (Jerven 2013, Chap. 3, 2014, 2): an approach that tries to assess the impact of the political and economic context in which statistics are produced on their design and use.[6] In order to be accurate such an analysis cannot ignore the historical specificities of African states. Catherine Boone (2003) has convincingly shown with reference to Ghana, Ivory Coast and Senegal that the exercise of power by African states, and the economic and political strategies arising from the interaction of rulers with local conditions, resulted in an "uneven institutional topography". This paper suggests the wide variations identified by Boone at the institutional level within the nation-state were reflected in the ways in which planners designed household budgets in different parts of the country, resulting in what is called an "uneven statistical topography".

The first section of this paper places the rise of household budget surveys within the history of Ghanaian economic statistics. The second section discusses some of the problems arising from the construction of the surveys, and shows how the choice of the location for the surveys closely mirrored the political interests of those in power. The third section analyses the construction of household budget surveys in urban areas, arguing that in this case household budget surveys were mostly used as a tool to measure expenditures while dismissing differences among the sources and compositions of incomes. The fourth section looks at the introduction of household budget surveys in the cocoa producing areas, and claims that in this case the construction of income–expenditure tables mirrored a broader attempt of the state to reduce its uncertainty about agricultural production figures, and reform the institutional framework in which the production of cocoa took place through the provision of credit to the farmers. The concluding section summarises the interplay between state ambitions and the evolution of household survey work at this key period in Ghana's history.

The rise of household budget surveys as a tool of enquiry

Statistics in Africa is as old as colonial rule itself. Since the late nineteenth century, colonial administrations under British rule published yearly *Blue Books* with basic statistical information on trade, health, education and, occasionally, production and prices. Following the spectacular success of Ghanaian cocoa for export, the need was felt for more accurate information about agriculture, leading in 1928 to the reorganisation of the Department of Agriculture and the inclusion of a new section devoted to statistical work. G. Auchinleck, the Director of Agriculture, forcefully stated: "In a country of illiterate farmers, no exact information is obtainable unless special arrangements are made for obtaining it, and no impartial information is available unless Government issues it" (Gold Coast Colony 1932, 19). The 1930s were characterised by a tension between the demand for more standardised and detailed data (Clauson 1937, 3–4) and less financial resources available for statistical work (Gold Coast Colony 1934, 15–16).

If the Great Depression already provided a strong incentive to collect more and better statistics, the Second World War had an even greater impact on the importance attached to statistical knowledge in the African colonies. The Colonial Economic Advisory Committee (CEAC), in charge since 1943 for providing recommendations to both colonial administrations and the Colonial Office on matters of economic and statistical policy, aptly summarised the prevailing intellectual atmosphere:

> Hardly any colonial government in the past has consciously planned the development of its territory. Law and administration have been the favourite sons, education and public health the not so favoured daughters. […] This approach to colonial administration belongs to an era that is passed. ("CEAC (44) 16 Appendix II … ", BLPES CEAC 4/7)

Although there were wide divergences between the more conservative views prevailing at the Economics Department of the Colonial Office under the direction of Sydney Caine and the more interventionist positions expressed through the CEAC (especially by W. Arthur Lewis) on issues as different as agriculture, foreign capital, secondary industries and the role of the state in promoting development (Ingham 1992, Tignor 2006, Chap. 2), there was an unanimous call for more and better evidence on the colonial economies. This gained further momentum after the demise of the CEAC and the creation of institutions like the Colonial Economic Development Council (CEDC) and the Colonial Economic Research Committee (CERC), which recognised that "Colonial statistics were quite inaccurate and misleading" ("Colonial Economic Research Committee … ", BLPES CERC 1/1) and attached much importance to the need of building a wider and more accurate statistical basis to inform policy action. Furthermore, the demand and the supply of more economic data in the postwar world was also a consequence of the creation of international organisations like the United Nations, the International Monetary Fund and the International Bank for Reconstruction and Development. These institutions contributed to the consolidation of an international epistemic space, in which knowledge about African economies could be gathered, packed and travel more easily (Speich 2011).

It was in this context that the most important change in the institutional landscape in which statistics were constructed in Ghana took place: the establishment of the Office of the Government Statistician. After a brief phase in which different alternative institutional arrangements were compared, it was finally agreed that "the object to be aimed at is a self-contained Statistical Office, not subordinated to any one Department, but serving and working with all Departments which require statistical information or interpretation in any form in the course of their duties" ("Telegram from the Secretary of State … ", PRAAD RG 2/1/62, 51 [archivist's page number]). The early years of the Office of the Government Statistician, which was formally established in 1948, were characterised by a fervent activity; the production of economic statistics witnessed both an increase in its technical sophistication and an expansion in its domain of inquiry. A part of the work of the statistical office consisted in the creation of macroeconomic statistics. In 1952 what was expected to be a simple report on the conditions and the bottlenecks of the building industry, prepared by Dudley Seers and C. R. Ross of the Oxford Institute of Statistics and published under the auspices of the Office of the Government Statistician, ended up pioneering the construction of national income accounts and social accounting matrixes for the Gold Coast economy (Seers and Ross 1952). The publication in 1953 of the first *Economic Survey of the Gold Coast*, resulting from the cooperation of the government statistical service with the Ministry of Finance included "for the first time an estimate of the Gold Coast's balance of payments and capital investment" (Gold Coast Ministry of Finance 1953, Foreword).

But the construction of macroeconomic statistics did not constitute the area to which the statistical service devoted most energies and work. Beginning in 1952 the Office of the Government Statistician started preparing a new series of Statistical and Economic Papers to make available the results of special inquiries and publish information "of significance in relation to the general economic life of the Gold Coast" (Gold Coast Office of the Government Statistician 1953a, iii). It is striking to note that the first seven papers, accounting for the whole period under consideration,[7] were all inquiries based on household budget surveys. They are presented in Table 1.[8]

The main reason behind the rise of budget surveys as a statistical instrument has to be found in the increasing concerns of colonial governments, from the 1940s on, with African poverty and welfare.[9] Budget surveys were perceived as a reliable basis for the construction of a consumer price index and the most rigorous tool for "measuring standards of living and variations in consumption patterns" (Colonial Office 1951, 13). Furthermore, given the scarce financial resources available for statistical work in the African colonies, budget surveys could serve simultaneously different purposes, including checking the population figures obtained in censuses (Colonial Office 1954, 8) and provide additional data for the construction of national income accounts (Ghana Central Bureau of Statistics 1961, 3).

Constructing household budget surveys

Although household budget surveys were being increasingly perceived as useful tools to inform policy-making, the design of rigorous inquiries and the collection of data in the field posed many conceptual and practical problems. The first, and one that still haunts contemporary statisticians working on African economies, is an appropriate definition of "family" as an economic unit.[10] The minutes of the first conference of statisticians working in sub-Saharan Africa, which took place in 1951 in Salisbury (today's Zimbabwe), suggest that Ghana was one of the first countries attempting to tackle systematically this issue; A. B. Reisz, first government statistician of the country, stated that "the difficulty of defining the family was so complex in the Gold Coast that the family as a unit had been eliminated. Instead it had been decided to use the household group" ("Minutes of Conference of Statisticians ... ", PRO CO 852/1078/1, 36 [original typescript page]).[11]

A second crucial set of problems was related to sampling: while the advantages deriving from a rigorous process of random sampling were acknowledged, this was sometimes not feasible in practice. In the case of the agricultural survey of South-East Akim Abuakwa (discussed in the next

Table 1. Statistical and economic papers published by the Office of the Government Statistician (Gold Coast/Ghana), 1953–1960.

Paper number	Date of publication	Title of paper
1	September 1953	Agricultural Statistical Survey of South-East Akim Abuakwa, 1952–1953
2	December 1953	1953 Accra Survey of Household Budgets
3	June 1955	1954 Akuse Survey of Household Budgets
4	March 1956	Sekondi-Takoradi Survey of Population and Household Budgets, 1955
5	March 1956	Kumasi Survey of Population and Household Budgets, 1955
6	July 1958	Survey of Population and Budgets of Cocoa Producing Families in the Odu-Swedru-Asamankese Area, 1955–1956
7	December 1960	Survey of Cocoa Producing Families in Ashanti, 1956–1957

Source: Gold Coast Office of the Government Statistician (1953a, 1953b, 1955, 1956a, 1956b) and Ghana Office of the Government Statistician (1958, 1960).

section), random sampling was not possible for the lack of a complete list of villages (Gold Coast Office of the Government Statistician 1953a, 2). The way in which the selection of samples was conducted in practice incorporated many extra-statistical considerations. The First Conference of Colonial Government Statisticians, which met in London in 1950, agreed that the "necessity to gain the confidence of the public would sometimes imply the choice of a larger budget sample than was scientifically required" (Colonial Office 1951, 12). This observation points at the political undertone of the practice of statistical work, and stresses the crucial importance of gaining the trust of the subjects observed if accurate information had to be collected.[12] A monumental survey of Yoruba cocoa farmers in Nigeria published in 1956 under the auspices of the Nigerian Cocoa Marketing Board reveals that the procedure of random sampling could not be adopted, among other reasons because "there was no certainty of even likelihood of obtaining the cooperation of the headmen and farmers in villages chosen at random" (Galletti, Baldwin, and Dina 1956, xxiv).[13]

The history of Ghanaian statistics provides several examples of the extent to which the collection of statistics involved attempts on part of the investigators to build trust in the subjects observed. In 1932, during a study of the cocoa producing village of Akokoaso, before the inquiry could begin a meeting with the chiefs, the elders and the villagers had to be held to explain the reasons why such an inquiry was undertaken, and convince the villagers that the government had no other goal than that of gathering knowledge about agricultural yields, labour costs and other sociological data. W. H. Beckett, the author of the survey, not only had to rely on the contacts established during his previous work in Akokoaso as a District Agricultural Officer, but he felt the need to send two months before the beginning of the inquiry "an African Overseer [...] to form contacts" (Beckett [1944] 1979, 1). Sometimes the necessary trust could not be established, with detrimental consequences: reporting about her 1943 study of standards of living in Accra, economist Peter Ady wrote that the house-to-house visits necessary for the inquiry were met with misunderstanding and hostility, to the point that "abuse has sometimes been violent, and the continuation of the queries has taken great personal courage" ("Letter of Peter Ady to the Secretariat ... ", PRAAD RG 3/1/253, 2 [archivist's page number]). Furthermore, the atmosphere of distrust in which statistical work took place in colonial Ghana was not limited to the interaction between observers and observed subjects, but sometimes infected also the technologies of measurement. In occasion of the 1952 survey of South-East Akim Abuawka, "compasses and chains were found to arouse suspicion of farmers" (Gold Coast Office of the Government Statistician 1953a, 5). This forced the statisticians to come up with a second-best way of measuring the extension of the plots, consisting in pacing "along each side of a farm, observing the general shape at the same time, and then [plotting] the results on a grid using a scale of 50 yards to the inch [...]. From the grid the total farm area was read off in acres" (Gold Coast Office of the Government Statistician 1953a, 5). It is likely that this resulted in a loss of accuracy.

Although actual statistical work involved a good deal of contingencies, negotiation and trust building, all the budget surveys under analysis shared certain formal features. They were all comprised of two parts: "first an enumeration of a fairly large proportion of the total population and second a detailed budget record over a period of one month covering a smaller sample of families drawn from those visited during the population enquiry" (Gold Coast Office of the Government Statistician 1956b, 1). Moreover, the budget records were created by filling in tables listing the elements that were identified as the main sources of income and expenditure for the families selected in the second part of the survey. Finally, the inquiries relied on the work of a large number of local enumerators and interviewers including temporary staff and members of the permanent field organisation of the statistical office, with the exact number depending on the size of the survey area and the final sample selected. The employment of a large number of enumerators, although placing an additional strain on the limited funds available for statistical work, was largely a consequence of the fact that widespread illiteracy made unviable the option of sending printed questionnaires and asking people to compile them. On the other hand, considering the strong incentives on the part of the observed subjects to underreport or overreport, face-to-face data collection was also useful for increasing the accuracy of the information collected.[14]

Yet, in spite of this common structure, there was a certain variety in the main problems addressed by the survey and in the extent to which these were supplemented by other cognitive tools. What accounted for the differences among the surveys under examination is the theme of the next sections. Before turning to this, the geographical distribution of the surveyed areas should be noted.

Indeed all household budget surveys in the period under consideration took place in the southern and central regions, to the exclusion of the northern ones, which included some of the poorest areas of the country.[15] One of the few contemporary economic studies available about the Northern Territories, prepared by the agricultural economist John R. Raeburn for the Colonial Office (rather than for the Office of the Government Statistician) presented a picture of underdevelopment and backwardness with limited prospects of change:

> Disease and slave raiding have resulted in the depopulation of large areas of land which are reported to be fertile, while elsewhere increases of population have led to misuse of land. […]
> Production of crops, livestock and forest products is limited in all areas by long dry season. […] All areas are subject to risks of poor crops due to insufficient or ill-timed rainfall during the wet season. […]
> So far no mineral deposits of considerable economic value have been reported. […] It is unlikely that supplies of underground oil exist. […]
> Production and incomes are not only low: they are also unstable. (Raeburn 1951, iii, 2, 3, 7)[16]

Considering that the household budget surveys emerged in the 1950s as the most rigorous tool available for gaining information about welfare conditions, the statistical neglect of the Northern Territories is perhaps symptomatic of the region's remoteness from what the rulers in Accra identified as the cores of their political and economic interests. The "uneven political topography" described by Boone (2003) resulted also in an "uneven statistical topography": the household budget surveys prepared by the statistical office closely mirrored the will of the state, constrained by scarcity of human and material resources that could be employed to count people and resources and measure incomes and expenditures, to extend its power over different parts of its territory.[17] It is in this sense that the uneven statistical topography institutionalised by the household budget surveys assumed a spatial and geographical connotation.

Measuring expenditures: household budget surveys in urban areas

Four of the five household budget surveys published between 1953 and 1956 dealt with urban areas. The use of statistics to assess living conditions in urban areas did not begin with the 1950s household budget surveys; instead it should be placed in a longer history of empirical studies promoted by the colonial administration to measure the impact of price controls and assess urban welfare during the Second World War (Gold Coast 1942; Gold Coast 1943). In spite of the fact that a 1945 inquiry into the costs of living in Accra noted that, unlike traders, fixed income groups "suffered a steady deterioration in their standards of living" ("Wages & Standards of Living. Accra 1945", PRAAD ADM 5/3/52/15, 12 [original typescript page]), the government proved unable to protect urban purchasing power from postwar inflation. The discontent of urban consumers reached its climax in 1947, and exploded leading to the so-called Accra riots. The riots in Accra, which shortly afterwards spread to other main urban areas of the country, abruptly accelerated decolonisation. Kwame Nkrumah, who had been jailed by the British for contributing to mobilise discontent, was the leader of the Convention People Party (CPP), which won the 1951 election. The 1951 election de facto marked the end of colonial rule and the beginning of an hybrid phase in which Nkrumah served as leader of the government business, before the country could achieve full independence from British rule in 1957.[18] The point that should be taken here is that Nkrumah knew all too well how crucial the support of urban constituencies was for the survival of his government.[19]

Thus it should not come as a surprise if a great deal of the statistical work conducted in the 1950s was connected with attempts at measuring the welfare of urban communities.[20] An early project that involved the new Office of the Government Statistician was the survey on bread consumption in Accra, prepared in cooperation with the Medical Department in September 1950. The slim survey, amounting to little more than 10 pages, found that bread, cassava and corn were "generally the food with the highest frequency of consumption"; that bread was being consumed at least once a day (although not excessively, to the point of becoming dangerous for the organism due to its low vitamin content); and that the main sources of bread were either local bakeries or itinerant market women. In no recorded case did home baking serve only household consumption ("Report on a Survey on Bread Consumption", PRAAD RG 4/1/124, 6–7 [archivist's numbers]). Yet the statistical methodology of the survey left much to be desired: although the authors admitted that "the use of a statistically random sample would be a great improvement", the sample of households interviewed consisted of families already known to the Medical Department (PRAAD RG 4/1/124, 4, 7 [archivist's numbers]).

The five household budget surveys published by the Government Statistician between 1953 and 1956 constituted an attempt to provide more rigorous and systematic information on the expenditures and welfare of urban populations. The first of these surveys took place in the rural area of Akim-Abuakwa, but the location was selected because it constituted "an important source of food supply for Accra and other towns" (Gold Coast Office of the Government Statistician 1953a, 2). Far from showing a deep concern with the welfare of rural producers, the Akim survey bluntly stated that "the principal agricultural problem in the Gold Coast at the present time is the supply of foodstuff to growing urban communities" (Gold Coast Office of the Government Statistician 1953a, 25). The Akim-Abuakwa survey represents an early example of "multipurpose sample survey" (Battacharya and Potakey 1969, 1): besides income and expenditure tables for the sample families, it incorporated estimates of food crop production and the results of road checks to analyse the export of food to the cities. One of the main purposes of the enquiry became the measurement of the gap between the production and the local consumption of food crops such as cassava, maize, plantain, yam and palm fruit, plus other "miscellaneous crops" like bananas and oranges (Gold Coast Office of the Government Statistician 1953a, 8). Although the relationship between production and consumption was very much dictated by the seasonality of the crops, overall it was found that in the survey period, from June 1952 to May 1953, the difference between production and consumption amounted to approximately 15,000 tons of food crops (Gold Coast Office of the Government Statistician 1953a, 10) – which could potentially find their way to urban markets. Following the publication of the Akim-Abuakwa survey, and in line with the government's concerns with urban food prices, the Office of the Government Statistician devoted four subsequent household budget surveys to the study of urban conditions.

The four survey locations included the capital Accra in 1953 (Gold Coast Office of the Government Statistician 1953b) and Kumasi, the second largest town in the country, in 1955 (Gold Coast Office of the Government Statistician 1956b), both obvious choices. For the other two surveys the government selected localities it saw as iconic representations of its attempts to modernise the economy. Thus Akuse was selected because of its proximity to the Volta River, which was the theatre of the most ambitious development project undertaken in Ghana: the construction of a dam that could provide electricity for the whole country (Gold Coast Office of the Government Statistician 1955, 1). Sekondi-Takoradi (Gold Coast Office of the Government Statistician 1956a) in turn, was not only the capital of the Western Region, but also one of the most developed infrastructural nodes of the country, hosting a port-harbour and constituting a terminal point of the railway linking Accra and Kumasi. The statistical office was trying to identify the features of the "typical" urban worker, whose income was not too high or too low, and would mostly derive from wage labour. The choice to focus on wage labourers was made under the assumption that the income of traders would follow more closely price fluctuations, and therefore did not require a separate analysis. However, it was soon discovered that this was not necessarily the best choice for all the survey areas, as the percentage of waged labour differed widely from location to location. Certainly the waged worker was representative in the cases of Accra and Sekondi-Takoradi, where the portion of the population earning their main income from wage labour was, respectively, 57 per cent "due to the employees of Government and commercial firms" and 69 per cent due to port and railway activities (Gold Coast Office of the Government Statistician 1956b, 4). In Kumasi, though, this choice did not turn out to be appropriate. After examining the results of the population survey "it was decided not to limit the budget sample to wage earning families as was done in Accra and Sekondi-Takoradi, as these formed only 34% of the total" (Gold Coast Office of the Government Statistician 1956b, 4). In spite of these differences in sampling method, the statistical office, following the completion of the household survey in Kumasi, produced a comparative picture of income and expenditure levels and of income percentages spent on different classes of goods (see Table 2).

The statistical construction of the "typical" urban worker was made easier by focusing on the composition of expenditures rather than on the composition of income, which instead proved to be more heterogeneous. Not only, as it has been indicated above, did the percentage of wage earning households vary greatly across the samples; among the wage earners this kind of income accounted for a wide range of the total income, spanning from the 22 per cent observed in Kumasi to the 90 per cent recorded in Sekondi-Takoradi. The notion of *urban* typicality emerging from the surveys of Accra, Sekondi-Takoradi and Kumasi was reinforced by the explanation given for the lower level of expenditures observed in Akuse (although their composition was fairly similar with those of other cities): "more rural conditions prevailed" (Gold Coast Office of the Government Statistician 1956b, 11).[21] Yet, the conceptual unevenness embedded in the construction of household budgets emerges fully when one contrasts the design and implications of urban surveys with those prepared for the cocoa producing areas.

Measuring production, income and credit: household budget surveys in the cocoa producing areas

Following the completion of the household budget surveys in the urban areas, the statistical office turned once again to the rural world with the publication of the *Survey of Population and Budgets of the Cocoa Producing Families in the Oda-Swedru-Asamankese Area, 1955–1956* (Ghana Office of the Government Statistician 1958), and the *Survey of the Cocoa Producing Families in Ashanti, 1956–1957* (Ghana Office of the Government Statistician 1960). As it is clear from the titles, unlike the food farming communities described in the Akim Abuakwa survey, the object of inquiry in these cases was the cocoa producer. At the beginning of the Swedru survey the authors state that, following the completion of surveys in the urban areas, it became apparent that "economic information about cocoa producers was a more urgent requirement than an extension of the urban investigations and attention was shifted to the rural areas" (Ghana Office of the Government Statistician 1958, 1).[22] The urgency to introduce household

Table 2. Comparative levels of income and expenditure in surveys of four urban areas of Gold Coast/Ghana, 1953–1955.

		Accra 1953	Akuse 1954	Sekondi-Takoradi 1955	Kumasi 1955
Sample size (number of households)		570	163	546	570
Average earnings[a] (survey month)		£16.8	£12.13	£11.10	£17.18
Average monthly expenditures[a] on home consumption		£15.14	£10.8	£12.9	£ 14.2
Wage as a percentage of earnings		67%	46%	90%	22%
Category of expenditure (% of total expenditures)	Local food	49.2	51.5	52.3	52.3
	Imported food	8.8	5.7	5.4	5
	Total food	58	57.2	57.7	57.3
	Clothing	12.1	17.3	14.8	13.8
	Drink and tobacco	6.1	6.6	5.1	4.2
	Fuel and light	4.7	4.6	6	6.2
	Services	5.8	5.9	4.9	5.8
	Rent and rates	5.4	2.2	6	7.5
	Durable goods	3.6	2.7	2.5	2.1
	Miscellaneous	4.3	3.5	3	3.1
	Total	100	100	100	100

Source: Gold Coast Office of the Government Statistician (1956b, 11–12).
Note: [a]Until 1958, when the Ghanaian pound was introduced (usually indicated as G£), the country used the British West African pound. This currency was traded at parity with the British pound and it was indicated simply as £ in the surveys. It can be assumed that the amounts listed here are nominal values, as there is no evidence that indexation was adopted.

budgets in Swedru and Ashanti was firmly grounded in the political and economic importance of cocoa. The Ministry of Finance acknowledged:

> The significance of cocoa production to the Gold Coast economy requires no underlining, since cocoa makes up about two-thirds of the value of the export trade. Even this figures [sic] does not emphasise sufficiently the dependence of the country on the cocoa crop. Not only is the cocoa industry by far the largest single direct source of income, but other sections of the economy such as transport and distributive services, depend directly or indirectly on its prosperity, and it provides a large part of the public revenue. (Gold Coast Ministry of Finance 1953, 15)

Such rich wealth was the object of a fierce redistributive struggle: the cocoa money that could have contributed to the development of Ashanti, where most of the cocoa trees were located, was being taken away and redistributed by the government for the economic development of "the nation". Initially this took place through the operation of the Cocoa Marketing Board. The Cocoa Marketing Board was officially established by the colonial government in 1947, with the aims of acquiring foreign exchange and stabilising the income of the farmers.[23] The Cocoa Marketing Board acted in a regime of monopsony, being granted by law the task of purchasing all the cocoa produced by the farmers and selling it on the world market. However, the Cocoa Marketing Board paid the farmers a price that was inferior to the one prevailing in the world market, thus cumulating large surpluses that were used to finance the government's expenditures. Before he was elected in 1951, Nkrumah and the CPP had managed to mobilise rural discontent by claiming that, with their victory, the surpluses accumulated through the Cocoa Marketing Board would be given back to the farmers.[24] Soon it became obvious that this would have not happened: indeed large cocoa producers "turned against the CPP as early as 1952, when it became clear that the state would have used the cocoa marketing board as a mechanism of state accumulation, rather than returning Ghana's cocoa surpluses to the farmers" (Boone 1995, 29). As a consequence the cocoa producers in the Ashanti region, where one-quarter of the Gold Coast population lived, mounted an opposition. The most evident expression of this was the formation, in 1954, of the National Liberation Movement, which called for the secession of Ashanti from the rest of the Gold Coast.[25] Catherine Boone argues convincingly that the opposition to the central government was not a reaction to a specific price conjuncture, but rather to the government's redistributive principles: "Crystallisation of the anti-CPP opposition [...] occurred when Ghanaian cocoa producers incomes were stable (1951–1954) during which time the flow of state patronage to the rural areas increased" (Boone 1995, 29). To cope with this heated political situation, Boone observes:

> the regime of Kwame Nkrumah sought to establish centralised control over a state apparatus that reached deep into localities, governing the cocoa belt intensively through a dense network of official institutions that insinuated state power into the micro-level dynamics of local political economies. (Boone 1995, 7)

The strategies adopted by the government were extremely varied, and included the formation of agricultural cooperatives, systematic attempts to incorporate the chiefs into the CPP (and try to de-stool those who refused),[26] the institution of new monopsonistic agencies (like the Cocoa Purchasing Company) and the provision of credit. These actions by the government to appropriate the wealth of the cocoa producing areas and integrate the farmers in a more extensive network of state institutions had several consequences for the way in which the statistical office designed the surveys of Swedru and Ashanti. Household budget surveys in the cocoa producing areas became tools to double-check cocoa production figures, provide a more rigorous assessment of farmers' income and quantify the impact of the newly established state institutions in the economic life of the areas under examination.

Let us start with production figures. Despite the fact that African economies were largely agricultural, the quality of agricultural statistics was very unsatisfactory: the 1951 conference of statisticians working in countries south of the Sahara agreed that "as regards crop statistics, most countries are still grappling with the elementary problem of providing a suitable system of collecting regular statistics of acreage and output" ("Conference of Statisticians in Countries in Africa ... (Draft Report) ... ", PRO CO 852/1078/2, 18 [original typescript page]). Even if the Gold Coast compared favourably in terms of statistical coverage with many other colonies represented at the conference, in the first Economic and Statistical Survey the Ministry of Finance candidly admitted that "the coverage of statistics on agricultural activities does not at the present permit a detailed comparison between production in 1952 and 1951" (Gold Coast Ministry of Finance 1953, 17). Besides the administrative problems, such as shortage of trained staff, that made the collection of any kind of statistical information in sub-Saharan Africa particularly difficult, those in charge of the collection of data on agricultural production were facing additional obstacles. Communal ownership of the land, the subsistence basis of agriculture and the practice of mixed cropping were usually the main obstacle listed ("Conference of Statisticians in Countries in Africa ... ", PRO CO 852/1078/2, 18–21 [original typescript pages]).[27] Certainly the statistical information existing in the Gold Coast about cocoa, even preceding the introduction of household budgets, was much more accurate than that available for food crops. A report on the reorganisation of the statistical office after independence admitted that "so far, no general statistical information is available about agriculture in Ghana except in the case of crops which are mainly exported" (Ghana 1960, 21). Although some of the problems identified by the 1951 conference of African statisticians still applied to cash crops, the existence of the Cocoa Marketing Board, which purchased what was assumed to be the totality of the crop output, provided for more accurate statistical information about cash crops than food crops. Of course, this worked only under the assumption that the marketing board was actually able to locate and purchase 100 per cent of the cocoa produced in the country.[28]

In view of the relatively weak informational capabilities of the colonial state, this was by no means a given: part of the importance attached to the introduction of household budgets in the cocoa producing areas was the opportunity they provided to check the figures constructed by the Cocoa Marketing Board. This was made possible by comparing the Board's figures with those obtained from the household budget surveys using the following formula:

Average declared cocoa production per budget family (loads) * total number of cocoa owning families * total districts / sample districts = total cocoa production [in] survey area. (Ghana Office of the Government Statistician 1958, 17, 1960, 10)

The application of this formula to the Swedru area (35.3 * 8,201 * 225/90) produced a figure of 724,000 loads (or 19,400 tons), while the reported purchase of the Cocoa Marketing Board amounted to 32,000 tons. Since the survey region could have produced so much cocoa only if its yield was 30 per cent higher than elsewhere, it was likely that the cocoa purchased in Swedru by the marketing board included crop produced in other regions and bought on its way to the ports (Ghana Office of the Government Statistician 1958, 17). This seemed a reasonable assumption but, given the lack of precise data on acreage, or more extensive crop movement statistics, it could not be conclusively tested.[29] Thus the household budget survey became an instrument pointing out the limits of existing knowledge and suggesting further hypotheses that needed to be tested.

Another important difference between surveys in cocoa producing areas and the four surveys discussed in this paper's previous section was the development of a more sophisticated way of conceptualising income. As acknowledged by a postcolonial report about the field surveys prepared by the statistical office in the 1950s, the household budgets in cocoa producing areas differed from those conducted in urban areas in one important aspect: "In the other family budget surveys, income data was recorded mainly as a check of the expenditure information and was not a primary concern of the investigation" (Ghana Central Bureau of Statistics 1961, 79). Unlike the relatively simple income classifications used in the urban surveys, the quantification of income in Swedru and Ashanti was based on several distinct measures: gross cocoa income (equal to the value of the cocoa sold), gross farming income (equal to the gross cocoa income plus the income deriving from the sale of other farm products) and total gross farming income (equal to the gross farming income plus incomes deriving from other sources such as wage labour, rent from property and petty trading). Total receipts were the sum of these three entries, plus cocoa grants, sales of property, loans and other remittances received. The net farming income was the difference between gross farming income and farming costs, while the net income was the difference between gross earned income and total costs. Finally, the overall budget was the result of subtracting total payments from total receipts. The conceptual apparatus used to calculate rural incomes is shown in Table 3.

The inclusion of credit and debit positions in the calculation of receipts and payments should be noted. This, which was not considered in any of the surveys discussed so far, must be understood against the background of the crucial importance attached to the provision of credit by the government in order to gain the political support of cocoa farmers. Admittedly, the indebtedness of the Ashanti cocoa farmers was, already in the 1920s, a concern of the British colonial administration, principally because they feared that the repayment of onerous loans would have a negative impact on the quality of cocoa, resulting in a loss of market share (G. Austin 2005, 300).[30] But Nkrumah's CPP took more aggressive action, not only

Table 3. Receipts and payments table used for surveys conducted in cocoa producing areas of Ghana, 1955–1957.

RECEIPTS	Sales of farm produce	Cocoa
		Foodstuffs
		Livestock
		Gross farming income (A)
		Petty trading
		Work on own account
		Rent from property
		Wage incomes
		Total gross earned income (B)
		Cocoa grants
		Sales of property
		New loans
		Repayment of loans given
		Other remittances received
		TOTAL RECEIPTS (C)
PAYMENTS		Share payment to caretakers
		Payment to labourers
		Other cocoa harvesting costs
		Farming costs (D)
		Trading purchase for resale
		Costs of materials for crafts
		Total costs (E)
		Domestic expenditure
		Loan repayments
		Loans given
		Payments on property purchased
		Other payments
		TOTAL PAYMENTS (F)
	NET FARMING INCOME (A-D)	
	TOTAL NET EARNED INCOME (B-E)	
	OVERALL BALANCE ON BUDGET (C-F)	

Source: Ghana Office of the Government Statistician (1958, 68) and Ghana Office of the Government Statistician (1960, 54).

expanding the amount of formal credit available to the small farmers, but setting up a series of institutions (most notably the Cocoa Purchasing Company) that could extend the state's reach in the countryside and replace other sources of credit such as European brokers and "informal" institutions. The household budget surveys then became in the cocoa producing areas a tool to quantify the farmers' dependence on the state in contrast with other sources of credit, and perhaps more generally their degree of integration in the network of state-sponsored institutions. This was made possible by collecting data on receipts and payments over the course of the survey and decomposing the loans taken and given according to the source, as shown in Table 4.

The performance of the CPP government in extending its control over the countryside was mixed. From a political point of view alone it could be considered a success: the National Liberation Movement, which was literally competing with the central government in providing credit to the farmers (Boone 2003, 168), lost the 1956 election. However, the fate of most of the loans made to farmers by the Cocoa Purchasing Company in 1954–1955 was not to be repaid (Boone 2003, 168). Furthermore, the Ashanti survey confirms that the state had not yet succeeded in

Table 4.   Average new loans taken and repaid per sample family during the survey period, classified according to type of loan and loan source.

			Total (shillings)
New average loans per family taken during the survey period	Type of loan	Pledged farms	5.5
		Advance on crop	54.7
		Other	32.3
		Total	92.5
	Source of loan	Cocoa Purchasing Company	4.8
		Co-operatives	9.5
		Firms and brokers	32.9
		Other	45.3
		Total	92.5
Average loans per family repaid during the survey period	Type of loan	Pledged farms	180.4
		Advance on crop	425.5
		Other	178.5
		Total	784.4
	Source of loan	Cocoa Purchasing Company	75.3
		Co-operatives	127.9
		Firms and brokers	246.5
		Other	334.7
		Total	784.4

Source: Ghana Office of the Government Statistician (1960, 74).

eradicating the presence of alternative sources of credit. From the data reported in Table 4 it is possible to calculate that the cooperatives and the Cocoa Purchasing Company accounted only for 15 per cent and 26 per cent of new loans and loan repayments respectively.[31] Similar results were obtained in the Swedru survey: of the new loans on average 17 per cent came from the purchasing company, 3 per cent from the cooperatives, 52 per cent from firms and brokers and 28 per cent from other sources (Ghana Office of the Government Statistician 1958, 30). Most of the credit provided to cocoa farmers came from what the statisticians included in the residual category of "other", typically comprising other farmers and relatives.[32] The Swedru and Ashanti surveys thus represented not only the cognitive locus where a more precise measurement of the state's influence on the economic life of the cocoa farmers was made possible by double-checking marketing boards figures, measuring incomes and identifying sources of credit. The surveys also provided a clear indication that the CPP government had not managed to fully bring to the countryside the structural transformation it had envisaged for it.

Conclusion

This paper has provided an historical reconstruction of the evolution of household budget surveys in late colonial Ghana. It has shown that household budgets emerged as an important kind of statistical inquiry in the 1950s. It has argued that household budget surveys institutionalised what has been called an "uneven statistical topography". This unevenness can be observed at two levels. First, it can be seen in the geographical distribution of sampling areas. Given the limited amount of funding and trained personnel available for statistical work, the selection of the sampling location was more likely to reflect the political and economic relevance of the different areas of the country to those in power, than any strictly statistical notions of "typicality" – which in principle could have allowed inferences to be made from the sample to the whole population. Second, while sharing the use of income–expenditure tables, household budget surveys were far from being a homogenous statistical tool. Following the modification of income–expenditure tables from Akim-Abuakwa to the main cities, to the cocoa producing areas of Swedru and Ashanti reveals the flexibility of the concept of household budgets, as well as the extent to which the cognitive tools and the conceptual grids that were adopted reflected the political and economic agenda of the government.

A few years after the achievement of independence from British rule in 1957, Ghana turned to socialism. This shift envisaged a much more pervasive role for the state in economic life, and raised even higher the importance attached to economic planning and the collection of accurate statistics in designing and implementing economic policy. In spite of the change in ideological discourse, the construction of household budget surveys in the 1950s provided a formidable learning experience for the postcolonial state. Looking back at the 1950s household budgets, the Central Bureau of Statistics (as the Office of the Government Statistician was renamed between 1960 and 1961) explicitly acknowledged their "unevenness":

> It would have been very helpful if the urban area surveys had included a classification of income similar to that in respect of the cocoa enquiries […] It would have also been better if a standard classification of income and expenditure had been used. (Ghana Central Bureau of Statistics 1961, 80)

In spite of these shortcomings the statistical office concluded that household budget surveys represented a successful tool in penetrating the countryside and gaining information on agricultural production, on which African states largely depended but about which they knew so little (see for example Ghana Central Bureau of Statistics 1961, 35).With the expansion of funding available for statistical work, the organisational framework on which the ad hoc enquiries of the 1950s relied had to be expanded and extended to cover the whole country, thus becoming an important part of a cognitive apparatus eager to collect more detailed information about "the private sector of the economy" (Ghana Central Bureau of Statistics 1961, 36).

Certainly more research is needed on the reasons that led African states to see and represent their economies the way they did, the limits and potential of these representations, the extent to which they were shaped by the purposeful actions of the subjects observed and the actual impact of statistical information on policy formulation and implementation. These questions are beyond the scope of this paper. However, it is hoped that this historical inquiry into the construction of household budget surveys represents a step towards a more precise assessment of the informational constraints of African states, and thus a more balanced appraisal of their role in economic development.

Acknowledgements

Previous versions of this paper were presented at the conference "African Economic Development: Measuring Success and Failure", Simon Fraser University (18–20 April 2013) and at the Graduate Thesis Workshop of the Economic History Department, London School of Economics and Political Science (1 May 2013). Besides the organisers and participants to these workshops, the author would like to thank for insightful comments Lars Boerner, Federico D'Onofrio and an anonymous referee. Special thanks to Leigh Gardner and Mary Morgan, my PhD advisors, and to Morten Jerven. The usual disclaimer applies. Financial support from the Economic History Society, which contributed to fund the archival research for this paper, is gratefully acknowledged. Finally, I would like to express my gratitude towards the LSE British Library of Political and Economic Science, the Public Records Office (London), and the Public Records and Archives Administration Department (Accra branch) for the permission to reproduce their material, and to their staff for the kind help offered over the course of this research.

Biographical note

Gerardo Serra is a PhD student in the Department of Economic History at the London School of Economics and Political Science. His research interests are the history of economics, colonial and post-colonial African economic history, and the political economy of development and planning.

Notes

1. This literature is too vast to be summarised here. Recent influential works include Herbst (2000), Mkandawire (2001), Young (1994) and Bayart (2009).
2. On the other hand it should be noted that the knowledge that Hayek thought relevant for the construction of a "rational economic order" could not be strictly quantified: "the sort of knowledge with which I have been concerned is knowledge of the kind which by its nature cannot enter into statistics and therefore cannot be conveyed to any central authority in statistical form" (Hayek 1945, 524).
3. In his influential history of statistics, Porter (1995, xi) wrote that "geographical limitations are perhaps less forgivable than the temporal ones, and the history of colonialism, of international organisations and of centrally planned economies all provide extremely rich material for the history of quantification". There is little doubt that Africa could provide a valuable collection of case studies to develop the lines of research suggested by Porter.
4. Throughout the paper "Gold Coast" and "Ghana" will be used interchangeably.
5. For a broad overview of the scope and breadth of recent historical research on decolonisation, see the articles collected in Le Sueur (2003).
6. An excellent example of this approach in relation to family expenditure surveys in the United States is Stapleford (2007).
7. Although the last two papers were published after independence, the beginning of the actual surveys took place before that date.
8. Table 1 excludes a small survey that was realised in 1951–1952 in a selection of villages in the Akwapim area. While certainly it was not published in the *Statistical and Economic Papers* of the Office of the Government Statistician, unfortunately the author has not even been able to find a draft or an unpublished copy in the Ghanaian archives. What is known about it is only that "the scale of the enquiry was too small to field [sic] quantitative results, but it provided a valuable indication of the items which could be reliably recorded in such enquiries" (Ghana Central Bureau of Statistics 1961, 2).
9. For further discussion, see Iliffe 1987 (especially Chap. 11), and Cooper (2002, Chap. 5).
10. A classic account of this is Hill (1986, Chap. 7). Similar problems were faced by colonial economists attempting to construct national income accounts. Phyllis Deane, for example, wrote about her fieldwork in Northern Rhodesia (Zambia): "The principal difficulty in surveying was that the sleeping household, the producing household and the spending household all represented different combinations and permutations within one wide family group" (quoted in Morgan 2011, 313).
11. Other conceptual problems experienced in designing the surveys discussed in the minutes of the statistical conference included the pervasive presence of retribution in kind, differences among tribes in patterns of income and expenditures, the communal holding of capital and items such as bicycles and clothing, the lack of understanding of the purpose of budget enquiries and the high labour turnover ("Minutes of Conference of Statisticians of Countries in Africa … ", PRO CO 1078/1, 33–36 [original typescript pages]).
12. As rightly pointed out by Maas and Morgan (2012, 15): "Social statistics and classifications are always the outcome of strategic interactions that are politically loaded". In a most fascinating work, Roger J. Bowden (1989) has gone as far as to construct a series of game theoretical models to represent the strategies involved in the creation of statistical information. While further research is needed to explore the role played by observers in shaping the strategic interaction with the observed subjects and establishing trust in the making of African statistics, there are studies which deal with this problem with reference to other geographical contexts. D'Onofrio (2012) for example addresses it in the context of the making of agricultural statistics in early twentieth-century Italy.
13. Thanks to an anonymous referee for bringing this valuable source to my attention.
14. Indeed, the practice of self-reporting has serious repercussions on statistical accuracy. For a study of this aspect in the context of American household surveys see Stapleford (2012).
15. This can be seen even more clearly in the map presented in Ghana Central Bureau of Statistics (1961, v).

16. A recent historical assessment largely confirms Raeburn's view: "This area has a history of chronic malnutrition and enduring poverty, even if it has not suffered massive famine mortality" (Destombes 1999, 4).

17. This does not imply that there was no attempt whatsoever to develop the Northern Territories. For example, in 1950 the colonial administration established the Gonja Development Corporation to increase food output and mechanise agricultural production (Miracle and Seidman 1968, 5).

18. This is an oversimplified, shortened version of the story. For extensive discussion of the politics of decolonisation in the Gold Coast the best departure point probably remains the classic work by D. Austin (1970).

19. The postcolonial history of Ghana presents a counterexample. The devaluation of the cedi in 1971 under Kofi Abrefa Busia, making the food consumed in the towns more expensive, led to wide discontent and eventually to the fall of the government and the seizure of power by the military (Bates 1981, 31).

20. It should be noted that attempts at measuring income and expenditures did not exhaust the range of statistical enquiries conducted in urban areas. In 1955, for example, the Ministry of Industries prepared a survey of industrial enterprises in Accra. The category "industrial enterprises" in this case was not confined to industrial plants, but included economic activities as different as laundries, mechanical repair shops, bakeries and shoe repair establishments. The survey itself simply consisted in a list of enterprises classified according to sector and the number of persons employed by each ("Accra Survey, 27 June–30 July", PRAAD RG 7/1/359, 1[archivist's page number]).

21. The low expenditures observed in Akuse was also derived from the fact that the survey had been conducted "about two months before the beginning of Christmas expenditure" and thus "people were saving in preparation for the festive season" (Gold Coast Office of the Government Statistician 1956b, 12). While some recent historical work (Andersson 2002) has pointed out that the postcolonial division between "urban" and "rural" can be traced back, among other things, to the inheritance of a conceptual apparatus developed by the colonial administrations, further research is needed in uncovering the role of statistics in this process.

22. The production of economic surveys in the cocoa producing areas became in the same years an increasingly important object of study at the Economics Research Division of the University College of the Gold Coast (later University of Ghana). See for example Hill (1957) and McGlade (1957).

23. However, the issues that led to the institution of the Cocoa Marketing Board can be traced back to the consequences of the Great Depression, the cocoa hold ups of 1937–1938 and wartime measures on cocoa production and exports. For further discussion of the constitution of the Cocoa Marketing Board see Meredith (1988) and Alence (2001).

24. For further discussion on this and the role of the CPP in mobilising rural discontent see Danquah (1994).

25. A propaganda leaflet of the same year stated: "Ashanti produces more cocoa than the colony. IS THERE ANY COCOA IN THE NORTHERN TERITORRIES [sic]? NO! Why should Government tax cocoa farmers to develop the country in which Ashantis suffer most?" (quoted in Allman 1990, 266).

26. For a detailed exploration of the relationship between Nkrumah's regime and the chiefs, see the excellent study by Rathbone (2000).

27. Furthermore, specific crops presented additional problems. In spite of its crucial importance as a staple food in the West African diet, cassava was extremely difficult to count because, being a tuber, it was buried underground. Hill (1986, 34) notes that cassava "is often cultivated in tiny plots and in mixtures so that no West African country can have the faintest idea of how much is produced".

28. For a review of the scope of the crops statistics produced by colonial West African marketing boards, see Bauer (1954).

29. A crop movement survey, including both vehicle and lorry checks, was then in fact organised between 1957 and 1958 (Ghana Central Bureau of Statistics 1961, 59).

30. For an extensive discussion of the history of the making of the Ashanti cocoa economy, see G. Austin's book, especially chapters 7 and 15. The study of credit was already a feature of surveys in the cocoa producing areas that preceded the formation of the Office of the Government Statistician. See for example Beckett ([1944] 1979, Chap. 5 and 6).

31. Similar findings were observed in postcolonial studies. Shortly after independence the amount of loans provided by the Cocoa Purchasing Company in Ahafo amounted to almost 7 per cent; more than 85 per cent was still provided by local farmers and relatives (G. Austin 2005, 389).

32. A more detailed classification of "informal" credit sources to cocoa farmers is presented by McGlade (1957, 14) in her survey of the Cape Coast area. Out of the 48 creditors identified, 32 were farmers with no other occupation, seven farmers with other occupations and four were cocoa brokers.

References

Unpublished archival sources

Colonial Science Collection, British Library of Political and Economic Science (BLPES), London School of Economics and Political Science

"CEAC (44) 16 Appendix II Memorandum Referred to in Paragraph 24. Some Aspects of the Flow of Capital into British Colonies", 1944. In BLPES CEAC (Colonial Economic Advisory Committee) 4/7, "Some Aspects of the Flow of Capital into British Colonies", 31.

"Colonial Economic Research Committee, Advisory Panel on Colonial National Income Studies, Minutes of the First Meeting Held in the Colonial Office on Thursday 16th December 1948 at 2.30 pm in room n. 337, Church House". In BLPES CERC (Colonial Economic Research Committee) 1/1.

Public Records Office (PRO), London

"Conference of Statisticians in Countries in Africa South of the Sahara (Draft Report), Salisbury (Southern Rhodesia) 30th July–7th August, 1951". In PRO CO 852/1078/2. Commission for Technical Co-operation in Africa South of the Sahara. African Statistical Conference, 1951. Report of the Conference.

"Minutes of Conference of Statisticians of Countries in Africa South of the Sahara, Salisbury, Southern Rhodesia 30th July–7th August 1951". In PRO CO 852/1078/1. Commission for Technical Co-operation in Africa South of the Sahara. African Statistical Conference, 1951. Agenda and Minutes of Meetings.

Public Records and Archives Administration Department (PRAAD), Accra branch

"Accra Survey, 27 June–30 July". In PRAAD RG 7/1/359. Survey of Industrial Enterprises Accra.

"Letter of Peter Ady to the Secretariat of State of the Colonies, 6th March 1946". In PRAAD RG 3/1/253. Social and Economic Survey of Ghana by Miss Peter Ady of the Colonial Research Council.

"Report on a Survey on Bread Consumption". In PRAAD RG 4/1/124 Survey of Bread Consumption Accra.

"Telegram from the Secretary of State of the Colonies to the Office administering the Government of the Gold Coast, 24th January 1947". In PRAAD RG 2/1/62. Establishment & Strength Government Statistician.

"Wages & Standards of Living. Accra 1945". In PRAAD ADM 5/3/52. Report on wages and standards of living in Accra 1945 by Miss Peter Ady.

Published sources

Alence, R. 2001. "Colonial Government, Social Conflict and State's Involvement in Africa's Open Economies: The Origins of the Ghana Cocoa Marketing Board, 1939–46." *Journal of African History* 42 (3): 397–416.

Allman, J. M. 1990. "The Youngmen and the Porcupine: Class, Nationalism and Asante's Struggle for Self-Determination, 1954–1957." *Journal of African History* 31 (2): 263–279.

Andersson, J. A. 2002. "Administrators' Knowledge and State Control in Colonial Zimbabwe: The Invention of the Rural–Urban Divide in Buhera District, 1912–1980." *Journal of African History* 43 (1): 119–143.

Austin, D. 1970. *Politics in Ghana, 1946–1960*. London: Oxford University Press.

Austin, G. 2005. *Labour, Land and Capital in Ghana: From Slavery to Free Labour in Asante, 1807–1956*. Rochester: University of Rochester Press.

Bates, R. H. 1981. *Markets and States in Tropical Africa: The Political Basis of Agricultural Policies*. Berkeley: University of California Press.

Battacharya, C. G., and P. N. Potakey. 1969. *A Study of Cocoa Farming and Cocoa Farmers in the Eastern Region of Ghana Using an Integrated Household Survey*. Institute of Statistical, Social and Economic Research, University of Ghana, Legon, Technical Publication Series No. 8.

Bauer, P. T. 1954. "Statistics of Statutory Marketing in West Africa." *Journal of the Royal Statistical Society. Series A (General)* 117 (1): 1–30.

Bayart, J.-F. 2009. *The State in Africa: The Politics of the Belly*. Cambridge: Polity.

Beckett, W. H. [1944] 1979. *Akokoaso: A Survey of a Gold Coast Village*. New York: AMS Press.

Boone, C. 1995. "Rural Interests and the Making of Modern African States." *African Economic History* 23: 1–36.

Boone, C. 2003. *Political Topographies of the African State: Territorial Authority and Institutional Choice.* Cambridge: Cambridge University Press.

Bowden, R. J. 1989. *Statistical Games and Human Affairs: The View from Within.* Cambridge: Cambridge University Press.

Clauson, G. L. M. 1937. "Some Uses of Statistics in Colonial Administration." *Journal of the Royal African Society* 36 (145): 3–16.

Colonial Office. 1951. *First Conference of Colonial Government Statisticians 1950: Report.* London: His Majesty's Stationery Office.

Colonial Office. 1954. *Report on the Second Conference of Colonial Government Statisticians, 1953.* London: Her Majesty's Stationery Office.

Cooper, F. 2002. *Africa since 1940: The Past of the Present.* Cambridge: Cambridge University Press.

D'Onofrio, F. 2012. "Making Variety Simple: Agricultural Economists in Southern Italy, 1906–1909." In *Observing the Economy: Historical Perspectives*, edited by H. Maas and M. Morgan. o*History of Political Economy, Special Supplement* 44 (1): 93–113.

Danquah, F. K. 1994. "Rural Discontent and Decolonisation in Ghana, 1945–1951." *Agricultural History* 68 (1): 1–19.

Desrosières, A. 2003. "Managing the Economy." In *The Cambridge History of Science, Volume 7: The Modern Social Sciences*, edited by T. M. Porter and D. Ross, 553–564. Cambridge: Cambridge University Press.

Destombes, J. 1999. *Nutrition and Economic Destitution in Northern Ghana, 1930–1957. A Historical Perspective on Nutritional Economics.* Department of Economic History, London School of Economics and Political Science, Working Paper No. 49/99.

Falola, T. 1996. *Development Planning and Decolonization in Nigeria.* Gainesville: University Press of Florida.

Ferguson, J. 1994. *The Anti-Politics Machine: Development, Depoliticization and Bureaucratic Power in Lesotho.* Cambridge: Cambridge University Press.

Galletti, R., K. D. S. Baldwin, and I. O. Dina. 1956. *Nigerian Cocoa Farmers: An Economic Survey of Yoruba Cocoa Farming Families.* Oxford: Oxford University Press on behalf of The Nigerian Cocoa Marketing Board.

Ghana.1960. *Report of Committee on Creation of Central Bureau of Statistics.* Accra: Office of the Government Statistician.

Ghana Central Bureau of Statistics. 1961. *Field Survey Work in the Ghana Statistics Office.* Statistical and Economic Papers No. 8. Accra: Central Bureau of Statistics.

Ghana Office of the Government Statistician. 1958. *Survey of Population and Budgets of Cocoa Producing Families in the Oda-Swedru-Asamankese Area, 1955–1956.* Statistical and Economic Papers No. 6. Accra: Office of the Government Statistician.

Ghana Office of the Government Statistician. 1960. *Survey of Cocoa Producing Families in Ashanti, 1956–1957.* Statistical and Economic Papers No. 7. Accra: Office of the Government Statistician.

Gold Coast. 1942. *Report on the Enquiry into the Costs of Living in the Gold Coast Held in January 1942.* Accra: Government Printer.

Gold Coast. 1943. *Report of the Commission of Enquiry into the Distribution and Prices of Essential Imported Goods (With an Appendix Setting Forth the Action which the Government Proposes to Take to Implement the Recommendations Contained Therein).* Accra: Government Printing Department.

Gold Coast Colony. 1932. *Report on the Department of Agriculture for the Year 1931–1932.* Accra: Government Printer.

Gold Coast Colony. 1934. *Report on the Department of Agriculture for the Year 1933–1934.* Accra: Government Printer.

Gold Coast Ministry of Finance. 1953. *Economic Survey 1952.* Accra: Government Printer.

Gold Coast Office of the Government Statistician. 1953a. *Agricultural Statistical Survey of South-East Akim Abuakwa, 1952–1953.* Statistical and Economic Papers No. 1. Accra: Office of the Government Statistician.

Gold Coast Office of the Government Statistician. 1953b. *1953 Accra Survey of Household Budgets.* Statistical and Economic Papers No. 2. Accra: Office of the Government Statistician.

Gold Coast Office of the Government Statistician. 1955. *1954 Akuse Survey of Household Budgets.* Statistical and Economic Papers No. 3. Accra: Office of the Government Statistician.

Gold Coast Office of the Government Statistician. 1956a. *Sekondi-Takoradi Survey of Population and Household Budgets, 1955*. Statistical and Economic Papers No. 4. Accra: Office of the Government Statistician.
Gold Coast Office of the Government Statistician. 1956b. *Kumasi Survey of Population and Household Budgets, 1955*. Statistical and Economic Papers No. 5. Accra: Office of the Government Statistician.
Hayek, F. A. 1945. "The Use of Knowledge in Society." *The American Economic Review* 35 (4): 519–530.
Herbst, J. 2000. *States and Power in Africa: Comparative Lessons in Authority and Control*. Princeton: Princeton University Press.
Hill, P. 1957. *An Economic Survey of Cocoa Farmers in Kwahu*. Economics Research Division, University College of Ghana, Cocoa Research Series No. 6.
Hill, P. 1986. *Development Economics on Trial: The Anthropological Case for Prosecution*. Cambridge: Cambridge University Press.
Iliffe, J. 1987. *The African Poor: A History*. Cambridge: Cambridge University Press.
Ingham, B. 1992. "Shaping Opinion on Development Policy: Economists at the Colonial Office during World War II." *History of Political Economy* 24 (3): 689–710.
Jerven, M. 2013. *Poor Numbers: How We Are Misled by African Development Statistics and What to Do about It*. Ithaca: Cornell University Press.
Jerven, M. 2014. "The Political Economy of Agricultural Statistics and Input Subsidies: Evidence from India, Nigeria and Malawi." *Journal of Agrarian Change* 14 (1): 129–145.
Le Sueur, J. D., ed. 2003. *The Decolonization Reader*. London: Routledge.
Maas, H., and M. Morgan. 2012. "Observation and Observing in Economics." In *Observing the Economy: Historical Perspectives*, edited by H. Maas and M. Morgan. *History of Political Economy, Special Supplement* 44 (1): 1–24.
McGlade, C. 1957. *An Economic Survey of Cocoa Farmers in the Cape Coast Area*. Economics Research Division, University College of Ghana, Cocoa Research Series No. 4.
Meredith, D. 1988. "The Colonial Office, British Business Interests and the Reform of Cocoa Marketing in West Africa, 1937–1945." *Journal of African History* 29 (2): 285–300.
Miracle, M. P., and A. Seidman. 1968. *State Farms in Ghana*. Land Tenure Center, University of Wisconsin, Madison, LTC no. 43.
Mkandawire, T. 2001. "Thinking about Developmental States in Africa." *Cambridge Journal of Economics* 25: 289–313.
Morgan, M. 2011. "Seeking Parts, Looking for Wholes." In *Histories of Scientific Observation*, edited by L. Daston and E. Lunbeck, 303–225. Chicago: University of Chicago Press.
Porter, T. M. 1995. *Trust in Numbers: The Pursuit of Objectivity in Science and Public Life*. Princeton: Princeton University Press.
Raeburn, J. R. 1951. *Report on a Preliminary Economic Survey of the Northern Territories of the Gold Coast*. London: Colonial Office.
Rathbone, R. 2000. *Nkrumah and the Chiefs: The Politics of Chieftaincy in Ghana, 1951–1960*. Oxford: James Currey.
Scott, J. 1998. *Seeing Like a State: How Certain Schemes to Improve the Human Condition Have Failed*. New Haven: Yale University Press.
Seers, D., and C. R. Ross. 1952. *Report on Financial and Physical Problems of Development in the Gold Coast*. Accra: Office of the Government Statistician.
Speich, D. 2011. "The Use of Global Abstractions: National Income Accounting in the Era of Imperial Decline." *Journal of Global History* 6 (1): 7–28.
Stapleford, T. 2007. "Market Visions: Expenditure Surveys, Market Research and Economic Planning in the New Deal." *Journal of American History* 94 (2): 418–444.
Stapleford, T. 2012. "Navigating the Shoals of Self-Reporting: Data Collection in US Expenditure Surveys since 1920." In *Observing the Economy: Historical Perspectives*, edited by H. Maas and M. Morgan. *History of Political Economy, Special Supplement* 44 (1): 160–182.
Tignor, R. L. 2006. *W. Arthur Lewis and the Birth of Development Economics*. Princeton: Princeton University Press.
Tooze, A. J. 2001. *Statistics and the German State, 1900–1945: The Making of Modern Economic Knowledge*. Cambridge: Cambridge University Press.
Young, C. 1994. *The African Colonial State in Comparative Perspective*. New Haven: Yale University Press.

Des revenus nationaux pour l'Afrique? La mesure du développement en Afrique occidentale française dans les années 1950

Vincent Bonnecase

CNRS, Science politique, Les Afriques dans le monde, IEP, Pessac, France

RÉSUMÉ   Cet article interroge les modalités concrètes de production des premiers revenus nationaux en Afrique occidentale française dans les années 1950, leur signification pour les contemporains et les usages antagoniques auxquels ils ont donné lieu. Il montre que ces chiffres, hautement incertains au regard de leurs conditions de calcul et du point de vue de leurs propres concepteurs, n'en ont pas moins été rapidement utilisés par différents acteurs, à des fins d'évaluation comptable des politiques coloniales ou de comparaison internationale des niveaux de développement.

ABSTRACT   This article investigates the methods used for producing the first national revenues in French West Africa during the 1950s, their significance today and the controversial usages which they have led to. The article demonstrates that these figures, highly uncertain in terms of how they were calculated and conceived, were nevertheless rapidly used by different actors to different ends, be it for colonial policy or for comparing international levels of development.

Introduction

C'est sans doute une étrange entreprise que de vouloir, en l'an de grâce 1953 et dans un pays de l'Union française où les services officiels de statistique ne sont même pas implantés aux échelons territoriaux, s'attaquer au problème qui figure parmi les plus ardus des économistes modernes : le calcul du revenu national. (Direction générale des Finances de l'AOF, « Essai de récapitulation des éléments connus à Dakar pour servir à un calcul du revenu national de l'AOF », Dakar, 1953)

En 1953, la Direction générale des Finances de l'Afrique occidentale française (AOF)[1] entreprend, pour la première fois dans l'histoire de la fédération, de procéder au calcul du revenu national de ce territoire de près de 500 000 km² et d'environ 16 millions d'habitants. Cette initiative, « étrange » au regard de ses propres initiateurs, s'inscrit dans un triple contexte à la fois politique, idéologique et économique. Tout d'abord, à l'échelle de l'AOF elle-même, les autorités coloniales se sont lancées depuis 1946 dans une nouvelle politique d'investissement et de planification qui réforme totalement les relations financières entre la métropole et les colonies : alors que celles-ci avaient jusqu'alors, en vertu d'un principe d'autonomie définie par la loi des finances de 1900, largement autofinancé par le biais de la fiscalité locale leur propre équipement, ce dernier repose désormais également sur les fonds métropolitains (Coquery-Vidrovitch 1982). Ensuite, à l'échelle de la métropole, l'après-guerre voit s'accroître le rôle régulateur de l'État dans les politiques économiques, lesquelles se retrouvent dotées d'un nouveau langage : la comptabilité nationale. Cette évolution induit une valorisation des grands agrégats, au premier rang duquel le produit intérieur brut, désormais établi de manière routinière à des fins de prévision économique globale et de fixation des politiques publiques (Desrosières 2003a). Enfin, à l'échelle internationale, l'émergence d'une idéologie du développement (Rist 1996) va de pair avec une nouvelle demande pour des indicateurs permettant la mesurabilité et la comparabilité des conditions d'existence dans le monde : les espaces coloniaux en particulier se retrouvent inscrit dans une hiérarchisation internationale des niveaux de vie dont ils étaient, jusqu'alors, globalement exclus (Bonnecase 2011).

L'objectif de cet article est de proposer une contribution à l'histoire des indicateurs productifs et à leur place dans la mesure du développement, en revenant sur l'élaboration des premiers revenus nationaux en AOF dans les années 1950, au moment de ce qu'on a pu appeler le colonialisme tardif. Il ne s'agira pas, dans une optique rétrospective, de mettre en question ces indicateurs à la lumière de leurs critiques actuelles (Destremeau et Salama 2002; Bourmaud 2011), mais de les replacer dans les controverses de l'époque en interrogeant à la fois leurs conditions concrètes d'élaboration, le sens qui a pu leur être donné par les contemporains et les premiers usages politiques qui ont été les leurs. Je m'appuierai pour cela, outre la littérature s'inscrivant dans une « sociologie historique de la quantification » (Desrosières 2008a), sur trois principaux types de sources : d'abord, les premières études du revenu national effectuées en AOF, et plus largement en Afrique française, sous l'égide du gouvernement général de la fédération et du ministère de la France d'outre-mer; ensuite et en amont, les données sollicitées dans ces études et préalablement collectées dans le cadre des pratiques routinières de l'administration; enfin et en aval, les discours politiques à plus large diffusion dans lesquels les revenus nationaux ont figuré dès les années 1950, peu après leur élaboration.

Trois questions traverseront cet article. La première porte basiquement sur la propension des premiers revenus nationaux à décrire la réalité économique de l'AOF. On peut vite être amené à affirmer, en s'appuyant sur les doutes formulés à cet égard par les enquêteurs (doutes que l'on peut en même temps facilement retrouver dans n'importe quelle enquête de ce type) que ces chiffres ne veulent pas dire grand-chose au regard de leurs modalités d'élaboration. Mais il ne me semble pas moins important de prendre au sérieux, au moins au départ, la prétention descriptive des premiers concepteurs du revenu national et les débats méthodologiques suscités par cette prétention.

La deuxième question porte sur le caractère spécifique qu'a pu revêtir le revenu national dans un contexte colonial et développementaliste, alors que les gouvernements des pays industrialisés procédaient également, à l'époque, à l'élaboration ou à la révision de leurs propres comptabilités nationales. Il conviendra à ce titre de mettre en rapport la signification et l'utilité prêtées à ces chiffres en AOF et celles qui peuvent leur être prêtées au même moment en métropole ou au sein des organisations internationales.

La troisième question, liée à la précédente, porte sur le rôle politique des premiers revenus nationaux africains, derrière leur aspect technique tels qu'ils se donnent à voir (Ferguson 1990). En figurant une certaine idée du progrès, ces chiffres ont incontestablement concouru à valoriser les politiques économiques menées sous le colonialisme tardif et à orienter les politiques attendues pour atteindre le développement. Mais cela ne suppose pas pour autant un processus intentionnel et univoque de la part des multiples acteurs ayant participé à l'émergence des premiers revenus nationaux africains, comme si les uns et les autres s'étaient attachés à mettre en place une machine bien huilée : il s'agira bien au contraire de montrer les multiples décalages, désaccords et luttes de sens auxquels cette émergence a donné lieu dès les années 1950.

Des richesses coloniales à la richesse nationale

Comment mesure-t-on les richesses aux colonies avant que l'émergence du revenu national dans les années 1950? Même si ce n'est qu'en 1945 qu'est mis en place en AOF un service de la Statistique, les autorités coloniales s'attachent, dès la conquête, à « gouverner par les nombres » (Desrosières 2008b). En matière de production, chaque secteur d'activité, qu'il soit taxé de « traditionnel » ou de « moderne », fait l'objet, depuis les années 1920, d'une comptabilisation annuelle extrêmement précise, à défaut d'être fiable, sans que nécessité soit ressentie d'une quantification globale. Là est ce que je voudrais en premier lieu montrer : l'apparition du revenu national en AOF dans les années 1950 ne résulte pas de nouvelles modalités de calcul de la production, de la mise en place de nouveaux dispositifs d'enquêtes, ni même d'une reconsidération d'un certain nombre d'activités qui auraient été auparavant ignorées; elle découle d'une nouvelle signification générale donnée à différentes statistiques productives qui jusqu'alors étaient dotées de fonctions bien différenciées et qui, après la Guerre, sont agrégées en un indice synthétique pour satisfaire une nouvelle demande politique.

Mesurer les richesses avant le temps du revenu national

Si l'on revient sur les années qui précèdent l'émergence d'un revenu national pour examiner la manière dont les services coloniaux calculent la valeur de la production en AOF, tous les secteurs ne sont pas également considérés, à l'instar de ce qui a été observé ailleurs, en particulier en Afrique britannique par Morten Jerven (2011). C'est en la matière, et dans la logique du Pacte colonial, la production destinée aux exportations qui fait office de secteur privilégié : si le Sénégal ou la Côte d'Ivoire sont plus « riches » que la Mauritanie ou que le Niger, c'est que l'une, principalement par l'arachide et l'autre, par le café et le cacao, fournissent davantage de richesses à la métropole que les deux dernières. Ces productions destinées à l'exportation font l'objet d'une comptabilisation rigoureuse, non seulement parce qu'elles figurent le rendement économique de ces différentes colonies au sein de l'Empire, mais aussi parce que c'est sur les droits d'entrée et de sortie des produits commercialisés que repose la fiscalité indirecte, laquelle fournit l'essentiel des ressources du budget fédéral. Cette mise en exergue du secteur d'exportation au sein de la production procède donc tout à la fois d'une mesure de l'apport colonial à l'économie impériale mais aussi, plus concrètement, de la gestion financière des colonies.

Outre la production destinée à l'exportation, la Direction générale des Finances dispose également de données précises sur les « exploitations à caractère industriel », les bénéfices desquels sont également imposés.[2] L'un et l'autre constituent – avec les productions assurées par les services administratifs – le secteur dit « moderne », par opposition aux secteurs dits « traditionnels », lesquels comportent principalement l'agriculture de subsistance, l'élevage et l'artisanat destiné aux marchés locaux. En considérant que le paradigme racial structure bien des pratiques coloniales (Reynaud-Paligot 2006), il est tentant de voir dans ce dualisme une représentation racialisée de la production coloniale avec, d'un côté, celle qui intéresse les métropolitains et, de l'autre, celle, dévaluée, qui ne concernerait que les indigènes. Ce serait cependant une erreur de penser que seule la première fait l'objet d'une comptabilisation précise par les services coloniaux, en tout cas pour ce qui est de l'Afrique française. La production indigène, en particulier la production vivrière, donne tout autant lieu à une élaboration régulière de chiffres depuis au moins 1926.[3] Mais outre que ceux-ci entretiennent un lien plus incertain avec la réalité au vu de la faiblesse de l'appareil statistique mais aussi de bonnes raisons qu'ont les populations de se méfier des opérations comptables des administrateurs (Alpha Gado 1988, 250–255), leur usage au sein du gouvernement colonial est tout autre.

Cet usage est de deux ordres. Les statistiques vivrières ont tout d'abord une fonction idéolo-gique : sachant que l'administration coloniale fonde une partie de son autolégitimation sur sa pro-pension à nourrir les populations colonisées – l'idée selon laquelle les famines ont cessé avec la colonisation est un leitmotiv des discours administratifs durant les années 1930, depuis les com-mandants de cercle jusqu'aux ministres (Hardy et Richet 1933) – elles concourent à façonner l'image d'un État colonial grenier. Il ne s'agit que d'une projection : dans les faits, ces chiffres ne parviennent absolument pas à déjouer les crises alimentaires et, lorsque celles-ci arrivent, ce n'est que rétrospectivement, à la lumière de ses manifestations concrètes, que l'administration en prend acte, réécrivant les statistiques de manière à les faire coller à la réalité empiriquement perçue (Bonnecase 2009). La seconde fonction des statistiques vivrières est fiscale, non que la production agricole soit imposée,[4] mais qu'elle donne une indication sur le niveau de ressources des populations rurales. L'histoire de la colonisation est traversée par des débats relatifs au niveau de l'imposition directe – la capitation – prélevée en argent sur les collectivités. Évaluer la pro-duction indigène est un outil d'ajustement global de l'imposition, que ce soit pour la rendre moins lourde – c'est ainsi l'un des enjeux qui animent la conférence des gouverneurs généraux convoquée en 1936 sous le Front populaire,[5] – ou au contraire pour l'augmenter (Ancian 1952).

Si l'administration coloniale dispose donc d'une multitude de données chiffrées pour évaluer différents pans de la production dans les années 1940, elle ne dispose pas de donnée synthétique qui relie les unes et les autres dans un même nombre. Cela ne constitue que partiellement une spécificité coloniale : il convient de relativiser cette absence d'agrégat à l'aune d'une plus large histoire des revenus nationaux. Dans les pays industrialisés, ce n'est qu'à partir des années 1930 que le revenu national commence à faire l'objet d'une comptabilisation précise par les pouvoirs publics, alors qu'émerge l'idée selon laquelle il appartient aux États de piloter l'équilibre macro-économique : selon les innovations théoriques formalisées par Keynes, l'éco-nomie apparaît désormais comme un grand tout articulé par quelques grands flux, lesquels deman-dent à être traduits en chiffres synthétiques (Desrosières 2003a). Pour chacun des pays industrialisés, on peut dater précisément cette irruption d'une statistique globale dans la gestion politique de l'économie : aux États-Unis, le Sénat préconise pour la première fois en 1934 d'établir des « estimations du revenu national » dans le contexte de la crise de 1929. En Grande-Bretagne, après des initiatives discrètes dans les années 1930, l'établissement des comptes nationaux se systématise à partir de 1941, à des fins de rationalisation de l'effort de guerre (Desrosières 2003b). En France, l'évolution est plus tardive puisque, si les initiatives pla-nificatrices du gouvernement de Vichy vont de pair avec une tentative de rénovation de la statis-tique productive,[6] ce n'est qu'avec la création du Commissariat du Plan en 1945, puis de l'INSEE (Institut national de la statistique et des études économiques) en 1946, qu'émerge la comptabilité nationale moderne (Fourquet 1980).

Vu sous cet angle, l'initiative de 1953 en AOF pourrait n'être lue que comme la simple décli-naison, avec sept années de décalage, de la nouvelle demande d'agrégats formulée en métropole dans le nouveau contexte keynésien d'après-guerre. Mais outre que, au regard des conditions de conception des chiffres et de leurs usages politiques, les premiers revenus nationaux de l'AOF sont assez différents de leurs homologues métropolitains (comme on le verra ultérieurement), ils apparaissent également autrement plus novateurs. Si la comptabilité nationale est nouvelle en 1945 dans la métropole, le revenu national n'en a pas moins donné lieu à de multiples évalu-ations depuis le dix-septième siècle ainsi que le rappelle André Vanoli (2002, 20–47). Pareilles évaluations, presque toujours d'initiative privée, étaient principalement mues par des motivations internes de réforme mais pouvaient aussi répondre à une recherche de prestige et de comparaison internationale (Studenski 1958). Cela est plus patent encore si l'on se réfère non pas au calcul des flux productifs mais à celui des patrimoines nationaux. De nombreux tableaux comparatifs en la matière sont dressés au dix-neuvième siècle, alors que la statistique internationale est en plein essor (Brian 1989), pour comparer le niveau de fortune des pays touchés par l'industrialisation. Dans l'entre-deux-guerres, une comparaison est même établie dans le cadre de la Société des Nations (SDN) pour évaluer les richesses respectives des États-Unis et des principales puissances européennes (Vanoli 2002, 383). Mais les colonies ne sont pas conviées dans cette comparabilité internationale, laquelle reste « géographiquement limitée aux seuls pays civilisés » (Horvath 1972, 289).

L'émergence d'un revenu national en AOF, tout en s'inscrivant dans un mouvement plus général de valorisation des agrégats économiques dans le monde au sortir de la Deuxième Guerre mondiale, traduit donc quelque chose de plus spécifiquement nouveau dans un contexte colonial : la possibilité de placer les colonies, par le chiffre, dans un même *continuum* que les pays non colonisés et de les comparer à ces derniers.

Une nouvelle demande d'indicateur global

Il s'agit dès lors de s'interroger sur les raisons de cette innovation statistique ou, plus précisément, sur les nouvelles demandes politiques à laquelle elle répond. Deux facteurs principaux, liés l'un à l'autre parce qu'ils s'inscrivent l'un et l'autre dans le nouveau contexte développementaliste de l'après-guerre, peuvent être invoqués. Le premier, déjà évoqué, est endogène et relève de la mise en place de la nouvelle politique volontariste d'investissements coloniale. Le second, exogène, réside dans la nouvelle demande internationale d'indicateurs à des fins de comparaison internationale et de mesure du développement.

En premier lieu, ce n'est pas un hasard si le premier service de statistique créé pour l'AOF en 1945 se prénomme service de la Statistique *et* du Plan : c'est le gonflement des investissements publics et la nouvelle politique de planification mise en place dans le cadre du nouveau Fonds d'investissement pour le développement économique et social (FIDES) qui suscitent une nouvelle demande statistique, notamment sur la production. On retrouve le même phénomène en Afrique britannique où les premières études du revenu national, à commencer par celle menée en 1948 par Phyllis Deane (1948) pour la Rhodésie du Nord, sont sous-tendues par la nouvelle politique d'investissements mise en place au début de la décennie à la suite du *Welfare and Development Act* de 1940 (Cooper 2004, 40–41). Idéalement – c'est-à-dire, selon la logique qui prédomine au même moment dans les comptabilités nationales métropolitaines – il appartiendrait désormais aux statisticiens de faire le bilan des ressources disponibles dans les colonies, mais aussi d'en prévoir les différentes attributions. En pratique, la chose est plus malaisée dans le cadre de l'AOF ainsi que l'exprime la Direction générale des Finances dans son rapport de 1950 :

> Si la perfection sollicite qu'il soit établi un bilan des ressources du pays et qu'ensuite, en fonction d'une politique déterminée, l'autorité fixe la part de ces ressources à attribuer à la consommation privée, à la consommation publique et au développement du capital de l'AOF, il est bien difficile, en l'état actuel des renseignements statistiques et des moyens d'investigations du pays, de faire autre chose que de l'empirisme légèrement corrigé par quelques observations de base.[7]

Sont ici énumérés les trois éléments qui fondent, en métropole, le calcul du revenu national en fonction de la demande finale (la consommation, la dépense publique et les investissements), laquelle est précisément privilégiée pour calculer le revenu national dans le cadre des nouvelles politiques keynésiennes (Desrosières 1994, 384). Or, s'il apparaît difficile, au tout début des années 1950, de transposer une telle démarche en AOF, c'est pour des raisons de faisabilité pratique, mais aussi parce que son utilité n'apparaît pas aussi évidente.

Plutôt qu'à planifier l'attribution à venir des ressources disponibles, le calcul d'un revenu national répond, dans l'optique de la Direction générale des Finances, à deux préoccupations plus immédiates. Le premier, classique comme on l'a vu, réside dans l'évaluation de la ponction fiscale. Pareille préoccupation est ancienne : dans les rapports financiers des années 1940, il est régulièrement question de mesurer « l'effort fiscal » des différentes colonies; mais à l'époque, le niveau d'imposition est rapporté, faute d'autre référent, à la population dans son ensemble.[8] Avec l'évaluation du revenu national, il devient possible à « la puissance publique d'avoir au moins une idée de la ponction qu'elle prélève par l'impôt sur [le] produit » et de s'assurer que « celle-ci a atteint sa limite ».[9] La deuxième préoccupation consiste, plus qu'à planifier par avance l'attribution des ressources disponibles, à mesurer après coup la croissance économique induite par les investissements, partant du principe, selon les termes de la Direction générale des Finances de l'AOF en 1953, que « l'on ne peut valablement parler d'accroître un revenu dont on ne connaît pas au moins l'ordre de grandeur ».[10] Cette attente est clairement exprimée deux ans plus tard par la Direction des Affaires économiques et du Plan du ministère de la France d'outre-mer :

> Les données fragmentaire dont nous disposons laissent deviner une très large expansion de la richesse publique et une élévation rapide du niveau de vie dans les territoires d'outre-mer depuis la mise en application du premier programme du plan de l'après-guerre, [...] mais il serait plus démonstratif encore d'accuser la signification de ces indices de l'activité économique en dégageant de leur ensemble et de la masse des autres données numériques existantes un chiffre unique pour chaque territoire et pour chaque année, celui qui traduirait ce qu'on appelle ordinairement, dans les pays d'Europe, le revenu national.[11]

Ainsi, plus qu'un outil de planification et de prévision des politiques publiques, selon la logique qui prévaut au même moment en métropole, le calcul du revenu national dans les colonies traduit la volonté gouvernementale d'évaluer les effets induits par la nouvelle politique d'investissement colonial sur la production locale et les conditions de vie des populations colonisées. Pareille optique demande à être replacée dans la profonde crise de légitimité qui affecte l'Empire colonial français dans l'après-guerre : sans qu'il soit nécessairement dans l'intention des premiers concepteurs des revenus nationaux de répondre directement à cette crise, leurs travaux n'en ouvrent pas moins la possibilité de prouver par le chiffre, pour la première fois dans l'histoire de la colonisation, l'impact positif de la politique coloniale sur la richesse globale des colonies et de ses habitants. C'est d'ailleurs ce qu'en retiendront, après les Indépendances, les statisticiens français chargés de mettre en place les comptabilités nationales des nouveaux États africains, cette fois à des fins affichées de planifications des politiques de développement :

> Les [premiers] travaux relatifs au produit intérieur brut [...], quand ils furent entrepris, avaient pour objet essentiel d'apprécier le niveau de vie en Afrique de l'Ouest. [...] Par le détour du produit intérieur, on cherchait en fait à appréhender les utilisations finales intérieures – ou plus exactement leurs contreparties en termes de revenus. (Haubert 1969, 43–44)

En second lieu, cette quête de légitimation par les chiffres est également sous-tendue, de manière exogène, par une demande internationale. L'une des principales activités des nouvelles organisations onusiennes mises en place à partir de 1945 consiste à produire une standardisation des savoirs à des fins de comparabilité internationale d'une part et de mesurabilité du développement d'autre part. Chaque organisme spécialisé agit en ce sens dans son propre domaine : la FAO (Food and Agriculture Organization) par exemple, s'attache tout à la fois à standardiser la collecte de données sur la production agricole dans le cadre de grands recensements décennaux mondiaux, et à produire de nouvelles normes de besoins alimentaires *minima* à l'aune desquelles mesurer et comparer les niveaux d'alimentation dans le monde. Cette démarche s'inscrit dans la lignée d'une dynamique déjà à l'œuvre dans l'entre-deux-guerres sous l'égide de la SDN mais qui, pour l'essentiel, ne concernait que les pays européens et nord-américains. L'une des grandes préoccupations onusiennes de l'immédiat après-guerre consiste à inclure les territoires désormais « sous-développés » dans l'espace de comparabilité induit par la statistique internationale, rompant ainsi la barrière d'incommensurabilité qui séparait jusqu'alors les colonies et les métropoles (Bonnecase 2011) : sous le prisme du développement, les conditions de vie dans le monde sont désormais posées comme étant tout à la fois mesurables, comparables et rattrapables.

L'une des questions qui agitent les instances internationales résident alors dans la question des critères adéquats : sachant que la Charte des Nations unies proclame que l'activité économique et sociale internationale doit tendre à instaurer « de meilleures conditions de vie »,[12] il s'agit tout à la fois de préciser ce que recouvrent cette notion et les méthodes qui doivent permettre de mesurer son élévation. En mai 1949, l'Assemblée générale adopte ainsi une résolution demandant au Conseil économique et social d'examiner « la situation sociale dans le monde » à partir « d'indices quantitatifs de satisfaction de besoins dont l'existence est universellement reconnue ».[13] Trois ans plus tard, le Conseil économique et social établit un premier « rapport sur la situation sociale dans le monde et les niveaux de vie en particulier » dans lequel « le revenu national par habitant » est « considéré comme un indice des niveaux de vie », même si « on ne s'est pas encore nettement mis d'accord sur ce qu'il fallait entendre au point de vue international par "niveau de vie" ».[14] Parallèlement une nouvelle résolution de l'Assemblée générale des Nations unies prie le Conseil économique et social de « faire élaborer des méthodes et des techniques statistiques appropriées de manière à faciliter au maximum le rassemblement et l'emploi de données pertinentes afin que le Secrétariat général puisse publier régulièrement des rapports annuels indiquant, en chiffres absolus, les changements intervenus dans tous les pays en ce qui concerne les conditions de vie ».[15]

Suite à cette résolution, un comité de six experts est réuni en juin 1953 par le Conseil économique et social afin de travailler à « la définition et l'évaluation des niveaux de vie du point de vue international ».[16] Des membres de l'OIT (Organisation international du travail), de l'UNESCO (Organisation des Nations unies pour l'éducation, la science et la culture), de la FAO et de l'OMS (Organisation mondiale de la santé) participent également aux réunions de travail. Le comité s'appuie en outre sur les avis formulés par une trentaine d'universitaires, de ministres ou d'anciens ministres, majoritairement d'Europe et des États-Unis, plus marginalement d'Asie du Sud ou d'Amérique latine.[17] Outre le bienfondé de la démarche dans son ensemble et le « risque de « préjugé ethnocentrique » qu'elle comporte – parce que « l'emploi d'un système de valeurs uniforme et universel pourrait conduire à « sanctionner sur le plan international les progrès techniques réalisés dans l'Occident » –, l'une des principales controverses touche à la pertinence d'un « indice unique du niveau de vie global ». Le revenu national apparaît à cet égard comme « un indicateur relativement complet » tout en pouvant susciter des « conclusions assez fausses sur les différences qui existent entre les niveaux de vie des diverses régions du monde », d'une part parce qu'il est difficile de « mesurer la parité de pouvoir d'achat et [de] convertir les monnaies nationales », d'autre part parce qu'une « partie des biens et services ne relèvent pas de la consommation marchande ». En revanche, le comité cible la « variation du revenu national par habitant » comme étant l'un des principaux indicateurs permettant de mesurer « l'évolution du niveau de vie général » d'une population dans un même pays, à défaut de permettre des comparaisons internationales pertinentes.[18] On retrouve là des débats par la suite maintes fois repris, parfois dans une prétention novatrice, au sein des organisations onusiennes, des instances académiques ou des médias internationaux et qui, finalement, ont d'emblée fait partie de l'histoire du revenu national comme indicateur de niveau de vie.[19]

Deux choses importantes ressortent de ce retour sur les conditions d'émergence du revenu national en AOF. D'une part, cette émergence constitue une rupture dans l'appréciation des richesses coloniales en ce qu'elle ne connaît pas de précédents comparables aux prémices de la comptabilité nationale en métropole. D'autre part, elle répond à des demandes hétérogènes où se mêlent des considérations internes anciennes – en particulier ce qui touche à la fiscalité – et un nouveau souci de mesurabilité des niveaux de vie dans le monde. Il paraît important d'insister sur le fait que le revenu national n'a pas été doté après coup de cette dernière signification, ainsi que le suggère Alain Desrosières (2012) à propos des seuls pays industrialisés : en Afrique tout au moins, cette valeur d'indicateur de niveau de vie, aussi controversée soit-elle, a été présente au moment même de l'élaboration des premiers revenus nationaux.

Quels chiffres et pour quoi faire?

Je voudrais maintenant interroger les conditions concrètes d'élaboration des premiers revenus nationaux en AOF et les usages qui ont pu être les leurs à la toute fin de la période coloniale. Si un terme permet de relier l'un et l'autre des deux questionnements, c'est celui de décalage : d'un côté, le calcul des premiers revenus nationaux donne lieu à de nombreuses controverses, tant relatives aux méthodes employées qu'à la fiabilité des résultats obtenus; de l'autre, cela ne les empêchent nullement de valoir comme preuves et d'être politiquement investis, parfois de manière antagonique, notamment à des fins de valorisation ou de contestation de la politique coloniale.

L'incertitude des chiffres, des méthodes et de leurs concepteurs

Les deux premières études du revenu national en Afrique française, hormis deux précédents en 1952 pour les seuls territoires du Cameroun et de Mauritanie,[20] sont menées en 1953 et en 1955. La première est un « Essai de récapitulation des éléments connus à Dakar pour servir à un calcul du revenu national », établi par un administrateur colonial, André Auclert, pour le compte de la Direction générale des Finances de l'AOF.[21] Il s'agit d'une compilation des données productives disponibles, lesquelles sont converties en valeur monétaire et synthétisées en un « revenu par tête » pour l'AOF et chacune des colonies qui composent la fédération. Celle-ci se retrouve ainsi, pour la première fois de son histoire, inscrite dans une hiérarchisation internationale des niveaux de vie en fonction du revenu national (Tableau 1). La deuxième s'inscrit dans un plus large « Essai de détermination du revenu national des principaux territoires d'outre-mer », mené sous la direction d'un administrateur de l'INSEE, Boris Maldant. Outre l'AOF, sont évaluées les productions respectives de l'Afrique équatoriale française (AEF), du Cameroun et de Madagascar pour les années 1947 et 1953.[22] Ce dernier choix n'est pas fortuit puisqu'il s'agit des limites du premier plan de développement mis en œuvre dans le cadre du FIDES, dont il s'agit ainsi d'évaluer les effets sur la richesse globale de ces territoires.

L'une et l'autre de ces deux études sont significatives des controverses méthodologiques et, finalement, des incertitudes qui marquent l'établissement des premiers revenus nationaux dans les colonies africaines. L'une des principales interrogations porte sur les « termes récalcitrants », autrement dit les secteurs productifs dont la mesure pose le plus problème, soit qu'ils soient non marchands, soit que leur qualité même de « production » prête à contestation. Apparaissent ainsi principalement comme « récalcitrants » dans les colonies africaines l'autoconsommation paysanne, les services rendus par les ménages à eux-mêmes et les logements occupés par leurs propres propriétaires. La prise en compte de chacun de ces termes dans le calcul du revenu national donne lieu à des débats qui dépassent les limites de l'Empire français, s'inscrivant ainsi dans les nouvelles formes de connexions inter-impériales qui se dessinent après la Guerre (Kent 1992). Concernant l'autoconsommation paysanne, se posent à la fois le problème de son évaluation quantitative et celui de sa transcription en valeur marchande. Si ces questions, derrière leurs aspects techniques, renvoient à des enjeux éminemment politiques, il ne semble pas que

Tableau 1. Quelques revenus nationaux dans le monde en 1953.

Territoire	Revenu par tête en francs CFA
Arabie Saoudite (1949)	5 250
Yémen (1949)	5 250
Éthiopie (1949)	6 650
Afghanistan (1949)	8 750
Pakistan (1949)	8 925
AOF (1951)	9 400
Inde (1949)	9 450
Bolivie (1953)	10 000
Pérou (1949)	11 130
Argentine (1948)	15 240
Brésil (1950)	22 810

Source : Centre des Archives d'outre-mer (CAOM), BIB-SOM, Direction générale des Finances de l'AOF, « Essai de récapitulation des éléments connus à Dakar pour servir à un calcul du revenu national de l'AOF », Dakar, 1953.

cette économie domestique ait été sciemment dépréciée par les premiers concepteurs des revenus nationaux en Afrique française pour des raisons idéologiques, à l'instar de ce qu'observe Morten Jerven (2011) à propos de l'Afrique britannique : on verra à ce titre que les services coloniaux avait plutôt intérêt à présenter les chiffres de PIB les plus hauts possibles – économie domestique inclue – ne serait-ce que pour valoriser leur propre politique de développement. La valeur à donner aux services rendus par les ménages à eux-mêmes fait également débat : alors qu'une partie des premiers investigateurs supposent que ces services sont particulièrement importants en Afrique – dans la mesure où de nombreuses activités telles que le puisage de l'eau, la coupe du bois ou la transformation des céréales, fournies par des professionnels en Europe, sont assurées par les ménages dans les territoires africains[23] –, telle n'est pas la position retenue par André Auclerc et Boris Maldant, d'une part parce que « la quasi-totalité des femmes [africaines] concourent à la production agricole mesurable » et d'autre part « parce que les besognes ménagères constituent des services relativement sommaires »[24]. Concernant enfin l'évaluation du revenu que rapporte à son propriétaire la possession d'un logement qu'il habite et pour lequel il ne paye pas de loyer (ce qui est le cas de la totalité des populations rurales), André Auclerc s'inspire des études faites par Phyllis Deane (1948) sur « le revenu des cases » en Rhodésie du Nord, pour en extrapoler les conclusions à l'AOF, en attendant « une enquête aussi localisée que possible afin de connaître le prix de revient de ce type de logement » dans la fédération.[25]

Une seconde interrogation touche, non pas aux méthodes de calcul, mais aux sources empiriques sur lesquelles reposent un certain nombre de données collectées, en particulier celles qui ont trait aux cultures vivrières, à la production pastorale et à la population. Pour ce qui est d'abord des cultures vivrières, les chiffres reposent ainsi, faute d'enquête par sondage,[26] sur l'estimation annuelle des rendements et des surfaces ensemencées par les agents des services agricoles. Sachant que ces derniers sont presque toujours amenés à extrapoler à l'ensemble des circonscriptions qu'ils ont à charge leurs observations effectuées dans quelques villages, les résultats restent de l'aveu du service de la Statistique de l'AOF assez aléatoires. L'évaluation des produits de l'élevage, ensuite, repose sur les recensements pastoraux à finalité fiscale, lesquels sous-estiment invariablement la réalité du fait des stratégies d'évitement développées par les éleveurs à l'égard des agents recenseurs. Pour pallier cette imperfection, les statisticiens établissent un « coefficient de sous-déclaration fiscale »[27] destiné à redresser la valeur de la production pastorale. La comptabilisation des populations, enfin, repose sur les recensements administratifs, lesquels visent d'abord à calculer le montant de l'impôt de capitation. Outre que les agents recenseurs ont tendance, dans ces conditions, à comptabiliser avec moins de zèle les classes d'âge non imposables, ils font eux-aussi l'objet de stratégies d'évitement qui visent à faire baisser les charges fiscales pesant sur les collectivités. Lors des premières enquêtes démographiques par sondage réalisées en Afrique francophone à partir de 1955, il sera ainsi fréquent de voir la population réévaluée de plus d'un dixième par rapport aux estimations administratives.[28]

Ces questionnements amènent finalement les statisticiens de la France d'Outre-mer à considérer avec prudence leurs premiers résultats et les conclusions que l'on pourrait en tirer, en matière d'accroissement de la richesse et de comparaison internationale. D'après l'étude publiée par le ministère en 1955 – la première à faire l'objet d'une diffusion par les services de la France d'outre-mer[29] –, le revenu national s'élève en 1953 à 13 600 francs CFA par habitant en AEF, à 13 800 francs en AOF, à 18 100 francs au Cameroun et à 23 400 francs à Madagascar (Tableau 2) et présente des taux de croissance globale compris entre 50 pour cent et 80 pour cent par rapport à 1947, année de lancement du premier plan du FIDES (Tableau 3).

Les auteurs de l'étude prennent toutefois soin de conclure dans ces termes :

> Ces récapitulations ne doivent […] pas être considérées comme une évaluation définitive du revenu national des territoires, et méritent de sérieuses réserves dans leur état actuel, car elles sont entachées de sous-estimations de toute sorte. […] Une particularité remarquable […] est l'alignement de la production par habitant de l'AEF sur le taux de l'AOF. Une telle constatation va à l'encontre des données classiques. […] Il est probable que sur le plan des niveaux de vie véritables, l'AOF devrait être créditée de 1 000 à 1 500 francs de plus […] relativement à l'AEF. […] On peut toutefois se demander si, *réellement*, les deux territoires n'ont pas des standings plus voisins qu'on le croit.[30]

Deux éléments ressortent de cet examen des conditions d'élaboration des premiers revenus nationaux en AOF. D'une part, les statisticiens chargés de leur élaboration, tout en répondant à des

Tableau 2.   La composition du revenu national en Afrique française en 1953.

	AOF	AEF	Cameroun	Madagascar
Activités des services publics	1 960	2 350	2 030	3 590
Produits d'exportation	2 380	1 910	3 540	3 140
Activités à l'importation	2 030	2 030	2 740	3 420
Activités locales affectées aux investissements	1 990	1 960	3 190	3 280
Produits de l'agriculture vivrière	4 380	3 670	5 720	7 770
Produits de l'élevage	1 110	1 680	880	2 220
Revenu national par habitant	13 800	13 600	18 100	23 400

Source : Centre des Archives d'outre-mer (CAOM), 1fides/69, Direction des Affaires économiques et du Plan du ministère de la France d'outre-mer, « Essai de détermination du revenu national des principaux territoires d'outre-mer (AOF, Cameroun, AEF, Madagascar) en 1947 et en 1953 », Paris, 1955.

Tableau 3.   La croissance en Afrique française de 1947 à 1953.

	AOF	AEF	Cameroun	Madagascar
Revenu national de 1947*	160 300 000	50 500 000	37 300 000	72 400 000
Revenu national de 1953*	271 800 000	71 300 000	67 000 000	110 800 000
Croissance globale de 1947 à 1953	+ 69%	+ 41%	+ 80%	+ 53%

*en francs CFA de 1953
Source : Centre des Archives d'outre-mer (CAOM), 1fides/69, Direction des Affaires économiques et du Plan du ministère de la France d'outre-mer, « Essai de détermination du revenu national des principaux territoires d'outre-mer (AOF, Cameroun, AEF, Madagascar) en 1947 et en 1953 », Paris, 1955.

préoccupations proprement productives dans le cadre de la planification coloniale, attribuent également à leurs chiffres une valeur de mesure des « niveaux de vie », conformément à ce qui a été observé à l'échelle internationale. D'autre part, ces chiffres peinent à faire autorité face à la réalité telle qu'elle est empiriquement perçue : l'alignement statistique de l'AOF sur le niveau de l'AEF apparaît ainsi éminemment suspect au regard des perceptions habituelles de la chose, à tel point que les statisticiens puissent inviter à se demander, au terme de leur étude, ce qu'il en est *réellement*.

Dire des vérités par les chiffres

Or, ces réserves n'empêchent nullement ces chiffres, une fois établis, d'échapper à leurs propres concepteurs, de valoir comme preuves et de signifier des vérités. Là est sur ce quoi je voudrais finir : les premiers revenus nationaux établis en AOF ont beau être quelque peu incertains, ils furent rapidement investis politiquement et cela, à des fins assez contrastées, voire parfois antagoniques. S'il n'est pas question de saisir ici la totalité des débats au sein desquels ont figuré ces indicateurs dans les années 1950, je voudrais juste cibler quatre usages qui en ont été faits.[31]

Le premier usage, le plus prévisible puisque là était l'attendu de départ, réside dans la valorisation de la nouvelle politique d'investissements coloniale par le ministère de la France d'outre-mer. Dans ce cas, plus que le revenu national lui-même, c'est son augmentation qui fait office d'indicateur privilégié. De 1946 à 1953, durant la mise en œuvre du premier plan du FIDES, cette augmentation atteindrait près de 9 pour cent par an en AOF. Cela permet aux statisticiens du ministère de conclure prudemment à un rôle positif du plan, lequel est « le seul élément nouveau d'après-guerre qui ait exercé une action assez marquée et assez continue pour rendre compte de la rapide expansion des revenus territoriaux en l'espace de ces six années ».[31] Pareil bilan comptable est en revanche relayé sans distance par une presse coloniale qui se félicite, revenus nationaux à l'appui, que « grâce à l'effort français, les niveaux de vie se [soient] élevés dans les colonies ».[32] Ces chiffres, que l'on peut également retrouver dans des livres d'histoire sur la colonisation (Ageron 1990, t.2, 453), concourent finalement, aux côtés d'autres statistiques, notamment médicales, à présenter le colonialisme tardif sous un jour favorable, celui du « renouveau » et des « réalisations tardives » (Bado 1996, 349). Il ne s'agit pas ici de nier le fait que les investissements français de l'après-guerre aient été synonymes d'accroissement de la production – et il n'est pas entré dans ma démarche de vouloir substituer aux statistiques officielles d'autres chiffres qui seraient les *vrais* chiffres de la croissance. Il s'agit juste de bien voir que les premiers revenus nationaux de l'AOF ont permis de figurer un succès malgré les incertitudes qui ont marqué leurs modalités d'élaboration.

Un deuxième usage, plus synchronique et davantage tourné vers les attentes internationales, consiste à inscrire les chiffres du revenu national sur une échelle de développement afin de mesurer la position relative de l'AOF par rapport à d'autres territoires. Un tel usage va là encore à l'encontre des réserves affichées par les statisticiens pour lesquels, si « la notion de niveau de vie moyen peut être dégagé en divisant le revenu national par le nombre d'habitants », le procédé reste « très critiquable en matière de comparaison internationale » (Fabre, Dubois, et Courcier 1958, 7). Pareil usage est en outre ambivalent puisque, selon le point de vue où l'on se place et les comparaisons que l'on mobilise, il est possible d'en tirer des conclusions plus ou moins favorables à la politique coloniale de la France. Cette ambivalence est perceptible dès 1953, alors que la Direction générale des Finances de l'AOF, munie de son premier revenu national, entreprend de dresser un tableau comparatif des niveaux de développement dans le monde (Tableau 1). D'un côté, elle admet que « le revenu par tête de l'AOF » est « caractéristique d'un pays sous-développé ». Mais de l'autre, elle met en exergue le fait que « des nations dites libres, devenues des accusateurs internationaux, sont également sous-développées, et souvent d'une manière plus grave ». Il apparaît ainsi utile à la Direction générale « de rappeler quelles sont les estimations connues du revenu national dans quelques pays sous-développés du monde parmi lesquels on trouve les plus farouches de nos détracteurs dans les assemblées internationales ».[33]

Or, il est possible, à partir du même indicateur, d'aller chercher des conclusions opposées. Un troisième usage, fait des revenus nationaux dans les années 1950, consiste ainsi à mettre en cause l'efficacité de la politique coloniale française en termes d'élévation des niveaux de vie. L'un des principaux courants critiques des investissements métropolitains dans les colonies est connu : il s'agit du cartiérisme, du nom du journaliste Raymond Cartier qui, dans trois articles publiés par *Paris Match* en août et septembre 1956, met en cause la nouvelle politique coloniale d'après-guerre. Ce qui est moins connu, c'est la manière dont ce discours mobilise les propres chiffres de l'administration coloniale pour les retourner contre elle. Ainsi, selon Cartier :

> En Haute-Volta, on touche aux niveaux de vie les plus bas de l'Afrique française. Le revenu moyen du paysan mossi est évalué à 5 000 francs CFA, soit 10 000 francs métropolitains par an. Sur les marchés, les femmes vendent des œufs microscopiques et des poignées d'arachides que l'on paye avec des vieilles pièces en bronze d'aluminium d'un ou deux francs. C'est pour le commun de ces pauvres gens qu'on croit nécessaire d'édifier des halles en béton, hautes comme une cathédrale! […] Malgré la Côte d'Ivoire, qui relève la moyenne en se rapprochant du bien-être de l'Espagne, le niveau de vie de l'AOF ne dépasse pas celui de l'Inde, et il tombe, en Haute-Volta, à l'étage du Yémen. (Cartier 1956)

Ces assertions – jusqu'aux exemples invoqués – ne sont rien d'autre que la mise en mots du tableau statistique établi par la Direction générale des Finances de l'AOF trois ans plus tôt. Cela illustre finalement la manière dont le débat public métropolitain s'empara assez rapidement du revenu national et de la quantification des niveaux de vie pour en faire un argument global, à charge ou à décharge, de la politique coloniale française en Afrique. Or, il convient en dernier lieu d'interroger l'usage de ces chiffres par les premiers destinataires de cette politique, en l'occurrence les populations colonisées. Là encore plusieurs directions différentes ont pu être prises dans les discours des syndicats et des partis africains durant les dernières années de la colonisation. Si l'on se focalise d'abord sur l'écart entre les colonies et la métropole, le revenu national par habitant peut d'abord être invoqué pour signifier une inégalité foncière. Mais il ne me semble pas que cet usage des chiffres soit répandu entre 1953 et l'indépendance. Dans les plateformes des principales formations politiques interterritoriales constituées en AOF, ce sont d'autres indicateurs – en particulier le taux de mortalité infantile ou celui de la ration calorique – qui font office d'arme statistique en matière de comparaison avec la métropole.[34] Si l'on se focalise ensuite sur la structure interne des revenus nationaux, les nouveaux savoirs permettent de quantifier des écarts entre différentes populations qui, jusqu'alors, n'avaient jamais été mesurés : il peut être ainsi affirmé, à la fin de la décennie, que « le niveau de vie » dans la fédération est en moyenne près de 40 fois plus élevé chez « les blancs » que chez « les noirs », en admettant que « les revenus des secteurs modernes échoient principalement aux premiers » tandis que ceux des « secteurs mixte et traditionnel » reviennent aux seconds (Capet et Fabre 1957, 13). Si l'on se focalise enfin sur l'augmentation de la production dans les années 1950, le revenu national peut être invoqué pour négocier de meilleurs traitements, notamment en terme salarial, avec l'administration. Là est davantage la position des syndicats de la fédération qui, tout en indexant une augmentation du coût de la vie, arguent de la croissance économique – et des bénéfices des entreprises – pour exiger l'augmentation des salaires.[35] En tout état de cause, cela invite aussi à voir dans l'émergence des revenus nationaux à la fin de la période coloniale une nouvelle opportunité discursive pour les acteurs politiques africains.

Conclusion

Trois éléments, qui se dégagent de cette histoire des premiers revenus nationaux en AOF, peuvent être mis en perspective à la lumière de travaux récents. Premier élément, ces chiffres sont incertains au regard de leurs conditions de production. Cela ne constitue que moyennement une surprise : plusieurs auteurs, et essentiellement Morten Jerven pour l'Afrique anglophone, ont déjà montré que les chiffres de la croissance pouvaient parfois se réduire à de simples jeux d'écriture, soit qu'il y ait faiblesse de l'appareil statistique, soit qu'il y ait changement dans les modalités de calcul ou même, parfois, volonté délibérée de travestissement (Jerven 2009, 2010). Ces jeux sur les chiffres constituent en outre nullement une réalité spécifiquement africaine ni même spécifiquement coloniale, pas plus qu'ils ne se cantonnent à un passé révolu (Data 2009). L'histoire que j'ai ici racontée est finalement relativement banale : elle traduit la propension de chiffres, une fois établis, à poursuivre leur propre histoire, indépendamment de leurs propres concepteurs et à revêtir des significations que ces derniers n'y avaient pas nécessairement mis. Second élément, ces chiffres ont eu une place importante dans la justification tardive de la colonisation, à un moment où celle-ci souffrait d'un déficit marqué de légitimité. Cela incite à lire les revenus nationaux, non pas seulement comme des outils descriptifs, même imparfaits, mais aussi comme des biais de gouvernement et de légitimation. C'est ce que fait Béatrice Hibou (2011) à propos du cas tunisien, lorsqu'elle lit les indicateurs macro-économiques comme les composants d'un récit statistique – celui du « miracle » – lequel était devenu central dans l'appareil idéologique de l'État benaliste et la fabrique du consentement. Sans vouloir transférer au colonialisme tardif les caractéristiques de ce régime autoritaire, tout au moins peut-on affirmer que les premiers chiffres du revenu national s'inscrivent également dans un récit statistique, celui du succès tardif de la politique économique de la colonisation, dont on peut se demander s'il n'a pas, plus tard et par contraste, contribué à écrire un autre récit, celui de la faible croissance des pays africains après les indépendances. Troisième élément, le revenu national a fait office, dès les années 1950, d'indicateur des niveaux de vie en Afrique sans que ce soit son seul usage, ni que cet usage-là soit autant publicisé qu'il ne le sera par la suite. Il ne me semble pas, à ce titre, que l'on puisse clairement distinguer, ainsi que le fait Alain Desrosières (2008b, 18–19) sur la base d'observations européennes et américaines, un premier usage expert du revenu national focalisé sur sa signification macroéconomique et un usage grand public plus récent qui ferait du revenu national un indicateur de richesse. Dès les années 1950 – et pour ce qui est de l'Afrique –, l'un et l'autre de ces deux usages se sont d'emblée mélangés et la propension du revenu national à figurer le niveau de vie a fait l'objet de controverses, dont on peut observer les prolongements jusqu'à aujourd'hui.

Notice biographique

Vincent Bonnecase est docteur en histoire et chercheur en science politique au Centre national de la recherche scientifique à Bordeaux (France). Il a travaillé sur l'histoire de la mesure de la pauvreté en Afrique coloniale et postcoloniale. Il a notamment écrit *La Pauvreté au Sahel. Du savoir colonial à la mesure internationale* (Paris, Karthala, 2011). Il travaille désormais sur les mobilisations contre la vie chère en Afrique contemporaine.

Notes

1. L'AOF est l'une des deux grandes fédérations coloniales détenues par la France en Afrique. Établie en 1895, elle regroupe le Sénégal, la Mauritanie, le Soudan français (Mali), le Niger, la Guinée, la Haute-Volta (Burkina Faso), la Côte d'Ivoire et le Dahomey (Bénin).
2. Archives nationales du Sénégal (ANS), 2G50.40, Contrôle financier de l'AOF, « Rapport sur les budgets de l'AOF », Dakar, 1950.

3. C'est à partir de 1926 que les services de l'Agriculture de l'AOF doivent, par arrêt du gouvernement général, comptabiliser le volume de la production agricole chaque année dans chaque colonie.
4. Il existe toutefois une taxe sur le bétail.
5. ANS, 17G255, ministère des Colonies, « Rapport sur la Conférence des gouverneurs généraux », Paris, 1936.
6. La loi du 6 avril 1941 portant sur le plan d'équipement national prévoyait un plan d'investissement de 10 ans dans les colonies.
7. ANS, 2G50.40, Direction du Contrôle financier de l'AOF, « Rapports sur les budgets de l'AOF », Dakar, 1950.
8. ANS, 2G48.105, Direction du Contrôle financier de l'AOF, « Rapport sur la situation budgétaire de l'AOF au 30 juin 1948 », Dakar, 1949.
9. Centre des Archives d'outre-mer (CAOM), BIB-SOM, Direction générale des Finances de l'AOF, « Essai de récapitulation des éléments connus à Dakar pour servir à un calcul du revenu national de l'AOF », Dakar, 1953.
10. Centre des Archives d'outre-mer (CAOM), BIB-SOM, Direction générale des Finances de l'AOF, « Essai de récapitulation des éléments connus à Dakar pour servir à un calcul du revenu national de l'AOF », Dakar, 1953.
11. CAOM, 1fides/69, Direction des Affaires économiques et du Plan du ministère de la France d'outre-mer, « Essai de détermination du revenu national des principaux territoires d'outre-mer (AOF, Cameroun, AEF, Madagascar) en 1947 et en 1953 », Paris, 1955.
12. ONU (Organisation des Nations unies), Chartre des Nations unies, San Francisco, 1945, préambule.
13. ONU, Assemblée générale, résolution n° 280-III du 13 mai 1949.
14. ONU, Conseil économique et social, « Rapport préliminaire sur la situation sociale dans le monde et les niveaux de vie en particulier », New York, 1952.
15. ONU, Assemblée générale, résolution n° 527-VI du 26 janvier 1952.
16. Il comprend Raymond Firth et Philip Hauser, respectivement professeurs d'anthropologie en Angleterre et de sociologie aux États-Unis, Erland Hofsten et Alexander Moraes, chefs de service statistique en Suède et aux États-Unis, M. V. Rao, directeur d'un Institut d'Économie politique en Inde, et Louis-Joseph Lebret, directeur de la revue *Économie et humanisme* en France.
17. Parmi les experts sollicités, on peut trouver, outre plusieurs universitaires aux États-Unis, des personnalités aussi diverses que Sumitro Djojohadikusomo, ministre des Finances de l'Indonésie, Henri Labouret, ancien administrateur colonial français, et Josué de Castro, auteur brésilien du premier ouvrage nommément consacré à la faim dans le monde (Castro 1951).
18. ONU, Conseil économique et social, « Rapport sur la définition et l'évaluation des niveaux de vie du point de vue international », New York, 1954.
19. Pour une résurgence récente et fortement médiatisée de ces débats, voir Fitoussi, Sen, et Stiglitz (2009).
20. Ces deux études menées sous la direction de deux administrateurs de l'INSEE – Jules Leveugle pour le Cameroun et Louis Marciniak pour la Mauritanie – se focalisent davantage, voire exclusivement dans le premier cas, sur la production marchande (Fabre, Dubois, et Courcier 1958).
21. CAOM, BIB-SOM, Direction générale des Finances de l'AOF, « Essai de récapitulation des éléments connus à Dakar pour servir à un calcul du revenu national de l'AOF », Dakar, 1953.
22. CAOM, 1fides/69, Direction des Affaires économiques et du Plan du ministère de la France d'outre-mer, « Essai de détermination du revenu national des principaux territoires d'outre-mer (AOF, Cameroun, AEF, Madagascar) en 1947 et en 1953 », Paris, 1955.
23. C'est notamment le point de vue défendu par Jules Leveugle (1953).
24. CAOM, BIB-SOM, Direction générale des Finances de l'AOF, « Essai de récapitulation des éléments connus à Dakar pour servir à un calcul du revenu national de l'AOF », Dakar, 1953.
25. CAOM, BIB-SOM, Direction générale des Finances de l'AOF, « Essai de récapitulation des éléments connus à Dakar pour servir à un calcul du revenu national de l'AOF », Dakar, 1953.
26. Hormis quelques précédents au début de la décennie, les premières grandes enquêtes par sondage sur la production agricole et, plus largement, sur les niveaux de vie des populations sont menées en 1954-1955 en Côte d'Ivoire (« Enquête sur la subdivision de Bongouanou ») et en 1956-1958 au Sénégal (« Mission socio-économique du Sénégal ») et au Soudan français (« Mission socio-économique du Soudan ») (Bonnecase 2011).
27. Ce coefficient de sous-déclaration est lui-même calculé en recoupant les données des recensements et celles des campagnes anti-épizootiques, supposées plus conformes à la réalité, dans les zones où ces deux opérations sont menées de manière disjointe.

28. Cette réévaluation atteint jusqu'à 23% en Haute-Volta (République de Haute-Volta, ministère de l'Économie nationale, « Compte-rendu de l'exécution de l'enquête démographique par sondage, 1960-1961 », Ouagadougou, 1962).
29. L'étude de 1953 n'est pas publiée.
30. CAOM, 1fides/69, Direction des Affaires économiques et du Plan du ministère de la France d'outre-mer, « Essai de détermination du revenu national des principaux territoires d'outre-mer (AOF, Cameroun, AEF, Madagascar) en 1947 et en 1953 », Paris, 1955.
31. CAOM, 1fides/69, Direction des Affaires économiques et du Plan du ministère de la France d'outre-mer, « Essai de détermination du revenu national des principaux territoires d'outre-mer (AOF, Cameroun, AEF, Madagascar) en 1947 et en 1953 », Paris, 1955.
32. CAOM, 1affpol/2186, « L'information de la France d'outre-mer », 23-24 septembre 1956.
33. CAOM, BIB-SOM, Direction générale des Finances de l'AOF, « Essai de récapitulation des éléments connus à Dakar pour servir à un calcul du revenu national de l'AOF », Dakar, 1953.
34. ANS, 17G611, Gouvernement général de l'AOF, rapports et documentation sur les congrès interterritoriaux des partis politiques, 1956.
35. ANS, 17G272, Gouvernement général de l'AOF, rapports et documentation sur l'activité syndicale en AOF, 1955.

Références

Ageron, R., dir. 1990. *Histoire de la France coloniale*. 2 tomes. Paris : Armand Colin.

Alpha Gado, B. 1988. « Sécheresses et famines au Sahel. Crises alimentaires et stratégies d'autosubsistance en Afrique sahélienne. » 3 tomes. Thèse de troisième cycle, Université de Paris 7.

Ancian, G. 1952. *Budgets et niveaux de vie des cultivateurs betsiléos*. Paris : École nationale de la France d'Outre-Mer.

Bado, J.-P. 1996. *Médecine coloniale et grandes endémies en Afrique*. Paris : Karthala.

Bonnecase, V. 2009. « Avoir faim en AOF. Investigations et représentations coloniales (1920-1960). » *Revue d'histoire des sciences humaines* 2009 (21) : 151–174.

Bonnecase, V. 2011. *La pauvreté au Sahel. Du savoir colonial à la mesure internationale*. Paris : Karthala.

Bourmaud, P., dir. 2011. *De la mesure à la norme : les indicateurs de développement*. Bangkok-Lausanne : Presse de l'Institut français du Proche-Orient – Bangkok Services Network.

Brian, É. 1989. « Statistique administrative et internationalisme statistique pendant la seconde moitié du XIXe siècle. » *Histoire et mesures* 4 (3/4) : 201–224.

Capet, M., et R. Fabre. 1957. *L'économie de l'AOF depuis la guerre*. Paris : Imprimerie Guillemot et de Lamothe.

Cartier, R. 1956. « En Afrique noire avec Raymond Cartier. La France sème ses milliards, les Africains disent : c'est bien tard. » *Paris Match*, n° 384, 25 août.

Castro, J. de. 1951. *Geopolítica da fome*. Rio de Janeiro : Casa do Estudante do Brasil.

Cooper, F. 2004. *Décolonisation et travail en Afrique. L'Afrique britannique et française*. Paris : Karthala.

Coquery-Vidrovitch, C. 1982. « Le financement de la "mise en valeur" coloniale : méthode et premiers résultats. » Dans *Études africaines offertes à Henri Brunschwig*, dirigé par J. Vansina, C.H. Perrot, R. Austen, et Y. Person et al., 237–251. Paris : Éditions de l'École des hautes études en sciences sociales.

Data, L. 2009. *Le grand trucage. Comment le gouvernement manipule les statistiques*. Paris : La Découverte.

Deane, P. 1948. « The Measurement of Colonial National Incomes : An Experiment. » National Institute of Economic and Social Research, Occasional Papers 1948 (7). Cambridge : Cambridge University Press.

Desrosières, A. 1994. *La politique des grands nombres. Histoire de la raison statistique*. Paris : La Découverte.

Desrosières, A. 2003a. « Historiciser l'action publique : l'État, le marché et les statistiques. » Dans *Historicités de l'action publique*, dirigé par P. Laborier et D. Trom, 207–221. Paris : Presses Universitaires de France.

Desrosières, A. 2003b. « Naissance d'un nouveau langage statistique entre 1940 et 1960. » *Courrier des statistiques* 2003 (198) : 41–52.

Desrosières, A. 2008a. *Pour une sociologie historique de la quantification. L'argument statistique I*. Paris : Presses de l'école des mines.

Desrosières, A. 2008b. *Gouverner par les nombres. L'argument statistique II*. Paris : Presses de l'école des mines.

Desrosières, A. 2012. « La mesure du développement. » Travail présenté à Conférence d'introduction au colloque du GEMDEV/UNESCO, Paris, 1–3 février.

Destremeau, B., et P. Salama. 2002. *Mesures et démesure de la pauvreté*. Paris : Presses Universitaires de France.

Fabre, R., G. Dubois, et M. Courcier. 1958. « Comptes économiques 1951–1956. Compte-rendu sommaire de travaux effectués depuis 1951, concernant certains États d'Afrique et de Madagascar. » Tiré à part d'*Outre-mer*, édité par le service de la Statistique du ministère de la France d'outre-mer.

Ferguson, J. 1990. *The Anti-Politics Machine : "Development", Depolitization and Bureaucratic Power in Lesotho*. Cambridge : Cambridge University Press.

Fitoussi, J.-P., A. Sen, et J. E. Stiglitz, dir. 2009. *Rapport de la Commission sur la mesure des performances économiques et du progrès social*. Paris : Ministère français de l'Économie, de l'Industrie et de l'Emploi.

Fourquet, N., dir. 1980. *Les Comptes de la puissance : histoire de la comptabilité nationale et du Plan*. Paris : Éditions Recherches, coll. Encres.

Hardy, G., et C. Richet, dir. 1933. *L'alimentation indigène dans les colonies françaises, protectorats et territoires sous mandats*. Paris : Vigot frères éditeurs.

Haubert, M., dir. 1969. *Matériaux pour une analyse de la croissance dans l'Ouest africain*. Paris : Institut d'étude du développement économique et social.

Hibou, B. 2011. « Macroéconomie et domination politique en Tunisie. Du "miracle économique" benaliste aux enjeux socio-économiques du moment révolutionnaire. » *Politique africaine* 124 : 127–154.

Horvath, R. 1972. « Le concept de statistique internationale et son évolution historique. » *Revue Internationale de Statistique* 40 (3) : 281–298.

Jerven, M. 2009. « The Relativity of Poverty and Income : How Reliable Are African Economic Statistics? » *African Affairs* 109 (434) : 77–96.

Jerven, M. 2010. « Random Growth in Africa? Lessons From an Evaluation of the Growth. Evidence on Botswana, Kenya, Tanzania and Zambia, 1965–1995. » *Journal of Development Studies* 46 (2) : 274–294.

Jerven, M. 2011. « Users and Producers of African Income : Measuring the Progress of African Economies. » *African Affairs* 110 (439) : 169–190.

Kent, J. 1992. *The Internationalization of Colonialism. Britain, France and Black Africa, 1939–1956*. Oxford : Clarendon Press.

Leveugle, J. 1953. *Étude du revenu et des comptes du Cameroun en 1951 : principaux résultats, méthodes*. Paris : Ministère de la France d'outre-mer.

Reynaud-Paligot, C. 2006. « Usages coloniaux des représentations raciales (1880-1930). » *Cahiers d'histoire. Revue d'histoire critique* 2006 (99) : 103–110.

Rist, G. 1996. *Le développement. Histoire d'une croyance occidentale*. Paris : Presses de Sciences Po.

Studenski, P. 1958. *The Income of Nations. Theory, Measurement, and Analysis : Past and Present*. New York : New York University Press.

Vanoli, A. 2002. *Une histoire de la comptabilité nationale*. Paris : La Découverte.

Measuring the Sudanese economy: a focus on national growth rates and regional inequality, 1959–1964

Alden Young

Department of Africana Studies, University of Pennsylvania, Philadelphia, PA, USA

ABSTRACT What effect did the adoption of national income accounting as a planning technique have on economic policy-making in Sudan during the first half of the 1960s? This article draws on extensive archival evidence from the World Bank Archives, the British National Archives and the National Records Office in Khartoum, Sudan. The main conclusion is that national income accounting heightened planners' awareness of income inequality between Sudan and other states, but lessened their awareness of regional inequality within Sudan. This article takes the Ten Year Plan of Economic and Social Development, 1961/62–1970/71 as a case study for how policy-makers implement plans that magnify inequality in the name of development. The conclusion offers some suggestions for the connection between growing regional inequality and the October 1964 coup.

RÉSUMÉ Quel effet l'adoption d'un système de comptabilité nationale des revenus comme méthode de planification a-t-elle eu sur la politique économique du Sudan au début des années 1960? L'examen des archives de la Banque mondiale et des archives nationales de la Grande-Bretagne et du Soudan démontre que cette comptabilité a pu sensibiliser les planificateurs à la différence de revenus entre le Sudan et d'autres États, mais non aux inégalités régionales internes au pays. Le cas du Plan décennal pour le développement économique et social 1961/62–1970/71 illustre bien que les plans adoptés avaient pour effet, au nom de développement, d'augmenter les inégalités. La conclusion fait l'hypothèse qu'il existe d'un lien entre la croissance des inégalités régionales et le coup d'État d'octobre 1964.

Shortly after Sudan's independence in 1956, Sudanese policy-makers found themselves confronting a problem common to many developing countries, particularly in Africa: how to meaningfully distribute the benefits of site-specific investments throughout a vast territory with a dispersed population (Lewis 1965). After all, at independence policy-makers in Khartoum were confronted with responsibility for governing what had previously been the largely autonomous regions of the Anglo-Egyptian Sudan as a united territory. Sudan, which was nearly one-third the size of India but contained only 12 million people in 1960, became, and would remain until the state's partition in 2011, the largest country in Africa.

Income inequality plagued the country. The central triangle from Omdurman to Kosti and Sennar not only dominated the nation's politics, but also was significantly richer than the rest of the country, with a per capita income of over 100 pounds (LS 100) compared with an income of significantly less than the national average of LS 30 in many parts of southern and western Sudan (Daly 2007, 185–189). Yet, despite the vast amounts of income inequality that plagued the newly independent Sudan, economic growth rather than equity became the dominant concern of financial policy-makers in Khartoum. While retrospectively it is tempting to frame the aims of development during the era of decolonisation in Africa and Asia as being primarily about improving the living standards of each newly independent country's citizens following years of colonial neglect, to think of development in such terms is to forget about the new ability of policy-makers to compare their state's performance against the performance of neighbouring states and the competitive environment this created (Speich 2011; Reinert 2011, 1). It was in this context that, during the years between 1956 and 1958, Sudanese politicians and policy-makers became invested in the expansion of irrigated cotton production. This was widely understood by policy-makers to be the fastest and most secure means of increasing the income available to the government in order to build more robust state institutions, speeding the moment when Sudan arrived at an institutional level of development comparable to that of its imagined peers.

However, investing the majority of the government's income in the expansion of irrigated cotton not only meant ignoring and likely exacerbating regional inequality within Sudan, it also meant increasing the government's vulnerability to an inherently unreliable source of income. Between 1956 and 1959, when finance officials primarily used the national budget and the government's reserves of foreign exchange to evaluate the performance of economic policies, rapid fluctuations in these figures made it difficult to sustain a consensus in favour of continued investment in the expansion of cotton. However, the use of national income statistics to formulate investment plans based on future targets expanded the horizon for policy-makers to estimate a potential return on investment, and in the process made what had previously appeared an uncertain investment, in irrigated cotton, appear certain once again. Yet, because national income accounting produced simple and quantifiable targets, finance officials and their political masters were tempted to use indicators such as the per capita growth rate as meaningful proxies for the success of government policies and the health of the wider economy. Healthy growth rates blinded officials during the early 1960s to rising regional inequality and the stagnating or declining livelihoods of individual Sudanese citizens as a result of their government's policies, which emphasised investment over consumption.

This study takes seriously questions about policy-making and bureaucracy in postcolonial Africa. Placing it outside of much of the literature on the African state, which seeks to explain the failure of the African state as a result of it either being too weak or too strong in relation to an often poorly defined "society" (Herbst 2000; Young 1997). Scholars have often insisted on imagining the state as rapacious and predatory, with official institutions that served little purpose other than legitimisation and patronage (Bayart 1993, 211; Chabal and Daloz 1999).[1] The point here is not to argue that postcolonial states were not rapacious, but to question whether the study of their institutions can so easily be dismissed. Rather than being purely decorative, the bureaucracy and its practices, particularly planning, served to structure elite conflict and bargaining. Plans were formulated over and over again, because planning and the vocabulary of economic development determined which demands upon the state were legitimate (Morgan 2008, 6–7; Cooper 1998). Plans and planning defined the boundaries of consensus, much as the discourse of development, speaking the idiom of economics, established the language of negotiation.[2] That the technocratic language of planning, not the sloganeering of politics, often defined which policies could be implemented highlights the importance of looking at which kinds of statements national income accounting made it easy to communicate and which the language of income accounting obscured. While the bargains reached among the elite were often functional, the rules and tools of economic planning structured how bargains were reached (Jerven 2011; Bonnecase 2011).

The central argument in this article is that once policy-makers began to evaluate economic policy on the basis of changes in per capita GDP over time, they became more acutely aware of the disparity between the wealth of the Sudanese state and that of other states. At the same time, this metric made policy-makers less aware of the growing disparities in wealth within Sudan. Consequentially, the manner in which data were presented exacerbated the biases that policy-makers already held, as it focused their attention on accelerating economic growth at the expense of inequality.

Two impulses lay behind finance officials' decision to use changes in national income to judge the economic performance of the government after 1958. The first was an international evolution in the practice of economic data gathering and reporting during the 1950s. This evolution was marked by the widespread adoption of practices like national income accounting and the calculation of per capita GDP (Speich 2011; Jerven 2013; Okigbo 1989). However, international norms alone do not explain the adoption in 1958, and subsequent prominence in policy-making of national income accounting;[3] instead, circumstances within Sudan made a shift in the calculation of the state's economic performance imperative.

The second impulse was increased fluctuation in the price of cotton. From 1954 until 1958, fluctuations in the price of cotton created doubt about Sudanese officials' budgetary projections, and therefore reopened the debate about the state's investment decisions. Finance officials believed that moving away from a focus on the annual contribution of the cotton crop to the country's budget and particularly its reserves of foreign currency would strengthen the argument for continued investment in irrigation. Because national income accounts attempted to tabulate the totality of economic activity within a particular economy, finance officials could use these data to model the future impact of investing in cotton cultivation on the economy as a whole, demonstrating how much growth would occur in the future as result of immediate sacrifices.

Finance officials believed that if they demonstrated that capital-intensive investment over a short period of time could raise national living standards, despite a few years of sacrifice, political support for their investment plans could be maintained. During the 1950s, riots had repeatedly plagued the three cities of Khartoum, Khartoum North and Omdurman as the various political parties jockeyed for power and protested the increased sacrifices in individual consumption necessitated by an emphasis on savings and investment in increasing production in the cotton-growing sector (Al-Amin 2005).

At independence, the political elite in Khartoum believed that the economic basis of the new state of Sudan could be agriculture, and particularly the export of raw cotton. They expected the price of cotton to continue increasing as it had during the first half of the 1950s. However, in 1954 the rate of increase began to level off, and when the price began to decline in 1957, Sudanese officials were forced to search for new sources of revenue both for the state and the political parties that were rivalling one another for leadership. Beginning in 1954, Sudanese officials committed themselves to funding the expansion of state-managed cotton irrigation schemes. These schemes were to become the cornerstone of national development efforts. The concentration of political and economic authority in Khartoum after the achievement of self-government in 1954 allowed the bureaucracy of the newly independent Sudan to decide how the government's resources should be spent. The government decided to expand irrigation in the south-western region of the Gezira plain, planning an undertaking that became known as the Managil Agricultural Extension Scheme. Managil consumed most of the state's development budget from 1955 until the scheme ended in 1962. The construction of the Roseires Dam, a major goal of which was to provide additional water to Managil, was not finished until 1967. The decision to emphasise Managil, which had the side-effect of exacerbating existing regional inequality, was supported despite fluctuations in the price of cotton and the negative impact of those fluctuations on the government's balance sheet by faith in finance officials' ability to project the economic growth that this investment would eventually produce.

Within political circles in Khartoum, the decline in the price of cotton that occurred from 1957 was not a cause to emphasise alternative types of development, such as the production of new cash crops such as sisal, tobacco, tea or even livestock. Instead, finance officials continued to believe that these alternatives would produce a sub-par return on investment in comparison to exporting cotton. In addition, these types of investments would have required a dramatic shift in the types of infrastructure investments that were supported by the state. A new push to upgrade Sudan's transportation infrastructure and improve the connections between the various peripheries of the country would have meant supplanting the current focus on building irrigation works in the most developed areas of the country. This policy change was rejected during the late 1950s and again during the early 1960s, when planning according to national income targets became the norm in Khartoum.

Senior members of the Sudanese bureaucracy remained committed to their prior policy decisions, despite the realisation in 1957 by finance officials that the decreases in the price of cotton would prevent the government from being able to finance the Managil Scheme – upon which its development agenda rested from domestic sources alone. A scapegoat was needed, and was quickly found. The political parties were blamed for increasing spending on consumption, which could have been directed towards investment. Among the supporters of the military coup on 18 November 1958, one of the key justifications was that the political leaders lacked the discipline necessary to develop the Managil Scheme, and to hold off the frivolous demands emerging for investment in the periphery.

The senior officers in the military, who replaced the civilian government for the first time in November 1958, believed that economic growth, particularly within the region of the country spanning from Omdurman to Kosti and Sennar, would create increased political and social stability in the core regions of the country, and that stability in the periphery would follow, if not immediately. The size of the cotton sector, and its location in the most politically influential area of the country, meant that even with the application of new techniques of economic measurement, the success of the cotton producers continued to represent the fortune of the Sudanese economy in the eyes of government officials in Khartoum.

At first glance, the shift in the way in which officials described, measured and demonstrated the country's economic performance might appear to be unrelated to whether civilian politicians or military officers ruled in Khartoum. However, the changes in economic reporting were related to the changes in government, as both were a response to the same problem. The declining and increasingly unstable price of cotton threatened the political and economic hegemony of the cotton elite. This elite had inherited political power as the British departed. In the years after Sudan achieved self-governance in 1954, the political power of the cotton-growing elite reinforced its economic power. Consequently, the government poured the vast majority of its resources into the cotton sector, overwhelmingly located in the central riverain area from Kosti to Omdurman to Sennar. This area, when expanded to include the stretches of the Nile extending north from Khartoum to the border with Egypt and along the Atbara River, was the homeland of the political elite. That the most economically and politically advanced regions of the country overlapped was not a coincidence. In part this region's economic privilege was insured by its ability to continually receive the majority of the state's investments. Initially, finance officials were able to take for granted that the expansion of the Managil scheme would be in the interest of the state and of Sudanese society at large. However, demand shifts and volatile cotton prices combined to create doubts about the wisdom of the government's investment decisions, and therefore necessitated greater clarity about how the state's policies actually benefited Sudanese society. The introduction of national income accounting and a focus on the growth rate were both attempts by state officials to justify their policies to increasingly restless constituencies.

The rise of Sudan's Ministry of Finance and Economics

Between 1946 and 1964, finance officials went from being government auditors to the articulators of plans against which the government's legitimacy was measured. They did this by transforming a fragmentary and disjointed Anglo-Egyptian Sudan into a national economy. Finance officials began by asserting that they had the authority to coordinate the planning process for the entirety of Sudan without deference to the prerogatives of local or imperial actors. In the process of evaluating individual projects for inclusion in the five year plans that finance officials designed, they transformed the meaning of development in Sudan. Projects that emphasised the protection of distinct populations were de-emphasised in favour of those benefitting Sudan as a whole. Finance officials developed an evaluative framework for their own use, which determined the viability of projects and their suitability for government funding by measuring these projects' impact on the central budget; however, it was not until the 1959 that a unified Sudanese economy became institutionalised.

The military buttressed its legitimacy by claiming that it was putting fiscally responsible technocrats in power in the place of feckless civilian politicians. Military leaders made use of new tools such as national income accounting to proclaim that their regime would also be accountable. In the Ten Year Plan of Economic and Social Development 1961/62–1970/71, finance officials articulated clear and measurable goals, and they expected that if these goals were met the regime would be rewarded for its sound economic stewardship by Sudan's people. Instead, despite increasing the growth rate, completing Managil and making sustained progress on the Roseires Dam, in October 1964 the military regime was faced with angry crowds in the streets of Khartoum. The October Revolution had begun and the military had lost its mandate to rule. The senior army officers in Khartoum surrendered in stunned disbelief to the crowds in the capital, in part because they had always assumed that unrest would occur only in the economically marginalised, peripheral regions of the country. They had already begun a pacification campaign in the south and were prepared to sustain it. Finance officials and their military overlords had assumed that economic growth would assure legitimacy in the wealthiest parts of the country, and therefore were largely silent when it did not.

The Ten Year Plan of Economic and Social Development, 1961/62–1970/71

The military government made a strong commitment to the new model of national planning. Aside from questions about bureaucratic capacity, the principal complaint of planners had been that they were unable to devise an appropriate means of measuring, evaluating and calibrating the impact of the government's economic policies.

The major innovation in planning under the military was the introduction of national income estimates in Sudan. National income accounts made it possible to compare the wealth of various nations across time, and thus, the thinking went, allowed political leaders to demonstrate with hard figures how successful their policies were. The publication of economic growth statistics effectively became an annual referendum on the political leadership of the country. Depending on the calculations undertaken, economists and statisticians claimed that the resulting figures could be used to understand the production and distribution of a society's economic welfare as well as to highlight how the different units of the economy and society fit together (Studenski 1958). Moreover, as pointed out by the economist Paul Studenski, "the concept of national income is social in nature and differs fundamentally from the private concepts of individual, family, or group incomes" (Studenski 1958, 165). The implication was that national income accounting gave the authors and the policy-makers who depended on these accounts a new social object: the nation, in whose name they could act. It was the ability of military leaders to claim that they were acting in the name of the nation that justified the abrogation of the electoral system, which was premised on aggregating individual preferences.

The national income statistics that finance officials produced were aggregates, numbers that described the average and the norm rather than the individual experience. While technically, national income accounts were composed of three separate calculations that needed to match, in Sudan as in many developing countries only two calculations were made. The first calculation is often referred to as the "output method" and the second was called the "expenditure method" (Department of Statistics 1959). The output method was a tabulation of the value of all of the goods and services produced in a given economy, while the expenditure method calculated the total amount of money spent on goods and services. Both calculations were used by finance officials to estimate the total income of the economy, because output, expenditure and income should all be equal in a given economy. The major innovation undergirding national income accounting was imagining that the income of a whole society could be accounted for similarly to the way a single business balanced its books (Vanoli 2005). Even as the general formulas for calculating national income became increasingly standardised, the intrusion of politics was clearest in "the problem of deciding which receipts of money or of goods and services to include in the concept and computation of national income and which to exclude". The estimator was inevitably forced to rely on arbitrary "escapes from theoretical and practical difficulties", accounting challenges that were compounded by theoretical questions about which activities qualified as economic and which activities should properly be considered non-economic and therefore non-countable (Studenski 1958, 166). These decisions about what to count and how to count directly impacted how finance officials and the public evaluated economic policy, especially the economic plans crafted by the military. For instance, when Sudanese historian Al-Amin 'Abd-Rahman points to the positive aspects of the Abboud regime he emphasises Abboud's success in increasing the growth rate, assuming that the lives of ordinary people became easier as a result (Al-Amin 2005).

It was in the context of an improving economy that work on a comprehensive development plan for Sudan began to bear fruit (Economic Planning Secretariat 1962, 1). These efforts were coordinated by 'Abd al-Rahim Mirghani, deputy permanent under-secretary within the Ministry of Finance. The economic council headed by the president of the Supreme Council for the Armed Forces, the prime minister and key cabinet members determined policy. Policy proposals were designed by the development committee, which was composed of the senior civil servants from the different ministries.

The earlier efforts at development planning took the form of an enumeration of desirable capital projects with their estimated price tags, which were then compared with a series of projections about the amount of revenue that the government would be capable of raising over a defined period of time (Mirghani 1983, 10). The new 1961 development plan included a macroeconomic framework within which the plan's proposals were situated and against which their impact was estimated.[4] The primary innovation in this iteration of planning was that all of the various proposals developed by government departments and units were:

> subsequently embodied in a uniform set of summaries and schedules, showing the aims of each proposal, the required investment amount and its phasing, its contribution to the national income, its effects on the balance of payments [and] administrative requirements. (Economic Planning Secretariat 1962, 1)

A special World Bank mission and Special Adviser to the Under Secretary for Economic and Social Affairs of the United Nations, Dr W. H. Singer, then evaluated the macroeconomic framework developed by the economic planning unit inside of Sudan's Ministry of Finance to ensure that the plan met emerging international norms. According to Mirghani's introduction to the published Ten Year Plan, the aim of the plan was to ensure that Sudan's economy "not only expand[ed] at an accelerated rate but ... at the same time reach[ed] the stage of self-sustaining growth" (Economic Planning Secretariat 1962, 2).

The publication in March 1959 of *The National Income of Sudan: 1955/56*, Sudan's first series of national income accounts, allowed the military government to equate economic success with political legitimacy. C. H. Harvie and J. G. Kleve, the leaders of the Department of Statistics in Sudan, oversaw the publication of the national accounts with the help of 11 Sudanese assistants (Harvie and Kleve 1959, 1). Sudanese experts followed the lead of the national income surveys carried out in Nigeria (1950–1951) and Tanganyika (1952–1954). Many of the assumptions of the studies carried out in those two countries informed the best practices that became used in Sudan (Morgan 2011; Prest and Stewart 1953). Technical advice about how to shape government budgets and accounts for national income accounting came from several United Nations publications, including *A Manual for the Economic and Functional Classification of Government Transactions* (United Nations Department of Economic and Social Affairs 1958).

In his announcement of the Ten Year Plan, the Minister of Finance and Economics – speaking in the name of the military revolutionary council – stated, "Amongst the most important targets that the blessed Revolutionary Government pursued and is still pursuing is the improvement of the standard of living of the citizens through the development of the resources of the Country." The metric of success was per-capita income growth (Economic Planning Secretariat 1962, 3). Previous plans had been collections of public sector capital investments, without a clear estimation of the effects of capital spending on "over-all magnitudes like national income, balance of payments, government revenues, employment, etc." (Poduval 1963, 2). This plan was to be comprehensive. Minister of Finance Ahmed defined comprehensive planning thus:

> Comprehensive economic planning is basically a scientific study of the circumstances and problems that hinder the progress of society, and assessing the natural and human resources available, and drawing out the right projects which aim at changing those circumstances and dealing with these problems in the light of the available resources. It is therefore a process of defining and knowing the problems and resources of society and the best use and effective mobilisation of these resources to achieve a stage of progress accepted by society as a target to be achieved in a certain period of time. (Economic Planning Secretariat 1962, 4–5)

Ahmed meant that comprehensive planning attempted to measure the impact of investment decisions, and not simply to establish a schedule of capital spending.

Finance officials believed that what was required for economic development was an increase in the accumulated capital base of a particular country. These suppositions allowed economists and other policy-makers to focus on the ratio of "required" investment to desired growth. The formula was provided as follows:

> A country that wanted to develop had to go from an investment rate of 4 percent of GDP to 12–15 percent of GDP. Investment had to keep ahead of population growth. Development was a race between machines and motherhood. (Easterly 1997, 4)

This model made it possible to make hypothetical calculations along the following lines. If a country pushed its rate of investment up to 12 per cent of GDP, it could increase its GDP by perhaps 3 per cent per year. Assuming population growth of 2 per cent per year, it could as a result achieve a per capita growth rate of roughly 1 per cent per year. Sudanese policy-makers set a target of growing the capital-intensive sectors of their economy by 3 per cent during the first years of the 1960s, which meant that they would have to find adequate inflows of capital (Mirghani 1983, 29). However, there was a widespread belief in the international community that poor countries could not achieve such high rates of investment from their own savings alone, and therefore would need not only to suppress domestic consumption but also to turn to foreign aid (Easterly 1997). It was the failure of the parliamentary system to create a political climate in which either of these objectives appeared possible that paved the way for and legitimated the military coup.

Success was quantified. Per-capita income was projected to rise from LS 28–30 to LS 65 by the end of the plan period. This would allow Sudan to surpass the per capita income of Morocco and Tunisia and bring it into the range of such countries as Turkey. The projected figures also demonstrated that the wealth divide within the country was quite large, with some regions, particularly western and southern Sudan, considerably below the LS 28–30 per-capita income range.[5] Other areas of the country, particularly the area within the triangle formed by Omdurman, Kosti and Sennar (including the three towns of Omdurman, Khartoum and Khartoum North), as well as the Gezira district, had much higher per capita incomes. This was the area of maximum state investment due to irrigation schemes such as Gezira and Managil, and it already enjoyed incomes above that of Turkey, in the range of LS 65–75 per capita (Economic Planning Secretariat 1962, 40). It was expected that by the end of the plan period the per capita of this triangle could reach levels as high as LS 110, much higher than the projected national per capita GDP of LS 37. This would be "very high by African standards and probably sufficiently high to sustain self-generating growth" (Federation of British Industries 1963, 4). Unequal growth was justified by the assumption that if one continued to invest in the most capital-intensive parts of the economy, growth would eventually spread to other portions of the economy through savings:

> For although at first sight the "imbalance" in the economy between the modern part and the traditional part might be criticised, particularly in respect of the difference in per capita incomes, the Plan in fact turns this imbalance to advantage by using the resulting higher rate of domestic savings in the modern sector to develop both parts of the economy. (Economic Planning Secretariat 1962, 43)

It was estimated that during the life of the plan the proportion of the population of Sudan involved in the modern sector of the economy would rise from one-quarter to possibly one-third. As the modern sector of the economy grew, finance officials expected that the profits derived from it would increasingly be available to fund the development of other parts of the economy, creating a virtuous cycle and leading to a higher national income overall (Economic Planning Secretariat 1962, 43–44). For the planners, the aim of the development strategy was essentially the realisation of a "big push" to propel the most economically advanced sectors and regions of the economy forward (Poduval 1963, 2).[6] The "big push" did not aim for economic equitability and stability, but rather for growth.

The objective of the plan was to transform a poor economy with a low national income, a total dependence on cotton, idle manpower in the south, east and west of the country, little skilled manpower, unknown resources and a rudimentary industrial base into a growing and increasingly wealthy economy. Planners wanted the population to transition from the traditional sector of the economy toward the modern sector of the economy. They also aimed to diversify the economy. Noticeably missing from Sudanese diversification plans were theories of import substitution based on heavy industrialisation. Instead planners intended for industrialisation initially to be confined to processes that were complimentary to the agricultural sector, such as the light processing of agricultural goods. A major component of reducing imports was also agricultural diversification, because while largely self-sufficient in the production of foodstuffs, Sudan imported large amounts of tea, coffee, sugar and wheat (Federation of British Industries 1963, 2). Finance officials such as Mamoun Beheiry and John Carmichael of the Economic Planning Secretariat assumed that for the foreseeable future Sudan would remain an agricultural exporting economy (Economic Planning Secretariat 1962, 6). Unlike many developing countries, Sudan's policy-makers recognised the limitations of their domestic market and never intended to shift the basis of the economy from agriculture to manufacturing. Rather, the government hoped to produce more agricultural products for domestic consumption and at the same time increase agricultural exports in order to fund greater quantities of imports (Federation of British Industries 1963, 2–3). Planners thought the most promising path toward import substitution was agricultural diversification into such commodities as coffee, rice and sugar, decreasing the need importing these products (Economic Planning Secretariat 1962, 29).

The limitations of the Ten Year Plan

The publication of a national census and the country's first national income survey in 1959 allowed Sudanese finance officials for the first time to evaluate their economic policies according to their impact on the country's national income (Harvie and Kleve 1959). And the Ten Year Plan published in 1962 became the first official statement that the goal of state economic policy was to increase the income of the whole country, and thus making the growth rate the prime indicator of policy success (Economic Planning Secretariat, 1962). Sudanese policy-makers would attempt for the first time to calculate the impact of government spending on economic activity, and not simply the impact of individual enterprises on the government's balance sheet. The success of economic policy, specifically the large-scale investment in cotton cultivation, would now be measured by the extent to which this investment increased national income.

Despite the fact that the vast majority of capital expenditure was indeed allocated to a small number of projects in the central region of Sudan, finance officials presented the plan to the public through radio broadcasts and speeches as an initiative that would benefit the entire country. Officials acknowledged that the focus would remain on "a wedge-shaped fertile clay plain ... situated in the center of the country and ... widening toward the East" (Economic Planning Secretariat 1962, 10).[7] The plan was comprised of more than 260 individual projects, including coffee schemes in Equatoria and experiments with rice cultivation in Bahr el-Ghazal (Economic Planning Secretariat 1962, 27). Yet, despite generic statements about "attention to the development of backward areas in all parts of the country especially the South", the plan denied funding to major infrastructure projects in the western, eastern and southern regions of Sudan.[8] Although coffee and rice cultivation could play vital roles in import-substitution, as late as the 1964/65 budget money had only been allocated for surveying potential coffee estates in Equatoria and establishing a pilot scheme for rice production in Bahr el-Ghazal.[9] The decision to minimise funding for economic development and social services in southern Sudan would have dramatic consequences, because it increased the alienation of communities there from the state, even as military conflict was escalating in the south as a consequence of demands for political autonomy.

The resistance to shifting scarce capital from the expansion of the major pre-existing agricultural schemes to improvements in the transportation network further demonstrated the extent to which a limited number of cotton schemes in central Sudan could be represented as the national economy. Sudanese policy-makers continued to debate the merits and challenges of both an integration of additional regions of Sudan into the existing export economy and a rapid increase in the export potential of the major irrigated schemes. From a purely accounting perspective, increased investment in transportation was considered financially unsound. In a sparsely populated country, an adequate transportation network was judged to be an unaffordable luxury. However, without affordable transportation the expansion of agricultural production into new regions was unprofitable and therefore the development of new regions of the country could not proceed without loss-making investments (Economic Planning Secretariat 1962, 99) In fact, officials of the International Bank for Reconstruction and Development (IBRD) highlighted the inadequacy of the transportation network as "a bottleneck in the development of Sudan".[10] At the same time, the

IBRD's transportation analysts were sceptical about the financial feasibility of extending the network to new regions of Sudan.[11] The justification for ignoring the development of the economic peripheries within Sudan came from planners' acceptance of the division of the economy into a modern and a traditional (that is, subsistence, or "domestic") sector. They assumed that the traditional sectors of the economy would eventually wither away, to be replaced by the modern sectors of the economy. Indeed, statistics reported between 1956 and 1961 demonstrated that the modern sector grew twice as fast as the traditional sector, which seemed to bear out their expectations (Economic Planning Secretariat 1962, 13).

However, the statisticians tasked with using national income accounts to measure economic performance relied on a limited set of data. They had good access to data about commodities produced for export, because of the relative ease of acquiring those statistics. The over-representation of cotton production in general economic statistics encouraged Sudanese officials to overestimate the extent to which the Omdurman–Kosti–Sennar triangle was the engine of the national economy. Consequently, officials made very little effort to collect data about the traditional subsistence sector, and it was estimated to account for as much as 36 per cent of the country's GDP (formally, finance officials did factor this sector into their calculations).[12]

The line between the traditional (or domestic) sector of the economy and the modern (export) sector was also unclear. Even within the most capital-intensive agricultural schemes, such as Gezira and Managil, farmers devoted a significant amount of their labour and capital to producing grains for subsistence. The cultivators of groundnuts and gum arabic in the western regions of Sudan were often not considered to be part of the modern economy because they employed "traditional" methods of production, even though both crops were highly profitable and sold to international buyers. Because planners did not consider these to be modern sectors of the economy, they did not invest state resources in improving the small-scale production of such cash crops as grains, gum arabic or groundnuts. Abdel Rahim Mirghani, citing his own and his colleagues' reading of Dudley Seers's ideas about "uneven development", believed that capital, labour and land should be steered toward the modern sectors where their productivity could be raised (Mirghani 1983, 28–31).

The financial strain

The vulnerability of the Sudanese economy was evident. The development expenditures programmed within the Ten Year Plan required an additional LS 95 million in loans from abroad, and the LS 56 million already received required interest payments of 5 per cent over the next 15 years. The plan's chief architect, 'Abd al-Rahim Mirghani, expected the burden on the Sudanese economy to be massive. He hoped that the industrialised countries would be lenient in the terms of their loans.[13] One key issue was whether the capital spending the government had embarked upon would produce self-sustaining growth. A second critical question was whether concentrating the bulk of the state's investments in a few development schemes would pay off and yield returns that could be distributed in a sustainable manner. This was particularly important because projections of government revenue during the plan period did not call for taxation to play a major role in raising state revenue (Poduval 1963, 3).

Despite the doubts, by the 1964/65 fiscal year, the first four phases of the Managil Extension Scheme had been successfully completed, providing substantially increased export capacity. However, the Roseires Dam was still under construction. The foreign currency component of the dam project totalled LS 17,722,841. The principal loans for it were secured from the IBRD, the International Development Association and the Federal Republic of Germany. The cost of actually constructing the Roseires Dam continued to rise as of 1964/65, as did the cost of completing the Khashm el-Girba Dam (Department of Economic Planning 1965, 33–35).

Despite the increased cost of these projects, the 1963 IRBD Mission to Sudan concluded that the plan was realistic and that "the proposed sale of investment would be within the capacity of the country, provided it could obtain suitable aid from abroad".[14]

The objectives of the Ten Year Plan were not expected to resolve Sudan's foreign exchange vulnerability in the short term. Experts expected that the programmes included within the plan would magnify existing problems. The formulators of the plan understood that Sudan would incur a deficit in its balance of payments. This would require new capital inflows of upwards of LS 150 million (Poduval 1963, 2). One attempt to address this problem was to devote domestic foreign exchange reserves exclusively to the problem of managing short-term fluctuations in the international commodity markets (Economic Planning Secretariat 1962, 46). Heavy capital spending on development projects, the need to service foreign loans and lower than expected income from exports all meant that there was heavy pressure to reduce other government expenditures on items such as social services and employment.

Reasons for the failure of the Plan and the fall of the Abboud regime

By November 1963, the Sudan IBRD Consultative Group, composed of the principal Western creditors to the country, began to express concerns about the country's ability to fund the implementation of its development plan.[15] Sudan had a relatively modest deficit in its balance of payments in 1963 after a poor cotton harvest in 1962.[16] Another fear was that the government would be unable to control its expenditures. The Group also identified the concentration of development programmes in the central region of the country. However, the group praised Sudanese officials for their willingness to emphasise commodity-producing projects over social investments.[17]

The optimistic forecast of cotton harvests on which the plan was based did not materialise, and by January 1964 the government of Sudan was forced to seek additional loans from international lenders to fund its development programme.[18] To increase its legitimacy internationally and domestically, in November 1963 the Abboud regime had created a Central Council, an advisory board of civilian experts, to augment the Supreme Council of the Armed Forces as it made executive decisions. By April 1964, however, the Abboud regime faced increased criticism about its economic stewardship, often from members of its new council (Bechtold 1976, 205). A major complaint raised by the government's critics was that the Khashm el-Girba scheme was significantly over cost, while at the same time Egypt was delaying payment of the compensation it had promised Sudan for the flooding of Wadi Halfa.[19] The government tried to cover the unexpected expenses by raising taxes on some tenant farmers.[20] The Ministries of Defence, Interior and Information, which were favoured by the governing army officers, were consistently overspending their budgets. Criticisms of the government were further fuelled by political tensions in southern Sudan, where the decision to cease investing in local economic and social projects exacerbated the ongoing conflict between the periphery and the core regions of the country. Open warfare broke out in the southern region during the early 1960s (Yusuf Fadl Hasan 1967, 504). However, the immediate concern was not simply the generation of budget surpluses, but finding more foreign exchange for the country to devote to accelerating its development plans.[21] Still, the military regime often won praise from foreign investors for ensuring political stability and for its ability to produce consistent budget surpluses (Federation of British Industries 1963, 23).

A superficial analysis of aggregate economic indicators such as the GDP made the Abboud regime's economic stewardship appear modestly successful. During the first five years of the Ten Year Plan, Sudan's GDP increased by 20 per cent. Excusing the steep economic decline associated with the collapse in 1957–1958, however, the Sudanese economy scarcely grew any faster during the first years of the Plan than it had during the previous years of civilian rule. To judge whether the military's policies were successful, it is necessary to examine the five years after the military came to power in October 1964. During the period 1965–1971, after the military relinquished power, GDP expanded by 30 per cent (Niblock 1987, table A10). The transitional civilian government that came to power in 1965, following the revolution of October 1964, was formed by the National Front for Professionals and made up of members willing to pursue new social and economic policies. However, by April 1966 the traditional parties such as the Umma and the National Unionist Party (NUP) had resumed control of the government and began to carry out economic policies that were in general alignment with the Ten Year Plan (Niblock 1987, 226–229; Daly 2007, 189). Therefore, the resulting acceleration in the growth rate in 1965–1971 can be attributed in part to the framework developed by the planners (Daly 2007, 185–189).

Yet this raises the question of why the military regime fell. Bechtold writes that it occurred:

> surely not because of economic pressures, for the slight drop in foreign exchange reserves affected very few people at the time, and whatever inconvenience resulted was definitely outweighed by the considerable rise in the standard of living since 1958. (Bechtold 1976, 213)

One possible answer can be found by examining the outbreak of violence on 21 October 1964 at the University of Khartoum. This followed a meeting about the government's failed strategy in the south. Recognition among large segments of the Khartoum elite that the military government's strategy of politically and economically marginalising the periphery was a failed strategy precipitated the end of the Abboud regime (Mahgoub 1974, 188–192).[22] The drive for increased economic growth favoured the concentration of development in a few defined areas, but such concentration did very little to address questions of regional equity. Therefore, even as economic growth resumed, political unrest continued to fester.

As fighting escalated between the central government and an increasingly complex group of separatist movements in southern Sudan in 1963, the distrust and unfamiliarity that had marked relations between the Arabised elite in Khartoum and the largely mission-educated African elites of southern Sudan was exacerbated. At the 1965 Khartoum Conference on the Southern Sudan, Aggrey Jaden, the president of the Sudan African National Union, proclaimed:

> The Sudan falls sharply into two distinct areas, both in geographical areas, ethnic groups, and cultural systems. The Northern Sudan is occupied by a hybrid Arab race who are united by their common language, common culture, and common religion; and they look to the Arab world for their cultural and political inspiration. The people of the Southern Sudan, on the other hand, belong to the African ethnic group of East Africa ... There is nothing in common between the various sections of the community; no body of shared beliefs, no identity of interests, no local signs of unity and above all, the Sudan has failed to compose a single community. (Shepherd 1966, 195)

When Aggrey made this statement in the mid-1960s, it was clear to many northern and southern Sudanese people that the attempt to suppress issues of regional and local identity in the name of national economic development had hopelessly failed. At a forum on 9 September 1964, noted member of the Muslim Brotherhood and lecturer in the Faculty of Law at the University of Khartoum, Dr Hasan al-Turabi, argued that the "southern question" could never be resolved without addressing issues surrounding Sudan's democracy and centralisation. Turabi challenged the legitimacy of the military regime, and after a series of public meetings at the University of Khartoum the military attempted to reassert its authority. The conflagration that ensued on 21 October eventually led to the overthrow of the government (Yusuf Fadl Hasan 1967, 505). By April 1965, the United Front, dominated by the Umma and the NUP, had come to power. These two parties continued many of the economic policies of the Abboud regime, as well as its civil war in the three southern provinces of Sudan (Nyquist 1965, 263–272).

In the Sudanese case, national income accounting decreased the visibility of regional inequality, and therefore reinforced a tendency of the governments in Khartoum to invest capital in a manner that exacerbated regional inequality rather than alleviating it (Mollan 2008). The presentation of economic data made it easy for finance officials and military leaders to believe that policies that accelerated the growth rate strengthened the county as a whole. However, economic growth was not the principal way in which the population judged their well-being. Officials encountered mounting political and social discontent in the early 1960s, which culminated in severe riots in Khartoum in 1964 and the subsequent fall of the military regime.

Reframing the aim of government policy, away from particularistic measures such as the amount of revenue generated by the export of particular commodities and towards a commitment to counting the total economic activity taking place within the country, in theory allowed finance officials to reflect a broader spectrum of the potential drivers of growth in their measurements and eventual decision-making. When national income was divided by the population, it provided the real GDP per capita figure, which when compared with previous years, resulted in the growth rate (Jerven 2013). Aggregate indicators, such as GDP, created a uniform image of economic progress, despite the presence of stark inequality within Sudan. These indicators' inability to reflect regional inequality often had the effect of justifying policies that reinforced it. In part, regional inequality was the result of decades of government decisions to invest in certain areas of the country and not in other areas (Weinstein 2008). The conventions of national income accounting, and the addition of a statistical office to the central government rather than to the regional authorities, made it easier to visualise the inequality in wealth between Sudan and Britain or Sudan and Turkey than to recognise, for example, the inequalities between the Omdurman–Sennar–Kosti triangle and the rest of the country (Speich 2011; Weinstein 2008).

Biographical note

Alden Young is a Mellon Postdoctoral Fellow (2013–2015) in Africana Studies at the University of Pennsylvania. His research uses political and administrative history to interrogate the postcolonial state. Currently he is examining the post-1964 disillusionment with the Sudanese state as a vehicle for political, social and economic transformation and the search for alternatives forms of community. In 2013 he completed his PhD in history at Princeton University.

Notes

1. Thus, Bayart (1993) has asserted that it is a waste of time to study the institutions of the African state, the legal edifices of the state being little more than a shell to hide criminality; moreover, he claims, the international nature of the political networks of clientelism often makes state institutions irrelevant.
2. Roberto Unger makes a similar point about elite instrumentalisation of legal discourses: "The subtlety in this conversion of vision into vocabulary and of vocabulary into strategy is that the strategic imperative requires the agent to continue speaking the vocabulary of the vision in which he has ceased to believe. In so doing, he fails fully to grasp the hidden restraints implicit in his supposedly strategic language" (Unger 1996, 52, 54–55). Similar arguments have been made about the usefulness of elections, even if flawed or held under authoritarian regimes. They reinforce the ideal of an orderly state contracting with rational individuals. The repetition of the event becomes important in part because of the widespread awareness in each iteration of shortcomings and of the necessity for constant improvement; see Willis and El Battahani (2010, 191–212) and Young (1993, 299–312).
3. Beginning in 1947, the United Nations sought to create a system of national income accounts that could be standardised and used by all member states, to further the project of international comparison.

In 1953, these standards were enshrined in a manual, which could be followed by the statistical offices of various states. For a basic timeline of the development of national income accounts see the website of the United Nations Department of Economic and Social Affairs (available at http://unstats.un.org/unsd/nationalaccount/hsna.asp). The second reason for the spread of national income accounting was that it became a necessity for UN membership, as the basis on which member-country dues would be calculated (Studenski 1958, 152, 155).

4. The macroeconomic framework included a new iteration of the national income accounts prepared by the Department of Statistics that specifically focused on producing data about capital formation, the output of manufacturing and capital/output ratios. A study of the structure of the Sudanese economy was also undertaken, as well as papers focusing on the building and construction potential of the government machinery and the availability of skilled labour. The principal Sudanese officials working on these studies within the Ministry of Finance were 'Abd al-Rahim Mirghani and Mohammed Khogali (Letter. Abdel Rahim Mirghani to Arie Kruithof, IBRD, October 16, 1961, "Sudan Railway Project – Negotiation 01," Box # 172012B).

5. Another feature of the national income accounts was the inclusion of Sudan on a United Nations list of countries ordered by each country's per capita income. Of the 15 countries listed, the United States ranked at the top and Tanganyika at the bottom. Using numbers for 1956, the US had a per capita income of LS 717, while using 1954 data Tanganyika had a per capita income of LS 17. Sudan was calculated to have the same income per person as Kenya, LS 27, and to have an income that was higher than that of Pakistan, India and Nigeria, as well as Tanganyika. However, the income of the Sudanese was significantly lower than that of the Egyptians, calculated in 1956 to be LS 40, and significantly below the per-capita income of the Union of South Africa and the European countries (Department of Statistics 1959, 9).

6. For more on the history of the "big push" idea, see Arndt (1987, 58).

7. The Ten Year Plan provided details: "Although the arable land in Sudan is estimated at about 100 million acres, only slightly over 7 million acres are cropped. The most developed land agriculturally is the fertile, central clay plains growing practically all cotton. To the west of this, is the 'quoz' area in Kordofan and Darfur provinces where gum arabic and oilseed crops are grown; to the east, are flooded silt plains of Gash and Tokar Deltas, irrigated by seasonal streams, sowing principally cotton and dura (sorghum). The southwest region, chiefly the Equatoria Province, in the tropical rainfall belt, has laterite soil, viable for various tropical crops. In the arid and semi-arid areas in the north, cultivation is confined to the Nile Basin with a uniform cropping pattern consisting of a mixture of food and cash crops" (Economic Planning Secretariat 1962, 27).

8. The finance minister's broadcast statement, included in the published Ten Year Plan, noted that work would not proceed on the Khartoum–Port Sudan Road, the Regeneration of Suakin, the extension of Railway Line from Wau to Juba, the exploitation of the Jebel Marra Lands, and the extension of a railway from Nyala to Geneina. Several smaller industrial projects were also not funded (Economic Planning Secretariat 1962, 8–9).

9. Similarly, aside from surveying and visits by experts, little work was done in Jebel Marra despite the discovery of water in good quantities (Department of Economic Planning 1965, 5–31).

10. Memo Mr. Burney to Files. "Sudan – General Negotiations," January 29, 1963, WBG "Sudan Railway Project – Negotiations 01," Box # 172012B.

11. Letter. Cecil Hutson to J. A. McCunniffe, October 3, 1960, WBG [World Bank Group] "Sudan – Expansion of Railways and Water Transport Facilities Project – Administration 03," No. 1741655, Box # 172007B.

12. In Sudan, subsistence agricultural production was included in the calculation of per capita income. These prices were figured by deriving the sum at which agricultural products were sold directly from the farm without including marketing and transportation costs. Statistics on subsistence farming were biased toward figures that documented the production of tenants on the major exporting estates, who were allowed to use part of the land to produce foodstuffs, which were often also sold in the market. The farm gate value is typically lower than the retail price consumers pay, as it does not include costs for shipping, handling, storage, marketing and profit margins of the involved companies (Department of Statistics 1959, 9).

13. "As you know it is now generally recognized and accepted by the industrialized countries that the needs of the underdeveloped countries for capital to finance their development plan should be met by a major part by soft loans otherwise the success of their developmental effects will be endangered" (Letter. Abdel Rahim Mirghani to Sayyid Mohammed Hamad el Nil, "Second Sugar Factory at Kashm

el Girba," November 15, 1962, WBG "Sudan – Expansion of Railways and Water Transport Facilities Project, Administration 04," Box # 172007B).

14. Note. From Sir D. Ormsby Gore, "Inward Saving Telegram from Washington to FO: IBRD – Sudan," July 27, 1963, TNA [British National Archives] FO 371/172364.

15. The Consultative Group was chaired by the IBRD and composed of representatives from the Washington embassies of Belgium, France, Germany, Italy, Japan, Netherlands, Switzerland, the United Kingdom, the State Department of the United States and US Agency for International Development (USAID) (Letter. From Washington, Sir D. Ormsby Gore to FO, "Addressed to FO Telegram No. Eager 232 Saving of November 29: Sudan IBRD Consultative Group," TNA FO 371/172364).

16. "The Sudan's total imports in 1962 were LS 89 million and total exports LS 79 million, of which LS 48.5 million were cotton and cotton seed. This deficit on the visible balance of payments is modest, bearing in mind the development of the Plan and the amounts of foreign aid available" (Federation of British Industries 1963, 3).

17. From Washington, Sir D. Ormsby Gore to FO, "Addressed to FO Telegram No. Eager 232 Saving of November 29: Sudan IBRD Consultative Group," TNA FO 371/172364.

18. Memo. M. A. Burney to Hendrik Van Helden, "Sudan Loan Application for the SR." January 27, 1964. WBG. "Sudan – Railway Project – Negotiations 01," Box # 172012B. In the beginning of February 1964, 'Abd al-Rahim Mirghani travelled to Washington in order to explain the difficulties that the Republic of Sudan was having carrying out the Ten Year Plan. Letter. Pierre L. Moussa to Mamoun Beheiry, February 27, 1964, WBG "Sudan – Expansion of Railways and Water Transport Facilities Project – Administration 04," Box # 172007B.

19. Egypt was in need of IMF stabilisation funds in 1964 to meet some of its external debts (Memo. From Commercial Department, British Embassy in Khartoum, July 4, 1964, TNA FO 371/178613; Letter. From A. D. Parsons to P. H. Laurence, April 14, 1964, TNA FO 371/178613; Letter. From M. P. V. Hannam to R. W. Munro, July 24, 1964, TNA FO 371/178613).

20. The rate of withdrawal was raised from 5 to 10 per cent for tenants in the Tokar Delta (Memo. Department of Finance and Economics, "Decision of the Council of Ministers, the 456 Meeting," June 21, 1964, NRO [National Record Office, Khartoum] Finance 3-A/28/6/22/).

21. Note. Maurice Bart to Mr. G. Stewart Mason, August 25, 1964, WBG "Sudan – Second Railway Project – Negotiations 02," Box # 172012B.

22. For a detailed account of the resistance to the Abboud regime and the events of October 1964, see Yusuf Fadl Hasan (1967, 491–509). Bechtold (1976, 202) writes that "economically, [the Supreme Council of the Armed Forces] performed with considerable efficiency; politically, increasing ineffectiveness marked its tenure".

References

Al-Amin, 'Abd al-Rahman. 2005. '*Al-Fariq Ibrahim 'Abbud wa 'Asruhu al-Dhahabi* [Lieutenant General Ibrahim Abboud and the Golden People]. Khartoum, Sudan: 'Abd al-Rahman Ahmed 'Isa.

Arndt, H. W. 1987. *Economic Development: The History of an Idea*. Chicago, IL: University of Chicago Press.

Bayart, Jean-Francois. 1993. *The State in Africa: The Politics of the Belly*. New York: Longman.

Bechtold, P. K. 1976. *Politics in the Sudan: Parliamentary and Military Rule in an Emerging African Nation*. New York: Praeger.

Bonnecase, Vincent. 2011. *La Pauvreté au Sahel: Du Savoir Colonial à la Mesure Internationale*. Paris: Karthala.

Chabal, Patrick, and Jean-Pascal Daloz. 1999. *Africa Works: Disorder as a Political Instrument*. Bloomington, IN: Indiana University Press.

Cooper, F. 1998. "Modernizing Bureaucrats, Backward Africans, and the Development Concept." In *International Development and the Social Sciences: Essays on the History and Politics of Knowledge*, edited by Frederick Cooper and Randall Packard, 64–84, Berkeley, CA: University of California Press.

Daly, M. W. 2007. *Darfur's Sorrow: A History of Destruction and Genocide*. Cambridge: Cambridge University Press.

Department of Economic Planning, Ministry of Finance and Economics, Republic of Sudan. 1965. *The Ten Year Plan of Economic and Social Development 1961/62–1970/71: Explanatory Memorandum on 1964/65 Development Budgets*. Khartoum, Sudan: Government Printing Press.

Department of Statistics (HQ Council of Ministers). 1959. *National Income of Sudan (In Brief). 1955/56*. Occasional Statistical Paper No. 2. Khartoum, Sudan.

Easterly, W. 1997. *The Ghost of Financing Gap: How the Harrod–Domar Growth Model Still Haunts Development Economics*. World Bank Development Research Group, Policy Research Working Paper 1807. Washington, DC: World Bank.

Economic Planning Secretariat, Ministry of Finance and Economics. 1962. *The Ten Year Plan of Economic and Social Development, 1961/62–1970/71*. Khartoum: Government Printing Press.

Federation of British Industries (FBI). 1963. *Assessment of Sudan's Ten Year Plan*. London: FBI.

Finance Department, Sudan Government. 1946. *Five Year Plan for Post-War Development*. Khartoum, Sudan.

Finance Department, Sudan Government. 1953. *The Sudan Development Programme 1951/56*. Khartoum, Sudan: Government Printing Press.

Hajj Hamad, Muhammad Abu al-Qasim. 1980. *Al-Sudan: al-Ma'ziq al-Tarikhi wa Afaq al- Mustaqbal* [Sudan: Historical Dilemmas and Future Horizons]. Beirut, Lebanon: Dar al-Kalimat lil Nashr.

Harvie, C. H., and J. G. Kleve. 1959. *The National Income of Sudan 1955/56*. Khartoum: Department of Statistics.

Herbst, Jeffrey. 2000. *States and Power in Africa: Comparative Lessons in Authority and Control*. Princeton, NJ: Princeton University Press.

Jerven, M. 2011. "Users and Producers of African Income: Measuring African Progress." *African Affairs* 110 (439): 169–190.

Jerven, M. 2013. *Poor Numbers: How We Are Misled by African Development Statistics and What to Do About It*. Ithaca, NY: Cornell University Press.

Lewis, W. A. 1965. *Politics in West Africa*. Oxford: Oxford University Press.

Mahgoub, M. 1974. *Democracy on Trial: Reflections on Arab and African Politics*. London: Deutsch.

Mirghani, A. R. 1983. *Development Planning in the Sudan in the Sixties*. Khartoum: University of Khartoum Press.

Mitchell, T. 2002. *The Rule of Experts: Egypt, Techno-Politics, Modernity*. Berkeley, CA: University of California Press.

Mollan, S. 2008. "Business, State and Economy: Cotton and the Anglo-Egyptian Sudan, 1919–1939." *African Economic History* 36: 95–123.

Morgan, Mary S. 2008. *"On a Mission" with Mutable Mobiles*. Department of Economic History, Working Papers on the Nature of Evidence: How Well Do "Facts" Travel? 34/08. London: London School of Economics and Political Science.

Morgan, M. S. 2011. "Seeking Parts, Looking for Wholes." In *Histories of Scientific Observation*, edited by Lorraine Daston and Elizabeth Lunbeck, 303–326. Chicago, IL: University of Chicago Press.

Niblock, T. 1987. *Class and Power in Sudan: The Dynamics of Sudanese Politics, 1898–1985*. Albany, NY: SUNY Press.

Nyquist, T. E. 1965. "The Sudan: Prelude to Elections." *Middle East Journal* 19 (3): 263–272.

Okigbo, P. C. 1989. *National Development Planning in Nigeria, 1900–92*. Oxford: James Currey.

Poduval, R. N. 1963. "Sudan's Ten Year Plan of Economic and Social Development. Institute of National Planning Memo No. 333, May 29." Cairo: United Arab Republic Institute of National Planning. Accessed January 30, 2014. http://www.econbiz.de/Record/sudan-s-ten-year-plan-of-economic-and-social-development-poduval/10002657592.

Prest, A. R., and I. G. Stewart. 1953. *The National Income of Nigeria, 1950–1951*. London: HM Stationery Office.

Reinert, Sophus. 2011. *Translating Empire: Emulation and the Origins of Political Economy*. Cambridge, MA: Harvard University Press.

Shepherd, G. W., Jr. 1966. "National Integration and the Southern Sudan." *Journal of Modern African Studies* 4 (2): 193–212.

Speich, D. 2011. "The Use of Global Abstractions: National Income Accounting in the Period of Imperial Decline." *Journal of Global History* (6): 7–28.

Studenski, P. 1958. *The Income of Nations. Theory, Measurement, and Analysis, Past and Present: A Study in Applied Economics and Statistics*. New York: New York University Press.

Unger, Roberto Mangabeira. 1996. *What Should Legal Analysis Become?* New York: Verso.

United Nations Department of Economic and Social Affairs. 2012. *Historic Versions of the System of National Accounts*. Accessed June 16, 2012. http://unstats.un.org/unsd/nationalaccount/hsna.asp.

United Nations Department of Economic and Social Affairs. 1958. *A Manual for the Economic and Functional Classification of Government Transactions*. New York: United Nations Press.

Vanoli, A. 2005. *A History of National Accounting*. Amsterdam: IOS Press.

Weinstein, B. 2008. "Developing Inequality." *American Historical Review* 113 (1): 1–18. doi: 10.1086/ahr.113.1.1

Willis, J., and A. El Battahani. 2010. "'We Changed the Laws': Electoral Practice and Malpractice in Sudan since 1953." *African Affairs* 109 (435): 191–212.

Young, C. 1997. *The African Colonial State in Comparative Perspective*. New Haven, CT: Yale University Press.

Young, T. 1993. "Elections and Electoral Politics in Africa." *Africa* 63 (3): 299–312.

Yusuf Fadl Hasan. 1967. "The Sudanese Revolution of October 1964." *Journal of Modern African Studies* 5 (4): 491–509. http://dx.doi.org/10.1017/S0022278X00016372

The bureaucratic performance of development in colonial and post-colonial Tanzania

Felicitas Becker

Department of History, University of Cambridge, Cambridge, United Kingdom

ABSTRACT This article examines change and continuity in development measures concerning cassava in a poor Tanzanian region over a period of 80 years. It shows ambivalent and dubious ways of reasoning about the causes of and solutions to poverty related to these measures, and argues that the persistence of such problematic arguments is understandable if one considers their political usefulness. Local officials have always had to safeguard their own viability in the eyes of their superiors in the administration, as well as those of local audiences. For them, "development" has become a focus of political performances that serve to reinforce their legitimacy.

RÉSUMÉ Cet article se penche sur les variations dans les mesures du développement de la culture du manioc dans une région pauvre de la Tanzanie sur une période de 80 ans. L'étude met en relief les raisonnements ambigus et douteux sur les causes de la pauvreté, et sur les solutions à y apporter, qui sont sous-jacents à ces données. Ces raisonnements s'expliquent toutefois si on en examine l'utilité politique. Les fonctionnaires locaux ont toujours dû protéger leurs arrières face à leurs supérieurs, tout en maintenant une apparence d'indépendance face aux populations locales. Pour eux, le développement est une arène où les jeux politiques servent à renforcer leur légitimité.

Introduction

The present article examines the connection between development planning and assessment on the one hand and Tanzanian local politics on the other. It seeks to explain the recurrence of questionable and often poorly argued for assertions, especially when it comes to the conditions of increasing agricultural production among officials and experts concerned with development. Its main argument is that these ways of reasoning would make more sense if we think of them as political rhetoric – an element of what could be called political theatre – rather than the economic, agricultural or technical assessments they claim to be.

The study is set in the Lindi and Mtwara regions in Tanzania's south-eastern region. This area is best known for two large-scale interventions, namely the "Groundnut Scheme" in the late 1940s and 1950s, and the villagisation campaign of the 1970s (Hogendorn and Scott 1981; and, on groundnuts and villagisation, Lal 2011). Both are typically described as clear failures in function to their developmental aims, although they are wrought with unintended consequences. The present article, however, focuses instead on recurring, small scale projects which have taken place since the 1920s and is concerned with a crop that is rarely ascribed much developmental potential: the cassava root. These ongoing and modest efforts provide an alternative perspective to the history of development that is less dominated by top-down intervention from the centre. Arguably, they also provide some insight into why the ambitious top-down models seemed so attractive at times.

The discussion covers both the colonial and the postcolonial period, and the assertion that the forms of "political theatre" which occurred in both inevitably demonstrates continuity between the two. This continuity is real, but should not be overstated. In both the colonial and postcolonial periods, the dynamics of political theatre, as understood here, were driven by local officials' efforts to manage conflicting expectations: those of their superiors at the political centre on one hand, and of their local subjects or citizens on the other. But as administrative and political structures and the sources of political legitimacy changed greatly with the transition to independence (Iliffe 1979; Mamdani 1996), so did the character of the political performances they helped frame. One could say that they moved from the stage of "studio theatre" during the colonial period to the "big stage" in the following period.

The relationship between development and the politics of so-called developing nations has engendered lively discussion in Africa and beyond. One important strand of this discussion concerns the way development, according to some, sustains dysfunctional political regimes, especially by financing their patronage networks (van de Walle 2001). The present article acknowledges that development projects can adopt a character of patronage when undertaken by officials. It does not, however, share the assumption that the political structures within which these officials work are inherently dysfunctional or illegitimate. Moreover, the political theatre with which I am concerned here is not merely an accompaniment to the doling out of patronage, but one that sustains and, at times, supplants patronage.

My main interest is in the way the invocation of development has helped, over time, to sustain a severely under-resourced local state and how this has shaped the way development is understood or conceptualised. This line of enquiry has to be related also to accounts of development as a way to expand the presence of the state – to constitute "governmentalities", to use Foucault's (1991) term, while "whisking political realities out of sight", in James Ferguson's evocative phrase (Ferguson 1994, xv). The ability of technocratic language of development to obscure the political character and implications of so-called development projects has been ably demonstrated by other authors besides Ferguson, including Li (2007) and Mitchell (2002).

I lack space here to do justice to the diverse ways in which these authors characterise the relationship between development and state power, but I can at least highlight the importance of another of Ferguson's observations: namely, that the "state" in this context cannot be taken as a unitary agency with unitary goals (Ferguson 1994, 273–277). Rather, development enables "a knotting or a coagulation of power" (Ferguson 1994, 274) in which different agents participate in pursuit of different aims. The ultimate effects of the particular processes initiated may not conform to the aims of any one of these actors. Thus, "governmentality" here does not denote a rationalisation of aims and powers, but rather an understanding of the way in which the powers of state and non-state actors combine to remain both effective and diffuse.

The present article, then, seeks to enrich analyses of the "anti-political" effects of development by tracing how a developmental discourse with ostensibly apolitical content is made to do obvious political work. It presents yet another configuration of developmental expertise and politics. In the present case, there is no South African Leviathan in the background as there was for Ferguson, less concentrated imperial interests as there were in Mitchell's Egypt, and no oppressive anti-communist discourse as there was for Li. The focus here is on administrative officials for whom development was a pursuit among many, and who sought to make the most of their inevitable involvement with it. For them, the discourse of development could do political work even if it appeared to deny the political character of the social and policy processes to which it referred.

In other words, similar to the situations examined by the authors mentioned above, planning documents are just as interesting for what they leave out as for what they contain, for what they obscure as for what they highlight. As elsewhere, experts' language fails to acknowledge the political character of social intervention in the name of development. But I will argue that the invocation of development by administrative officials, especially in public, is widely understood as a political act; as part of what I call political theatre. The depoliticisation of development by technocratic language does not preclude its deployment in contexts whose political character is hard to deny, and quietly recognised by participants.

This state of affairs need not even be seen as contradictory. As observers from Weber (1988) to Orwell (1949) and Cooper (2005) have reminded us, the content of a concept can be very different from the work it does. Arguably, the configuration of developmental rhetoric and political practice examined here is just one of many possibilities in the encounter of developmental aims and organisations with African states. Catherine Boone (2003) has made clear that one African state may use a variety of different stratagems to maintain its presence in its rural peripheries. Following her, what I am about to describe can be seen as one register among others of African politics.

Location and institutional context of the study

The area discussed here, the colonial "Southern Province", the Lindi and Mtwara regions of Tanzania, followed the trajectory of many parts of Africa that lacked either mineral deposits or a profitable cash crop during the colonial period characterised by economic stagnations and an increase in exported labour. Relatively low-lying, the climate is hot and fairly dry; the presence of tsetse flies interferes with cattle keeping. In parts of the area surface water is scarce; soils are often either sandy or excessively clayey and the population is unevenly distributed and often scarce (Land Resources Development Centre [LRDC] 1979). Localised famine early in the British period necessitated relief and established the region as an unproductive drain of financial resources according to officials at the Centre. By the late colonial period, the area had become a "Cinderella region" (Iliffe 1979). The incoming independent government proposed special measures to change this, but did not succeed in breaking the vicious circle of isolation, lack of profitable exports and lack of investment.

The possibility of this region expressing developmental interest in a crop as marginal to agricultural commodity markets as cassava is itself partly a reflection of the difficulty of establishing and maintaining attractive alternatives. Cassava was tried for want of options. But the rationales for seeking to change cassava production changed greatly over time, keeping partly with administrative concerns and partly with current trends in development. The changing agendas attached to cassava – which will be considered in greater detail below – included famine prevention, soil and forest conservation, income generation and participatory development.

All of these strategies were presented as ways to address the poverty of this region, yet, as I hope to show, they were based on divergent accounts of the causation of this poverty, and hence differ in ways to address it. In particular, the aetiologies of poverty used were deeply ambivalent about the role of rural producers in the causation of poverty. At times, rural people are presented as part of the problem: they are "thriftless" in the language of colonial officials or passive or traditionalist in that of postcolonial officials (Ellis and Biggs 2001). In other cases, they are discussed rather as victims of a situation beyond their control, while the problems lie with infrastructure, climate, soils and markets. Elements of both can combine in the same planning document. Similarly, the solutions that were proposed combined elements of approaches that would contradict one another if stated together. Some suggestions focus on inputs, on technical solutions such as new crops or ways of processing. Others are educationalist, focused on changing rural people and in particular their agricultural practices.

Such forms of contradictory reasoning, which combine arguments with a good deal of tension between them, are not all that unusual in political discourse. It is worth emphasising that their occurrence does not indicate an unusual degree of hypocrisy among the actors involved, nor does it betray grand conspiracies. Nevertheless, this jumbling together of disparate rationales is useful to officials and experts in a pragmatic or improvised sort of way. As readers of development planning documents will have noted, these documents tend to foreground a single or a small number of issues as the crucial ones through which a problematic can be addressed. The juxtaposition of different analyses and strategies then facilitates shifts between different core issues, and thereby between development projects.

The possibility of making such shifts in turn was important to officials who had reason to worry about their viability within the political system of which they formed part. In the interwar period, they had to demonstrate a commitment to the often conflicting goals of public order, efficient tax collection and fiscal prudence to their paymasters in the colonial capital (Gardner 2012 on taxation; Berman and Lonsdale 1992 on the conflicting aims of "men on the spot"). Since the postwar period, they have been under pressure to demonstrate their commitment and effectiveness as agents of development (Schneider 2003).

Switches between different accounts of poverty and development helped officials manage expectations, explain failures, and sustain ambitions by reformulating them. Different intellectual fashions adopted by experts, who faced their own legitimacy issues, helped keep development discourse fresh. The following section will explore the way successive agendas attached to cassava cultivation helped local officials and experts manage their relations with the political centre. A last section will then examine the way the development discourse has helped them manage relations with local audiences.

Cassava, agricultural intervention, local officials and institutional change

A New World crop, cassava probably entered the region under discussion from the Portuguese-influenced areas south of Tanzania. When colonialism was established, the crop was common in parts of the area under discussion, while grains formed the staple food elsewhere (Fuchs 1905). From the late 1920s, administrators took an interest in it as a "famine safety" measure, trying to enforce the cultivation of minimum acreages with the help of "Native Authorities". This use of cassava was widespread in British Africa at the time (Hodge 2007 for Tanganyika, in particular; Maddox 1986).

Intermittent food shortages nevertheless persisted. Occasionally, local officials explicitly blamed "thriftless" or "idle" Native Authorities for failing to enforce cassava cultivation. In the words of an official report: "this area ... has been subject to famine before and is inhabited by a thriftless people who in spite of repeated warnings are content to live from hand to mouth and have little, if any, reserves of cassava".[1] In fact, the part of the province that depended most heavily on cassava for sustenance, the Makonde Plateau, was actually less prone to food shortages than other regions, and was often a destination for those seeking food. Yet the blame-mongering officials failed to take into account the actual reasons why cassava was not a panacea for food shortages. Propagated through fresh cuttings, this root is harder to disseminate than its grains. Moreover, it thrives only in light, sandy and not too wet soils, which were uncommon in the region discussed (LRDC 1979). Some of the areas affected by recurrent shortage were clearly not suited to it.

Yet, for local officials, focusing on cassava planting campaigns – and Africans' failure to engage in them – had advantages. Food shortage caused a great deal of embarrassment to the officials in whose districts it occurred and endangered their career prospects (Perham 1976; Lumley 1976). Cassava cultivation was a concrete and apparently simple counter measure. Further, a focus on cassava distracted from the dilemma officials faced between ensuring tax collection and preventing famine. Most villagers in this region paid their taxes by selling grain in the absence of other cash crops. This meant that they made themselves more vulnerable to food shortage by serving their tax obligations. As efficiency in tax collection was no less important to a district officer's good standing than reduction of famine; they faced conflicting goals.

In the early 1930s, an agricultural officer tried to address the problem directly by experimenting with alternative, non-grain cash crops.[2] But he found that these experiments were difficult to finance, as the Centre was reluctant to spend money on a region that had already cost so much in famine relief and delivered such low returns in tax. Moreover, every cash crop faced the same difficulty with market access due to poor transport infrastructure, and again funding to improve this infrastructure was not forthcoming from the Centre.[3] Emphasising the need for peasant effort in cassava cultivation was a much safer way to frame food security problems than examining these political constraints.

Somewhat ironically, it appears that cassava nevertheless came to contribute to food security not through locally enforced cultivation, but by entering the regional food market. Cassava flour mills came into wider use during the Second World War, when food security was at a political premium. Cassava flour, more easily transportable than the whole root, could then plug holes in the food supply caused by the exportation of more sought-after grains to politically or strategically more important parts of the colony or empire.[4] During the boom in demand for foodstuffs that followed the war, cassava finally became a cash earner. In 1948, the district officer in Newala on the Makonde plateau, the district most geared towards cassava cultivation, reported that cultivators "were able to market over 3000 tons of this crop which in the past was, save in times of famine, well-nigh unmarketable".[5] In other words, the official policy of cassava cultivation as a food security measure never appeared to have made much difference to a crop whose uses were shaped by the vagaries of soils, climate, markets and taxation. Nevertheless, for local officials there were at times advantages to invoking this policy.

Urgency and optimism: the independence period

Here, as elsewhere in Tanzania, the years between the foundation of the Tanganyika African National Union in 1954 and independence in 1961, were marked by an expectation that things could only get better. The technocratic optimism of this period has been much remarked on (Cooper 1996). In the region under discussion, the greatest economic change was the rise of a cash crop more profitable than grain; that is, the cashew nut. It added to the general optimism. Instead of specific aims such as famine prevention and tax collection, there was a general sense that "more is better"; production increases were routinely expected and implicitly taken as a good thing.

This optimism, though, also created new pressures on provincial officials. They had to demonstrate commitment and success, and arguably could expect less understanding from superiors who were less willing to accept "natives" shortcomings as an explanation for failure. In this sprit, in 1961 an agricultural officer deployed to this area transmitted to Dar es Salaam the "production targets" he had set for the province. Referring to one district, Lindi, he stated that:

> minimum acreages to be cultivated by each family have been laid down as a result of which it has been found possible to set the following district production targets for the next five years:

present	average	estimated 1962	1967 (tons)
Pulses	700	450	1500
Cassava	100	150	2000
Sesame	2500	4500	7000

(Tanzania National Archive [TNA] Acc 498/D30/23 3-year development plan, 1961/62–1963/64, 8–9)

These increases (twenty-fold over six years in the case of cassava) were supposed to be achieved by increasing acreage, better "crop husbandry", new seeds and some limited use of new technology. Implicitly, the plan presupposed peasants' ability to significantly increase labour input, and heavily relied on it to meet its aims.

The plan also stated the need for investment in transport so as to ease marketing, in keeping with demands made since the 1930s.[6] Here, the discussion acknowledges that cultivators faced difficulties beyond their ability to affect change: poor access to markets threatened to make their bulky, low-value trade goods unviable. The report does not, however, acknowledge that marketing problems could form a real disincentive to increase production. Rather, the acknowledgment of marketing problems coexists with a heavy emphasis on cultivators' increased effort. The author claims that extended circumcision ceremonies and "absentee landownership" limited production in Lindi district. He states that "an approach has been made" to the District Council to "change" these practices, without acknowledging that "unused" land was an integral part of the fallow system universal in local agriculture. Similarly, when writing on the neighbouring district of Mtwara, he announced his intention:

> To arrive at a standard minimum acreage for every cultivator to aim at and to try to get him to cultivate this area by the use of TANU and the TANU Youth League who will be taught to step out acres, and who will try to cajole more effort out of farmers by making public examples of those who do not try and models of those who do.[7]

Again, the emphasis is on extracting "effort" from cultivators. The "forecast" given above thus seems like an ambitious statement of intent rather than a reasoned assessment of what is possible. As in the colonial period, one senses the writer's eagerness to make a good impression on the addressees of the report. What has changed is the writer's notion of what constitutes a good impression: it is not about demonstrating compliance with famine safety measures or deflecting blame for failure to do so; instead, there is a general emphasis on growth and on improvement.

Yet the limiting factors unresponsive to peasants' efforts became very evident later in the decade. Cassava flour had quietly established itself as a minor export earner – in 1963, Newala district was selling it to Poland and (presumably East) Germany.[8] A "bumper" harvest in 1966, however, showed up the limits of the market for this crop. In the words of Newala's agricultural administrator:

> Generally, in crop production and taking cassava crop in particular, the year 1966 was the most favourable crop season ever had before. Total production of this crop, is without doubt, the highest on record. ... For a marketing period of 2 months only [...] saleable tonnage had gone up to 23,000 and this was probably a third of the total produce expected for the year [...] The co-operative societies were faced with a trouble of how they could get rid of such a surplus harvest. ... it was then ruled by the Government that the only solution of such surplus production, was to reduce the price per kg. Of dried cassava from -/19 to -/12. This ruling, of course did not meet favourable welcome in the hearts of district's farmers and it was unanimously and adversely agreed by the farmers not to offer

any more of this crop for marketing. At this date, a good lot of cassava is commonly found here and there with no economic value. The state has arisen ill feelings in the hearts of most individual farmers and has come out like a common song sung by many that the agricultural staff encourage the expansion of acreages for increased production but cannot find market for the produce. It is indeed a very serious affair, and it speedily leads to a draw back by some farmers ... [9]

One senses how official optimism collides with the realities of infrastructure and of the market.

Compared to the colonial period, though, there is also a change: the writer appears anguished about his standing *vis-à-vis* his local audience: the cultivators. He comes close to pleading with his superiors on their behalf. In this regard, the report indicates the changed political dynamic of the postcolonial period. In the postcolonial dispensation, officials were under increased pressure to demonstrate or promise developmental success to their local audiences. Yet, in an ongoing process of parallel reasoning, assertions that cultivators had to increase effort, exculpating local officials at the centre, also persisted. This juxtaposition of different lines of reasoning is further traceable in discussions of the relationship between cassava cultivation and conservation.

Cassava cultivation, conservation and participation

In the run-up to independence, cassava became caught up in a then widespread strand of development rhetoric: soil conservation. Tilley (2011) and Hodge (2007) have shown how a concern for soil conservation arose from imperial debates on the productivity and fragility of tropical environments and populations. On the ground in east Africa, the policies arising from these concerns had major political repercussions. Labour-intensive measures such as ridging caused rural discontent, which added to the support for demands for independence (Anderson 2002; Giblin and Maddox 1996).

In the region under discussion, soil conservation became the subject of a flurry of bylaws in the 1950s, part of a broader "drive" for improvement in a region by then recognised as disadvantaged (Liebenow 1971). At first, conservation intervention took the form of simply prohibiting cultivation. Making the Makonde escarpment a forest reserve was first mooted in 1954, in connection with a large scale scheme to improve water provision on the plateau (Liebenow 1971). In 1963, the then agricultural officer for Mtwara, J.A. Whitehead, had written about the Makonde Plateau that:

> [S]oil conservation ... is practically unknown. ... protecting steeper slopes by not cultivating them meets with strong opposition. ... the position in Newala in some parts gives cause for serious concern ... tons of top soil will be lost ... if the people do not become alive to the dangers of cultivating the escarpment soon.[10]

Four years later, another agricultural officer, who signed himself Hilalo, stated that the "evil custom" of cultivating on the slopes continued, and suggested making a bylaw against it.[11]

Suggestions to protect the Makonde escarpment by removing cultivation lingered in the 1970s and 1980s, alongside afforestation projects and attempts to expand cassava production for the market without regard to conservation. Yet, when the regional government in Mtwara re-examined the problem in 1991, they presented the relationship between cassava cultivation and conservation as mutually beneficial rather than antagonistic. In a document entitled "Soil and Water conservation project in Makonde Plateau", produced by the Regional Commissioner's Office in Mtwara in November 1991, planners projected that *thanks to* conservation efforts, dried cassava production would triple from 1 tonne/hectare to 3 tonnes/hectare in five years, through "improved management".[12] The price of such flour would, it was claimed, rise from 10 to 25 TZS per kg.

The measures proposed to achieve this consisted in the "reservation" – that is, removal from agricultural use – of land around a dozen wells on the plateau, afforestation especially in so-called "shelter belts" and general "coordination of services".[13] Why they would have such a dramatic effect on cassava production, in an area where land was reported to be under stress from overuse, is not explained. But the references to improved management and integration of services (presumably referring to the agricultural extension services used by cultivators) suggest that once again a combination of new inputs and farmers' effort is supposed to be the cause of change. Thirty eventful years apart, then, we find a similar mixture of technocratic optimism and voluntarist reliance on peasant effort in this 1991 planning document as in the future production estimates from 1961. In both cases, the planning documents make more sense as pieces of political rhetoric than as assessments of economic state and potential.

Nevertheless, in some ways the 1991 document contrasts with the earlier ones. In particular, it invokes "participatory" planning and implementation. To understand the antecedents of this feature of the 1990s view, it is helpful to remember the policy transitions that occurred between the mid-1970s and the early 1990s. While villagisation in the 1970s constituted an extremely top-down approach to development (Hyden 1981; Scott 1999), its economic failure created openings for international development agencies that emphasised a more consultative approach (Jennings 2002).

In the region under discussion, this new influence took the form of a Finnish-funded agency known as Rural Integrated Programme Support (RIPS; Government of Finland and Government of the United Republic of Tanzania 1998, a title closely aligned with the integrated rural development then pushed by the World Bank). Until the mid-2000s, RIPS would be the dominant international development presence in this region. Influenced by the "farming systems" approach, it had a programmatic orientation towards aiming for close integration into the social contexts where it worked, and towards supporting small scale projects thought to be in accordance with the priorities of villagers. Thus, when the 1991 report states that "the project is participatory and heavily relies on successful involvement of the target groups in decision making and project implementation",[14] the Regional Commissioner's office is both integrating conceptual developments in the field and talking the talk of its main sponsor.

The paragraphs following this statement, nevertheless, specify that every cultivator involved in the project would be obliged to plant trees and follow new bylaws on soil and water conservation. These measures were to be accompanied by demonstration plots, training, seminars, field days and the use of cinema, posters and pamphlets. In other words, traditional top-down elements, some in use since the 1930s, have not actually gone away. The participatory elements represent the newest "layer" in plans that bear traces of decades of development thinking. They enabled the project to pass as new, thus promising, in 1991. But the insistence on peasant effort was unchanged since the 1960s. The main innovation by RIPS lies with the way in which consultation was formalised and recorded: the elaborate protocols for soliciting and recording villagers' input through transect walks and chapatti diagrams, and the insistence on repeating such assessments in the course of a project.

Overall, it is hard to tell what influence, if any, policy interventions had on the development of cassava cultivation. Such figures as are available do suggest that over the long term, since the 1930s, production has increased significantly. This is hardly surprising considering that the number of cultivators who depended on it for sustenance also greatly increased in these decades. We know that marketing measures did influence farmers' planting choices, as the events of 1966 show. Yet reports from the villagisation period suggest that the "closer planting" of cassava then pushed by agricultural advisors had adverse effects, as it eased the spread of disease. The 1977 land use study also clearly started the persistence of marketing constraints, in terms of processing facilities, transport and international prices. Either way, neither the insistence on peasant effort nor the association between conservation and expansion of cassava cultivation that officials proposed ever becomes very plausible.

We have seen, then, how cassava has repeatedly become the focus of interest for development experts, their colonial forerunners and local officials. This recurrent interest was shaped partly by policy fashions emanating from the centre: food security; conservation; and participation. But it was also driven by the institutional dynamics that local officials had to manage, in particular, their need to legitimate themselves to the centre and to donors. In this context, measurements and planning documents do not so much reflect real outcomes and possibilities as the efforts of provincial officials at favourable self-representation. Yet to understand why the conflicted agendas and dubious claims around cassava as an object of development persisted, we also have to examine the legitimating role of invocations of development in interactions between local officials and rural populations.

The rhetoric of development and postcolonial politics in rural Tanzania: development as political performance

That there is a theatrical, performative element to postcolonial African politics is almost a journalistic cliché: it is only too evident in such larger-than-life characters as Mobutu or Idi Amin. In some ways, this is due to the weight of history, as performative politics clearly predated colonialism (Haugerud 1997; Glassman 1996). But it also draws strength from aspects of the present (Haugerud 1997). For Tanzania especially, performative elements in the independence campaign and in postcolonial protest movements have been recognised (Geiger 1997; Tripp 1997), as has the political subtext of performances not explicitly political (Askew 2002).

Yet it should be clear that these performative elements do not hark back simply to an "African" political culture. Rather, they have distinctly colonial roots. The famous thesis of the "invention of tradition" in colonial Africa (Hobsbawm and Ranger 1983) was originally demonstrated with reference to theatrical practices celebrating the British Empire in Africa (Ranger 1983). Nevertheless, one source of strength for performative politics lies in the pervasiveness of performative aspects in everyday life, especially in a context where privacy is hard to come by. The practice of conveying additional meaning to verbal content through tone, accompanying gesture or facial expression serves to compensate for the difficulty of making openly evaluative comments on others in the absence of secure privacy. The political performer thus has a highly perceptive audience to work with.

The political performances that I have in mind are mostly quite low key affairs, worlds away from either "Empire Day" celebrations of yore or Mobutuesque splendour. They occur in the regular pursuit of governance in the Tanzanian countryside and very often take the form of public meetings, typically prompted by the arrival of a visitor: a high level official; a vaccination team; a foreign expert; or even a researcher. While low-key, they are nevertheless quite choreographed, with seating and speaking orders, specific gestures of respect and the use of elevated language. Reference to *maendeleo,* progress, is an inescapable part of these occasions. Occurrences as mundane and, arguably, retrograde as the work of street food traders or a small-town beauty contest may be glossed as signs of "progress" in this context. More often, though, reference is made to developmental aims and projects, such as the ones discussed above.

These occasions can be read as political performance not only because they have precedents in the performative politics of the independence era and the public displays of power that were official visits in the colonial period (Ranger 1983; Deutsch 2002). The main point is that rather than facilitating concrete developmental measures, they elaborate, embellish and at times even replace them, and in the process help reaffirm a commonality of purpose (the purpose being *maendeleo*) between officials and audiences.

Much of the literature on rural politics in Africa at large and Tanzania in particular could make the reader wonder why such reaffirmation should even be needed. With the exception of the villagisation period (Hyden 1981) and spasmodic rural protest often concentrated in relatively wealthy or well-connected locations (Kelsall 2000) rural politics here tend to be seen as fairly quiescent. After several rounds of multiparty elections, voter support for the ruling party has held up well outside Zanzibar. An explanation for this quiescence is also easily available in the continuing dominance of the ruling party in terms of resources to disburse, hence rural patronage, and the density of its grassroots organisation, going back to the single-party period (on grassroots organisation, see Bryceson 1993, 11–22; Tripp 1997).

There seems to be little reason, then, for government to make an effort to keep rural voters on-side beyond election period patronage. But this picture of rural quiescence is misleading, for at least three reasons. Firstly, despite the predictability of national elections, the local elections instituted under the villagisation era village constitutions were more competitive and matter locally. Secondly, electoral dominance did not translate into smooth compliance between elections; technocrats' complaints of villagers' foot dragging are not purely rhetorical. Thirdly, and following from that, patronage is no panacea for dealing with rural audiences; officials here actually have *persuading* to do. For this purpose, political rhetoric and performance play a crucial part, and "development" is a core trope in it.

The legacy of villagisation in village politics is quite contrary to the authoritarian character of the campaign itself, as it entailed the entrenchment of an elective element in rural administration. Villages and village wards elected their executive authorities and these elected officials liaise with the appointed ones. Village elections, moreover, were more likely to be genuinely competitive than those for parliament. Personality could beat party loyalty at this local scale, and parties poorly represented in parliament may still gain a smattering of village council seats (Vaughan Hassett 1984; Seppaelae 1998; and from personal communications: Omari Bakari Chanyunya, [Rwangwa-Nachingwea, then chairman of Nachingwea sub-village, interviewed 12 October 2003]; I. Makota [Rwangwa-Nachingwea, chairman of opposition party Chadema, interviewed 14 October]; Ali Sefu Marongora [Rwangwa-Kilimahewa, former village chairman, interviewed 9 October]; and I.B. Namachi [Rwangwa-Dodoma, sub-village chairman, interviewed 10 October]). This situation makes the local officials attentive to their electorate. By extension, the appointees working with them have to reckon with the sensibilities of the electorate if they want to support (or undermine) local notables.

Moreover, these local electoral politics tie the working of village administration very visibly into the sphere of life that Goran Hyden (1981, passim) termed the "economy of affection": the informal networks of support and control; of patronage; patriarchy; but also of competition that could make and unmake candidates in such elections (Falk Moore 1996; Seppaelae 1998). The balance of power between these and the local arms of the state, their mutual dependence or independence, are a crucial aspect of the postcolonial order, and were very fluid (Boone 2003). One of the spaces in which they have conducted their relationship is that of political performance (see Geiger 1997; Iliffe 1979 for the mid-twentieth century).

Next, we need to consider the issue of everyday compliance. Even if rural officials did not have to worry about the way villagers voted, they still needed them to turn up for vaccination campaigns, to deliver their cash crops at the prices available, to come out to greet visitors from on high and prettify the village beforehand, and so on. Non-compliance was widespread in the early 2000s concerning the so-called "development levy" (Tripp 1997; Becker 2013); producers do seek to withhold crops from the market if prices are disappointing (Chachage and Nyoni 2001); public standoffs occur around the activities of healers, with authorities alternating between heavy-handed interference and reluctance to intervene even where a healer threatens life (Langwick

2001). The invocation of "peasant conservatism" only goes so far in providing excuses to officials embarrassed by such occurrences.

Officials' need to deal with such events brings us to the limits of political patronage: it is too elaborate and expensive a tool to deal with all these issues. Doling out resources is undeniably a crucial task of the local state; up to a point the notion of the state and ruling party buying consent is appropriate. In emergencies, it has been since the colonial period, as the history of famine relief shows.[15] It became routinised in the late-colonial period, already in the name of development (Liebenow 1971), and while definitions of and prescribed paths towards development have changed, in one guise or another the expectation of resources for the purpose has stayed in place. But a local official cannot bring out a promise of resources, let alone material goods, every time he (or occasionally she) needs to call a meeting or find volunteers.

It is in this context that public invocations of shared development goals and its celebratory performances become important. In a way not totally unfamiliar to people working in cash-strapped public institutions in Europe, the relative shortage of resources to hand out tends to make the ceremony surrounding the handover more, not less, elaborate. Public meetings to explain the nature of new development measures need particular care if the measures themselves are disappointing.

In fact, public meetings and invocations of development take place even where there is nothing to actually dole out. They serve to publicly and collectively affirm the aim shared between officials and villagers (see Haugerud 1997 for an analysis of equivalent processes in Kenya). The doling out, the invocation of development and political performance come together in a particular kind of rhetorical political practice, in which the relationship between villagers and local officialdom is one of mutual dependency. The invocation of the shared aim of "development" helps both sides stake their claims on the other side and justify their accession to the other side's demands.

None of the above is particularly surprising as long as we accept that discursive, combative, ideologically influenced and popular politics have a place in rural Africa: that officials and politicians at times have to *persuade* rather than buy consensus with hand outs. If this proposition sounds exotic, this is partly because of the sort of portrayal of rural dwellers, as unenlightened bumpkins who sometimes "make an effort" but much too often don't, that is so evident in some of the planning documents above. It is in itself an ideological heritage from the late colonial period, when African cities became defined as the sites of progress and the countryside, by contrast, as the realm of stagnant subsistence (Cooper 1996, 202–216).

There is no need, therefore, to think of bureaucratic practice as somehow "perverted" by performance. In a way, every visa or welfare office is a stage dedicated to a performance that is about power (the right to ask questions) and compliance (the obligation to answer). But in rural Tanzania, performance also serves to manage the persisting incapacities, the sheer poverty, of the rural state. Officials may find themselves working out of thatched mud huts. Cars, petrol, paper, pens and stamps are often in short supply. The expanding mobile phone network, while compensating for the dearth of landlines in the countryside, burns a hole into budgets. Reporting and record-keeping, while at times elaborate, are not necessarily rewarded with resources from on high. If, then, the term "development" once was grounds for mobilisation to improve lives and show the world what Africans could do, it has become a common denominator that helps villagers and their administrators keep interactions civil in the face of a long history of mutual demands and frustrations.

Conclusion

Taking a long view, then, we find a great deal of continuity in the nature of poverty in this region, and in the way officials sought to counter and account for it. The lack of high-value export crops and reliable transport, and the fickleness of international markets with regard to the available cash crops, remain a problem throughout. In the accounts of poverty and recommendations for development, meanwhile, the most palpable continuity is the tendency to fall back on ideas of rural peoples' shortcomings, their lack of effort or understanding, and the need to extract effort from them. Yet, throughout the decades, references to such ideas also coexist uneasily with analyses of the structural constraints rural producers faced.

There is, however, also always something new. The focus of attempts to counter the persistent problems moves between innovation in crops and other inputs, infrastructure investment, education, conservation and more. Ways of describing the same problem change. The result is a peculiar mixture of the old and the new, and of institutional memory (returning, for instance, to the idea of protecting the Makonde escarpment) with official amnesia (the latter evident, for example, in failure to acknowledge the reasons why past attempts at protecting the escarpment came to nothing).

These ambivalences make sense if we take into account the institutional and political pressures that local officials faced. They had to propose feasible interventions and promise success while also allowing for possible and actual failure. They had to propose alternatives to promising but financially unfeasible interventions such as road-building. In this context, measurement and planning were intimately connected, and at times subservient, to political rhetoric and performance.

The character of these political performances, though, changed significantly from the colonial to the postcolonial period. As Achille Mbembe (2001) reminds us, the colonial state's sovereignty was based on conquest, thus not answerable to the populations over which it was exerted. Concomitantly, before independence the rhetoric of development is shaped predominantly by local officials' need to explain themselves to the colonial centre; in the present case, Dar es Salaam. After independence, this need does not go away, but it now competes with the need to convincingly address local audiences. Local officials now had to actively project power and to persuade, rather than fall back on the sovereignty of conquest. Ultimately, then, the "poor numbers" used by local planners are not only the outcome of the lack of resources so vividly described by Jerven (2013). Rather, the exactitude of their figures is of less concern to them than these figures' political usefulness.

It is worth stressing again that stating this does not imply blatant deception of the part of the people who make or use these figures. Nor do I mean to imply that local officials pursue development goals to simply legitimise their positions. Rather, its uses in local politics constitute but one level at which the practice of development functions; a welcome side effect as much as a planned intervention. To characterise this kind of effect, we can draw on Ferguson's characterisation of development practices as "knots" in webs of power relations: they encompass many interested parties and their intentions, from agricultural producers to officials to experts to buyers to national politicians, but they are not directed by any one of these parties. "Governmentality" here manifests less as the active pursuit of "a whole series of specific finalities" (Foucault 1991, 100; see Li, 2007) than as government letting a local political practice emerge from the efforts of provincial planners and their audiences.

Our case study therefore also has implications for understanding the role of provincial peripheries in the grand-scale practice of development. Historians and critics of developmental practice have traced the emergence of developmental concepts from the interaction of a set of institutions at the imperial and colonial centres (Hodge 2007; Tilley 2011). "Think tanks" and government departments in London and the British "home counties" communicated with imperial research institutions such as the agricultural school in Trinidad to put concepts such as "soil conservation" into circulation. After the Second World War UN institutions took on a similar function (Arndt 1987; Escobar 1994). Yet, while it is true that notions such as this arrived in places such as

Lindi and Mtwara fully formed and had to be integrated into local planning, the evidence examined above shows that local officials deployed these concepts in ways that suited them: according to both the constraints they faced and the ambitions they pursued.

Perhaps the tendency of developmental concepts and practices to take on lives of their own out in the provinces helps understand intermittent attempts at grand-scale intervention. Both the groundnut project and villagisation can, in a way, be understood as attempts to break the cycle of smaller-scale development projects becoming "sucked into" the everyday world of practical and political constraints on one hand, and alternative uses of development practice on the other. On these occasions, the centre sought to reassert control – and failed.

That "development" and related concepts escape the control of their planners and take on a life of their own among the target populations has been demonstrated very clearly (Ferguson 1999; Howard Smith 2008). The present study has focused on the role of official local "intermediaries" in the development process. Putting them into the picture makes visible an additional "layer" to the relations between development and politics. In the present case, as in those described by Ferguson (1994) and Li (2007), the explicit content of the development process, the social and technical processes involved become depoliticised. The rhetoric employed strips them of their power dimensions and reduces them to purely technical and practical problems. Yet, at the same time, the performative deployment of this rhetoric has recognisably political overtones and uses. Not only are the powers that be openly present and invoked at these choreographed public invocations of development; mutual consent and reaffirmation is palpably at stake. The politics is negotiated rather than confrontational, but it is there.

The observer may be tempted to consider the kind of political performance posited above as part of a "Tanzanian exceptionalism". The peaceful stability and pronouncedly "pro-poor" orientation of Tanzania's postcolonial regime, especially in its initial period under Nyerere, has often been noted. It has also, rightly, been questioned. Recently the authoritarian tendencies of the regime have at times been very evident, especially but not only in Zanzibar (Becker 2013). The discursive, negotiated character of the political performances built around development can coexist with authoritarian enforcement and violence. The performative politics examined here is one of a number of options available for a weakly institutionalised and under-resourced rural state. As such, it can be found, *mutatis mutandis*, also elsewhere in Africa (Boone 2003; Haugerud 1997).

Biographical note

Felicitas Becker is University Lecturer in African History at the University of Cambridge, and has previously taught at SOAS, London, and at Simon Fraser University, Vancouver. Her research has two related foci: on Islam in East Africa since the late nineteenth century and on local and popular politics, with particular attention to its interaction with development. Her publications include *Becoming Muslim in Mainland Tanzania* (Oxford University Press, 2008), and "Remembering Nyerere: Political Rhetoric and Dissent in Contemporary Tanzania" (*African Affairs*, 2013). Further contributions can be found in *Africa*, *Journal of Global History* and *Journal of African History*.

Notes

1. Tanzania National Archives (TNA) 19365 vol. II no. 148: Provincial Commissioner, Southern Province to Chief Secretary, Dar es Salaam, 11 April 1938.
2. On these plans, see TNA 21695: report on a meeting between the Secretary for Native Affairs, Director of Agriculture, Provincial Commissioner, Senior Agricultural Officer Southeastern Circle, and the Assistant District Officers for Masasi and Newala, Lindi, September 25 1933.
3. TNA Acc 16/15/29: Report on agricultural schemes by Senior Agricultural Officer Latham to Provincial Commissioner, Lindi, 4 May 1936.

4. On the replacement of rice destined for export with cassava flour in the local diet, see TNA Acc. 491, A 3/3/1, Food supplies and famine reports p. 29: Provincial produce officer, Southern Province, to Tunduru District Commissioner, 25 August 1952.
5. TNA Acc. 16/11/260: Mikindani district, annual report 1948, p. 113.
6. E.g. TNA 19365, p. 78: Provincial Commissioner, Lindi to Secretariat, Dar es Salaam, March 1934.
7. TNA Acc 498/D30/23: 3 year development plan, 1961/62–1963/64, appendix b.
8. TNA Acc 494 A/AR/D/new, p. 37: Annual Report to Ministry of Agriculture, Mtwara Region, 1963, by J.A. Whitehead.
9. TNA Acc 494 A/AR/D/new: Annual Report for 1967, Newala district, agricultural division. 6 January 1968.
10. TNA Acc 494 A/AR/D/new, p. 37: Annual Report to Minister of Agriculture, Mtwara Region, 1963, J. A. Whitehead
11. TNA 494 A/AR/D/new: Annual Report for 1967 in Newala district, agricultural division. 6 January 1968.
12. "Soil and Water conservation project in Makonde Plateau", Regional Commissioner's Office, Mtwara, November 1991, annex 2. RIPS library, Mtwara.
13. "Soil and Water conservation project in Makonde Plateau", Regional Commissioner's Office, Mtwara, November 1991, annex 2. RIPS library, Mtwara, p. 9.
14. "Soil and Water conservation project in Makonde Plateau", Regional Commissioner's Office, Mtwara, November 1991, annex 2. RIPS library, Mtwara, p. 17–18.
15. See TNA file nr. 19365 "famine relief", on famines in the "Southern Province" in the 1930s; especially Provincial Commissioner Southern Province (Mr Hallier) to Chief Secretary, Dar es Salaam: Report on famine in Tunduru district, Lindi, 19 March, 1931, which details famine relief expenses for this famine episode.

References

Anderson, D. 2002. *Eroding the Commons*. London: James Currey.

Arndt, H. W. 1987. *Economic Development: The History of an Idea*. Chicago, IL: University of Chicago Press.

Askew, K. 2002. *Performing the Nation: Swahili Music and Cultural Politics in Tanzania*. Chicago, IL: University of Chicago Press.

Becker, F. 2013. "Remembering Nyerere: Political Rhetoric and Dissent in Contemporary Tanzania." *African Affairs* 112 (447): 1–24.

Berman, B., and J. Lonsdale. 1992. *Unhappy Valley: Conflict in Kenya and Africa*. Oxford: James Currey.

Boone, C. 2003. *Political Topographies of the African State*. Cambridge: Cambridge University Press.

Bryceson, D. 1993. *Liberalising Tanzania's Food Trade*. London: James Currey.

Chachage, S. L., and J. Nyoni. 2001. *Economic Restructuring and the Cashew Nut Industry in Tanzania: A Research Report*. Dar es Salaam: Tanzania Agricultural Situation Analysis (TASA).

Cooper, F. 1996. *Decolonisation and African Society: The Labour Question in French and British Africa*. Cambridge: Cambridge University Press.

Cooper, F. 2004. *Africa since 1940: The Past in the Present*. Cambridge: Cambridge University Press.

Cooper, F. 2005. *Colonialism in Question: Theory, Knowledge, History*. Berkeley, CA: University of California Press.

Deutsch, J.-G. 2002. "Celebrating Power in Everyday Life: The Administration of Law in Colonial Tanzania, 1890–1914." *Journal of African Cultural Studies* 15 (1): 93–104.

Ellis, F., and S. Biggs. 2001. "Evolving Themes in Rural Development, 1950s–2000." *Development Policy Review* 19 (4): 437–448.

Escobar, A. 1994. *Encountering Development: The Making and Unmaking of the Third World*. Princeton, NJ: Princeton University Press.

Falk Moore, S. 1996. "Post-socialist Micro-politics: Kilimanjaro, 1993." *African Affairs* 66 (4): 587–606.

Ferguson, J. 1994. *The Anti-Politics Machine*. Minneapolis, MA: University of Minnesota Press.

Ferguson, J. 1999. *Expectations of Modernity*. Berkeley, CA: University of California Press.

Foucault, M. 1991. "Governmentality." In *The Foucault Effect*, edited by G. Burchell, C. Gordon, and P. Miller, 87–104. Chicago, IL: University of Chicago Press.

Fuchs, P. 1905. "Die wirtschaftliche Erkundung einer Ostafrikanischen Suedbah", *Beihefte zum Tropenpflanzer* 6: 4–5.

Gardner, L. 2012. *Taxing Colonial Africa: the Political Economy of British Imperialism.* Oxford: Oxford University Press.

Geiger, S. 1997. *TANU Women: Gender and Culture in the Making of Tanzanian Nationalism.* Oxford: James Currey.

Giblin, J., I. Kimambo, and G. Maddox. 1996. *Custodians of the Land.* London: James Currey.

Glassman, J. 1996. *Feasts and Riot. Revelry, Rebellion and Popular Consciousness on the Swahili Coast, 1856–1888.* Oxford and London: James Currey.

Government of Finland and Government of the United Republic of Tanzania. 1998. *The Rural Integrated Project Support Programme: Phase Two Programme Evaluation.* Internal report, no publisher.

Haugerud, A. 1997. *The Culture of Politics in Modern Kenya.* Cambridge: Cambridge University Press.

Hobsbawm, E., and T. Ranger. 1983. *The Invention of Tradition.* Cambridge: Cambridge University Press.

Hodge, J. M. 2007. *Triumph of the Expert.* Athens, OH: Ohio University Press.

Hogendorn, J. S., and K. Scott. 1981. "The East African Groundnut Scheme: Lessons of a Large-scale Agricultural Failure." *African Economic History* 10: 81–115.

Howard Smith, J. 2008. *Bewitching Development: Witchcraft and the Reinvention of Development in Neoliberal Kenya.* Chicago, IL: University of Chicago Press.

Hyden, G. 1981. *Beyond Ujamaa in Tanzania; Underdevelopment and an Uncaptured Peasantry.* Berkeley, CA: University of California Press.

Iliffe, J. 1979. *A Modern History of Tanganyika.* Cambridge: Cambridge University Press.

Jennings, M. 2002. "'Almost an Oxfam in Itself': Oxfam, Ujamaa and Development in Tanzania." *African Affairs* 101 (405): 509–530.

Jerven, M. 2013. *Poor Numbers: How We Are Misled by African Development Statistics and What to Do About It.* Ithaca, NY: Cornell University Press.

Kelsall, T. 2000. "Governance, Local Politics and 'Districtization' in Tanzania: The 1998 Arumeru Tax Revolt." *African Affairs* 99 (397): 533–551.

Lal, P. 2011. "Between the Village and the World: Imagining and Practicing Development in Tanzania, 1974–75." PhD diss., New York University.

Langwick, S. 2001. "Devils and Development." PhD diss., University of North Carolina, Chapel Hill.

Li, T. M. 2007. *The Will to Improve: Governmentality, Development and the Practice of Politics.* Durham, NC: Duke University Press.

Liebenow, J. G. 1971. *Colonial Rule and Political Development in Tanzania.* Everton, IL: Northwestern University Press.

Land Resources Development Centre (LRDC). 1979. *Mtwara/Lindi Regional Integrated Development Programme – Report of the Zonal Survey Team in Phase 2. Vol. 1: Methodology and Physical Environment; Vol. 2: Farming Systems and Development Prospects.* Surbiton: Ministry of Overseas Development.

Lumley, E. K. 1976. *Forgotten Mandate: A District Officer in Tanganyika.* London: Hurst.

Maddox, G. 1986. "Njaa: Food Shortages and Hunger in Tanzania Between the Wars." *International Journal of African Historical Studies* 19 (1): 17–34.

Mamdani, M. 1996. *Citizen and Subject: Contemporary Africa and the Legacy of Late Colonialism.* Princeton, NJ: Princeton University Press.

Mbembe, A. 2001. *On the Postcolony.* Berkeley, CA: University of California Press.

Mitchell, T. 2002. *Rule of Experts: Egypt, Techno-politics, Modernity.* Berkeley, CA: University of California Press.

Orwell, G. 1949. *Nineteen Eighty-Four.* London: Secker and Warberg.

Perham, M. 1976. *East African Journey: Kenya and Tanzania, 1929–30.* London: Faber and Faber.

Ranger, T. 1983. "The Invention of Tradition in Colonial Africa." In *The Invention of Tradition,* edited by Eric Hobsbawm and Terence Ranger, 211–262. Cambridge: Cambridge University Press.

Rural Integrated Programme (RIPS). 1991. *Soil and Water Conservation Project in Makonde Plateau.* Mtwara: Regional Commissioner's Office.

Schneider, L. 2003. "Developmentalism and its Failings: Why Rural Development Went Wrong in 1960s and 1970s Tanzania." PhD diss., Columbia University.

Scott, J. 1999. *Seeing Like a State: How Certain Schemes to Improve the Human Condition Have Failed.* New Haven, CT: Yale University Press.

Seppaelae, P. 1998. *Diversification and Accumulation in Rural Tanzania.* Stockholm: Nordisk Afrikainstitutet.

Tilley, H. 2011. *Africa as a Living Laboratory.* Chicago, IL: University of Chicago Press.

Tripp, A. M. 1997. *Changing the Rules.* Berkeley, CA: University of California Press.

Van de Walle, N. 2001. *African Economies and the Politics of Permanent Crisis, 1979–99.* Cambridge: Cambridge University Press.

Vaughn Hassett, D. 1984. "Economic Organisation and Political Change in a Village of South East Tanzania." PhD diss., University of Cambridge.

Weber, M. 1988. *Gesammelte Aufsaetze zur Religionssoziologie, Band 1.* Tuebingen: UTB.

Economic calculations, instability and (in)formalisation of the state in Mauritania, 2003–2011

Boris Samuet

Sciences-Po/Centre d'études et de recherches internationales (CÉRI), Paris, France

ABSTRACT   This article describes the transformations of the state in Mauritania in 2003–2011 in terms of the concrete practices of economic policy management. It questions the relationship to the state in a context of massive informality and where circumvention of the rules and misappropriation are major political repertoires. Nevertheless, my observations suggest that it is useful to study the rules and formal procedures in concrete terms in order to decode the way that they structure power relations in Mauritania, and that this analysis can be used to investigate the transformations of the state. I propose a reinterpretation of Mauritania's political trajectory seen through the prism of the concrete practices of economic management. This reveals that, despite major deception in relation to macroeconomic figures revealed in 2005, technocratic activity continued in an "ocean of transgression".

RÉSUMÉ   Cet article rend compte des transformations de l'Etat en Mauritanie entre 2003 et 2011 par le biais des pratiques concrètes de la gestion des politiques économiques. Il questionne le rapport à l'Etat dans un contexte où l'informalité est massive et où le contournement des règles et l'arnaque sont des répertoires politiques majeurs. Néanmoins, mon constat indique qu'il est intéressant de décrypter la manière dont les règles et procédures formelles, étudiées au concret, structurent les rapports de pouvoir en Mauritanie, et que cette analyse peut servir à interroger les transformations de l'Etat. Je propose une relecture de la trajectoire politique nationale au prisme des pratiques concrètes de gestion de l'économie. Il en ressort que, même lors des importants mensonges sur les chiffres macroéconomiques, dévoilés en 2005, l'action technocratique a pu se maintenir dans un « océan de transgression ».

Introduction

In September 2004, the new governor of the Central Bank of Mauritania flew to Washington DC with a tough mission to complete. He had to confess to the World Bank and IMF officials that a massive statistical lie had taken place in Mauritania in the past few years. He had the president's approval to do so; Maaouya Ould Taya was losing his control over the administration as well as the economic and financial elite. Large amounts were spent off-budget and the foreign currencies reserves of the Central Bank were looted. After this "misreporting", the country underwent international sanctions; it had to launch a large process of reform and revision of all macroeconomic data, and a whole new national economic history emerged (Islamic Republic of Mauritania 2006). But despite this reformist strategy, Mauritania was entering a long period of instability. Taya was overthrown from power in August 2005 after heading the state for more than 20 years; his regime was followed by a transition (2005–2007), a democratic election (April 2007), a new coup d'état in 2008, a rectification period (2008–2009) and again a so-called democratic period (2010–). In this trajectory, instability, power struggles and the use of formal administrative and reformist practices are closely intertwined.

Drawing on the Mauritanian situation, I argue that analysing formal economic procedures and calculation practices helps us understand the way power is exercised, even in a context of massive informality and fraud.[1] In the *Report on the Revision of Macroeconomic Data 1992–2004*, not only did the government admit to faking its economic statistics over some 12 years, it also stated that during that period "macroeconomic management became increasingly inappropriate to the real situation, often with the advice of partners who had been misled, leading to the taking of measures that fostered imbalances instead of combating them" (Islamic Republic of Mauritania 2006, 7). It thus presented its management of economic policy as a structured process, consisting of "measures" and formal procedures, even if their transgression was rife. More generally, all successive regimes in Mauritania since 2003 have been characterised by predatory practices, while implementing "governance reforms" and conducing programs for the "moralisation of public life". Repertoires of transgression and circumvention have thus continuously cohabited with those of legalism and technocratic modernisation. I therefore argue that Mauritanian political transformations can be studied through the lens of its changing economic management procedures. In this direction, I propose to shed a new light on Mauritanian political trajectories over the period 2003–2011.

This article builds on the approach that sociologists and historians of quantification like Theodore Porter or Alain Desrosières have developed in non-African countries (Porter 1995; Desrosières 1998, 2003). Their works have shown that studying the state's statistical practices from a sociological perspective enables us to question the different "ways of acting on the economy" through numbers, as well as the political legitimacy associated with the production and use of these quantitative techniques. Adopting such a perspective requires observing the concrete practices of economic policy management.

This has not been widely done to analyse African countries and the so-called "developing world". In order to do so, I also draw on some anthropological works, like Jane Guyer's studies of calculation practices and numbers in African economies (Guyer 2004), and on a political sociology of the state in Africa derived from the works of Jean-François Bayart (Bayart 2009) and Beatrice Hibou (Hibou 2011a). This way I can shed a sociological and political light on the links between economic calculation practices, economic stories and national trajectories that some other researchers have approached in a more historical perspective, like Morten Jerven on national income (Jerven 2013) or Vincent Bonnecase on poverty (Bonnecase 2011). Therefore, while building on the Mauritanian case, I believe the present article should also help understanding other national situations, in Africa and more generally in countries managing their economies in close relations with international financial institutions, especially the International Monetary Fund (IMF).

Informalisation of the state and economic management procedures at the end of Taya's regime (2003–2005)

Institutions, informality and the exercise of power

At the beginning of the 2000s, Mauritania had spent a great many years as the "model pupil" of international organisations and adjustment. In 2003–2004, international institutions still regarded the country as having accomplished "an impressive array of structural and macroeconomic reforms" (IMF 2003, 6). Mauritania was allowed to participate in all the pilot schemes, for example drawing up one of the first Poverty Reduction Strategy Paper (PRSP) in Africa, and being a very early beneficiary of the Heavily Indebted Poor Countries (HIPC) initiative.

However, bureaucratic activities and state management in Mauritania have long operated in a context of massive informality and fraud. Macroeconomic policies offer a striking example of this: the scale of the circumvention reflected in the falsification of public accounts in the period 2000–2005 undermines the very principle of a state budget and, still more, of any possibility of steering the economy. Extra-budgetary expenditure reached 40 per cent of the budget in 2003, representing almost 12 per cent of official GDP at that time (Islamic Republic of Mauritania 2006). In 2004, three distinct budgetary exercises were carried out simultaneously, with none of the three annual accounts ever being closed, making it impossible to audit or monitor expenditure in any reliable way (IMF 2005, 16). An analysis of this type of situation forces us to leave normative concepts aside, notably in dealing with institutional logics.

Indeed the official administrative functions are often illusory. Until 2005, the Ministry of Economic Affairs and Development (MAED) owed much of its prestige not to its role as "coordinator of social and economic policies", but to the management of many development projects for which it was given direct responsibility in a largely discretionary manner. One of these projects involved the richly funded unit in charge of education reform, which was placed under the authority of the MAED, thereby escaping that of the Ministry of Education. The Ministry of Fisheries, which collected fines and payments while running the trade in fishing licences, was also a site of major powers since, contrary to regulations, it did not pass on these "public receipts" to the Treasury. Conversely, the upper ranks of the police depended largely on funding from "outside" the state, and more precisely on the national transport federation, which was in the hands of businessmen from the president's tribe, who had a monopoly in the sector at the time.[2] More generally, as in many countries coming out of adjustment, the proliferation of agencies, commissions, semi-public businesses and major projects made the public sector appear highly fragmented into a great many coveted centres of power and, to some extent, comprising a set of obscurely structured "fiefs". The bureaucratic work of the public administration was thus underpinned by a situation in which institutional functions were often dominated by power relations and access to resources.

Several elements can help to explain how Mauritania could be a "good pupil" while showing signs of massive informality in its public management. Mauritania only played the card of democratisation and of the docile acceptance of structural adjustment after a particularly traumatic period in the 1980s, marked by the ethnic violence of 1989 that was a legacy of the difficult birth of a young "frontier state", prey to many centrifugal forces (Ould Ahmed Salem 2004), and in which the state played a central role. Since the 1980s, the Mauritanian regime has taken refuge in stabilisation through a tribal management of public resources (Marchesin 1992), containing the deep socio-political rifts using authoritarian and clientelist practices (N'diaye 2006). By maintaining it status of the "good pupil", it thus often set itself apart in order to ensure a flow of income from outside, which was necessary both for security (Jourde 2007) and to supply government clients. At the beginning of the 2000 decade, Mauritania was managing its many political and social tensions by harvesting the fruits of its "model pupil" status and keeping up the appearances of reform.

Of course, there is nothing new about a situation in which aid goes hand in hand with authoritarian, and clientelist domination, giving rise to a "reformist façade".[3] But the way the different repertoires combined in Mauritania is far from anecdotal interest. On the one hand, Mauritania is a open society, Nouakchott being a city of salons where information always gets out in rumours and where many people and groups are aware of what the authorities and business get up to. But at the beginning of the 2000s, the regime's chosen weapons were silence and weasel words. Censorship of the press was frequent, by virtue of a law of 1991[4] that was not abolished until the democratic transition of 2006, and the apparatus of repression was omnipresent, with social and political life regulated by "information bulletins". When, it was discovered in 2004 that public sector data had been widely instrumentalised – which was a sign of the major disorder that prevailed in the economic and financial administrations – silence reigned. Economic management practices preserved an appearance of normality, but they were in fact also submitted to discipline and surveillance. For example, the simple mention of a parallel exchange market in a newspaper would be censored, although this market was massive and functioned openly, and the IMF had no more permission to mention it than the newspapers.[5] Similarly, since the retail price index was falsified, discussion of the causes of inflation was taboo. The most ordinary economic practices provided occasions for both massive circumvention and authoritarian practices.

Hence, while infringements were widespread until the end of the Taya era, the rules were more or less formally preserved, and they even acted as tools of power and oppression.

In these years, Mauritania was also subject to a great deal of informality linked to a rush to appropriate the multiple national rents. In the forefront was the prospect of the arrival of the oil industry, officially announced by Taya on 28 November 2002, which led to a doubling of the state budget by 2010. Although hopes of an oil boom soon disappeared, their effects on the economy were massive, notably through highly optimistic forecasts that made the national market "attractive". They generated a great deal of national and international investments (in construction, infrastructure and services, for example) and an accompanying housing boom. In addition, fishing, iron ore industry and the development aid contributed to make public money abundant and providential (Ould Ahmed Salem 2008). The state, to use the expression of Abdel Wedoud Ould Cheikh, could be compared to a "boutique structure" (Ould Cheikh 2006). This obviously had multiple consequences for economic management, as attested by the mechanisms for falsifying data that I shall describe below.

Informalisation and economic management procedures: the falsification of economic and financial statistics

Informal management of resources at the heart of the economic fiction

By 2003, the falsification of the macroeconomic accounts had reached an impressive scale: as shown by the re-evaluation undertaken in 2005 and 2006, the money supply was twice as big as that shown in the official statistics. The currency reserves, officially representing 12 months of imports, in fact covered two weeks. The figures had been falsified since 1992 at least, and on a grand scale since 1995 (Islamic Republic of Mauritania 2006). They masked illegal uses of public money, the provision of funds to private individuals and fraudulent access to the currency reserves. Several types of mechanism were used: so-called extra-budgetary expenditure, in other words public expenditure carried out by the Treasury but without legal authorisation; the anarchic opening of credit facilities with the Central Bank; debits to the Treasury's accounts at the Central Bank without the knowledge of the Ministry of Finance; privileged access to the exchange market for some individuals; and so on. From 1995, many of these sums initially corresponded to military expenditure ordered by the president of the republic.[6] In addition, some major public programmes operated off-budget, such as the emergency food programmes of 2003 and 2004. Lastly, as discovered later, particularly lucrative operations were carried out behind the back of the Central Bank for the profit of individuals. For example, credit facilities were made available to primary banks without justification in 2001 and 2002, as was widely publicised when some of the country's most important businessmen belonging to the tribe of the former president were sent to prison in 2009 (Cherif 2009).

The role of the IMF in national economic calculation procedures

The management of financial and economic policies also involved formal procedures. The IMF teams notably played a crucial part in the process of constructing the economic picture. Their interventions provided the underlying procedures on the basis of which policies were developed and to which administrative activity was linked. As a recipient of IMF loans until 2005, Mauritania was also subject to the constant "monitoring" of its policies and statistical indicators by IMF teams, who went to Nouakchott at least three or four times a year. They worked closely with the Mauritanian authorities, providing very concrete support to the development of economic policies: they discussed the consistency of the figures; the techniques used to produce them; how they should be interpreted; the technical hypotheses on which they were based; and so on. Ultimately, the IMF teams actually validated the economic policies and statistical data on which access to funds was based.[7] So we can say that the statistical fiction that remained in place for over 15 years really was built up before their eyes. The question is not even whether or not these officials knew whether the figures were flawed. The fact is that they were continuously monitoring the methodologies and building the base on which the fiction was elaborated by the government.

We can go even further. Government departments talked to each other very little in the years 2003–2005. The withholding of information was at its height at the end of the Taya era. During this period interministerial cooperation, and even that between divisions and departments within a single institution, was completely blocked by the impossibility of gaining access to the other side's information, which was totally inconsistent and, therefore, kept highly secret. For example, just as it was extremely difficult for the national accounts unit of the National Office for Statistics (ONS) to obtain information from the customs directorate of the Ministry of Finance, so it was sometimes very difficult, within the ONS itself, to gather detailed figures in relation to prices, although these were produced by another unit in the same building. Meanwhile, a bureaucratic coping system was established to get round the barriers: so, when officials from the MAED were granted the privilege of obtaining data that ONS departments could not get hold of – such as information on fishing and customs – they would pass them on to their colleagues and vice versa. Many administrative relationships were contingent on the small details of everyday office life, interpersonal relationships, friendships and even tribal relationships. The same was true, in a more exacerbated form, when it came to defining "economic policy": for example, the budgetary forecasts prepared by the Ministry of Finances were transmitted to other ministries only with difficulty, including to those colleagues who were theoretically closest, such as those at the Ministry of Economy. In such an opaque context, formulating any economic policy was a very delicate matter; administrative compartmentalisation, opacity and informality reigned against a background of false accounting.

But, at the same time, the IMF and its procedures played a key role in coordinating the Mauritanian technical work. As an IMF member Mauritania was under statutory obligation to pass on data to the IMF teams, who thus created centralised sets of figures that no national institution could have put together. The procedures by which macroeconomic policies were formulated thus radiated out from around the IMF teams. They alone were able to produce an overall view of the economy and put together all the pieces of the puzzle. In practice this meant that procedures for formulating economic and financial policy existed, but were not centralised within the government. The formalisation process was broadly coordinated, more or less unknowingly, by the IMF itself. This is a crucial observation: rather than being a carefully planned and fully controlled construction, the lie was based on an "anarchy" of bureaucratic procedures (Blum and Mespoulet 2003) deployed around a set of international procedures and rules.

Putting an indistinguishable reality into numbers

This confusion was reinforced by the fact that the misuse of resources was a haphazard affair. To borrow the words of a former high-ranking official, for a long time it was so easy to open illegal credit facilities at the Central Bank, that all those who were in a position to do so "helped themselves from the till". When the new governor, Zeine Ould Zeidane, arrived in July 2004, 95 per cent of open accounts were not legitimate.[8] Where the budget was concerned, the mechanisms seem equally haphazard: major emergency programmes conducted on an entirely extra-budgetary basis and run from high up in the administration (for example at the time of the droughts of 2003, or the anti-locust campaigns of 2004) coexisted with the processing of everyday expenses, which managers would unofficially send to the budget office because it was simpler and more flexible to do so. Accelerated and extra-budgetary procedures would be used to acquire a ream of paper or for the reception of an important guest. It was easier to incur expenses using exceptional budget procedures ("automatic debit letter" or "request for immediate payment") and thereby circumvent the entire monitoring system.

Thus, lies happened while – and partly because – a multiform and largely unrecorded reality was to be quantified in figures. The national and international economic experts, by putting a largely indistinguishable reality into numbers, were at the same time guardians of the norms and producing the fiction. Sometimes, however, the gap would become too large and the existence of a real lie would become obvious. For example, in 2003 and 2004, the authorities claimed to have enough foreign currency reserves to convert the entire official money supply, while at the same time the parallel exchange rate was constantly rising, a sign that the monetary authorities did not have enough hard currency to stabilise the Mauritanian currency (ouguiya).

This enables us to understand better how the Mauritanian government was able to say, in 2006, that it had formulated its economic policies on the basis of erroneous data. The formal economic procedures were intrinsically meshed with the means to circumvent them. We also understand that IMF procedures had structured the production of economic aggregates, because they obliged the government to put the economy into numbers. The figures were flawed because they could not account for the informal mecanisms driving the economy, but they reflected the use of international methods.[9]

The collapse of the fiction

The fiction fell apart between 2004 and 2005, in the context of a broad movement to deligitimise Taya's power. In the national administration, international organisations or economic spheres, everybody knew that the statistics were very fragile, so it was not a real surprise. It was, for example, widely known that price statistics or external trade statistics were not accurate because of the use of flawed methods (Samuel 2011). However, the scale of the lies was much greater than anybody could guess. The starting point for the "discovery" of the fiction was a change of regulation at the IMF (safeguards assessment policy), which, in 2003, led the fund's departments to ask for an entirely routine audit of the Central Bank's foreign exchange reserves. But the Mauritanian authorities refused, for fear of being unmasked, particularly as the foreign exchange reserves were one of the most heavily falsified indicators. The authorities thus tried to gain time and kept the IMF at bay in 2003, and again in 2004. But in the struggle a corner of the veil of deceitful statistics was gradually lifted, revealing illegal practices that proved central to the spiral ending in Taya's downfall.

By this time, the plundering of public resources, which had taken place on an unprecedented scale from 2000, started to have untenable consequences. First, the decidedly "expansionist" budgetary and monetary policies and the trade in currencies caused a wave of inflation and devaluation of the ouguiya; this caused the prices of food and imported products to shoot up, fostering a sense of frustration and exacerbating discontent among Mauritanian people. Numerous tensions emerged among the elite in the battles over the appropriation of resources; for example, around the fallout from oil exploitation (Augé 2007; Bensaâd 2007). And when Taya, who appointed Zeine Ould Zeidane as governor of the Central Bank in the summer of 2004, played the card of confessing its lies at the IMF, the regime made enemies of some of the businessmen closest to the centres of power, who had done very well out the system. Therefore, Taya was ultimately left behind in the race for appropriation of resources. The regime was rendered still more unstable by the security situation – an attack by the GSPC (Salafist group for preaching and combat) shook the north of the country in the summer of 2004 – and by the consequences of the presidential election fiasco of 2003, which saw Taya re-elected at the price of all kinds of repression used against the opposition and his political opponents (Bensaâd 2006). These events in turn encouraged the falsification of the figures, since massive military spending was carried out off-budget in 2003 and 2004, to which expenditure on the electoral campaign was added. All in all, the economic fiction was fuelled by a series of elements that combined to delegitimise the regime, while the discovery of the deception made the government's position worse, creating a vicious circle.

So, beyond its purely technical significance, the revelation of the falsification of the figures and the end of the economic fiction should be understood as the collapse of a mode of domination. While the revelation of the fiction was triggered and caused by the reserves audit, it represented a far more complex and multiform event.

Technocrats and the exercise of power: accumulation and modernisation of the state

In an apparent paradox, however, a relative technocratic autonomy cohabited during Taya's era with procedural anarchy. In a manner similar to the role played by the IMF officials in the statistical fiction, technocratic language was omnipresent inside the administration. The work of the technocrats involved wielding economic language in an environment marked by pervasive transgression, but the presence of a technocratic ethos was actually not incompatible with deception, not even with power struggles.[10]

Technical knowledge and the modernisation market

Administrative engineering was central to an important "market in modernisation". Technocratic operations received a great deal of finance, both from the state and in the form of aid provided by international donors as part of "capacity building" and "institutional development", which had been development watchwords since the late 1990s.

Very large sums were indeed devoted to modernising the state. The resulting modernisation market undoubtedly engendered a "rent-based economy", leading to spending on a plethora of dubious projects, consultations that were not properly targeted, and the organisation of workshops with their attendant buffets and directors' fees. But to describe the political economy of reform and modernisation, we need to go further. For example, when a World Bank Trust Fund finances the production of a "poverty profile" or a "poverty map", as it did in 2004, and this to the tune of several hundred million dollars, should we see it as no more than a wafer-thin technocratic facade? Not necessarily. To do so would be to neglect that, even in the Mauritanian sociopolitical context, managers and leaders of the economic and financial administration do share a technocratic interpretation of reality and, to a certain extent, a belief in the power of technique to underpin ways of governing. To this extent it is possible that "aid rents", despite being reappropriated in many different ways, may lead to the adoption of "modernising" practices, informed by knowledge and skills. We can even seek to identify elements of a "demand for modernisation" in this market (Hibou 2011b).

The example of macroeconomic forecasting provides an interesting example of this demand. The macroeconomic modelling that has proliferated in Mauritania in the last 10 years is an invariant of capacity building projects, even though the figures were long falsified, and are anyway largely produced at the interface with the IMF. A range of international experts have nevertheless been called on from time to time by the Ministry of Economic Affairs, the ONS and Ministry of Finance to launch a new study in search of the right model. Organisations approached by the ministries have included the World Bank, the French Statistical Institute, Afristat or the African Development Bank. How should this be understood? In practice, methods of macroeconomic forecasting are of major practical and symbolic importance to directors and top officials in the Ministries of the Economy and Finance (Samuel 2011).

One aim in improving them is to gain greater power in negotiations with the IMF and the World Bank. Moreover, forecasting structures a raft of relationships within the administration. It provides the basis for collaboration (through the transmission of statistical data) and simultaneously for emulation between departments, even in the unstable, compartmentalised conditions we have described. The different Directorates of Finances, Planning and the Central Bank thus compete to have their forecasts prevail, for example in relation to taxation during the preparation of annual exercises such as the budget, and exchange these forecasts either directly or through the IMF. In addition, models also play a part in international activities, since experiences are exchanged between the teams of forecasters and economists of different countries in sub-Saharan and North Africa, and indeed between oil producing countries,[11] which meet at many international and regional seminars. So we can see why in Mauritania there is consequently not only a demand, but also, in a sense, a "race for models".

When use of the Model of the Mauritanian Economy (MEMAU),[12] Mauritania's historical model hosted by the MAED, gradually fell away, its replacement gave rise to a great many projects. While the fortunes of these research projects differed, some produced concrete results (such as the so-called Tablo model, a recent updating of MEMAU, and the World Bank's Poverty Analysis Macroeconomic Simulator [PAMS] model). Beyond the objective to help making the best possible decisions, the sophisticated "ritual" of quantification was driving Mauritanian economists (Power 1999).

All this suggests that a technocratic ethos based on expertise and a certain understanding of ways of "managing the economy" (Desrosières 2003) could exist within administrative departments, and drive their work, even in a context of informality. The expertise market was not even linked solely to the availability of external funding and "extraversion rents". In the modelling field, projects emerged that were financed entirely from within Mauritania. For example, the Explorer Center, set up in 2003–2004, used its own funds to bring in French researchers and ran sessions financed by the Mauritanian state. Moreover, bonuses were long paid to managers and public agents in the economic and financial departments who were working to establish macroeconomic forecasts. This contextualisation of modelling can of course be applied, to different degrees, to many other techniques. Typically, some instruments in fashion in the development world, such as "medium-term expenditure frameworks", exerted an attraction over administrative departments (Samuel 2009). This attraction exerted by technical productions, rarely considered in discussions of the work of administrative departments in Africa, was very real, however paradoxical.

The emergence of an elite of experts

It is also notable that technocratic and technical competences led to the formation of dominant groups, even if their skills were later lost in an administration operating primarily through the interplay of influence and accommodation. So, for 10 years a small group of high-ranking officials with the profile of international experts controlled Mauritania's finances, steered the economy and guided the "reforms" from within a small club of relatively stable economic and financial institutions (MAED, ONS, Mauritanian Centre for Policy Analysis [CMAP], Ministry of Finance, Central Bank of Mauritania [BCM]). The managers of these institutions worked very closely together and were generally products of the major French universities and schools (such as the École national d'administration [ÉNA]); they had often taken the same courses and had since developed a sense of solidarity, or even a kind of corporatism. The functioning of the Mauritanian administrative system facilitated the rapid rise of technocrats, some very brilliant, who were of course appreciated by donors and lenders and ran the country from the administrative departments of the economics and finance ministries. Some also moved on to the political stage.

This was true of Zeine Ould Zeidane who, in a few years, moved from running a macroeconomic model in a small planning department office to the post of prime minister. In the course of this rise, he built up a reputation for technical skill[13] (and people skills, since he is married to the daughter of General Boukhreiss, one of Taya's closer allies). But in this he followed a long line of politicians who made their careers on, among other things, their image as technocrats, such as former Prime Minister Sidi Mohamed Ould Boubacar, who owed his reputation to his image as a considered and enlightened expert, and Mohamedou Ould Michel, who has just retired but was still an advisor to the 2007 elected President Sidi Ould Cheikh Abdallahi after a long career under Taya.

Of course, I am not seeking to turn these figures into virtuous "heroes", but to emphasise that, contrary to what is generally believed (Banégas and Warnier 2001), "models of success" also value the role of technocratic competence in driving successful careers and relationships of domination. By the way, legitimation by competence combines with other repertoires of power. Director and later Minister of Planning Abdallahi Ould Cheikh Sidya was the illustrious descendant of a marabout family and an ÉNA graduate who long remained typical of the elite and was respected as much for his prestigious birth as for his competent image. That he was, as head of Planning before 2004, one of the architects of the great falsification operation did not affect his prestige. There is nothing unusual about this combination between trickery, technical and aristocratic repertoires in Mauritania (Ould Ahmed Salem 2001).

So the profiles of technocrats can provide a source of legitimacy, even when circumvention of the rules is the rule itself. In the moral economy of trickery (*tcheb-tchib*) described by Zekeria Ould Ahmed Salem (2001), technical dexterity and understanding are certainly not discredited; indeed, they are very useful to the *el-gazra*, the squatter skilled in the use of deceit to appropriate public resources. This confirms what Jean-François Bayart has shown about the Cameroonian *feymen*, who use their skills in trickery at the interface between the state, global procedures and deeply rooted social values (Bayart 2004; Bayart, Ellis, and Hibou 1999; Malaquais 2001); it also confirms Beatrice Hibou's findings that the social value of trickery is often to be seen at the heart of formal economic management procedures (Bayart, Ellis, and Hibou 1999). What the Mauritanian case tells us here goes one step further, however: even in a situation where the fraud is massive, technocratic skills can be valued for themselves and be combined with deceit in the everyday management of the state.

Of course, appointments are often based on influence, nepotism and tribal and ethnic criteria (Marchesin 1992). Very often, managers find their careers blocked because of their ethnic or tribal origins, which may influence the course of their entire careers (Ould Cheikh 1998). But competence and technical skills are nonetheless evident criteria in the rise of many Mauritanian figures and underpin one vision of the state and government. From this point of view there is no inevitable contradiction between the valuing of competence, the modernising ethos and transgressive management practices in the administration, in which these same officials are also involved, as I shall show.

Overlaps between positions of "reform" and accumulation

An instrumental reading would assume that governance reforms seek to prevent the diversion of funds and quest for gain. But an analysis "from below" (Bayart, Mbembe, and Toulabor 2008) of administrative practices shows on the contrary that the repertoires of modernisation can combine with those of peculation in the everyday management of public administration. The first example is the private consultancy work undertaken by many officials.[14] All technically effective officials can expect to gain consultancy contracts in the specialist fields they work in as public servants, and of course render their administrative posts profitable through the revenue generated by their private work.

This means that they are also "development brokers" profiting from the governance market (Bierschenk, Chauveau, and Olivier de Sardan 2000; Lewis and Mosse 2006; Blundo and Le Meur 2009). I shall return to this later, as another, less obvious overlap must be noted. The accumulation of different administrative functions sometimes enables individuals to combine a number of assignments that give them direct responsibility to manage resources with work on administrative engineering and reform intended to improve governance. Because activities in both fields are performed by the same people, they can be subject to a kind of vertical integration, thereby creating wide margins for manoeuvre. A paradigmatic illustration of this is offered by the directorate of education and training projects, which, until 2007, was in charge of reforming the education sector.[15] This directorate monitored all the governance reforms in the education sector, carried out periodic evaluations of aid programmes, but it was also responsible for the effective use of a large share of the funds provided by the International Education for All Initiative. It long had control over extrabudgetary funds, an arrangement often criticised for its opacity (the aid provided for this programme was "budgetised" in the donors' eyes, but it made only a rapid detour through the Treasury coffers).

The man who was long the director of education and training, Weddoud Kamil, is known for his technical abilities – he is an international expert on education planning – but was much criticised for the opacity of his management. We should mention that he is also the brother-in-law of Maaouya Ould Taya. In practice, such situations are common. People at the MAED prepare the state's investment budget, supervise the transfer of funds to project heads and prepare the statistics that are used to evaluate macroeconomic performance and respect of expenditure ceilings. The same people are thus in a position both to promote the new tools of rigour – for which they benefit from training and capacity building programmes – to manage the funds, and to falsify the figures, so they develop a highly polysemous relationship to the "sums". Such mechanisms explain how, in Mauritania as in almost all the countries of Africa, state investment figures are systematically underestimated in order to get round the ceilings set by the IMF.

"Marginal gains" and technical skills

We could even go so far as to state that certain economic policy operations can in fact be assimilated into "transactions", combining predatory activities with the mobilisation of skills and knowledge. We have heard witnesses speak of extreme cases in which statistical tables relating to the public finances were bought from high-ranking civil servants by international officials. The justification given was that these tables were not immediately accessible and required a degree of expertise. In addition, they were vital to the writing of an evaluation report that had to be drawn up by the international financial institutions. Furthermore, the figures were produced at the very period of the statistical lies. Such cases are very interesting, because they combine many elements in a single "transaction": technical competence; individual interest; "privatisation" of the administration (Hibou 2004); production of the economic fiction; working methods of international organisations. Such mechanisms – which very precisely materialise the "marginal gains" described by Jane Guyer in elucidating the functioning of what she calls "formalities" (Guyer 2004) – help us understand how a concrete combination of different and apparently contradictory repertoires can operate within procedures for the "management" of the public finances.

Therefore, an ethos of modernisation can blossom in the shadow of networks of influence, all in the name of promoting a state underpinned by law and rationality. The polysemous, ambivalent nature of reforms and technocratic activities also explain how forms of domination can emerge out of modernising activities. It also contributes, more or less paradoxically, to lay the foundations for a certain kind of "technocratic legitimacy" (Hibou 2011b).

I now turn to the dynamics of formalisation and informalisation of the state to analyse the trajectories of the power after the end of the Taya regime, in August 2005.

The "transition to democracy" (2005–2008): power struggles and reformist feats

In August 2005, President Taya was overthrown by his own colonels, whose leader, Ely Ould Mohamed Vall, took over as head of a military council for justice and democracy (CMJD) and raised many hopes with a policy of transition to democracy. During the transition period, among a broad series of reforms, the economic figures were corrected and a new economic history was built with the help of the international organisations, as witnessed by the *Report on The Revision of Macroeconomic Figures 1992–2004* (Islamic Republic of Mauritania 2006). Such reforms undoubtedly conferred a high degree of legitimacy on the transition, but they remained ambivalent, the priority of the government being to restore the international trust and the flow of international aid as quickly as possible. Mauritania reconnected indeed with the IMF in the first half of 2006, benefiting from debt rescheduling only a few months later, but away from this visible activity the greater part of the administration was kept in a state of relative apathy. The "democratic" period opened with the presidential elections of April 2007 that brought President Sidi Ould Cheikh Abdallahi to power. The Consultative group meeting held in Paris in December 2007, originated in the period of the CMJD, is an interesting moment to relocate technocratic issues within the economic and political trajectory of Mauritania.

The return of the "model country"

During 2006, the work that had been halted after the fall of Taya was gradually restarted in the summer of 2005. The PRSP, left dormant by the transition government was restarted on the insistence of donors, who needed a programme on which to base their support for the transition and democratisation. Meanwhile, discussions with the IMF and the World Bank also raised again the need for a "medium-term expenditure framework" (MTEF) in order to identify the broad choices for state expenditure. The demand for planning was thus very high. A working group on the MTEF met in 2006, comprising the Ministries of the Economy and Finance and various peripheral actors. But the exercise proved complex and laborious. The transition and its major political manoeuvres were underway; elections were in prospect and large-scale administrative studies were out of favour with the economic and financial directorates. In addition, the macroeconomic data revision was still fresh, whereas the preparation of an MTEF demanded an unprecedented abundance of details. Mauritania was also bringing in its first oil receipts and plans for the use of budgetary resources were far from settled. Moreover, collaboration between the administrative directorates of the Ministries of the Economy and Finance proved difficult, and the working group did not really seem to be a priority for those involved. All these elements made the exercise difficult.

However, the resident representative of the World Bank, who had recently arrived in the country, was working hard to turn Mauritania into an example of "best practice"; he probably also wanted to use his time there as a launching pad for his own rise through his organisation. To this end he planned to promote the development of a collaborative Country Assistance

Strategy (CAS) for the World Bank, which would then make it possible to set up a "model" Consultative group. Once the Mauritanian transition was well underway, the representative's plan had certain attractions; in particular, it was giving weight to the reprise of partnerships between the government and donors, who were actively sponsoring democratisation.

For this it was crucial to have an MTEF as the underlying programme. But work on the MTEF in the Ministry of Finance and the MAED was behind schedule. The resident representative became impatient. Eventually, wearied by the lack of success encountered by his initiative, he looked around for alternative solutions and seized the opportunity offered by other ongoing works to get round the difficulties. In the absence of any good and proper programme of the MTEF type, he fell back on far simpler, more general calculations of the sums necessary to reach the Millennium Development Goals (MDGs). At the time, such works were in preparation by both the the United Nations Development Programme (UNDP) and the World Bank. This was not on the same scale as the MTEF, but it made it possible to start discussions. He enjoyed the crucial support of the Minister of Economic Affairs, Mohamed Ould Abed, a high-flying civil servant, graduate of the ÉNA and *éminence grise* of many reforms carried out by the government since the late 1990s.

So a major exercise was carried out in 2006–2007 involving donors, the state administration and civil society to plan Mauritania's development strategies. The initiative generated major events: in March 2006 large gatherings were organised using video-conferencing in multiplexes in several countries. The exercise was in tune with its time, giving rise to various presentations permitting the development of a form of language unconstrained by the empty bureaucratic rhetoric of the Taya era. As well as policies, debates focused on the functioning of Mauritanian society and its barriers, or the challenges of good management, in politico-technocratic arenas unused to such discussions. So the resident representative successfully pulled off his tour de force, driven by his personal ambitions and supported by the administration. This process, which remained technically unconvincing and very much focused on the World Bank, was nonetheless gradually transformed into a "technocratic feat" on the part of the regime.

The technocratic feat of a delegitimised regime: the Consultative group of December 2007

After the election of Sidi Ould Cheikh Abdallahi in April 2007, work began on the preparation of a Consultative group celebrating democracy. Work on the MTEF started up again. For the first time in Mauritania, detailed budgetary planning was undertaken, based on the PRSP and the funding intentions of the donors. The brand new Ministry of the Economy and Finance, reunified, provided the right framework for this kind of work, which required collaboration between the budget directorate and the directorate responsible for cooperation and planning. This collaboration went well, thanks to a great many senior executives who had been promoted while Zeine Ould Zeidane was prime minister. This time the sophisticated MTEF could be finalised. The preparation for the group achieved something hitherto unimaginable in the Mauritanian administration due to an impressive combination of favourable factors, including extensive involvement by donors, the input of highly experienced technocrats, a relative absence of barriers to the circulation of information and a "successful" democratisation that justified holding Mauritania up as an international example. The MTEF reflected a voluntarist development policy scenario and put the price of the "return of hope" at 1.6 billion dollars. The donors met at the World Bank's offices in Paris on 4, 5 and 6 December 2007, established their contributions and, in a major bureaucratic exercise, promised donations of 2.1 billion dollars; 500 million more than the sum requested by the government – a "democratisation bonus" as Zeine Ould Zeidane put it (Meunier 2007).

However, these plans were never realised, since Sidi Ould Cheikh Abdallahi was removed from power by Mohamed Ould Abdel Aziz in the summer of 2008. The coup d'état led to the suspension of all cooperation programmes for around a year, until the spring of 2009. But technocratic feats notwithstanding, a closer look shows that the Consultative group already contained all the seeds of the future instability.

In practice the Consultative group straddled the regime's internal divisions. As always, the government was a patchwork resulting from the horse-trading of appointments between the various currents and spheres. But the tensions derived from the post-electoral negotiations were particularly high. The government included military personnel from the CMJD, who got Sidi elected and imposed appointments on him, Sidi himself, who was bound by the political agreements he had made with other parties, and Zeine Ould Zeidane, who came third in the presidential election and had exchanged his support in the second round for the post of prime minister. The governmental equation was thus complex from the outset. The Consultative group gave Zeine an opportunity to impose his style through a technocratic process of which he was the prime embodiment. Indeed, the prime minister was counting on this to save his political future. He was in a very vulnerable position: he did not control his government and he was in dispute with the president, who had relieved him of the management of the most important dossiers, notably the return of refugees from Senegal, and the emergency food programme linked to the crisis of 2007–2008. So the Consultative group was very important to him, beyond the beauty of the exercise and its promises of development. But Abderrahmane Ould Hama Vezzaz, minister of the economy and finance and one of the president's men, also wanted to profit from the event, and the struggles were apparent at the time of the Paris meeting (Meunier 2008). The technocratic aspect, a key strength of Sidi's regime, thus appears at once as the element supposed to save the government's image and the focus of the internal quarrels that were destroying the same government's ability to govern (Ould Oumère 2007; Véridique 2008).

More seriously, this technocratic orientation crystallised the discontent of the Mauritanian people and helped speed up the regime's loss of legitimacy and credibility. The government was regularly accused of hiding behind piles of expert reports and being unable to meet expectations where the most important dossiers were concerned, in a context marked by intense social problems and rising prices (Tahalil Hebdo 2007). Furthermore, the reforms and good management that had been hoped for now seemed largely illusory. For example, complaints were mounting concerning the activities of President Abdallahi's inner circle, notably his wife Khattou Mint El Boukhary, who was accused of diverting public money intended for social policies via her charity. The Special Intervention Programme – a 169 million euro plan set up to alleviate the consequences of drought and rising food prices – was in practice carried out off-budget and gave rise to many instances of diversion of funds. The government had also started instrumentalising budgetary processes. The establishment of a computer program for monitoring expenditure, known as the Rachad application, symbolising the transparency of the public finances, was blocked for several months in 2007/08 in order to circumvent it.

It would probably be an exaggeration to suggest that the technocratic orientation of the regime was a cause of the subsequent divorce between government and citizens, but it was undeniably positioned at the intersection of several fault lines that caused the regime to fall. In one sense, the August 2008 coup d'état also signified the failure of a Mauritania that had played the card of formal procedures throughout the transition process. Although technocratic rhetoric was never a match for the social issues, the government had instigated sophisticated technical exercises and tried to profit from them through external rents and a modernising rhetoric that international donors often encouraged. But the main effect of this approach was to discredit the regime and increase disappointment. For a while technocratic constructions had maintained the fiction of successful transition, but at the same time they fuelled instability, disappointment and loss of legitimacy.

The Mauritania of Aziz: the economic procedures of a fragile country fighting against terror

After his coup in August 2008, General Abdel Aziz established a "rectificatory period". As justification for his coup d'état – perpetrated in the name of the "preservation of democracy" – he notably cited the former president's management practices and actions judged irresponsible for national security. Mauritania was shaken by terrorist attacks and preserving the country was one of his main justifications. He faced a strong internal and external opposition. But his skilful conduct of dialogue with the political parties opposed to the putsch (the "Dakar process") gave him legitimacy in the eyes of external partners (Antil 2010). On the national scene, a populist language and social rhetoric gave him some popularity after the coup, and facilitated his success at the ballot box organised in 2009.

Seen through the lens of economic and financial procedures, new modes of government seem to have emerged with Ould Abdel Aziz's regime.

Economic policies under the regime of Abdel Aziz: new "ways of acting on the economy"?

Today the MAED is often cited as an example of a weakened administration. While the Ministry of the Economy and Finance was once again separated into two parallel offices in the putsch of the summer of 2008 – as seen above, the ministry had been unified in 2007 in what appeared then as a good practice – the readoption of this structure did not bring about a return to the historic division of tasks. In the separation the Ministry of Economic Affairs and Development lost its historic role in preparing and managing the investment budget, which included all donor projects. In addition, since 2008 the posts of directors have been filled by a series of risky appointments. It became common that unconcerned and even incompetent individuals hold top positions within the ministry, which is unusual for a department that has long acted as a launch pad for high-flying administrative and political careers (Boluumbal 2011). As a result, its output is often judged to be at a standstill, by both aid agencies and former or current officials. This has led to the MAED appearing as something of an "empty shell" compared to its former power, which is a matter of regret for many observers. However, such a view seems a little hasty. Leaving aside any nostalgia, its functioning also seems to reflect a new way of "governing the economy".

First, as we have seen, for a long time one source of the MAED's power was the many very important development projects (in education, urban development, capacity building, and so on) that came under its direct responsibility. For years this situation had been criticised by international organisations as an infringement of governance, which pushed the government to hand these project cells over to sectoral ministries in 2007. However, these projects and programmes have recently been returned to the MAED. Some commentators have justified this measure by the insufficiencies of the sectoral ministries; but aside from such arguments, it remains the case that the MAED is once more playing a pivotal role, intervening in many different sectors, and indeed concentrating power in the hands of economic administrators. Furthermore, this move, which is somewhat reminiscent of the Taya period, seems to reflect a more general redeployment of state intervention in the economy, with a great many ramifications now developing. One major development under Aziz has been the proliferation of agencies, public enterprises and organisations. A national agency for monitoring major projects (ANSP), directly linked to the president's office, was created in 2010, with the task of monitoring and, theoretically, evaluating "presidential" projects, which are largely carried out off-budget. In 2011, a new financial arm of the state, closely linked with the MAED (the "Caisse des dépôts et de développe-ment") was created in order to finance large-scale projects and intervene in public enterprises. Many public enterprises (a dozen in the field of transport alone) have also been set up to pursue many different objectives, but their dubious justifications and opacity are criticised by both the opposition and the World Bank and the IMF (World Bank 2011, 23; Union des Forces de Progrès 2011). So we should read the evolution of the MAED in parallel to this pro-liferation of channels of economic intervention, which contributes to the expansion of the rhizome state (Bayart 2009) and recalls the atomisation of the public sector under Taya, which paved the way for informalisation.

Another factor suggests that the MAED has regained importance: judging by the organisation of a new round table of donors in 2010, the current strategy of the MAED for raising international finance appears very well thought, making it a masterpiece for the current regime. Unlike the 2007 Consultative group, the 2010 round table was called for by the national authorities, and the min-ister, Sidi Ould Tah, proved very skilful at organising the event in Brussels in July 2010. Different approaches were used with each of the different donor "types", with different issues at stake in each case. Western donors and international organisations affiliated to the OECD's Development Assistance Committee (DAC), heirs to the classic conception of development aid, were at the centre of the event. Then there were the Arab donors who, though they do not shun the delibera-tions of the OECD-aligned donors, have very different networks and modes of management. Interested above all in getting their money back, dialogue around policies did not interest them in the same way. So, they were given a separate round table, held a few weeks later. This was the second time this judicious format was adopted, the first being in 2007. Lastly, negotiations with the Chinese were different again, tending to operate in semi-commercial modes (around the eventual purchase of raw materials, for example) and remained separated. The possibility of a third round table for the Chinese has been frequently raised, more or less ironically, reflecting the many efforts made by the current minister to find Chinese finance, which have been a subject of sarcasm and debate.[16] The fact is that Chinese finance is important for the regime, both for the commission it generates, as denounced by many observers, and because it has become strategi-cally crucial in a context where European aid is drying up and there are uncertainties in relation to the Arabs (Quotidien de Nouakchott 2011a). Overall, the MAED appears highly effective in deploying the science of raising external finance.

But in a major contrast with the Consultative group, it was impossible, however, for the ser-vices of the MAED and Ministry of Finance to bring an MTEF or budgetary programme to the round table. One of the main reasons was the sudden transfer of functions between the Ministry of Finance and the Ministry of Economic Affairs. The departments no longer work readily together and, according to some managers, Ministry of Finance departments no longer want to collaborate with MAED planning units for the allocation of investment funds; meanwhile, the MAED no longer has the technical skills to undertake alone such a planning exercise. So, in contrast to the sophistication of the Consultative group of 2007, at the round table a simple list of "priority projects" requiring finance was put forward. True, this did form a basis for discussions with donors and in the MAED departments; no effort was spared to make it as "consistent" as possible with "needs". What is interesting in this situation, apart from the administrative compartmentali-sation that seems to have returned with a vengeance, is that such a list easily opens the door to various interventions and manipulations: indeed, after the MAED departments had done their work, the list was substantially amended to include promises and undertakings the president had previously given; many projects he had promised while touring the country were included in the national "priority investment programme". The new technocratic organisation of the MAED thus opens up new margins for discretionary actions, redeploying the power games sur-rounding technical procedures.

From "good pupil rent" to "security rent": the regime's international carte blanche

Aid issues are also posed today in radically different terms from those of the previous regime, due to the terrorist threat which served to justify the 2008 coup d'état. And it seems that this contributes to renewing the style of economic management as well. For the preparation of the round table, the government was able to focus on the problem of security in emphasising its need for finance, but it abandoned the fine figure-based models of the MTEF. The opening chapter of the report presented at the Round Table for Mauritania thus dealt with "geostrategic" issues, calling on the countries present to show "international solidarity" and fulfil their duty to "help each other" (Islamic Republic of Mauritania 2010, 10–15); an entire paper placed in the dossier distributed to the round table's participants was also devoted to this issue. So the rhetoric's seems to have changed, with the planning of development policies no longer being a priority, but support for the security becoming the cornerstone of arguments for raising finance.

In the context that has prevailed in Mauritania, these factors were indeed critical in the positioning of international actors (Antil 2010). The willingness of foreign donors to support Aziz's regime was obvious. The round table itself ended with promises of tremendous support (3.2 billion dollars). But more generally, the cooperation agencies seem to have given Aziz's regime carte blanche. The delegation from the European Commission had made in 2010 budgetary aid a priority, even if assurances in relation to governance were worse than ever, and though the same European Commission had always refused to grant budgetary aid for that very reason. Furthermore, some knowledgeable observers let it be understood that IMF departments were asked not to pay too much attention to Mauritania's record in 2010/2011, because the country was dealing with a tough security problem. If the international financial institutions have been generally lenient with the country in the past 15 years, this support went quite far. For example, this was supposedly the cause for an unexpected resignation of an IMF country economist in 2010. And informers inside public bodies confirmed that the Fund's teams have indeed proved less than meticulous in their enquiries, even in their methods of working with figures. So the regime seems to be enjoying new margins for manoeuvre thanks to the "security rent", which in turn would have very concrete repercussions for the conduct of economic monitoring activities.

Consultancy markets as a means of control

Another and last element supports my interpretation of the emergence of a new mode of government. Under Aziz, many high-ranking officials reputed to be competent have been bypassed on the pretext of their involvement in the "bad management" of the past. But this argument is primarily used to sideline particular people and maintain allegiances. As a result, many high-ranking skilled officials have sought refuge in consultancy work. It has indeed become commonplace to set up a consultancy and the market is flourishing. Several factors suggest that today consultancies occupy a space left vacant by the administration and that they have a stabilising role in the interplay of networks in the political arena. In the field of economics and statistics, some consultancies, such as that of Sidna Ould N'dah, former head of the national statistical office, and Didi Ould Biye, also a former high ranking official in the administration, seem in fact to be extensions of the administration. Sidna's city centre consultancy is today the lair of "former managers". The vast premises, with its offices, internet connection and conference room, has become an important meeting place. Sidna himself was one of Taya's high officials, ousted following the coup d'état of 2005. Today his consultancy enables him to tender for work and coordinate many different public activities, accumulating contracts with international organisations and the state. Sidna still talks like a "director general"; he uses "we" when talking to officials and when describing what the government should do in the future. In a sense he has remained a director general, while also being a consultant. He is moreover an active member of the National Pact for Development and Democracy – ADIL party, which includes many former top officials from the Taya period, having become allied with Sidi Ould Cheikh Abdallah. After the putsch of 2008, they did not support the seizure of power by Aziz and joined the National Front for the Defence of Democracy (FNDD). However, since then they have moved closer to the president, hoping to participate in public life. But Aziz, who claims to have broken with the former chiefs, is very cautious in relation to this party. He finally included it in the presidential majority, but his promises where appointments are concerned are barely kept. On the other hand, he has not blocked them either. And while Sidna has not exactly been co-opted by those in power, nor has he been left out; he has in a sense been put in reserve through the consultancy market, as have many of his peers. To the contrary, those who formerly held posts of responsibility and have not followed the desired political direction may be "ostracised" by being deprived of consultancy opportunities.[17] This shows how the market can be used as a means of control to regulate the political sphere. Today consultation is perhaps a way of recycling former elites and carrying out administrative work and, at the same time, in disciplinary terms, a way of keeping control over a section of the population and Mauritania's high-level technocrats by regulating their access to resources in a clientelist system. It represents both the margins for manoeuvre in modern Mauritania and some of the system's ways of accommodating and attenuating what is often authoritarian domination. But the price of all this is an ever-growing informalisation that proliferates around the formal procedures of economic management.[18]

Conclusion

I have described the transformations of the state in Mauritania in the period 2003–2011 by observing the concrete practices of economic policy management. I have proposed a reinterpretation of Mauritania's political trajectory. I have shown that under Taya's regime, despite major deception in relation to macro-economic figures revealed in 2004, calculation methods were structured around international surveillance procedures and IMF methods, even if transgression was pervasive. While economic reality was largely indistinguishable, technical expertise went hand in hand with deceit in concrete management practices, explaining how the fiction could arise. I also showed that the existence of an expert elite is central to understanding Mauritanian power relations at that time, and after. After Taya's downfall, the regime that emerged from the democratic elections of 2007 represented a dramatic change, bringing the Mauritanian technocratic elite into the limelight, enabling some technocratic achievements, like the Consultative group of December 2007. But the coup d'état of August 2008 signified the failure of a technocratic enterprise that had fostered a fiction of successful transition and concealed some real issues of power. Lastly, the current period has seen a reconfiguration of administrative processes in which, against the background of a serious degradation of working conditions, the authorities take advantage of flawed economic and financial procedures to use new margins for manoeuvre and to reinforce the atomised and clientelistic structure of the state, while adopting the moral high ground in the fight against rampant corruption. Therefore, it is possible to argue that the state, while managed in a discretionary and authoritarian manner, is developing new forms of informalisation.

Some general points also emerge. My observations suggest that it is useful to study the formal procedures of economic management in order to decode the way they structure power relations within the state, and that such an analysis can be used to investigate political legitimacy. Such observations are classical in Europe or America, following the seminal works of Theodore Porter (1995) or Alain Desrosières (1998), but it is not the case in Africa. Some patterns emerge, which should be confronted with other African cases to give a broader sociopolitical perspective on the economic fictions in Africa (Samuel 2009; Jerven 2013, Hibou 2011a). For example, it appears that the existence of a technocratic ethos is not incompatible with massive circumvention of the rules, nor even with power struggles. To the contrary, it reveals the coexistence and accumulation within the state of different relationships to the economy, combining trickery and technical expertise. Unlike most theories of neopatrimonial or failed states would present it, technical competence can be a legitimate repertoire and to some extent condition upward social mobility.

Acknowledgements

I would like to thank the Centre d'Études et de Recherches Internationales (CERI, Sciences-Po Paris) and the Fonds d'Analyse des Sociétés Politiques (FASOPO) who financed my fieldwork in Mauritania in 2011. This article also draws on extensive personal experience in Mauritanian economic and financial administrations during 2003–2007.

Biographical note

Boris Samuel holds a PhD in political science from Sciences-Po Paris (2013), and a Master's degree in economics and statistics from the École Nationale de la Statistique et de l'Administration Economique (ENSAE) in Paris. He has worked for 10 years as an expert in statistics, public finance and macroeconomics for various international organisations and governments in Africa. His research examines in detail technocratic practices across Africa and the Caribbean, to provide a historicised analysis of modes of government and power relations. Samuel is the General Secretary of the Fonds d'Analyse des Sociétés Politiques (FASOPO).

Notes

1. On the role of deceit and informality in Mauritania, see the work of Zekeria Ould Ahmed Salem (1999, 2001).
2. The monopoly was finally dismantled in 2006 under a strong pressure from the European Commission, which regarded it as a hindrance to transport development.
3. See, of course, the seminal work by Jean-François Bayart on "the politics of the belly" (Bayart 2009). See also the works on the neopatrimonial state, for example (Chabal and Daloz 1999) or analysis by political economists (Van de Walle 2001; Hibou 2011a).
4. The article 11 of the Legal order of 25 July 1991 on freedom of the press.
5. A growing gap between the official and parallel rates of foreign currencies (that is, the rates on the illegal market) is a sign of speculation and indicates that the country is running short of currencies.
6. According to a former Central Bank official, personal communication, Nouakchott, July 2011.
7. For an excellent analysis of the IMF's methods from a social science perspective, see Richard Harper (2007).
8. According to a former Central Bank official, personal communication, Nouakchott, April 2011
9. We can relate this with Jerven's reflection on the "production boundary", which shows the role of methodological choices in building an economic narrative (Jerven 2013)
10. Many studies have shown this in non-African cases (Porter 1995; Desrosières 2003; Terray 2003).
11. Indonesia offered support with the production of models in 2006 in the frame of the Projet d'appui à la gestion de l'énergie et du pétrole.
12. The MEMAU was created with the support of the German cooperation in the mid-1990s.
13. Until the year 2014, the Wikipedia page devoted to him has continuously mentioned these various technocratic feats, notably in relation to modelling.
14. Many works have described the role of consultancy markets and firms in the reform of the state: for example, on the United Kingdom (Power 1999) or France (Pierru and Henry 2012).
15. But part of the MAED rather than the Ministry of Education.
16. As in the case of the controversial fishing contracts with the Chinese company Poly Hondone (Quotidien de Nouakchott 2011b).
17. Personal communications, Nouakchott, January and April 2011.
18. On the link between "formalities" and "informalities", see the seminal work of Michel de Certeau (1984), and Hibou (2011b).

References

Antil, A. 2010. "Mohamed Ould Abdel Aziz l'alchimiste." *L'Année du Maghreb* 6: 357–372.

Augé, B. 2007. "Les enjeux du pétrole en Mauritanie." *L'Année du Maghreb* 3: 349–367.

Banégas, R. and J. P. Warnier. 2001. "Nouvelles figures de la réussite et du pouvoir." *Politique africaine* 82: 5–23.

Bayart, J.F. 2004. "Le crime transnational et la formation de l'État." *Politique africaine* 93: 93–104.

Bayart, J. F. 2009. *The State in Africa: The Politics of the Belly*. 2nd ed. Cambridge: Polity Press.

Bayart, J. F., S. Ellis, and B. Hibou. 1999. *The Criminalization of the State in Africa*. Oxford: James Currey.

Bayart, J. F., A. Mbembe, and C. Toulabor. 2008. *Le politique par le bas en Afrique noire*. Paris: Karthala.

Bensaâd, A. 2006. "Les répliques d'un coup d'Etat manqué." *L'Année du Maghreb* 1: 305–319.

Bensaâd, A. 2007. "Mauritanie: une révolution de Palais sur fond d'odeur de pétrole." *L'Année du Maghreb* 2: 323–336.

Bierschenk, T., J. P. Chauveau, and J. P. Olivier de Sardan, eds. 2000. *Courtiers en développement. Les villages africaines en quête de projets*. Paris: Karthala.

Blum, A., and M. Mespoulet. 2003. *L'Anarchie bureaucratique. Statistique et pouvoir sous Staline*. Paris: La Découverte.

Blundo, G., and P. Y. Le Meur, eds. 2009. *The Governance of Daily Life in Africa: Ethnographic Explorations of Public and Collective Services*. Boston, MA: Brill.

Boluumbal. 2011. Nominations au MAED: mes amis d'abord. *Boluumbal.org*, March 28.

Bonnecase, V. 2011. *La pauvreté au Sahel. Du savoir colonial à la mesure internationale*. Paris: Karthala.

Certeau, M. de. 1984. *The Practice of Everyday Life*. Berkeley: University of California Press.

Chabal, P., and J. P. Daloz. 1999. *Africa Works: Disorder as Political Instrument*, Bloomington, IN: Indiana University Press.

Cherif, B. 2009. Scandale de la Banque centrale de Mauritanie (BCM): pourquoi Ould Nagi a-t-il été arrêté?. *Le Quotidien de Nouakchott*, November 17.

Desrosières, A. 1998. *The Politics of Large Numbers: A History of Statistical Reasoning*. Cambridge, MA: Harvard University Press.

Desrosières, A. 2003. "Managing the Economy: the State, the Market, and Statistics." In *The Cambridge History of Science*, vol. 7, edited by T. Porter and D. Ross, 553–564. Cambridge: Cambridge University Press.

Guyer, J. 2004. *Marginal Gains: Monetary Transactions in Atlantic Africa*. Chicago, IL: University of Chicago Press.

Harper, R. H. R. 1997. *Inside the IMF: An Ethnography of Documents, Technology, and Organizational Action*. Orlando, FL: Academic Press.

Hibou, B., ed. 2004. *Privatising the State*. London: Columbia University Press.

Hibou, B. 2011a. *The Force of Obedience. The Political Economy of Repression in Tunisia*. Cambridge: Polity Press.

Hibou, B. 2011b. *Anatomie politique de la domination*. Paris: La Découverte.

IMF. 2003. *Staff Report for the 2003 Article IV Consultation, and Request for a Three-Year Arrangement Under the Poverty Reduction and Growth Facility*. IMF Country Report no. 03/314, June.

IMF. 2005. *Islamic Republic of Mauritania. Report on Non-Complying Disbursment*. Washington, DC: IMF.

Islamic Republic of Mauritania. 2006. *Rapport sur la révision des données macroéconomiques 1992–2004*. Nouakchott, June.

Islamic Republic of Mauritania. 2010. *La stabilité et le développement de la Mauritanie: un impératif pour la sécurité régionale et internationale*. Document for the Mauritanian Round Table, May 31.

Jerven, M. 2013. *Poor Numbers: How We Are Misled by African Development Statistics and What to Do About It*. Ithaca, NY: Cornell University Press.

Jourde, C. 2007. "The International Relations of Small Neoauthoritarian States: Islamism, Warlordism, and the Framing of Stability." *International Studies Quarterly* 51 (2): 481–503.

Lewis, D., and D. Mosse, eds. 2006. *Development Brokers and Translators: The Ethnography of Aid and Agencies*. West Hartford, CT: Kumarian Press.

Malaquais, D. 2001. "Anatomie d'une arnaque. Feymen et feymania au Cameroun." *Les Etudes du CERI* 77, June.

Marchesin, P. 1992. *Tribus, ethnies et pouvoirs en Mauritanie*. Paris: Karthala.

Meunier, M. 2007. "Interview de Zeine Ould Zeidane." *Jeune Afrique*, December 20.

Meunier, M. 2008. "Les hommes du président,."*Jeune Afrique*, March 31.

N'diaye, B. 2006. "Mauritania, August 2005: Justice and Democracy, or Just Another Coup?" *African Affairs* 105 (420): 421–441.

Ould Ahmed Salem, Z. 1999. *Fraude et piratage halieutique en Mauritanie*. Study for the French Ministry of Defence and CERI-Sciences Po, Paris.

Ould Ahmed Salem, Z. 2001. "'Tcheb-tchib' et compagnie. Lexique de la survie et figures de la réussite en Mauritanie." *Politique africaine* 82: 78–100.

Ould Ahmed Salem, Z. 2004. "Les marges d'un Etat-frontière. Histoire régionale, clôture nationale et enjeux locaux." In *Les Trajectoires d'un Etat-frontière. Espace, évolutions politiques et transformations sociales en Mauritanie*, edited by Z. Ould Ahmed Salem, 9–45. Dakar: Codesria.

Ould Ahmed Salem, Z. 2008. "Le partenariat Union Européenne-Afrique dans l'impasse? Le cas des accords de pêche." ASC Working Paper, 78, University of Leiden.

Ould Cheikh, A. W. 1998. "Cherche élite, désespérément … Evolution du système éducatif et (dé)formation des "élites" dans la société mauritanienne." *Nomadic Peoples* 2 (1): 235–252.

Ould Cheikh, A. W. 2006. "Les habits neufs du sultan: sur le pouvoir et ses (res)sources en Mauritanie." *Maghreb-Machrek* 189: 29–52.

Ould Oumère, M. F. 2007. "Groupe consultatif: la bataille de Paris fera-t-elle des victimes à Nouakchott?" *La Tribune* 378, December 12.

Pierru, F., and O. Henry, eds. 2012. *Le Conseil de l'Etat (1). Acte de la recherche en sciences sociales*, no. 193/3, Paris.

Porter, T. 1995. *Trust in Numbers. The Pursuit of Objectivity in Science and Public Life*. Princeton, NJ: Princeton University Press.

Power, M. 1999. *The Audit Society: Rituals of Verification*. 2nd ed. Oxford: Oxford University Press.

Quotidien de Nouakchott. 2011a. "Sidi Ould Tah dans les bras de Pékin." *Le Quotidien de Nouakchott*, January 6.

Quotidien de Nouakchott. 2011b. "Convention d'établissement MAED-Poly Hondone: quand le MAED parle chinois à l'Assemblée!" *Le Quotidien de Nouakchott*, June 5.

Samuel, B. 2009. "Le cadre stratégique de lutte contre la pauvreté et les trajectoires de la planification au Burkina Faso." *Sociétés politiques comparées* 16 (August).

Samuel, B. 2011. "Calcul macroeconomique et modes de gouvernement: les cas de la Mauritanie et du Burkina Faso." *Politique africaine* 124: 101–126.

Tahalil Hebdo. 2007. "Le glas a-t-il sonné pour Zeine Ould Zeidane?" *Tahalil Hebdo*, November 6.

Terray, A. 2003. *Des francs-tireurs aux experts. L'organisation de la prévision économique au ministère des Finances, 1948–1968*. Paris: Comité pour l'histoire économique et financière de la France.

Van de Walle, N. 2001. *African Economies and the Politics of Permanent Crisis, 1979–1999*. Cambridge: Cambridge University Press, 2001.

Union des Forces de Progrès. 2011. *Souveraine gabegie*. Nouakchott, April 21.

Véridique. 2008. "Conflit ouvert entre le PM et le ministre de l'Economie et des Finances." *Le Véridique*, June 22.

World Bank. 2011. *Islamic Republic of Mauritania Public Expenditure Review – Update*. PREM-Africa Region, Report No. 62082-MR, Washington, DC, May.

Reliable, challenging or misleading? A qualitative account of the most recent national surveys and country statistics in the DRC

Wim Marivoet and Tom De Herdt

Institute of Development Policy and Management, University of Antwerp, Antwerp, Belgium

ABSTRACT This paper presents a comprehensive assessment of the national information architecture in the Democratic Republic of Congo (DRC) between 1970 and 2010. In general, "the numbers" can be qualified as poorly reliable, though an important distinction should be made between aggregate country statistics and microlevel survey data. Whereas the latter inherently contain the purer and less manipulated pieces of information, the former have proven to be the result of an obscure blend of aggregation, estimation, permutation and negotiation, often with a weak informational basis. By contrast, survey data in the DRC are intrinsically of good quality and collected increasingly, although too many concerns remain about the poor accessibility of primary datasets, the fragmented metadata and the problematic sampling base to claim representativeness.

RÉSUMÉ Cet article présente une évaluation complète de l'architecture du système d'information nationale de la République démocratique du Congo (RDC) entre les années 1970 et 2000. Dans l'ensemble, les données sont peu fiables, bien qu'une distinction importante doive être faite entre les données agrégées au niveau national et les microdonnées d'enquête. Les premières sont le résultat d'un mélange obscur d'agrégation, d'estimation, de permutation et de négociation sur une base informationnelle pauvre. En revanche, les données d'enquête de la RDC sont d'assez bonne qualité et sont collectées de plus en plus fréquemment, mais, pour attester de leur validité, elles souffrent encore de trop nombreuses limites sur le plan de l'accès aux données originales, de la disponibilité des métadonnées et des plans d'échantillonnage.

Introduction

Although many scholars and development experts acknowledge the poor quality of sub-Saharan African data from which country statistics are derived and compiled in international datasets (Jerven 2013; Devarajan 2013; Henderson, Storeygard, and Weil 2012), they often use these derivatives at face value. One case in point is Gross Domestic Product (GDP) and its per capita equivalent, both of which are extensively used in the economic growth literature. To justify their use, two sorts of arguments are often put forward. The first one can best be para-phrased as "O.K., the data's lousy, but it's all we've got",[1] which values data not because of their intrinsic quality but rather because of their relative scarcity. The second argument tries to downplay the impact of potentially unreliable data by assuming errors to be randomly distributed and biases to be sufficiently reduced when enough data enter the analysis (Jerven 2013, 110).

Other scholars, however, tend to be more critical of these internationally compiled datasets but differ in how to deal with them. The more radical responses are either to shy away from this type of quantitative data analysis completely (Chambers 2007) or to rely on – literally – very indirect information like remote sensing and satellite data. The latter have been employed to correct or to estimate economic activity (Ghosh et al. 2010), economic growth (Henderson, Storeygard, and Weil 2012), land use and crop yield (Atzberger 2013) and health risks (Beck, Lobitz, and Wood 2000). A less drastic strategy to deal with potential data problems is to contextualise historically the information available. In his book, *Poor Numbers*, Jerven applies this approach to GDP estimates for many sub-Saharan African countries and finds that "[i]n large part, the information recorded in the [international] databases is the result of automatic data permutations, preliminary estimates, or negotiated numbers" (Jerven 2013, 28–29). Consequently, these numbers can only be meaningfully used if sufficient attention is paid to the historical recording of the underlying national account components.

In line with Jerven (2013), this paper will provide a qualitative and more contextual account of the Congolese information architecture. In particular, it will try to illuminate to what extent socio-economic survey data and a number of key statistics are reliable, challenging, or misleading. The period under investigation runs from 1970 to 2010 and the structure of this paper reads as follows. In the next section, the roots of some key statistics, such as GDP per capita, life expectancy and child mortality, will be explored and their reliability assessed. Thereafter, the paper will turn to national survey data to discuss their accessibility, quality and exploitation.

Development statistics

Let us start our inquiry into the data architecture of the DRC with an investigation of some key national development indicators. The World Development Indicators (WDI) database, which is the primary collection of development statistics compiled by the World Bank, was able to produce yearly estimates since 1970 (and even earlier) for GDP per capita, life expectancy and under-five mortality (see Figure 1). Contrary to expectations, the capacity of the Congolese administration did not seem to be much affected by the country's problematic history, a history which reads like a textbook example of state failure and economic decay (Young and Turner 1985; Marysse 2005; Herderschee, Kaiser, and Mukoko Samba 2012).

For GDP alone, this achievement is already immense, given the volatile economic outlook of the country (Bézy, Peemans, and Wautelet 1981; Maton, Schoors, and and Van Bauwel 1998; De Herdt 2002). For example, it must have been extremely difficult for those responsible at the national accounts department to measure correctly the real added value of an economy characterised by a chronic two-digit inflation rate with peaks well over 3,000 per cent during the early 1990s (Maton, Schoors, and and Van Bauwel 1998), while at the same time new currencies were introduced mid-year with conversion rates equalling 3 million old Zaire to 1 new Zaire (as was the case in October 1993).[2] Strangely enough, the time series for GDP per capita is both complete and far from jagged. The same completeness and smoothness can also be observed for life expectancy and child mortality. In the absence of routine registration of deaths, births and migrants, life tables for many developing countries are often obtained through sampling data (Lopez et al. 2001). Although several representative surveys on health and demography have been organised in the DRC (see below), they have been much more infrequent than the data would suggest.

As a result, and largely in line with conclusions drawn for other sub-Saharan African countries (Jerven 2013), one should be very reluctant to consider DRC's time series as a collection of pure

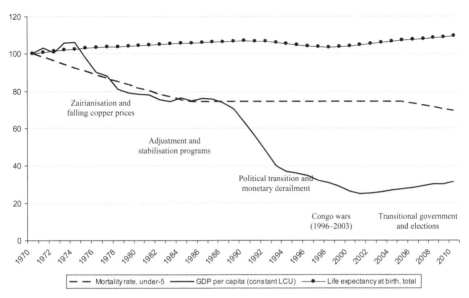

Figure 1.   Key development indicators for the DRC, 1970–2010.
Source: World Development Indicators (World Bank 2012).

data observations. This caution is all the more justified when considering the diverging trends between economic decline and human survival, as if a plane had crashed with only a few casualties (De Herdt and Marysse 1997, 214). In this section, we will try to dig deeper into this issue by disentangling the core and more robust pieces of information from those that have been estimated, extrapolated, or negotiated.

Gross Domestic Product per capita

Unlike many sub-Saharan African countries (Young 2012, 1), the smooth and complete time series of Congo's real GDP per capita does not really reflect what the World Bank itself calls gap-filling procedures (Jerven 2013, 22), automatic algorithms to fill out missing data. As a matter of fact, the UN Statistics Division said it only needed to estimate GDP data for the period 1970–1976 by applying a backward trend on the otherwise complete data series provided by Congo's Central Bank (BCC) (UNSTATS 2012). Curiously enough, the International Monetary Fund (IMF), which also relies heavily on the same information, states with respect to real GDP that "[d]ata prior to 2001 cannot be confirmed by national sources at this time" (IMF 2012). So, what else to conclude other than that data from BCC for the years before 2001 have been used and permutated by new IMF estimates? The same practice very much seems to be true for GDP estimates produced by the World Bank, which are constantly updated and revised, resulting in different figures for the same years depending on the exact date the data were downloaded (Jerven 2013, 124). As such, data permutation rather than gap-filling is a more accurate description of what mostly happens with GDP data from the DRC before they are each time read into international datasets.

Depending on the international organisation, research centre, or national administration, these data permutations follow different logics and objectives, and therefore do not result in fully comparable time series. Actually, the same national account information provided by the national authorities often gives ample room for interpretation to produce a specific series of estimates, reflecting what each actor may deem essential for analysis and comparison. Without entering into the nuts and bolts of these different logics, Figure 2 shows the range within which real GDP per capita should be situated, according to the most important sources. The bold solid line in the figure represents the WDI estimates (as downloaded in June 2012[3]) and the thin lines refer to the maximal and minimal estimates. Specifically, the upper bound is obtained by dividing the maximum value for real GDP reported in various official sources by the minimum value for population observed by these same sources, and the lower bound is obtained by doing the inverse.

Based on this information, three observations are important: (1) all conventional estimates of GDP per capita by and large point to the same overall negative trend; (2) despite some marked volatility during the 1980s, the estimates converge over time (especially after 1993) and the overall bandwidth becomes fairly narrow; and (3) the WDI estimates in general sit well midway between the upper and lower bounds of most official data. As a result, there should be little doubt about the reliability of the WDI estimates as well as the extent of economic decline that characterised the Congolese economy since the mid-1970s. Yet, no matter how reassuring this may seem at first sight, these official measures of GDP almost by definition ignore income activities taking place within the unobserved economy. For an idea of the possible size of this

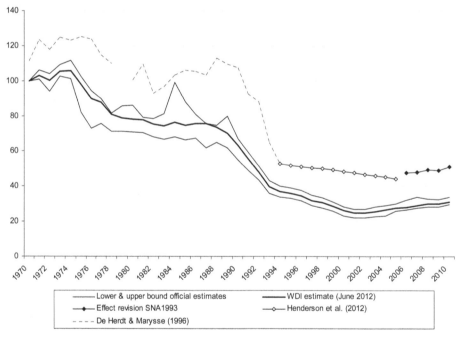

Figure 2.   Estimates of DRC's GDP per capita, 1970–2010[a], according to various sources.
Note: [a]All official estimates in constant prices and indexed at 1970.
Sources: GDP estimates based on World Development Indicators (World Bank 2012); World Economic Outlook (IMF 2012); National Accounts Main Aggregates Database (UNISTATS 2012); Maddison (2008); Total Economy Database (Conference Board 2013); Penn World Table (version 7.1.) (Heston, Summers, and Aten 2012); various reports and official website of the Central Bank of Congo (BCC 2013); Bézy, Peemans, and Woutelet (1981); Maton, Schoors, and Van Bauwel (1998); DSCRP2, Annex 3 (République démocratique du Congo 2011b); Henderson, Storeygard, and Weil (2012); and De Herdt and Marysse (1996). Population estimates based on World Development Indicators (World Bank 2012); National Accounts Main Aggregates Database (UNISTATS 2012); Maddison (2008); Total Economy Database (Conference Board 2013); Penn World Table (version 7.1.) (Heston, Summers, and Aten 2012); Ngondo, de Saint Moulin, and Tambashe (1993); and Maton, Schoors, and Bauwel (1998).

sector in the DRC, consider the three alternative time series in Figure 2, all having their merits and limitations.

The first one tries to correct for the unrecorded sector by using data on the mass of fiduciary and scriptural money within the Congolese economy (De Herdt and Marysse 1996). The results of this estimation exercise point to an informal sector that has gradually increased in size, from a share of the total economy of around 15 per cent in the first half of the 1970s to more than 40 per cent in the early 1990s. As such, the decline of recorded GDP over this period has been partly offset by a more vibrant informal sector, as indicated by the dashed line in Figure 2. The second time series is based on a statistical model developed by Henderson, Storeygard, and Weil (2012), who use satellite data on nighttime light to improve official income statistics. Following this procedure, annual GDP growth for the DRC between 1992–2003 and 2005–2006 on average would be 1.84 percentage points higher than the annual 0.52 per cent decrease as reported by the WDI (Henderson, Storeygard, and Weil 2012, 1019–1021). Assuming GDP data of De Herdt and Marysse (1996) to be accurate for 1994 combined with the most conservative population estimates, this revised annual growth rate would then result in a much smaller per capita income decline during this period, as could be observed by the white dotted line in Figure 2. The third alternative time series results from the DRC's recent exercise to upgrade its national account system from SNA1968 to SNA1993. This methodological shift also provided more tools to better record autoconsumption and informal income activities (Eurostat 2011, 103–111). As depicted by the black dotted line in Figure 2, preliminary[4] estimates of this revision would represent a near-doubling of GDP per capita (République démocratique du Congo 2011b). Irrespective of the exact degree, these alternative time series of GDP per capita in any case point to a considerable underestimation of true economic activity when current official data are taken at face value. Moreover, in the particular case of the DRC, the extent of underestimation is probably far larger than depicted in Figure 2. In effect, the unrecorded economy was very much a systemic phenomenon, as demonstrated by casewise evidence on unrecorded trading (MacGaffey 1987, 1991) and its eventual connection with the lingering conflict (Vlassenroot and Raeymaekers 2004), as well as by more systematic studies (Cour 1989). This economy was even part and parcel of the Mobutu regime's tactics of governance.[5]

Although the latter references much underscore the shallow nature of most GDP revisions, they do not, however, allow direct recalculation of GDP over a larger period of time or for the whole country.[6] We therefore focus here on the more complete national time series (Figure 2). Ultimately, the value of both the official and revised GDP estimates remains based on the quality of the underlying data provided by the Congolese administration. Therefore, to have a better view of this, it is essential to examine how the components of GDP per capita have been domestically produced in the first place.

Let us start with the GDP data. In theory, three approaches (production, income and expenditure) exist to derive the gross added value generated by all domestic actors in an economy. In most sub-Saharan African countries, however, the production approach is often favoured over the other two for lack of data. Moreover, instead of having three independent sources of information to measure GDP (so as to be able to distinguish one measure from the other when they diverge), one typically tries to obtain other macroeconomic aggregates, such as private consumption, C, by substituting the production-based GDP estimate into the generic entity $GDP = C + I + G + EX - IM$ (Jerven 2013, 12). An informant at the World Bank office in Kinshasa indeed confirmed that this kind of practice also applies to the DRC. The same informant also mentioned in passing that most national accounts of the DRC are simply subject to consensus, or, it appears, experts and consultants who sit together and decide on the size of the Congolese economy over a pint of beer.[7] At the same time, such a consensus strategy should not come as a surprise given the large amount of pure guesswork that seems to characterise the national accounting in the DRC.

Unfortunately, little of this information exists on paper, but what does exist indeed confirms the highly speculative nature of national accounting. In an attempt to provide provincial authorities with estimates of their local economy, the World Bank currently supports a methodology that derives the added value produced in each sector of the Congolese economy by applying a number of coefficients to final production in order to correct for intermediate consumption. These coefficients, however, are poorly specified (one for each of the eight broad sectors defined), static (they do not seem to change over time) and highly nominal across provinces (as no robust regional price index exists). Moreover, for the service sector, it seems that no such coefficient could be derived (leading to the unrealistic assumption that no intermediate consumption occurs in this sector) and that the correction for regional inflation was based on a national price index (Nintunze et al. 2012, 270–271). Assuming this newer methodology to be an improvement compared to previous practice, one can indeed raise several doubts about the reliability of older national account statistics.

The same speculative nature applies to the other necessary component of GDP per capita, namely population data. At present, nobody knows how many Congolese actually live in the DRC and all estimates are somehow based on the national census organised in 1984,[8] which was almost 30 years ago. Curiously enough, none of the international databases display the same figure for 1984 as the one officially announced by the National Institute of Statistics (INS) and the United Nations Development Programme (UNDP) (Institut National de la Statistique and Programme des Nations Unies pour le Développement 1991, 232). From then on, a spatially homogenous growth rate of around 3 per cent has been typically assumed to extrapolate the size of the Congolese population for the years between 1984 and 2010. Although this percentage comes close to the sub-Saharan African average (WDI 2012), there is little scientific justification for relying on this specific figure. Moreover, the mechanical nature of such updating is of course highly insensitive to the various local demographical events that have taken place since 1984, such as the death toll resulting from the conflict in eastern Congo (1997–2003)[9] or the mass expulsion of Kasaians from Katanga in 1992–1993 (Dibwe dia Mwembu 1999, 483–499). Given these arguments, and the need to have a sound sampling base for surveys (see below), it is difficult to overstate the importance of organising a new census (this has been scheduled now for 2014).

In summary, it should be clear that GDP per capita in the DRC is far from a series of pure data observations. As a matter of fact, GDP rather seems to be a list of negotiated figures based on information coming from an obscure estimation process, in which the formal sector's added value exclusively is proxied through a number of broad and static conversion rates for each sector in the economy. This GDP consensus is often then revised by several international organisations and research institutes, and divided by population estimates based on a sterile extrapolation of an outdated census. These permutations of GDP combined with the extrapolated population data give rise to the volatility as observed in Figure 2. Taking everything together, one can reasonably assume – from the revised estimates and other sources – that the economic decline was probably far less dramatic than depicted by the official bandwidth.

Statistics on human survival

A similar caution is appropriate when considering survival statistics. Figure 3 displays the time series for under-five mortality according to the WDI and the various survey interventions executed in the DRC. A first observation concerns the extent to which data have been extra- and interpolated to produce a complete time series. In fact, not more than five surveys (including the census) exist that allow a computation of mortality rates (see below). Only those data points that followed the same estimation technique and life table model as the WDI have been

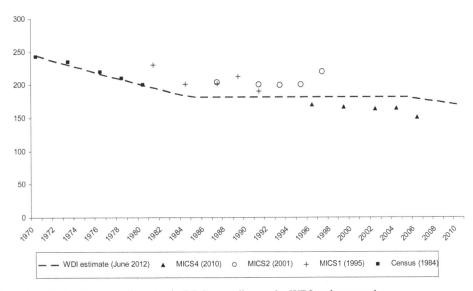

Figure 3.   Under-five mortality rates in DRC according to the WDI and survey data.
Note: All data on under-five mortality and life expectancy were derived using the indirect Brass estimation technique together with the North model of the Coale-Demeny life tables. The Demographic Health Survey (DHS) of 2007 made use of another estimation technique and therefore was discarded from this figure.
Sources: Based on World Development Indicators (World Bank 2012), Schneidman (1990), République démocratique du Congo (1996), République démocratique du Congo (2002), République démocratique du Congo (2011a) and IGME (2012).

retained in Figure 3. Remarkably, the survey data clearly differ from the WDI, both in terms of level and trend. Whereas the latter is characterised by a linear sequence of progress-stability-progress, the survey results are much more jagged, especially after 1980, when periods of progress and decline rapidly succeed one other. Furthermore, compared to the survey data, the WDI seem to underestimate mortality rates during the 1980s and early 1990s, and vice versa during the late 1990s and 2000s.

Unlike the previous discussion on GDP per capita, these dissimilarities among sources seem less straightforward to explain. Indeed, the only information available in the DRC to estimate mortality rates are survey records on child births and deaths. Therefore, it would seem reasonable to expect survey results and corresponding statistics in international datasets to be similar; of course, conditional upon the use of the same calculation method.

Further investigation has, however, revealed that the WDI series on under-five mortality is actually based on an estimation technique developed by the Inter-agency Group for Child Mortality Estimation (IGME). This technique attempts to harmonise estimates and trends over time by using all available sources per country (IGME 2007, 19–24). In the case of the DRC, the Demographic Health Survey (DHS) of 2007, with its direct calculation method and generally lower mortality rates, has been used as well. Not only may a difference in method explain why under-five mortality rates in the DHS were lower (and thus why WDI seemed to underestimate survey data during the DHS reference period), its problematic sampling base may also be an important factor. As will be discussed later in this paper, the DHS, in comparison with other household surveys, started from a 40/60 ratio between urban and rural populations that would give too much weight to the urban sector, thus resulting in biased and underestimated mortality rates for the period covered by this survey. And finally, even with the knowledge that DHS data were used as input for the IGME estimation, the strong linearity together with the long period of fixed mortality rates remain improbable, or at least give this series a rather fabricated look. Since information on life expectancy in the DRC is derived through survey data on child mortality, a similar discussion of trends and biases would apply to the corresponding WDI series.

Another potential bias of course relates to the overall quality of each survey intervention. In this respect, two important elements must be noted. First, data collection in conflict-prone areas typically entails an exercise of parallel sampling in order to lower the polltakers' exposure to risk. As a consequence, information coming from these areas may be positively biased, as the most deprived and risky areas are often excluded from the final sample. Second, the 1984 census was only incompletely processed. Compared to most other surveys that respond to an international demand to monitor global trends in poverty, health and education, the 1984 census was a much more nationally driven exercise, thus allowing the pursuit of a domestic agenda. Since this census was the first nationwide data collection after a series of controversial policies, measured progress in terms of people's living conditions would have been most welcome for the incumbent regime. More generally, the organisation of a census in Africa is often a political issue, as it reflects the relative power between different regions and ethnicities in a country (Gendreau 1990). Whether political motivations were really at play when processing the census data of 1984 is difficult to assess. However, the overall observation that the health prospects of the Congolese were not much impaired by the protracted economic crisis is largely built upon the trend derived from the 1984 census data. If indeed this information is only poorly reliable, the real health evolution would look less reassuring, as indicated by the other Multiple Indicator Cluster Survey (MICS) results.

Implications of "spurious" country statistics

"GDP is too important to be ignored and the numbers are too poor to be trusted blindly" (Jerven 2013, 115). From the discussion above, it should be clear that the second part of this quotation, taken from Jerven's study on African development statistics, also applies to the DRC in particular. The present section will therefore focus on the quotation's first part. Why is a correct measurement of development important, or, what are the direct consequences of Congo's spurious country statistics? In this respect, two sorts of implications can be distinguished: a political and a scientific one.

In political terms, measuring a country's development level is important for policy making as well as for the corresponding earmarking of national budget resources and international aid flows. Simply stated, if country statistics are erroneous, policy will be misguided. In a donor context, the example of Ghana is very illustrative: after revising its base year, this country's GDP increased by 60 per cent and consequently shifted from a low-income to a lower-middle-income country overnight (Jerven and Duncan 2012). In the DRC, the preliminary estimates of the upcoming shift to SNA1993 actually point to a similar increase of GDP.[10] Yet, given Congo's very low official GDP per capita compared to many other countries, this revision will not change its low income status or its lending opportunities. As a matter of fact, our own calculations indicate that the DRC would only move up from the last to the third last position, passing Burundi and Malawi.

Being last or not in international rankings has had huge importance indirectly, however, in terms of publicity and fundraising. In Kinshasa, the launch of UNDP's Human Development Report, as well as the International Food Policy Research Institute's (IFPRI) Global Hunger Index (GHI) of 2011, received considerable attention among policy makers and donors. In both reports, the DRC was assigned the least enviable rank, which promptly sparked debates on data reliability and construction. With respect to the Human Development Index (HDI), the local UNDP office in Kinshasa quickly identified the country's outdated system of national accounts (SNA1968) as the major source for this poor performance, while stressing at the same time that they had no hand in its data provision or computation. However, similar to the case of GDP per capita, our own calculations again suggest that this switch to SNA1993 would only result in raising the DRC to the fourth last position, ahead of Mozambique, Niger and again Burundi. Concerning the GHI, Congo's last position is mainly driven by the substantial increase in people who are undernourished, from 26 per cent in 1990–1992 to 69 per cent in 2005–2007 (IFPRI 2011, 49). These figures, taken from the yearly report of the Food and Agriculture Organization of the United Nations (FAO) yearly report on The State of Food Insecurity in the World (SOFI), were used without any modification by IFPRI to construct Congo's GHI. Evidently, when data receive an official stamp of approval, they are often used for many other purposes without much consideration (Jerven 2013). Fortunately for the Congolese, but unfortunately for those making a big fuss about Congo's extremely alarming nutritional status, the reality on the ground may be quite different. Indeed, many knowledgeable observers were surprised to see the DRC figuring at the bottom of the food security ranking. The next edition of the SOFI report in 2012 did not produce any estimate for the DRC, which in turn may reflect FAO's current concerns about data quality for this particular country. In the end, what matters is that the evolution sketched by an indicator should reveal something about the change in true living conditions experienced by people, rather than about a change in institutional rigor to produce or accept country statistics.

This brings us to the second major implication of spurious data, or, what to conclude scientifically from these national statistics in terms of their impact on the exact reading of Congo's history. In many instances, the problematic nature of DRC's country statistics leaves much room for interpretation, as noise seems to be a random attribute to most data. In a few cases, however, the direction of potential bias could be identified. The above discussion on GDP per capita revealed that the economic decline at least seemed very real, though its extent may have been somewhat exaggerated by the WDI series. On the other hand, the same WDI on child mortality and life expectancy may have sketched too optimistic a scenario about people's chances of survival. Combining both these elements, the difference between economic performance and human survival might have been less sharp in reality than depicted in Figure 1.

Everything depends of course on the quality and reliability of the underlying data used. At this point, survey data are often promoted as alternative and more accurate sources of information. Whereas survey data, by definition, come much earlier in the data production process (where they are closely monitored by international donors), national statistics not only are more politically sensitive but also entail a significant number of aggregation procedures that require sufficient resources of both the human and financial variety.

National household surveys

In the absence of a well-functioning administration to provide reliable statistics, household surveys can be very useful tools to get a better idea of a society's exact living conditions. Two main reasons for this preference stand out. The first one is intrinsic. In their report for the French government, Stiglitz, Sen, and Fitoussi (2009) explicitly recommend measuring economic performance and social progress by adopting a household perspective, rather than through a number of sterile macroeconomic indicators. As a result, national household surveys should take a more central role in measuring a country's living standards. The other reason is rather pragmatic and originates from the discussion above, in which survey data were often characterised as a collection of more primary and thus less manipulable pieces of information. However, whether survey data by definition are also less prone to other sources of spuriousness remains subject to debate. The current section will discuss all nationwide socioeconomic surveys executed in the DRC over the past 40 years.

Since the national census of 1984 (INS/PNUD 1991), several nationwide surveys have succeeded each other at an increasing pace, especially after the formal end of the conflict in 2003. In fact, after the census of 1984, two Multiple Indicator Cluster Surveys on the health and education of women and children have been conducted, one in 1995 (MICS1; République démocratique du Congo 1996) and the other in 2001 (MICS2; République démocratique du Congo 2002). Some years later, in 2004–2005, a so-called 1-2-3 Survey (Institut National de la Statistique, n.d.) on income, the informal sector and consumption was carried out, directly followed by a Demographic and Health Survey in 2007 (DHS; République démocratique du Congo 2008a) and a survey to conduct a Comprehensive Food Security and Vulnerability Analysis (CFSVA) in 2007–2008 (WFP/Ministère du Plan/INS 2008). More recently, in 2010, another MICS survey (MICS4) was conducted (République démocratique du Congo 2011a). Of course, many other household surveys exist, although their scope is often narrower either in terms of thematic or geographical coverage. Most noteworthy among them are the various demographic and budget surveys conducted in the 1970s, but which were limited to the western part of the country (see below).

In the following sections, the basic characteristics of each of these national surveys will be discussed in detail and their output will be evaluated in terms of their accessibility, quality and exploitation. For accessibility, we will focus on the publication date of the summarising report as well as on the availability of the underlying dataset. In terms of quality, it is worth making the distinction between primary data and metadata. Whereas the former will be checked by looking at aspects of internal coherence (for example between questionnaires, data and results), the latter refers to the accessibility and quality of all sorts of additional, but often very critical, information (such as sample design or coding information) or institutional support to obtain these elements. Concerning the exploitation of survey data, we will differentiate between political exploitation (relying on survey results to substantiate the analysis of policy documents) and academic exploitation (analysing primary datasets to create academic output). This type of academic visibility will be assessed through the Google search engine (http://scholar.google.be). Notwithstanding some other attempts to objectify, in the end this assessment is largely based on personal (field) experiences and observations over a period of time.[11] Table 1 provides a chronological summary of this qualitative assessment.

National census of 1984

After the demographic surveys supervised by Anatole Romaniuc in 1955–1957, very few efforts of this rigour have been made to keep the resulting demographical statistics up to date (Ngondo a Pitshandenge et al. 2003). Among these other initiatives, one could mention the administrative census of 1970 as well as two parallel studies executed in the western part of the country between 1975 and 1977.[12] The first of the two studies concerns a series of demographic and budget surveys executed in several major cities and the second is the EDOZA survey, which focused exclusively on demography within the remaining urban sector and the rural sector (Tabutin 1982).[13] Moreover, following the problematic events of the first years after independence, together with the administrative reorganisation of the country, a large part of the country's statistical base had either deteriorated or disappeared (Akoto Mandjale and Iba Ngambong 1992, 22). Given the controversy around the estimates stemming from the administrative census in 1970 (which de facto resulted in the elimination of the census from the country's demographic repertory), demographers interested in the most recent population data were often invited to study those of 1955–1957 (Kalombo N'Tambwe 1986). Consequently, the need to organise a national census in 1984 was genuine and its importance difficult to overestimate.

Table 1. Qualitative assessment of Congolese national survey data (1984–2010).

| Survey
- Year
- Size
- Budget | Basic characteristics | | General output | | |
	Actors - Principal(s) - Donor(s) - Executive(s)	Publication date of final report	Accessibility to raw data	Quality of (meta)data and institutional support	Political and academic exploitation
National census - 1984 - 30,729,443 individuals - Not available	- Government of Zaire - UNFPA - INS	One provisional report published seven years later	Not freely accessible	Not verifiable	Largely for internal use (and mainly employed as sampling base reference)
MICS1 - 1995 - 4,574 households - $124,750	- General Secretary of Plan - UNICEF, UNDP, WHO - INS	Published one year later	Not freely accessible	Disconnection between report and data Little information on the wealth index Little institutional support	- Hardly used for political and academic purposes
MICS2 - 2001 - 8,600 households - $1,300,000 (est.)	- Ministry of Plan - UNICEF/USAID - INS	Published one year later	Freely accessible through www.childinfo.org	Good data quality Little institutional support	- Poorly used for political purposes - Hardly used for academic purposes
1-2-3 Survey - 2004–2005 - 13,688 households - $2,260,547	- UPPE-SRP - WB, UNDP, French Cooperation, and others - INS, DIAL, AFRISTAT	No final report has been validated or published	Not freely accessible	Good data quality Price problem and highly scattered metadata Little institutional support	- Poorly used for political and academic purposes

(Continued)

Table 1. Continued.

Basic characteristics			General output		
Survey - Year - Size - Budget	Actors - Principal(s) - Donor(s) - Executive(s)	Publication date of final report	Accessibility to raw data	Quality of (meta)data and institutional support	Political and academic exploitation
CFSVA - 2007–2008 - 3,236 households - Not available	- Ministry of Plan - WFP, Citigroup, ECHO, and Belgian Cooperation - INS	Published the same year	Non-recoverable	Not verifiable	- Hardly used for political and academic purposes
DHS - 2007 - 8,886 households - Not publicly available	- Ministry of Plan and Health - USAID, DFID, UNICEF, and others - INS, Macro International	Published one year later	Freely accessible through www. measuredhs.com	Good data quality Sampling base problem Poor institutional support and problem of ownership	- Poorly used for political purposes - Hardly used for academic purposes
MICS4 - 2010 - 11,490 households - $2,115,000	- Ministry of Plan - UNICEF, UNFPA, WFP, USAID - INS	Published one year later	Freely accessible through www. childinfo.org	Good data quality Very good institutional support	- Poorly used for political purposes - Hardly used for academic purposes

Source: Based on information from the respective surveys.

So, how many Zairians were there at midnight on 30 June 1984? Following the huge endeavour that constituted the national census, one was finally able to answer this question with great precision: 30,729,443 individuals (INS/PNUD 1991, 232). However, it remained impossible, for example, to establish an age pyramid with the same precision. The reason for this abnormality relates to the processing methodology adopted:

> Due to certain constraints both of a technical and physical nature, the exploitation of census data was done following a two-step procedure: first, an exhaustive exploitation of the household sheet was pursued in order to obtain exact totals, and second, a *sample* of the individual questionnaires has been exploited to obtain more detailed information on individual characteristics. (INS/PNUD 1991, 229; emphasis added, my translation)

As a result, the corresponding descriptive analysis is rather one of a representative survey with error margins depending on the exact sample design; a sample which in total only covered 10 per cent of all the household records. Manifestly, the intention to exploit the remaining 90 per cent of census data still remains very present. However, until now there has not been any further extraction of data, or has a final report been published or a free access point to the 10 per cent of processed data been created (Ngondo a Pitshandenge et al. 2003, 172).

In light of these observations, it would be only fair to the many people involved in this census project to underline the following four critiques. First, covering but not processing 90 per cent of all household interviews is simply a flagrant waste of human and financial resources.[14] Second, the inaccessibility of the processed data (and lack of active dissemination to universities and research centres) has certainly also prevented the conduct of potentially rich and useful studies for policymakers. Third, one can also rightly consider the publication of a provisional report seven years after the census as an outdated event, at least in the sense that the embedded analysis involved a population that no longer existed at publication date. And finally, among the more implicit objectives of the census project of 1984 was the construction of a sampling base, allowing future sample designs to be nationally representative (Gendreau 1990). Given its incomplete processing, the error margins inherent in each sampling design and certainly those linked to specific subpopulations (such as women and children) will be unnecessarily wider.[15] As will be illustrated below, sampling experts in the DRC are still bearing the consequences of this unresolved issue.

Multiple Indicator Cluster Surveys in 1995 and 2001

During the long transition between the second and the third republic, two Multiple Indicator Cluster Surveys (MICS1 in 1995 and MICS2 in 2001) were carried out to assess the education and health conditions of children and women. The necessity to organise these surveys stems from the World Summit for Children, held in New York in 1990, at which common targets for 1995 and 2000 were set by 159 countries (République démocratique du Congo 2002, 1–2). Each of these surveys was largely financed by UNICEF, executed by the country's National Institute of Statistics (INS) and steered by a joint committee of public authorities and experts of UNICEF (République démocratique du Congo 1996, 2002). For both surveys, the sampling method was multistaged and stratified, the latter ensuring a minimum number of observations in each stratum (République démocratique du Congo 2002, 5). To this end, the national census of 1984 acted as the initial sampling base, despite its important shortcomings (see above) and despite the long interval that separates the MICS surveys from the census. However, during both surveys, the sampling base was gradually updated according to the altered realities observed on the ground (République démocratique du Congo 1996, 21; 2002, 7). Given the budgetary constraints in 1995, the sampling size comprised 4,574 households and was only strictly representative at the national and sector level (République démocratique du Congo 1996, 16). The MICS2 survey of 2001, on the other hand, covered 8,600 households and was also representative at the level of each of the country's 11 provinces (République démocratique du Congo 2002, 5–16).[16]

In contrast to the poor follow-up of the national census, voluminous descriptive reports were published one year after data collection, the availability of which is assured by a digital platform that also groups the underlying data and much additional documentation.[17] This state of affairs of course is a result of the international character and the central place occupied by children within the Millennium Development Goals (MDG). However, for MICS1, there seems to be an important discrepancy between the published results and the raw data.[18] Furthermore, the same MICS1 report makes reference to a composite index (which appears to be the precursor of the more well-known "wealth index" developed in the absence of more direct information on people's income or consumption), without, however, specifying the exact index components or the method of aggregation (République démocratique du Congo 1996, 36). With respect to MICS2, similar problems of consistency between data and report do not seem to exist, as survey results and wealth indices could easily be reproduced.[19]

As a result of these quality differences, and of the more limited representativeness of MICS1, it should not be surprising that the latter survey has barely been used for political or academic purposes. Indeed, only the national report on progress toward the MDGs (République démocratique du Congo 2010) and a local UNICEF report on the same theme (UNICEF-RDC 2011) have actually considered the MICS1 results. The results of MICS2 have been exploited a little more, with references in the country's first Poverty Reduction Strategy Paper, *Document de la stratégie de croissance et de réduction de la pauvreté* (DSCRP1), as well as in the draft version of DSCRP2. Concerning academic exploitation, Google Scholar only returns a very short list of publications that have used the data from MICS1 or MICS2.[20] At the origin of this meagre exploitation, one can identify at least the poor institutional support provided by UNICEF or INS to supply more detailed information when necessary, which forces interested researchers to establish personal relationships with various employees of these institutions.

1-2-3 Survey of 2004–2005

In order to expand the statistical repertoire for drafting the country's first DSCRP, the piloting unit behind this process (UPPE-SRP) ordered the organisation of a major budget survey in 2004–2005. Following the 1-2-3 methodology developed by the French research network on Development, Institutions and Globalisation (DIAL) and the Economic and Statistical Observatory of sub-Saharan Africa (AFRISTAT), this survey was conducted in three phases, each focusing on a different economic aspect: (1) employment; (2) the informal sector; and (3) household consumption. In total, 13,688 households were reached, those in Kinshasa as early in 2004 (the pilot phase of the survey), followed by the households in the rest of the country in 2005. Again, the INS has carried out the survey, but this time not less than five major donors sponsored the project (Institut National de la Statistique, n.d.). In the country's history, there has been no other budget survey of the same size and rigor, and the last initiative of this type dates back to the 1970s, when a number of major cities were surveyed (see above). Despite the huge potential to shed light on the varying microeconomic living conditions across the DRC, a final report on the major results has never been officially published and the datasets are still not freely available (although different versions of the latter do circulate).

For the data files indirectly obtained, the intrinsic quality as well as the coherence between raw data and results (as compiled within the tables of the provisional draft) seem to be fairly good.[21] However, several problems need to be mentioned. One of them is the issue of price data. In the third phase of the survey, households were asked to keep track of their daily food consumption in terms of quantities and prices for a period of around 15 days. However, because most of Congo's food retail relies on local units of volume (like *sakombi*, *ekolo* and *libanga*), and due to the variation of these units across the country, special teams were sent out to weigh the foodstuffs purchased. This would eventually have led to the construction of a standardised price index per food item and locality, by which nominal food consumption could be deflated. Unfortunately, this operation largely failed for several reasons. To name a few: the weighing of food items only occurred on two of the 15 days; the data files comprising this information contained a substantial number of outliers; and this exercise was not carried out in Kinshasa, where use was made of an already existing price list.

Another important problem of the 1-2-3 Survey is its poor ownership, which somewhat logically results from the multiple donors involved and the effect of which is felt in several ways. For example, the expertise and (meta)data of this survey are seriously fragmented over different public departments and their employees, all of them apparently controlling one or some vital parts but none of them having a full overview. This also explains why different versions of the same dataset are in circulation, some of which are more processed and purified than others.

These problems provide clear-cut explanations of why this survey remains highly under-exploited by policy makers and academics. To be sure, one cannot but be astonished that the information from the 1-2-3 Survey has not received more than the meagre analysis presented in the quantitative poverty diagnostic of the DSCRP1. On the other hand, the 1-2-3 data were essential to compute GDP estimates according to the newer SNA1993 (see above).

Comprehensive Food Security and Vulnerability Analysis of 2007–2008

A smaller survey, and for this reason probably also less well known, is the Comprehensive Food Security and Vulnerability Analysis (CFSVA), executed in 2007–2008 by the National Institute of Statistics (INS) and mainly financed by the World Food Program (WFP) to allow for a better targeting of its interventions. Its objective was to improve knowledge about households that suffer from food insecurity and those directly vulnerable to it. To this end, the CFSVA adopted a methodology that is theoretically framed within the livelihoods approach, and therefore data were collected on access and ownership of various sets of capitals and assets (WFP/Ministère du Plan/INS 2008, 24). Primary field data were collected in two stages: the first in 2007, covering five provinces, and the second in 2008, covering the remaining provinces. Unfortunately, the province of Kinshasa, together with the entire urban sector of all provinces, were not included in this survey. In total, the sample comprised 3,236 rural families, which were selected after stratification of the sample base into seven agroecological zones. As such, the results only relate to the country's rural sector and are representative at the stratum and provincial level (WFP/Ministère du Plan/INS 2008, 22–23).

Until now, the raw data of this survey could not be recovered, neither at the WFP headquarters in Rome nor at the local office in Kinshasa. Consequently, a quality check could not be performed. The CFSVA survey has therefore hardly been used for academic and political purposes.

Demographic and Health Survey (2007) and MICS4 (2010)

Two more national surveys were conducted to examine the level of education and health among women and children: the Demographic and Health Survey (DHS) in 2007 and the fourth generation of the Multiple Indicator Cluster Survey (MICS4) in 2010. The methodology followed by DHS is very similar to that of MICS4.[22] The DHS survey was financed by a group of donors (US Agency for International Development [USAID] being the most important one) and technically administered by Macro International, an American agency charged with the supervision of this type of survey around the world. By contrast, the MICS4 survey was largely run and financed by UNICEF. Given the international dimension of both surveys, official reports and data can be easily downloaded. The quality of the latter in terms of data consistency and coherence is generally very good.

Notwithstanding the many similarities between DHS and MICS4, there are also a few important differences that prevent a straightforward comparison of results. In this respect, three elements need to be mentioned. First, during and after the execution of the DHS survey, serious administration and ownership problems occurred. For example, the analysis of the final report was largely done without any involvement of local staff. Simply summarised by a local informant, the data were gathered in the DRC and studied in the USA, and the only parts of this entire operation that returned to Kinshasa were the final datasets and report. As a result, no one in Kinshasa seems able to provide more information on the exact construction of any particular indicator, as is the case for the wealth index. Even more astonishingly, Macro International itself seems unable to supply more detail on the construction of this index, because the corresponding syntax file allegedly could not be retrieved.[23] Given the magnitude of public funds directed to this survey, these problems are simply unacceptable. By contrast, high degrees of local ownership exist for the MICS4 survey and the institutional support provided by UNICEF in this respect is also very good.

Second, the incomplete processing of the 1984 census data (see above) has always bothered local sampling experts, but it became crucial during the period in which the DHS was prepared. As discussed above, the sampling base that originates from the census data would be updated by field observations each time a new survey was executed. However, during the execution of the 1-2-3 Survey in 2004–2005, serious disagreements arose around the last actualisation. Since no agreement seemed reachable in the short run, the sample design of the DHS had to be based on a projection of the last undisputed sampling base, which dated back to 2003 (République démocratique du Congo 2008a, 314). Meanwhile, before launching the MICS4 project, local demographers again agreed on a more updated version of the sampling base. The most important consequence of this episode relates to the marked difference in the relative size of the sectors. Whereas the sample design of the DHS assumed 40 per cent of all Congolese to be living in the urban sector (République démocratique du Congo 2008a, 314), the MICS4 survey assumed a 30/70 ratio between the urban and rural sector (République démocratique du Congo 2011a).

The impact of these varying sample designs on the final results is difficult to assess in general, as it will differ from one indicator to another. To illustrate this, consider Table 2, which compares the figures from 2001, 2007 and 2010 on the percentage of each province's population reported to live in the urban sector; those reported to own a radio; and the ratio of girls to boys in school (combining primary, secondary and tertiary education). Concerning the degree of urbanisation, Table 2 clearly indicates that the potential overestimation of the urban sector in 2007, compared to 2001 and 2010, is a common feature shared by all provinces (except for Orientale). As a result, one can assume that phenomena that are intrinsically related to the sector of residence will reflect this. Indeed, the percentage of households owning a radio is, nearly everywhere, substantially higher in 2007 than in 2001 and 2010. Since it is difficult to think of another reason why radio ownership first increases then decreases, it seems fair to attribute this trend to changes in the underlying sampling base. On the other hand, the impact of this sampling issue on variables with a less straightforward connection to the sector of residence is also less predictable. Indeed, the trend of gender balance in schooling clearly follows a different and more mixed pattern than was the case for radio ownership.

Table 2. Impact of a potentially biased sampling base: demographic data reported in three different years and surveys, by DRC province.

Province	% living in urban sector			% ownership of radio			Ratio girls/boys in school		
	2001	2007	2010	2001	2007	2010	2001	2007	2010
Kinshasa	100	100	100	55	70	69	99	97	100
Bas-Congo	22	30	15	34	59	55	100	101	107
Bandundu	13	21	13	21	38	32	92	85	98
Équateur	13	26	14	16	28	22	75	107	89
Orientale	21	15	18	28	34	38	92	96	99
North Kivu	12	25	20	10	50	51	80	100	95
Maniema	25	41	19	34	45	43	103	96	89
South Kivu	14	26	20	30	51	44	85	71	91
Katanga	41	56	29	24	47	40	88	97	83
Kasaï-Oriental	39	50	42	35	49	33	93	97	89
Kasaï-Occidental	23	35	13	31	40	24	80	85	83
Total	31	40	30	29	45	41	89	95	93

Source: Based on the MICS2 survey of 2001 (République démocratique du Congo 2002), the Demographic Health Survey (DHS) of 2007 (République démocratique du Congo 2008a), MICS4 2010 (République démocratique du Congo 2011a) and UNICEF-RDC (2011).

Third, several indicators are defined differently in DHS and MICS4. Apart from the difference in methods to obtain child mortality estimates (see above), the method of measuring school enrolment was also slightly different. Whereas the DHS relied on a more conventional indicator of schooling (République démocratique du Congo 2008a, 17), the MICS4 made use of "adjusted" enrolment rates, which also include children from a higher educational level than their age would indicate (République démocratique du Congo 2011a, 151).[24] Partly as a result of all this, the political as well as academic exploitation of both surveys remains rather poor.

Sampling base and national election data

Given its importance, the present section will focus once more on the country's problematic sampling base, this time by considering data coming from the national elections organised in 2006 and 2011. Despite the fact that election data are genuinely different from survey data, they do allow us to shed light on the credibility of either the sample base used in previous surveys or the election results. Indeed, in a society largely characterised by its informal nature, every interaction with the state becomes important for the day on which the latter again fully assumes its role. It is exactly within this logic that most Congolese tried at all costs to obtain their voting card; these were considered identity cards. Consequently, statistics on the number of people enrolled for the elections of 2006 and 2011 and their geographical distribution can be treated as a sort of census data; once, of course, they have been sufficiently corrected to account for the non-voting population.[25]

Table 3 presents the geographical distribution of the Congolese population between 1984 and 2011, adding election data to the sample base information used for surveys. Overall, the population more than doubled, from approximately 31 million to around 69 million inhabitants, over the period considered. This increase in population size corresponds to an average annual growth rate of 3 per cent. Compared with this, the annual rate for the period 1984–2006 is relatively low (2.7%), which may point to a possible underestimation of the real population size in

Table 3.   Geographical distribution of the Congolese population according to various surveys and election data, 1984–2011 (in thousands).

	Census 1984	MICS1 1995	MICS2 2001	1-2-3 Survey 2004–2005	Election 2006	DHS 2007	MICS4 2010	Election 2011
Kinshasa	2664	4787	6062	5751	5573	7567	7916	6182
Bas-Congo	1994	2835	3353	3207	2505	3224	4285	3054
Bandundu	3769	5201	6053	6304	6074	9212	7388	7318
Équateur	3576	4820	5561	5751	6293	8225	7559	8383
Orientale	4314	5566	6263	6581	6513	8488	7628	7772
North Kivu	5392	3453	4068	4479	5711	2632	6103	6967
Maniema		1205	1420	1548	1310	1974	1953	1819
South Kivu		2990	3522	3926	3907	2829	4968	4742
Katanga	3980	4125	6390	8737	8036	7501	11276	10570
Kasaï-Oriental	2646	3830	5114	4756	4578	7567	5731	5988
Kasaï-Occidental	2396	3337	4293	4258	4672	6580	4251	6100
Total	30731	42150	52099	55300	55173	65800	69059	68895
Annual growth rate (base=1984)	–	2.9%	3.2%	2.8%	2.7%	3.4%	3.2%	3.0%
% urban	28.0%	–	31.3%	30.4%	–	40.0%	30.3%	–

Note: This table was compiled by relying on the sample base information used in the different surveys. For the years 2006 and 2011, data on the number of people enrolled for the elections were inflated by a series of region-specific coefficients in order to include the non-voting population. These coefficients were derived from the 1-2-3 Survey (2004–2005). The CFSVA survey was not considered in this demographic overview as its coverage was limited to the rural sector.
Sources: Based on the census data from 1984 (INS/PNUD 1991), sample base information from the various surveys mentioned and election data as published by CENI (2012).

2006, at least when election data are taken for granted. A straightforward explanation for this observation may be a lack of interest by some people to register for the elections in 2006, or, more importantly, the many logistical difficulties encountered in doing so. In any case, the underestimation is still quite modest, if compared with the previous year,[26] which underscores our assumption that there was a massive rush to obtain voting cards.

On the other hand, for the period 1984–2007, the growth rate is relatively high (3.4%), which may indicate an overestimation of the population size in 2007. In this case, it is more difficult to find a convincing explanation for this deviant number. In fact, several demographic aspects of the 2007 survey are at least a little strange. First, compared to population trends observed in the sample base of other surveys, DHS seems to have considerably overestimated the population size in the provinces of Bandundu, Équateur and both the Kasaï, as well as strongly underestimating that of both Kivus and Katanga. Second, as discussed above, the DHS assumed that 40 per cent of all Congolese lived in the urban sector, a hypothesis that is not shared by any other survey. Therefore, and given the overall consistency observed between the population data originating from the national census, the several MICS surveys and the election results – which in total cover a period of more than 25 years – the DHS survey should only be used with a great deal of caution.

Conclusions

In most cases, data and datasets are not peer-reviewed. If, in addition, insufficient metadata is provided alongside, they become at least questionable, if not unreliable. Many aspects of the

Congolese information architecture between 1970 and 2010 indeed merit the latter label, though an important quality distinction should be made between country statistics and survey data.

Many country statistics on the DRC do not constitute a series of pure data observations, but result from multiple sorts of estimation, permutation and even negotiation of data. A case in point is GDP per capita, the primary country statistic to measure development, which has proven to be a very dubious outcome of an obscure estimation process unable to account for activities taking place in the sizeable informal sector. Furthermore, in cases in which a more direct comparison of primary data and aggregate statistics is feasible, clear discrepancies occur. This observation applies, for example, to several survival statistics, the construction of which should ultimately be based on survey data, but the aggregate statistics seem to point to a slightly more optimistic trend during the period of economic crisis compared to the microdata.

By contrast, survey information is particularly challenging to use, not so much because of the quality of primary data itself (which by and large is fairly good), but because of its limited accessibility, fragmented metadata, and other features that impede its exploitation. The most important issue in this respect is the problematic sampling base. All sampling designs since 1984 heavily depend on the scanty 10 per cent of census data that has been processed, and around which occasionally fierce commotion arises, as was the case for the DHS survey with its unconventional sampling base. Another area of major concern is price data, which are necessary to make meaningful welfare comparisons of household budgets. All this has certainly contributed to a glaring underexploitation of available survey data, both for political and academic purposes. To put it crudely, most surveys have only been used to write a descriptive report on some main observations before they end up at the back of a drawer, gathering dust.

The overall conclusion to draw from this more contextual reading of the Congolese data and statistics is that the numbers cannot be dismissed altogether, but must be used with utmost care and sufficient attention to the many warning signs that go with them.

Acknowledgements

The authors are grateful to the editors of this journal and two anonymous referees for their insightful and constructive comments. The authors also acknowledge the valuable input of Fidèle Bikangi, Dieudonné Vangu, Ronald van Dijk, Ivana Bjelic, William Prince, Milorad Kovacevic, Chris Rockmore, Guillaume Muhindo, Florence Marchal, Moise Tshimenga Tshibangu, Doris Wiesmann, Harold Vandermeulen and Stefaan Marysse. As usual, all errors remain the authors' sole responsibility.

Biographical notes

Wim Marivoet holds a PhD in applied economics from the University of Antwerp, Belgium. His research interests include welfare measurement, human development and coping strategies. Geographically, he has mainly published on the Democratic Republic of Congo (DRC).

Tom De Herdt is senior lecturer at the Institute of Development Policy and Management (IOB) at the University of Antwerp, Belgium. His research interests include capabilities, local governance and social norms. He has mainly published on poverty, governance and reconstruction in the DRC but has occasionally done work on Nicaragua, Rwanda and Cameroon.

Notes

1. This quotation comes from an international economic expert and forms the title of Gill's (1993) critique on the more conventional methods of (rural) poverty research.
2. Furthermore, to allow international comparisons, a conversion to international dollars is required, which has also proved problematic in case of the DRC (see De Herdt 2004, 25–26).

3. In line with the remarks above, the WDI (World Development Indicators) estimates for the years 2005–2010 downloaded in June 2012 indeed differ (slightly) from those downloaded in June 2013.

4. The precise status of this revision has been very confusing, and actually still is. For some time, the metadata of the WDI database certified GDP data of the DRC with an SNA1993 label. After some intense email traffic between Kinshasa, New York and Washington, a data specialist at the World Bank finally admitted that "the note in WDI is premature", and it was later modified to reflect current practice (which is SNA1968). However, the World Economic Outlook database of the IMF (versions October 2012 and April 2013) still erroneously state that the DRC already made this transfer to SNA1993 (see metadata of the World Economic Outlook).

5. This was more or less openly admitted by the chief of state: "Tout se vend et tout s'achète dans ce pays. Et dans ce traffic, le moindre accès au pouvoir public constitue un veritable instrument d'échange, convertible dans l'acquisition illicite de monnaie ou d'autres biens, ou dans l'évasion de toutes sortes d'obligations". Opening speech for the 11th extraordinary conference of the MPR, 25 November 1977.

6. An important exception to this might be Cour (1989).

7. This insight may at least also explain why official estimates increasingly converged over time, as noted in Figure 2.

8. Again, the metadata of the World Economic Outlook show sloppiness, as it states this last census occurred in 1983.

9. Besides, this death toll is also subject to serious debate, as estimates seem to vary between approximately 200,000 (Lambert and Lohlé-Tart 2008) and 4.6 million (Coghlan et al. 2008) casualties. A similar debate on numbers arose after the administrative census carried out in 1970, which further increased the need to organise a national census (see below).

10. This upward revision (based on the 1-2-3 Survey of 2004–2005) would amount to 57 per cent, and this same figure seems to apply to each year between 2006 and 2010 (République démocratique du Congo 2011b, annex 3). This latter aspect again underscores the fact that most series do not provide pure data observations but result from extrapolating a single observation to several successive years.

11. Overall, this paper draws on a research experience of more than seven years, including multiple short-term missions and one longer research stay with an internship at the National Institute of Statistics in Kinshasa.

12. For a more detailed historical overview of the country's demography between 1887 and 1992, see Akoto Mandjale and Iba Ngambong (1992, 13–32).

13. Whereas the second study was assigned to the Department of Demography within the Catholic University of Louvain, the first one was supervised by Joseph Houyoux of the Department of Sociology within the same university and largely financed by SICAI. Given their timing, their methodological comparability and their focus on household budget and assets, these city surveys offer a nice window to analyse the evolution in Congolese livelihoods over the period 1970–2010. In fact, Houyoux and his team repeated the same exercise in some cities in the eastern part of the country during the 1970s, as well as in Kinshasa in 1969 and 1986.

14. To give an idea, almost 1,000 people have been employed at the central headquarters in Kinshasa for an extended period of time, and not less than 45,000 individuals were directly involved in the field for several weeks (République du Zaïre 1982). On the financial side, it has been too complicated to determine the total cost of this census operation, but estimates for the upcoming census (scheduled for 2014) amount to 170 million dollars (Muhindo 2010). Both this estimate and the officially reported costs of many national surveys (as summarised in Table 1) seem high, even for Western standards, which may point to financial corruption. However, transportation of polltakers to the many remote corners of the country is very costly, and basic infrastructure (like electricity) and computer facilities at every cycle also often need updating.

15. For all national household surveys discussed in this paper, a stratified multistage sampling design typically applies. To stratify, each province (except for Kinshasa) is typically subdivided into three sectors, for which the following primary sampling units are used: (1) neighbourhoods in statutory cities; (2) other/smaller cities; and (3) collectivities of villages ("secteurs/chefferies"). For the latter two sectors, a second-stage sampling often procedes the final sampling of households, which may involve different (but often pragmatic) procedures.

16. Complementary to this sample and financed by USAID, another 1,683 families were surveyed to obtain data on immunisation coverage (République démocratique du Congo 2002, 7).

17. This platform is freely accessible after registration at www.childinfo.org. However, the raw data of MICS1 are not directly available on site, although they can be obtained upon request.

18. A more detailed investigation revealed that this discrepancy is probably due to an erroneous coding of some geographical variables for a limited number of observations. Unfortunately, without knowing the precise underlying data protocols, it was impossible to solve this issue.
19. However, a substantial (but isolated) problem exists for the majority of household assets surveyed in MICS2. More precisely, only a few assets were recorded in both the urban and rural sectors, despite their very large presence in both environments and their occurrence on both questionnaires.
20. One important exception in this respect is the National Human Development Report of 2008 (République démocratique du Congo 2008b), which made substantial use of the MICS1 and MICS2 datasets.
21. However, some modules within Phase 3 (like the one on material and financial patrimony [module 25] or on perceptions of living conditions [module 26]) do not seem to have been (correctly) conducted.
22. Given this methodological and thematic comparability, the DHS survey of 2007 can easily be considered as a MICS survey of the third generation, which then also explains the sudden shift from MICS2 to MICS4.
23. Moreover, even by relying on more general technical notes and those used for other sub-Saharan African countries, the reproduction of the wealth index was only possible for 79 per cent of all observations.
24. Unfortunately, this adjustment was not part of the previous MICS survey results either, which also complicates any straightforward comparison in this respect.
25. Similar to the selection bias introduced in many surveys' sample design, voter registration has likely been lower in many conflict-prone areas in the east of the country, which has been under the shifting control of rebels and insurgents of different kinds.
26. It involves a difference of less than 130,000 people, or around 0.2 per cent of the estimated population in 2004–2005.

References

Akoto Mandjale, E., and O. Iba Ngambong. 1992. "Démographie zaïroise (du début de la colonisation à nos jours)." In *Médecine et hygiène en Afrique centrale de 1885 à nos jours*, edited by P. G. Janssens, M. Kivits, and J. Vuylsteke, 13–32. Brussels: Fondation Roi Baudouin.

Atzberger, C. 2013. "Advances in Remote Sensing of Agriculture: Context Description, Existing Operational Monitoring Systems and Major Information Needs." *Remote Sensing* 5: 949–981.

Banque Centrale du Congo (BCC). 2013. "Production Intérieur Brut (PIB) constant au prix de 2000." Banque Centrale du Congo. Accessed August 19. http://www.bcc.cd/index.php?option=com_content&view=article&id=150:production-interieur-brut-pib-constant-au-prix-de-2000&catid=73:secteur-reel&Itemid=101

Beck, L. R., B. M. Lobitz, and B. L. Wood. 2000. "Remote Sensing and Human Health: New Sensors and New Opportunities." *Emerging Infectious Diseases* 6 (3): 217–227.

Bézy, F., J.-P. Peemans, and J.-M. Wautelet. 1981. *Accumulation et sous-développement au Zaïre 1960–1980*. Louvain-la-Neuve: Presses universitaires de Louvain (UCL).

Commission Électorale Nationale Indépendante (CENI). 2012. *Les élections présidentielles et législatives du 28 Novembre 2011 en RDC, Défis, stratégies et résultats*. Kinshasa: Commission Électorale Nationale Indépendante.

Chambers, R. 2007. *Poverty Research: Methodologies, Mindsets and Multidimensionality*. IDS Working Paper 293. Brighton: Institute of Development Studies.

Coghlan, B., R Brennan, P. Nagoy, F. Mulumba, C. Hardy, V. Nkamgang Bemo, T. Stewart, and J. Lewis. 2008. *Mortality in the Democratic Republic of Congo: An Ongoing Crisis*. New York: International Rescue Committee.

Cour, J.-M., 1989. *The Unrecorded Economy of Zaire and its Contribution to the Real Economy*. Washington, DC: International Monetary Fund.

Conference Board. 2013. "Total Economy Database." The Conference Board. Accessed August 19. http://www.conference-board.org/data/economydatabase

De Herdt, T. 2002. "Democracy & the Money Machine in Zaire." *Review of African Political Economy* 93/94: 445–462.

De Herdt, T. 2004. *Comment mesurer la pauvreté: Une déconstruction méthodologique de l'évolution de la pauvreté monétaire à Kisenso (Kinshasa RDC), 1997–2002*. Discussion Paper 2004-6. Antwerp: Institute of Development Policy and Management (IOB).

De Herdt, T., and S. Marysse. 1996. *L'économie informelle au Zaïre, (Sur)vie et pauvreté dans la période de transition*. Brussels: Institut Africain-CEDAF.

De Herdt, T., and S. Marysse. 1997. "Against all Odds: Coping with Regress in Kinshasa, Zaire." *European Journal of Development Research* 9 (1): 209–230.

Devarajan, S. 2013. "Africa's Statistical Tragedy." *Review of Income and Wealth* 59 (special issue): S9–S15.

Dibwe dia Mwembu, D. 1999. "L'épuration ethnique au Katanga et l'éthique du redressement des torts du passé." *Revue Canadienne des Études Africaines* 33 (2/3): 483–499.

Eurostat. 2011. *Essential SNA: Building the Basics*. Luxembourg: Publications Office of the European Union.

Gendreau, F. 1990. "À propos de recensement … comptes africains." *Politique Africaine* 40: 125–129.

Ghosh, T., R. L. Powell, C. D. Elvidge, K. E. Bough, P. C. Sutton, and S. Anderson. 2010. "Shedding Light on the Global Distribution of Economic Activity." *The Open Geography Journal* 3: 147–160.

Gill, G. J. 1993. *O.K., the Data's Lousy, But It's All We've Got (Being a Critique of Conventional Methods)*. London: International Institute for Environment and Development, IIED Gatekeeper Series 38.

Henderson, J. V., A. Storeygard, and D. N. Weil. 2012. "Measuring Economic Growth from Outer Space." *American Economic Review* 102 (2): 994–1028.

Herderschee, J., K.-A. Kaiser, and D. Mukoko Samba. 2012. *Resilience of an African Giant: Boosting Growth and Development in the Democratic Republic of Congo*. Washington, DC: World Bank.

Heston, A., R. Summers, and B. Aten. 2012. *Penn World Table (version 7.1.)*. Philadelphia, PA: Center for International Comparisons of Production, Income and Prices, University of Pennsylvania.

International Food Policy Research Institute (IFPRI). 2011. *Global Hunger Index 2011, The Challenge of Hunger: Taming Price Spikes and Excessive Food Price Volatility*. Washington, DC: International Food Policy Research Institute.

Inter-agency Group for Child Mortality Estimation (IGME). 2007. *Levels and Trends of Child Mortality in 2006*. New York: IGME (UNICEF/World HealthOrganisation/World Bank/UN Population Division).

Inter-agency Group for Child Mortality Estimation (IGME). 2012. "Child Mortality Estimates (CME Info) – Democratic Republic of Congo." Child Mortality Estimates. Accessed August 19, 2013. http://www.childmortality.org/index.php?r=site/graph&ID=COD_Congo%20DR

International Monetary Fund (IMF). 2012. "World Economic Outlook Database." International Monetary Fund. Accessed August 19, 2013. http://www.imf.org/external/pubs/ft/weo/2012/02/weodata/weorept.aspx?sy=1980&ey=2010&ssm=1&scsm=1&ssd=1&sort=country&ds=.&br=1&c=636&s=NGDP_R&grp=0&a=&pr1.x=24&pr1.y=8

Institut National de la Statistique (INS). n.d. *Enquête 1-2-3 (2004–2005)*. Kinshasa: INS (unpublished report).

Institut National de la Statistique and Programme des Nations Unies pour le Développement (INS/PNUD). 1991. "Zaïre: un aperçu démographique. Résultats du recensement scientifique de la population en 1984." *Zaïre-Afrique* 255 : 227–261.

Jerven, M. 2013. *Poor Numbers, How We Are Misled by African Development Statistics and What to Do about It*. Ithaca, NY: Cornell University Press.

Jerven, M., and M. E. Duncan. 2012. "Revising GDP Estimates in Sub-Saharan Africa: Lessons from Ghana." *The African Statistical Journal* 15: 13–22.

Kalombo N'Tambwe. 1986. *Avis et considérations sur les statistiques démographiques au Zaïre*. Kinshasa: Pragma Corporation.

Lambert, A., and L. Lohlé-Tart. 2008. "La surmortalité au Congo (RDC) durant les troubles de 1998–2004: une estimation des décès en surnombre, scientifiquement fondée à partir des méthodes de la démographie." Association pour le Développement de la Recherche Appliquée en Sciences Sociales. Accessed August 19. 2013. http://adrass.net

Lopez, A. D., O. B. Ahmad, M. Guillot, M. Inoue, B. D. Ferguson, and J. A. Salomon. 2001. *Life Tables for 191 Countries for 2000: Data, Methods, Results*. GPE Discussion Paper 40. Geneva: World Health Organisation.

MacGaffey, J. 1987. *Entrepreneurs and Parasites; the Struggle for Indigenous Capitalism in Zaire*. Cambridge: Cambridge University Press.

MacGaffey, J. 1991. *The Real Economy of Zaire; the Contribution of Smuggling and Other Unofficial Activities to National Wealth*. London: James Currey.

Maddison, A. 2008. *Historical Statistics of the World Economy: 1–2008 AD*. Accessed August 19, 2013. http://www.ggdc.net/maddison/Historical_Statistics/horizontal-file_02-2010.xls

Marysse, S. 2005. "Regress, War and Fragile Recovery: The Case of the DR Congo." In *The Political Economy of the Great Lakes Region in Africa, The Pitfalls of Enforced Democracy and Globalization*, edited by S. Marysse and F. Reyntjens, 125–151. New York: Palgrave Macmillan.

Maton, J., K. Schoors, and A. Van Bauwel. 1998. *Congo 1965–1997*. Ghent: University of Ghent.

Muhindo, G. 2010. "Journée africaine des statistiques: il faut 170 millions USD pour recenser la population congolaise." [Radio transmission.] Radio Okapi, November 18.

Ngondo, S., L. de Saint Moulin, and B. Tambashe. 1993. *Perspectives démographiques du Zaïre 1984–1999 et population d'âge électoral en 1993 et 1994*. Kinshasa: Centre d'Etudes Pour l'Action Sociale (CEPAS).

Ngondo a Pitshandenge, S., Ibrahima L. Diop, Daniel M. Sala-Diakanda, and Jean Wakam. 2003. "Anatole Romaniuc: Pioneer in African Demography." *Canadian Studies in Population* 30 (1): 163–177.

Nintunze, D., Moise Tshimenga Tshibangu, Boulel Touré, and Yves Birere. 2012. "Annexe A: Cadrage macroéconomique en provinces." In *Résilience d'un géant Africain: Accélérer la croissance et promouvoir l'emploi en République Démocratique du Congo, Volume I, Synthèse, contexte historique et macroéconomique*, edited by J. Herderschee, D. Mukoko Samba, and M. Tshimenga Tshibangu, 269–286. Kinshasa: Médiaspaul.

République démocratique du Congo. 1996. *Enquête sur la situation des enfants et des femmes au Zaïre 1995 (ENSEF-ZAIRE/1995)*. Kinshasa: INS/UNICEF.

République démocratique du Congo. 2002. *Enquête nationale sur la situation des enfants et des femmes (MICS2/2001)*. Kinshasa: INS/UNICEF.

République démocratique du Congo. 2008a. *Enquête démographique et de santé, République Démocratique du Congo 2007*. Calverton, MD: Ministère du Plan/Macro International.

République démocratique du Congo. 2008b. *Rapport national sur le développement humain: Restauration de la paix et reconstruction*. Kinshasa: Programme des Nations Unies pour le Développement.

République démocratique du Congo. 2010. "Rapport national des progrès des OMD." PNUD. Accessed August 19, 2013. http://www.cd.undp.org

République démocratique du Congo. 2011a. *Enquête par grappes à indicateurs multiples en République Démocratique du Congo (MICS4-RDC 2010)*. Kinshasa: INS/UNICEF.

République démocratique du Congo. 2011b. "Document de la stratégie de croissance et de réduction de la pauvreté de seconde génération (DSCRP2)." Republique Democratique du Congo. Ministère du plan et suivi de la mise en oeuvre de la revolution de la modernité. Accessed August, 19 2013. http://www.plan.gouv.cd/DSCRP2.php

République du Zaïre. 1982. *Recensement scientifique de la population: Aperçu général*. Kinshasa: Commissariat Général au Plan/Secrétariat National de Recensement.

Schneidman, M. 1990. *Mortality and Fertility Trends in Zaire*. Africa Regional Series IDP0080. Washington, DC: World Bank.

Stiglitz, J. E., A. Sen, and J.-P. Fitoussi. 2009. "Rapport de la commission sur la mesure des performances économiques et du progrès social." Commission on the Measurement of Economic Performance and Social Progress. Accessed August 19, 2013. www.stiglitz-sen-fitoussi.fr

Tabutin, D. 1982. "Evolution régionale de la fécondité dans l'ouest du Zaïre." *Population* 37 (1): 29–50.

UNICEF-RDC. 2011. *Les progrès vers l'atteinte des Objectifs du Millénaire pour le Développement en République démocratique du Congo*. Kinshasa: United Nations Children's Fund-Kinshasa.

United Nations Statistics Division (UNSTATS). 2012. "National Accounts Main Aggregates Database." United Nations Statistics Division. Accessed August 19, 2013.http://unstats.un.org/unsd/snaama/metasearch.asp

Vlassenroot, K., and T. Raeymaekers. 2004. *Conflict and Social Transformation in Eastern DR Congo*. Ghent: Academia Press.

World Bank. 2012. *World Development Indicators 2012*. Washington, DC: World Bank.

World Food Program/Ministère du Plan/Institut National de la Statistique (WFP/Ministère du Plan/INS). 2008. "République Démocratique du Congo, Analyse globale de la sécurité alimentaire et de la vulnérabilité (CFSVA), Données: juillet 2007 et février 2008." Programme Alimentaire Mondial. Accessed August 19, 2013. http://fr.wfp.org

Young, A. 2012. *The African Growth Miracle*. NBER Working Paper 18490. Cambridge: National Bureau of Economic Research.

Young, C., and T. Turner. 1985. *The Rise and Decline of the Zairian State*. Madison: University of Wisconsin Press.

The use, abuse and omertà on the "noise" in the data: African democratisation, development and growth

Dwayne Woods

Department of Political Science, Purdue University, West Lafayette, IN, USA

ABSTRACT   This article explores how "noisy" data are used by political scientists researching and publishing on Africa. It posits that the overwhelming evidence that most data on sub-Saharan Africa are "noisy" requires that the use of such data should always take account of this fact. The key analytical question addresses the nature and source, often unknown, of the "noise", and whether or not the errors are randomly distributed such that they do not lead to biased inferences. This critical assessment is done with a survey of several articles and their use of various international and national datasets concerning Africa.

RÉSUMÉ   Cet article discute des erreurs de mesure des données utilisées dans les publications et les enseignements sur l'Afrique subsaharienne en science politique. Tout indiquant que la plupart des données sur l'Afrique subsaharienne sont peu fiables, il soutient qu'on doit en faire un usage circonspect. L'analyse présentée s'intéresse principalement à la nature et à la source du « bruit » dans les données et tente d'estimer si les erreurs sont distribuées au hasard ou systématiques, auquel cas elles mèneront à des conclusions erronées. Sur la base de cette analyse, l'auteur pose un jugement critique sur une sélection d'articles pour la façon dont ils utilisent une diversité de banques de données internationales et nationales sur l'Afrique.

This article discusses the "noise" (or measurement error) in data used in political science publications and teachings on sub-Saharan Africa (SSA). It focuses in particular on the framing that justifies the use of and, at times, abuse of very "noisy" data. Specifically, I look critically at three types of data used by political scientists researching and publishing on sub-Saharan Africa[1]: national income, agricultural and quality of institutions data. This is done in surveying several key articles that employ the three aforementioned types of data to make rather bold causal claims about economic development, institutional capacity and urban bias across SSA. The article examines why the "noise" in the data is either downplayed or ignored – often justified with the proverbial comment that data are inherently "noisy".

This proverbial justification does not suffice when "noisy" data is synonymous with measurement error (Lee, Ridder, and Strauss 2010). "Noisy" data is defined as variables that do not exactly equal the variables of interest or are mismeasured. Thus, the key analytical issue is the nature and source, often unknown, of the "noise" and whether the errors are randomly distributed in such a way that does not lead to biased inferences. "Noise" is not always randomly distributed nor can it be easily set aside using statistical controls. In some instances, the "noise" is actually indicative of the lack of quality of the data. Without fully taking this aspect of the data into consideration, many studies are introducing bias into their analyses at the inception (Young 2009; Treier and Jackman 2008).

My survey of several articles and their use of various datasets is not an explicit critique of their empirical findings or of their theoretical claims and tested hypotheses. It is, however, a critical questioning of the failure by many who research and publish on SSA not to address more openly problems with the "noise" in the data that they use. In other words, do these articles treat it as a serious issue that a priori indicates that whatever their empirical results might be, they are in some ways biased because of the "noise" in the data? Or do they attempt to minimise the "noise" with different statistical techniques or claim that the "noise" is likely to be randomly distributed such that it does not bias anything systematically? The core argument in this article is that the overwhelming evidence that a lot of the data from or about SSA are "noisy" requires that the use of data regarding the continent should take account of this fact. My contribution is to bring these critical aspects of data use, abuse and omertà by political scientists to the forefront in African studies.

Conceptual issues with the use of data

The proverbial statement that there will always be "noise" in the data is self-evidently true. Thus the question is: what is the nature and sources of the "noise"? However, even before getting to the level of measurement, "noise" in the data should be treated as part of conceptualisation (Clarke and Primo 2012; Poovey 1998). In this regard, Schedler (2012a) makes a good point that judgment regarding the conceptual basis of the data we use should always be at the forefront. Schedler's contention overlaps with Peter Hall's (2003) injunction that everything of interest to social scientists cannot be measured in the same way. The nature and quality of data determine the kinds of methods and inferences that can be made. Inconsistent values, or numerous missing values in datasets, and unknown information about certain things such as the actual level of poverty, economic growth rate or population size in many sub-Saharan African countries strongly suggest that the incorporation of "noisy" data of this nature is an illustration of a failure in conceptual judgment.

The failure most likely arises from two imperatives that influence what is published and what is not. The first imperative is to prove a theory. General theoretical propositions are formulated in the language of hypothesis testing and then checked for robustness in relationship to the data (Shapiro 2002). Confidence in the theory and the data rests largely on statistical significance (Ziliak and McCloskey 2008). In a broad range of studies, statistical significance is treated as a confirmation of substantive theoretical claims and confidence in the quality of the data (Gerber and Malhotra 2008). While the issue of the source and quality of data is not limited to sub-Saharan Africa (Hawken and Munck 2009; Ross 2006; Roodman 2008; Herrera and Kapur 2007), Morten Jerven has shown (2009, 2011, 2012a, 2012b, 2013a, 2013b) that for SSA validity, quality and reliability issues are acute. In an early study of data issues, Lemke (2003, 121) highlighted the problems:

> Even when data are present, however, the problems of data quality could generate a significant African coefficient. There is evidence that data quality varies with the wealth of a country. James Dawson and coauthors report a strong negative correlation between GDP per capita and the extent of measurement errors in the Penn World Tables ... Well-established variables about growth, the permanent income hypothesis change when they adjust for the systematic bias in Penn World Tables data quality. It would be astonishing if similar systematic variation in data quality did not characterise the correlates of war datasets, the polity compilations, and so on.

Political scientists accept the idea that data do not speak for themselves. They understand that the collection of data and its coding and measurements are inherently problematic. Moreover, even before directly handling data, political scientists recognise that some degree of conceptualisation is required (Goertz 2008). Conceptualisation gets at a variety of issues: operationalisation of data, validity, quality, reliability and equivalence (Schedler 2012a). Unfortunately, while these elements are understood as essential to good data use, they generally fade into the background or are simply ignored in actual practice. Overall, issues of validity, operationalisation, reliability and equivalence are not invoked enough in work on sub-Saharan Africa, despite the fact that political scientists focusing on the continent are the first to highlight institutional weaknesses and other "pathologies" that undermine the quality and reliability of information.

Such critical observations are rarely extended to data on national income, population, agriculture, trade, institutional and poverty because political scientists rely primarily on international agencies for their data on Africa. They turn to the World Bank, the International Monetary Fund (IMF), UNESCO and the Penn World Tables. This degree of reliance on these bodies for data is somewhat ironic given the general consensus that bad and "noisy" data exist everywhere and these international bodies are nothing more than aggregators of national data. Moreover, the quality and reliability of data correlate strongly with a country's level of development and its overall infrastructural capacity in the collection and dissemination of data (Ponomareva and Katayama 2010; Dawson et al. 2001). As Dawson and his coauthors note about the Penn World Tables dataset: "error measurement is highly correlated with many variables of economic interests. It generally is least for countries with high levels of economic growth rates of output per capita and greatest at the other end of the spectrum" (2001, 989). They add that: "this systematic variation in the quality of data tends to bias test of relationships between levels of growth rates of income on the one hand and other economic variables – such as volatility of growth rates and consumption – on the other" (1008). Subsequent studies have abundantly confirmed these observations on the biasing effects of systematic error (Ponomareva and Katayama 2010; Hanoushek, Hajkova, and Filer 2008).

Yet, discussions of data use in relationship to SSA have not reflected the extent of the problem (Yeats 1990; Lemke 2003). In fact, far too many studies exploit various sources of political, social and economic data without bothering to reflect on the problematics of validity, quality, reliability and equivalence. At best, the problem of missing values will be mentioned and various statistical techniques will be employed to deal with the problem; however, the quality and reliability of the data which are not missing are rarely addressed. While the issues of validity, quality and reliability have drawn some attention in the social sciences (Mudde and Schedler 2010; Herrera and Kapur 2007), the subject of equivalence has been somewhat ignored. For example, it is assumed too easily that aggregated data on national income, trade and domestic taxation imply more or less the same thing across units of analysis. Despite recognition long ago that comparative analysis must consider equivalence at both the conceptual and the actual data level (Przeworski and Teune 1970), this is done too little in studies of sub-Saharan Africa (Jerven 2012a). In the following paragraphs, I will define and briefly summarise issues of validity, quality, reliability and equivalence in regard to data and SSA.

Validity and reliability

Validity goes to the heart of the data issue because, as Herrera and Kapur point out, it "refers to the relationship between theoretical concepts and collected information". In principle, political scientists are sensitive to validity and data because "the objective of information collection in ... research is to enable one to draw inferences and test theories" (2007, 366). In other words, data is just the means through the conceptualised relationship between cause and effect is measured. Thus, "if the connection between what is actually measured and what is purported to have been measured is tenuous (or absent altogether, in some cases), then the inferential relationship between cause and effect makes little sense" (367). Depending on our definition of concepts, different dimensions of the data are included or excluded in our measurements. Rarely do scholars agree on a single or uniform conceptual definition of what is being measured; therefore, this aspect of data validity is always open to question. Since this is so, it is somewhat surprising that measurement validity, as it relates to conceptual dimensions of the data and collection of data, is not always at the center in any data analysis.

Despite the fact that measurement validity is a basic conceptual principle, the use of imprecise or concept-inappropriate indicators remains widespread in the field. Herrera and Kapur (2007, 368) provide some telling examples of caste data – which was last collected in India for the 1931 census – still being used to explain contemporary phenomena. In SAA, they note that out-moded demographic data with margin errors often near 20 per cent are being used with little critical reflection on the distorting effects of such noise in the data. In addition, outdated and questionable measures of ethnicity have been used in a wide range of studies, often resulting in bold claims about how ethnic fractionalisation has hampered democracy or are a key factor in weak economic growth and development on the continent (Easterly and Levine 1997). Obviously, inferences of this kind are conditioned on the validity and reliability of the data (Hug 2013).

Closely tied to the subject of validity is reliability. Although there is a general trend among political scientists to turn to international, national and local sources for official data and then to rework the data – cleaning them up and re-dimensioning measurements to correspond more closely to concepts – the problem of reliability is not really addressed with this undertaking (Schedler and Mudde 2010). It is not uncommon for sources of data to have contradictory information. For example, as Herrera and Kapur (2007, 370) state: "the IMF's primary statistical publication, International Financial Statistics, provides many instances where the data of the same year in books from different years do not match". Or, "the World Bank offers data on GNP per capita growth rates for countries where underlying GNP data do not exist; they also report the share of agriculture in GDP for countries with non-existent GDP estimates" (370). Another example is educational data reported to UNESCO. These data on Africa suffer from huge gaps between years. Even for years in which educational information has been provided, it is sometimes inconsistent with information from previous years.

In a detailed analysis of cross-national differences in educational attainment, Nardulli, Peyton, and Bajjalieh (2012, 1) note:

> Data quality issues in the UNESCO archive are compounded by the fact that countries are not obligated to complete the questionnaire. Consequently, there is a considerable amount of missing data, though it varies by year, country, and region of the world. This is troubling because some of the missing data are systematic (i.e., non-random); they disproportionately affect poor countries or politically isolated entities that lack either the resources or the will to complete the survey. There is also a geographical bias; most of the countries lacking data are African, Asian, Middle Eastern or Southeast Asian; after the break-up of the Soviet Union much data are missing for the post-Soviet States.

As the above statement makes clear, the lack of reliability in the data is not random. There is a systematic bias in missing data from certain regions and within regions from specific countries.

Despite the potential bias effect of missing data (non-random), David Stasavage (2005) argued that democratic regimes in SSA spent more on primary education than non-democracies. Although he acknowledged the problem of missing data, he asserted that the use of imputation software for missing values had sufficed in dealing with the problem. This, however, is not the case since, in some instances, the missing values outnumbered the reported values substantially and the systematic bias aspect was not solved with statistical imputation techniques (Ross 2006, 866). The problem of the reliability of the data provided by many African governments and the numerous missing values in some cases make it difficult to believe that there was not systemic bias in Stasavage's regression of education by regime type.

Missing, incomplete or absent data obviously compound problems of validity. In many cross-national comparisons in which Africa is included: "data on key variables of interest to scholars and governments are either incomplete or simply not collected at all" (Herrera and Kapur 2007, 368). The use of proxies does not really help matters (Nathan 2005). Lemke underscores the difficulties in his 2003 assessment of the effect of missing, incomplete or absent data on scholarship on international relations and Africa's place in it. He highlights several earlier studies that used problematic data on Africa and consequently produced supposedly robust results that are suspect. For instance, the dyadic probability of war literature has produced results that are statistically significant and their estimated effects are consistent with theory. However, as Lemke (2003) notes, there is something amiss: the estimated variable for the Africa dyads suggests that countries on the continent are less likely to experience war than non-African countries. Prima facie there is something wrong in the data. Even if the popular perception of Africa as a continent mired in war and conflict is wrong, it is hard to believe that the region is more peaceful than the rest of the world. Evidently, missing and incomplete data were driving the dyadic conflict probabilities. The fact that these studies did not reflect on this type of systematic bias is surprising (Cramer 2006; Nathan 2005).

The source of bias is the data origin and not just the aggregation and dissemination (Schedler 2012b). Many developing countries simply lack the ability to provide quality data due to weak institutional capacity. Even when common "institutional norms" (Herrera 2010) concerning shared collection and accounting practices have been accepted, weak institutional capacity still matters for the introduction of systematic biases in national data. For instance, civil conflicts and major changes in political regimes often impede the state's ability and interest in collecting data. Angola, for example, went nearly a decade without providing any data to UNESCO on primary and secondary schooling (Nardulli, Peyton, and Bajjalieh 2012, 51). As Jerven (2013b) and others have pointed out, the quality, or lack thereof, of data produced by such states' statistical institutions often reflect the limited institutional capacity of the states themselves.

More significantly, as Herrera and Kapur (2007) underscore, the limited capacity of statistical agencies raises problems of endogeneity (Voigt 2013; Kurtz and Schrank 2007; Arndt and Oman 2006; Przeworski 2004). Endogeneity arises when the data are not external to what is being studied. While these data do not suffer from missing values per se, their quality and reliability are affected by weak institutions and collection processes. Efforts to get around this problem by relying on survey data of the quality of government and the rule of law only raises other issues of measurement error and bias (Van de Walle 2006).[2] While the quality of data and even the issue of reliability are not central to the World Bank governance data, problems of sample selection bias are real and, more importantly, the source of the data, based on aggregation of survey samples, raises questions about using them as an objective measurement of institutional capacity (Voigt 2013; Kurtz and Schrank 2007; Glaeser et al. 2004).

In an article using the World Bank's Country Policy and Institutional Assessments (CPIA), Bates and Humphreys (2005) test the logic of accountability and how it correlates with bad governance and lack of overall economic development in Africa. The authors make it clear that they are aware of the limitations of CPIA as a data source. In particular, they understand criticisms about the composite measures of validity and reliability. They claim to resolve these issues "by combining a Barro-like growth regression (which includes the policy ratings) with an empirical model of policy choice (which includes a measure of growth and other controls ...) into a single system of equations using three-stage least squares" (Bates and Humphreys 2005, 416). In doing so, they say they are able "to generate coefficients that provide measures of the relationship of policy to growth that partially account for endogeneity" (416). More importantly, these results indicate that "variation in our measures of policy choices are associated with large differences in growth rates: a one standard deviation shift in QUALITY and CPIA is associated with a shift of approximately 1.2 and 1.3 percentage points in growth rates, respectively" (416).

Underlying problems of what is being measured and how well the concepts of institutional quality map on to empirics, however, are not really addressed with this technique (Sanin, Buitrago, and González 2013). They persist because the national income data upon which the relationship between policy and economic growth is based has not been addressed. In many ways, all that this technique does is amplify the noise in the data. If there is a systematic bias in the reporting of growth rates by national governments in SSA, the coefficients and the standard deviation in the shift of policy quality and growth will mean little. The main point is not that Bates and Humphreys (2005) are necessarily wrong but that "noisy" data undermine the degree of confidence scholars can have in the generalisation they can make – especially when there are good conceptual reasons to doubt the purported empirical relationship (Jerven 2011).

Thus, Kurtz and Schrank's (2007, 551) strong criticism of this type of data is pertinent. They assert that their results show "that the data and conclusions found on the World Bank site – at least with respect to government effectiveness – are at best partial and at worst misleading" and that the noise in the measurements indicates "the beginning rather than the end" of efforts "to unpack the complicated relationship between growth and governance". Leaving aside the issue of the "noise" in the data, Rodrik (2012, 139) argues that little is to be learned from regressing economic growth on policy, since "what is special here is that policy endogeneity is not just an econometric nuisance but typically an integral part of the null hypothesis that is being tested". Consequently, "the supposition that governments are trying to achieve some economic or political objective is at the core of the theoretical framework that is subjected to empirical tests. In such a setting, treating policy as if it were exogenous or random is problematic not just from an econometric standpoint, but also conceptually" (139).

Equivalence

I believe that issues of validity, quality and reliability of data from Africa are often ignored or played down by social scientists because the primary motive for using such data is to establish causal equivalence (Jerven 2012a; Farrell and Finnemore 2009; Kenney and Williams 2001). Regression or logistic models are employed to tease out the relationship specified by some theory. Quantitative models need the data. Data themselves, however, are secondary to the agenda of testing theories. To use an analogy, data are the fuel that is needed to make the models run. Far too often the quality consistency for the use of a certain type of data is not taken into account (Mudde and Schedler 2010). Statistical models rely on some key assumptions, one of them being that the "noise" in the data is, more or less, randomly distributed or not systematic to the data themselves. For instance, it is assumed that national income data are naturally comparable across nation states. As an accounting category that, in principle, reflects the sum of the goods and services that transact in a given economy, this is true. However, the accounting equivalence becomes questionable once the variance in the capacity of states to record and measure their national economies is taken into account. In this sense, "noise" is no longer the typical measurement and reporting errors that all national accounts face. It is a more systematic problem of what is recorded, by whom and for what purposes (Morgan 2009).

In any case, the dominant interest is to assume at the theoretical and conceptual level a degree of equivalency across that which is measured (Sanin, Buitrago, and González 2013). The logic of equivalence is premised on the assumption that contextual effects can be minimised as long as one taps into the right co-variational relationship between variables. This logic is illustrated in Przeworski and Teune's (1967, 554) classic statement on equivalence:

> In formal terms, cross-national analysis is an operation by which a relationship between two or more variables is stated for a defined population of countries. In analysis, no proper names of societies or cultures are mentioned. The goal is not to "understand" Ghana or Cuba, not to describe Hitler, Stalin, Roosevelt, or Churchill, but to see to what extent external crises and internal control, military prowess and economic frustration, nationalism and persecutions, are related, and to know the generality of each relationship. Whether variables are related depends on the observations of Ghana, or Hitler. But these are the observations that are means to an end – the end of testing relationships between variables, even at the cost of obscuring some differences between specific units.

The prevailing discourse of the 1980s and 1990s on the bloated African state is a good illustration of a type of prior equivalence that often shapes interpretation of alleged facts. The view was that the African state was oversized and excessively bureaucratic. Its purported Leviathan characteristics were indicated in many empirical studies as the primary reason for the continent's lack of development and corruption. Tellingly, Arthur Goldsmith, in critical analyses of the African state and its oversized dimensions published in 1999 and 2000, informed us that we actually had very little hard data on the size and extent of most African bureaucracies. The data that did exist failed to support the idea of an oversized Leviathan. In fact, Goldsmith noted (1999, 520, 2000, 4) that in relationship to land mass and populations, many African state bureaucracies appeared to be undersized. Whether this claim is correct is secondary. What is primary is that a plethora of studies and policy prescriptions had been developed based on limited and weak data. The conceptual equivalence that Weberian-like bureaucracies have something to do with development was simply assumed and the conceptual baggage was transported to the continent with few asking the pertinent empirical question: what is the actual size and extent of African states? Moreover, in light of the absence of good statistics on the topic, what is it that is needed to get better data?

This drive to test theories leads political scientists to identify cases that they think are ideal for such purposes. While some effort is made at the theoretical level to identify the equivalencies of what is being measured across heterogeneous cases, the connection between the conceptual equivalence and the proxy data used is often underdeveloped or poorly conceptualised. Take for instance the effort to test political business cycles theory. Since Nordhaus's (1975) seminal article on political business cycles (PBC) theory was published nearly 40 years ago, a rather large literature has emerged within which various academics have attempted to put to the empirical test Nordhaus's core assertion that governments spend more during election cycles. Briefly, the model assumes "the electorate is backward looking and evaluates the government on the basis of its past track record". Consequently, as a result, "governments, regardless of ideological orientation, adopt expansionary fiscal policies in the late year(s) of their term in office in order to stimulate the economy" (Klomp and de Haan 2013, 330). The overall result after numerous studies testing this model is ambiguous. In short, no definitive evidence has emerged to support Nordhaus's (1975) core proposition. Nor has any definitive evidence been identified to categorically reject it. As a result, scholars have engaged in a kind of ratcheting up of sophistication of statistical techniques. Increasingly complex econometric models have been used to slice and dice the data, with the end result still being that of ambiguity. It is generally accepted in the literature that part of the problem arises from the "noise" in the data. Most studies of PBC have been limited to industrialised democracies, with the Organization of Economic Community Development Countries (OECD) the primary source for data.

In a perennial quest to test theory against the data, Block and his coauthors (Block, Ferree, and Singh 2003) have argued that sub-Saharan Africa was ideal for such purposes. They claimed that recent democratisation in Africa and the relative weakness of non-executive powers made the continent an appropriate place to test the model. They implicitly recognised in their study of elections and political business cycles that there were some serious issues with the economic data regarding sub-Saharan Africa budget reporting information to the IMF. The authors recognised difficulties in properly measuring automatic stabilisers, policy formulation and implementation capacity in SSA. They did not, however, believe that data issues outweighed their main objective, which was to test their theory that developing regions with weak institutions but strong executives were likely to engage in politicised spending in periods just before national elections. In the article, the authors stated that "the data used to test our hypothesis includes annual observations (1980–1995) for 44 sub-Saharan African countries (listed in Table 2), creating a panel of 704 country-year observations. Macroeconomic data are drawn from the IMF's International Financial Statistics" (Block, Ferree, and Singh 2003, 452).

Little attention was given to the source of the data, aside from a footnote noting that data were based on budget reports given to the IMF by national governments. However, there are indications that the quality and consistency of data on African government budget expenditures present serious problems. In a detailed study of budget institutions and fiscal performance, Gollwitzer-Franke (2011) points out that African budgets suffer from serious problems in terms of quality of information about them. It is not reasonable to assume that such wide variation in institutional quality did not affect the type of information sent to the IMF. In addition, Gollwitzer-Franke argues that the budget process in Africa is characterised by the following pathologies: "These include unrealistic budgeting, where the approved budget is commonly accepted as a farce; hidden budgeting, where the real budget is known only to a selected few" (119).

It does not matter if the pathologies described above are characteristic of all African states or only a minority of them. Only a few cases would suffice to distort the purported relationship between elections and budget cycles. Thus, an uncritical use of reported annual budget data from the IMF is clearly questionable. The conceptual equivalence established in political business cycle studies is that budget expenditures correspond to political choices tied to elections; however, the budget process itself suffers from opaqueness and instability. It is far from clear that the relationship specified by the authors' model holds in the data. Based on the criteria established by Gollwitzer-Franke to assess budget transparency and credibility, there is a great deal of variation that only partially corresponds to democracy and elections. For example, the author states that Niger and Togo performed well on her criteria, which suggests some confidence in their reported budget numbers, while Botswana, one of Africa's oldest democracies, did less well (2011, 123). What her examples suggest is that institutional capacity and governance can diverge considerably.

Significantly, a study by some economists at the International Monetary Fund found little in the way of support for the PBC thesis. What is particularly insightful from the study is its focus on the many confounding factors that affect political institutions, elections and budgetary expenditures. The authors of this study state that they find "no evidence that political institutions have any effect on the cyclical behavior of fiscal policy". In regard to the data on African institutions, they add that "this may be because institutional quality in sub-Saharan Africa is too low for any variation in political institutions to have much effect on fiscal decision-making or because those political variables do not vary much over time" (Lledó, Yackovlev, and Gadenne 2009, 15).

Making the data link: democracy, development and urban bias

The main use of institutional and national income data in the context of sub-Saharan Africa has been in studies that attempt to test how democratisation has shaped economic and social developments. Several studies have been undertaken to examine whether the transition to democratic regimes in some SSA countries has made a "measurable" difference (Glaeser et al. 2004). These studies are designed to capture temporal changes as well as engage cross-national comparisons. By temporal changes, I mean these studies focus on pre-and-post-democratisation and try to see whether or not economic growth has been better in those countries that have become democracies. What is noteworthy about many of these studies is that they depend on national income data as their primary indicator of economic growth or the lack thereof.

Most of these studies on the relationship between political change and economic performance rely on the Penn World Tables, despite some recent work showing inconsistent results across different regression analyses that use the Penn World Tables. Ciccone and Jarocínski (2010, 243) conclude from their assessment of this particular data source that results are "... sensitive to minor errors in measurement and [...] turn out to differ substantially depending on the income estimates that are being used". Bates and his coauthors, for example, feel so confident in the data that they conclude that the results of their analysis confirm the existence of a positive relationship between the level of democracy and income in sub-Saharan Africa. Overall, they find that "while the sign and significance of the coefficients on the measures of global trends remind us that the performance of Africa's economies are shaped by international forces, the sign and significance of the coefficient on income lends support to what the Granger causality test implies, that in Africa domestic political institutions affect the performance of economies" (Bates, Fayad, and Hoeffler 2013, 328).

When it comes to Africa, many authors feel confident that the relationship they have identified is robust. By employing a panoply of increasingly complex statistical methods and declarations of statistical significance (Wilson and Butler 2007), the underlying issues of what is being measured and how "noisy" the data are are largely ignored. Bates and his coauthors (2013), for example, do not ask at any point whether the noise in the Penn World data might or might not distort their conclusions. But they use the income data to confirm the major changes in institutional capacity and accountability that democratisation has brought about in many African countries. Briefly, Africans who live under democratic regimes are wealthier. The institutional effect is dramatic, they argue, because of the policy distortions of non-democratic regimes in the past. Whether or not democratisation has had the kind of impact they assert is an interesting finding, but it is undermined by the failure on the part of the authors to even mention the problematic nature of both the democratisation measures (Casper and Tufis 2003; Elgie 1998) and the Penn World national income data (Jerven 2013b).

Referring to Ndulu et al.'s (2008) extensive study of the endogenous policy shifts that have occurred in some African countries because of democratisation, Bates, Fayad and Hoeffler (2013, 329) claim that:

> Taken together, the policies were therefore biased against agriculture – the largest single industry in most of Africa's economies in Africa. One result was slow growth. The estimates reported in Ndulu et al. suggest that governments that adopted this mixture of policies lowered their country's rate of growth by nearly two percentage points per annum during 1960–2000.

The problem with their robust conclusions is that they are based on data that are shaky. A number of studies have highlighted the problems with the Penn database; thus, it is inexcusable that Bates and his coauthors spend no time on the subject (Jerven 2012a, 2012b). As stated earlier, any errors that arise from bad data are not likely to be just random; they are likely to be systemic. In fact, the systemic errors arise from the endogenous characteristics of how the data are collected and aggregated.

Bates and his coauthors (2013) simply ignore well established observations concerning problems with national income data. Young (2012, 696–697) begins his article on the "African Growth Miracle" with the following statement:

Much of our current understanding of the factors behind growth and development, and our continuing attempts to deepen that understanding, are based on cross-national estimates of levels and growth rates of real standards of living. Unfortunately, for many of the poorest regions of the world the underlying data supporting existing estimates of living standards are minimal or, in fact, nonexistent. Thus, for example, while the popular Penn World Tables purchasing power parity dataset version 6.1 provided real income estimates for 45 sub-Saharan African countries, in 24 of those countries it did not have any benchmark study of prices. In a similar vein, although the online United Nations National Accounts database provides GDP data in current and constant prices for 47 sub-Saharan countries for each year from 1991 to 2004, the UN Statistical Office, which publishes these figures, had, as of mid-2006, actually received data for only just under half of these 1,410 observations and had, in fact, received no constant price data whatsoever on any year for 15 of the countries for which the complete 1991–2004 online time series are published.

Interestingly, Young's main objective in his article is to argue that Africa has experienced more growth than has been previously accounted for; however, he makes a strong case that traditional sources of data are not reliable enough to make this case one way or another. Ciccone and Jarocínski (2010, 244) underscore Young's argument with their observation that "overall, our findings suggest that margins of error in the available income data are too large for empirical analysis that is agnostic about model specification. It seems doubtful that the available international income data will tell an agnostic about the determinants of economic growth". Here they are referring to the "noise" in global aggregate data, in which Africa's national income data are only part of a larger dataset.

That studies like Bates's fail to acknowledge research that has shown problems with the data suggests that these authors are more interested in supporting their theoretical claims than really engaging with the facts. Their assertion that there is a strong causal relationship between the onset of democratisation and economic growth (Kurtz and Schrank 2007) is all the more surprising given the problems with both institutional and national income measurements. Moreover, they claim that this spurt in growth due to democratisation has occurred in a limited time frame, since they believe that much of the growth of the late 2000s was driven by China's demand for commodities. And this observation is made as if Deaton (1999) and others (Sindzingre 2013) have not already shown the confounding effect that cyclical commodity prices have on economic growth and institutional dynamics. Nor do they cite or factor into their analysis significant critiques of placing too much causal "oomph" on institutions (Fortin 2012; Chang 2011; Engerman and Sokoloff 2008).

The focus on how democratisation and other institutional changes in SSA affect particular outcomes has shifted to the countryside. Bates and Block (2013) discuss how institutional changes in the 1980s has brought an increase in total factor productivity in the African rural sector, ending the stagnation that had characterised agricultures since the early 1960s. They make the claim that democratisation via competitive elections has led to a shift away from an urban bias towards policies more favorable to Africa's rural population (Bates and Block 2013, 378). A number of studies support Bates and Block's claim that there has been an increase in total factor productivity over the years (Alene 2010; Aboagye and Gunjal 2000), but some also highlight problems with the quality and consistency of the data and the difficulties that this poses in making generalisations about the magnitude and source of changes in the African countryside (Jerven 2013a; Olajide 2011; Beyerlee and Murgai 2001).

Whatever the exact relationship is between increased political competition and agriculture productivity in SSA, the fact remains that the primary source of data on the sector is poor. A consortium of international agencies has recently issued an action plan to improve data and knowledge about what has been happening in the African countryside. In a call to action the report highlights the following point:

The importance of the agricultural sector demands that its planning, management, and monitoring be based on sound evidence. This, in turn, requires the sustained availability of comprehensive, reliable, up-to-date, and consistent statistical data. In addition, these data need to be in a form that renders them intelligible and practicable for a variety of users. Unfortunately, agricultural statistical systems and data are in a sorry state in many African countries – the systems are weak, uncoordinated, insufficiently resourced, and essentially unsustainable. Further, their outputs are substandard in terms of quantity, quality, and dissemination. This is despite a number of statistical initiatives that have been put in place and implemented in Africa over recent years. The situation has been exacerbated by new and pressing data requirements to inform policy on emerging development issues such as food vs. bio-fuels, climate change and global warming, environment, and food security. (AFDb, ECA, and AUC 2011, executive summary, xiv)

In a separate article from the one he published with Bates in 2013 in the *Journal of Politics*, Block recognises that there are significant data problems. Block notes (2013, 7) that "the core data on agricultural outputs and inputs are drawn from the FAO online database. While often regarded as being of limited quality, these data are ubiquitous in studies of international agricultural productivity, as they are the only comprehensive and detailed source of cross-country data over a long period of time". Thus, the "noise" in the data is acknowledged but that does not seem to be a sufficient reason for treading cautiously and avoiding making the rather strong assertion that, in those countries which have established some degree of political competition, the purported "urban bias" has ended (Bates and Block 2013, 383).[3]

That this inference is based on such "noisy" and missing data is particularly noteworthy because the thesis of an "urban bias" itself was premised on limited and very "noisy" data. The call for correcting urban bias in SSA through structural adjustment was largely based on the Berg report (1981), which identified it as one of the key impediments to slow economic growth and rural stagnation in Africa. As Jerven (2013b, 167) states: "Berg acknowledged that the statistics he used in his report were only approximate, as statistical resources were lacking. He also pointed out the weak capacity to estimate food production". Ironically, structural adjustment weakened the already limited capacity of most African states to collect data on its agricultural sector. One of the major consequences of this weakening is that we still do not have good comprehensive data on agricultural production and poverty in the African countryside.[4]

Assessment and conclusion

The aim of this essay is to be critical but not dismissive of cross-national studies and the use of data. Data can be used for many different purposes. In some cases, data can be representative of something and in others they can be indicative of processes or trends. Goldsmith's study (1999), for example, provides some indication on how cross-national equivalence might be more effectively employed with weak data. Instead of starting from the theoretical assumption that all states are alike, it seems more appropriate to argue that states in richer countries are more likely to have certain shared characteristics and then use the data to assess what those characteristics are and how they connect to other things. States in poorer regions such as SSA are likely to share similar characteristics and data problems. Thus, our assessment of the actual size and quality of state institutions is likely to be biased by "noisy" data that arise from the very weaknesses of states in poorer countries. Moreover, the variation in the bias is more likely to be indicative of these states than a larger representative data of all states. Atkinson and Brandolini (2001) underscored this observation in their study on problems with data on income inequality among OECD countries. In this respect, intra-SSA comparisons are more likely to provide a better picture of states than a more global comparison that is premised on a problematic assumption of equivalence and, even more importantly, on questionable data.

National income data in most cross-national comparisons are used as if they were representative of a nation's wealth and productive capacities (Jerven 2012a, 2012b). Poor and weak data call into question the representativeness of such comparisons (De la Fuente and Doménach 2006; Deaton 2011). Establishing robust causality is difficult under the best of circumstances, but it is harder with very "noisy" data, whose noise often arises from systematic biases introduced in the way the data are collected and aggregated (Jerven 2013b; Moral-Benito 2012). Claims to have statistically parsed out the "noise" from the "signal" are not always convincing (Dawson et al. 2001). The constant revision and updating of data in rich countries should be enough of a warning that the use of data from poor developing countries to make blanketed and bold claims such as "Africa's lost decade" or "rural stagnation" is problematic. "Noise" in the data that we use as social scientists cannot be dismissed as just random or be assumed away, all things being equal, as a minor nuisance. Instead it requires a deeper reflection on the source of the data and how their use is tied into empirical efforts to establish causal complexity (Antonakis et al. 2010; Braumoeller 2003). Most social scientists will claim that they are interested in testing hypotheses against the background of some theory; however, "the cult of statistical significance" and assertions about the robustness of the given models suggest that establishing causality is what is really at play.

The selection, sources and quality of data matter for a simple reason. The datasets we choose are likely to affect our perception of the world. They are also likely to influence the descriptive and causal inferences we make. Most significantly for Africa, these inferences have real policy consequences on governance, development, poverty and well-being. Thus, if data (single or multiple) are available for a given research purpose and the quality cannot be established unambiguously, then it is imperative to reflect on the data's utility and the types of inferences that can be drawn (Mudde and Schedler 2010, 412). While it is now standard practice in quantitative comparative politics to test the robustness of empirical results, this technique has been confused with checking for "noise" and its distorting effect. The causal inferences made in cross-national research are often highly sensitive to the selection of explanatory variables, the choice of statistical techniques of data analysis and the non-randomness of measurement error – "noise" – in the data (Karcher and Steinberg 2013, 136). As Mudde and Schedler (2010, 412) nicely put it: "this is frustrating to the goal of the accumulative generation of knowledge".

Acknowledgements

I wish to thank Morten Jerven for making this publication possible.

Biographical note

Dwayne Woods is an Associate Professor of Political Science at Purdue University, Indiana, USA. His research interests include the political economy of development, democratisation and populism. His most recent publications are "Conditional Effect of Economic Development on Democracy – The Relevance of the State" (*Democratization*, 2012 [co-authored with Min Tang]) and "A Critical Analysis of the Northern League's Ideographical Profiling" (*Journal of Political Ideologies*, 2010).

Notes

1. Today, the continent suffers from a different tragedy than the "growth tragedy": a statistical tragedy. This may not sound as serious as the growth tragedy, but it too exerts a toll on Africa's poor. I just said that growth has picked up since the mid-1990s and, thanks to that growth, poverty is declining. The statistical tragedy is that we cannot be sure of either of these phenomena (Shantayanan 2013, 1).
2. Because of space limitations, this article does not discuss the "noisy" data on corruption and Africa, but these data suffer from similar problems. See Hawken and Munck (2009).

3. Bates's seminal 1981 book, *Markets and States in Tropical Africa,* was instrumental in establishing the "urban bias" thesis.
4. For more on telling the data what to say, see Mkandawire (2013).

References

Aboagye, Anthony, and Kisan Gunjal. 2000. "An Analysis of Short-Run Response of Export and Domestic Agriculture in Sub-Saharan Africa." *Agricultural Economics* 21: 41–53.

African Development Bank (AFDb), United Nations Economic Commission for Africa (ECA), Food and Agriculture Organization of the United Nations (FAO), and African Union Commission (AUC). 2011. *Improving Statistics for Food Security, Sustainable Agriculture, and Rural Development: An Action Plan for Africa, 2011–2015.* Tunis, Tunisia. http://www.afdb.org/fileadmin/uploads/afdb/Documents/Publications/Improving%20Statistics%20for%20food%20security_Sustainable_Agriculture%20and%20Rural%20Development.pdf

Alene, Agrega D. 2010. "Productivity Growth and the Effects of R&D in African Agriculture." *Agricultural Economics* 41: 223–238.

Antonakis, John, Samuel Bendahan, Philippe Jacquart, and Rafael Lalive. 2010. "On Making Causal Claims: A Review and Recommendations." *The Leadership Quarterly* 21: 1086–1120.

Arndt, Christiane, and Charles Oman. 2006. "Uses and Abuses of Governance Indicators." *OECD Development Center Studies*, 9–115. Paris: OECD.

Atkinson, Anthony B., and A. Brandolini. 2001. "Promise and Pitfalls in the Use of 'Secondary' Data-Sets: Income Inequality in OECD Countries as a Case Study." *Journal of Economic Literature* 39 (3): 771–779.

Bates, Robert H. 1981. *Markets and States in Tropical Africa: The Political Basis of Agriculture Politics.* Berkeley: University of California Press.

Bates, R. H., and Steven Block. 2013. "Revisiting African Agriculture: Institutional Change and Productivity Growth." *Journal of Politics* 75 (2): 372–384.

Bates, R. H., and Macartan Humphreys. 2005. "Political Institutions and Economic Policies: Lessons from Africa." *British Journal of Political Science* 35: 403–428.

Bates, R. H., G. Fayad, and A. Hoeffler. 2013. "The State of Democracy in Sub-Saharan Africa." *International Area Studies Review* 15 (4): 323–338.

Berg, Eliot. 1981. *Accelerated Development in Sub-Saharan Africa: An Agenda for Action.* World Bank Report No. 14030. Washington, DC: World Bank.

Beyerlee, Derek, and R. Murgai. 2001. "Sense and Sustainability Revisited: The Limits of Total Factor Productivity Measures of Sustainable Agricultural Systems." *Agricultural Economics* 26: 227–236.

Block, Steven A. 2013. "The Post-Independence Decline and Rise of Crop Productivity in Sub-Saharan Africa: Measurement and Explanations." Oxford Economics Papers, 23 March. doi: 10.1093/OEP/gpt010.

Block, Steven, A. K. Ferree, and S. S. Singh. 2003. "Multiparty Competition, Founding Elections and Political Business Cycles in Africa." *Journal of African Economies* 12 (3): 444–468.

Braumoeller, Bear F. 2003. "Causal Complexity and the Study of Politics." *Political Analysis* 11 (3): 208–233.

Casper, Gretchen, and Claudiu Tufis. 2003. "Correlation versus Interchangeability: The Limited Robustness of Empirical Findings on Democracy Using Highly Correlated Data Sets." *Political Analysis* 11 (2): 196–203.

Chang, Ha-Joon. 2011. "Institutions and Economic Development: Theory, Policy and History." *Journal of Institutional Economics* 7 (4): 473–498.

Ciccone, Antonoio, and Marek Jarocínski. 2010. "Determinants of Economic Growth: Will the Data Tell?" *American Economic Journal: Macroeconomics* 2 (4): 222–246.

Clarke, Kevin A., and David M. Primo. 2012. *A Model Discipline: Political Science and the Logic of Representation.* Oxford: Oxford University Press.

Cramer, Chrisopher. 2006. *War is Not a Stupid Thing: Accounting for Violence in Developing Countries.* London: Hurst & Company.

Dawson, James W., J. P. DeJuan, J. J. Seater, and E. F. Stephenson. 2001. "Economic Information versus Quality in Cross-Country Data." *Canadian Journal of Economics* 34 (4): 365–386.

De la Fuente, Angel, and Rafael Doménach. 2006. "Human Capital in Growth Regression: How Much Difference Does Data Quality Make?" *Journal of the European Economic Association* 4 (1): 1–36.

Deaton, Angus. 1999. "Commodity Prices and Growth in Africa." *Journal of Economic Perspectives* 13 (3): 23–40.

Deaton, A. 2011. "Measuring Development: Different Data, Different Conclusions?" In *Measure for Measure: How Well Do We Measure Development*. Proceedings of the 8th AFD-EUDN Conference, Paris, December, Chapter 1. http://www.princeton.edu/~deaton/downloads/deaton_different_data_different_conclusions_paris_2010.pdf

Easterly, William, and R. Levine. 1997. "Africa's Growth Tragedy: Policies and Ethnic Divisions." *Quarterly Journal of Economics* 11 (2): 1203–1250.

Elgie, R. 1998. "The Classification of Democratic Regime Types: Conceptual Ambiguity and Contestable Assumptions." *European Journal of Political Research* 33 (2): 219–238.

Engerman, Stanley L., and Kenneth L. Sokoloff. 2008. "Debating the Role of Institutions in Political and Economic Development: Theory, History, and Findings." *Annual Review of Political Science* 11: 119–135.

Farrell, Henry, and Martha Finnemore. 2009. "Ontology, Methodology and Causation in the American School of International Political Economy." *Review of International Political Economy* 16 (1): 58–71.

Fortin, Jessica. 2012. "Measuring Presidential Powers: Some Pitfalls of Aggregate Measurement." *International Political Science Review* 34 (1): 91–112.

Gerber, Alan, and Neil Malhotra. 2008. "Do Statistical Reporting Standards Affect What is Published? Publication Bias in Two Leading Political Science Journals." *Quarterly Journal of Political Science* 3 (2): 313–326.

Glaeser, E. L., Rafael La Porta, Florencio Lopez-de-Silanes, and Andrei Shleifer. 2004. "Do Institutions Cause Growth?" *Journal of Economics Growth* 9 (3): 271–303.

Goertz, Gary. 2008. "Concepts, Theories, and Numbers: A Checklist for Constructing, Evaluating, and Using Concepts or Quantitative Measures." In *The Oxford Handbook of Political Methodology*, edited by J. M. Box-Steffensmeier, H. E. Brady and D. Collier, 97–118. Oxford: Oxford University Press.

Goldsmith, Arthur. 1999. "Africa's Overgrown State Reconsidered: Bureaucracy and Economic Growth." *World Politics* 51 (4): 520–546.

Goldsmith, Arthur. 2000. "Sizing Up the African State." *Journal of Modern African Studies* 38 (1): 1–20.

Gollwitzer-Franke, Sophia. 2011. "Budget Institutions and Fiscal Performance in Africa." *Journal of African Economies* 20 (1): 111–152.

Hall, Peter A. 2003. "Aligning Ontology and Methodology in Comparative Research." In *Comparative Historical Analysis in the Social Sciences*, edited by J. Mahoney and D. Rueschemeyer, Chap. 11. Cambridge: Cambridge University Press.

Hanoushek, Jan, Dana Hajkova, and R. K. Filer. 2008. "A Rise by Any Other Name? Sensitivity of Growth Regressions to Data Source." *Journal of Macroeconomics* 30: 1188–1206.

Hawken, Angela, and G. Munck. 2009. "Measuring Corruption. A Critical Assessment and a Proposal". In *Perspectives on Corruption and Human Development*, edited by Anuradha K. Rajivan and Ramesh Gampat, vol. 1, 71–106. New Delhi: Macmillan India for UNDP.

Herrera, Yoshiko M. 2010. *Mirrors of the Economy: National Accounts and International Norms in Russia and Beyond*. Cornell: Cornell University Press.

Herrera, Yoshiko M., and Devesh Kapur. 2007. "Improving Data Quality: Actors, Incentives, and Capabilities." *Political Analysis* 15 (4): 365–386.

Hug, Simon. 2013. "The Use and the Misuse of the 'Minorities at Risk' Project." *Annual Review of Political Science* 16: 15–39.

Jerven, M. 2009. "The Relativity of Poverty and Income: How Reliable Are African Economic Statistics?" *African Affairs* 109 (433): 77–93.

Jerven, M. 2011. "The Quest for the African Dummy: Explaining African Post-Colonial Economic Performance Revisited." *Journal of International Development* 23: 288–307.

Jerven, M. 2012a. "An Unlevel Playing Field: National Income Estimates and Reciprocal Comparison in Global Economic History." *Journal of Global History* 7 (10): 107–128.

Jerven, M. 2012b. "For Richer or Poorer: GDP Revisions and Africa's Statistical Tragedy." *African Affairs* 112 (446): 138–147.

Jerven, M. 2013a. "The Political Economy of Agricultural Statistics and Input Subsidies: Evidence from India, Nigeria and Malawi." *Journal of Agrarian Change*. doi: 10.1111/joac.12025.

Jerven, Morten. 2013b. *Poor Numbers: How We Are Misled by African Development Statistics and What to Do About It*. Cornell: Cornell University Press.

Karcher, Sebastian, and David A. Steinberg. 2013. "Assessing the Causes of Capital Account Liberalization: How Measurement Matters." *International Studies Quarterly* 57: 128–137.

Kenney, Charles, and David Williams. 2001. "What Do We Know About Economic Growth? Or, Why Don't We Know Very Much?" *World Development* 29 (1): 1–22.

Klomp, J., and Jakob de Haan. 2013. "Do Political Budget Cycles Really Exist?" *Applied Economics* 45: 329–341.

Kurtz, Marcus, and Andrew Schrank. 2007. "Growth and Governance: Models, Measures, and Mechanisms." *Journal of Politics* 9 (2): 538–554.

Lee, Nayoung, Geert Ridder, and John Strauss. 2010. "Estimation of Poverty Transition Matrices with Noisy Data." Discussion Paper No. 576, August 16, Department of Economy, Pontificia Universidade Cathólica (PUC), Rio de Janeiro, 1–58.

Lemke, Douglas. 2003. "African Lessons for International Relations Research." *World Politics* 56: 114–138.

Lledó, V., Irene Yackovlev, and Lucie Gadenne. 2009. "Cyclical Patterns of Government Expenditures in Sub-Saharan Africa: Facts and Factors." *IMF Working Paper* 9 (274), 1–25. Washington, DC: International Monetary Fund. http://www.imf.org/external/pubs/ft/wp/2009/wp09274.pdf

Mkandawire, Thandika. 2013. "Neopatrimonialism and the Political Economy of Africa's Economic Performance: Critical Reflections." Institute for Futures Studies, Working Paper 1, 1–56. Stockholm: Institute for Future Studies. http://www.iffs.se/wp-content/uploads/2013/05/2013_1_thandika_mkandawire.pdf

Moral-Benito, Enrique. 2012. "Determinants of Economic Growth: A Bayesian Panel Data Approach." *Review of Economics and Statistics* 94 (2): 566–579.

Morgan, Mary S. 2009. "Seeking Parts, Looking for Wholes. History of Observation in Economics." *London School of Economics Working Paper Series* 1, 1–52. London: London School of Economics.

Mudde, Cas, and A. Schedler. 2010. "Introduction: Rational Data Choice." *Political Research Quarterly* 63 (2): 410–416.

Nardulli, Peter, Buddy Peyton, and Joe Bajjalieh. 2012. "Gauging Cross-National Differences in Education Attainment." International Political Science Association, Committee on Concepts and Methods Working Paper Series 57, 1–41. Amherst, MA/Mexico City: University of Massachusetts Political Science Department/Centro de Investigación y Docencia Económicas (CIDE).

Nathan, Laurie. 2005. "The Frightful Inadequacy of Most of the Statistics: A Critique of Collier and Hoeffler on Causes of Civil War." Crisis States Research Centre Discussion Paper No. 11. London: London School of Economics, 1–26.

Ndulu, B. J., S. A. O'Connell, R. H. Bates, P. Collier, and C. C. Saludo, eds. 2008. *The Political Economy of Economic Growth in Africa, 1960–2000*. New York: Cambridge University Press.

Nordhaus, W. 1975. "The Political Business Cycle." *Review of Economic Studies* 42: 162–190.

Olajide, Ajao A. 2011. "Empirical Analysis of Agricultural Productivity in Sub-Saharan Africa: 1961–2003." *Libyan Agricultural Research Center Journal of International* 2 (5): 224–231.

Ponomareva, Natalie, and Hajime Katayama. 2010. "Does the Version of the Penn World Tables Matter? An Analysis of the Relationship between Growth and Volatility." *Canadian Journal of Economics* 43 (1): 152–179.

Poovey, Mary. 1998. *A History of the Modern Fact: Problems of Knowledge in the Sciences of Wealth and Society*. Chicago: University of Chicago Press.

Przeworski, A. 2004. "Institutions Matter." *Government and Opposition* 39 (4): 527–540.

Przeworski, Adam, and H. Teune. 1967. "Equivalence in Cross-National Research." *Public Opinion Quarterly* 30: 551–568.

Przeworski, A., and Henry Teune. 1970. *The Logic of Comparative Social Inquiry*. New York: Wiley-Interscience.

Rodrik, Dani. 2012. "Why We Learn Nothing from Regressing Economic Growth on Policies." *Seoul Journal of Economics* 25 (2): 137–151.

Roodman, David. 2008. "Through the Looking Glass, and What OLS Found There: On Growth, Foreign Aid, and Reverse Causality." Center for Global Development Working Paper 137, 1–36. Washington, DC: Center for Global Development.

Ross, Michael. 2006. "Is Democracy Good for the Poor?" *American Journal of Political Science* 50 (4): 860–874.

Sanin, Francisco Gutiérrez, D. Buitrago, and A. González. 2013. "Aggregating Political Dimensions: Of the Feasibility of Political Indicators." *Social Indicators Research* 110 (1): 305–326.

Schedler, Andreas. 2012a. "Judgment and Measurement in Political Science." *Perspectives on Politics* 10 (1): 21–36.

Schedler, Andreas. 2012b. "The Measurer's Dilemma: Coordination Failures in Cross-National Political Data Collection." *Comparative Political Studies* 45 (2): 237–266.

Schedler, Andreas, and Cass Mudde. 2010. "Data Usage in Quantitative Comparative Politics." *Political Research Quarterly* 63 (2): 417–433.

Shantayanan, Devarajan. 2013. "African's Statistical Tragedy." *Review of Income and Wealth* 10: 1–7.

Shapiro, Ian. 2002. "Problems, Methods, and Theories in the Study of Politics, or What's Wrong with Political Science and What to Do About It." *Political Theory* 30 (4): 596–619.

Sindzingre, Alice N. 2013. "The Ambivalent Impact of Commodities: Structural Change or Status Quo in Sub-Saharan Africa?" *South African Journal of International Affairs* 20 (1): 23–55.

Stasavage, David. 2005. "Democracy and Education Spending in Africa." *American Journal of Political Science* 49 (2): 343–358.

Treier, Shawn, and Simon Jackman. 2008. "Democracy as a Latent Variable." *American Journal of Political Science* 52 (1): 2001–2017.

Van de Walle, Steven. 2006. "Comparative Statics: The State of the World Bureaucracies." *Journal of Comparative Policy Analysis* 8 (4): 437–448.

Voigt, Stefan. 2013. "How (Not) to Measure Institutions." *Journal of Institutional Economics* 9 (1): 1–26.

Wilson, Sven E., and David M. Butler. 2007. "A Lot More to Do: The Sensitivity of Time-Series Cross-Section: Analyses to Simple Alternative Specifications." *Political Analysis* 15 (2): 101–123.

Yeats, Alexander. 1990. "On the Accuracy of African Observations: Do Sub-Saharan Trade Statistics Mean Anything?" *World Bank Economic Review* 2: 135–156.

Young, A. 2012. "The African Growth Miracle." *Journal of Political Economy* 120: 696–739.

Young, Cristobal. 2009. "Model Uncertainty in Sociological Research: An Application to Religion and Economic Growth." *American Sociological Review* 74 (3): 380–397.

Ziliak, Stephen T., and Deirdre McCloskey. 2008. *The Cult of Statistical Significance: How the Standard Errors Cost Us Jobs, Justice, and Lives*. Ann Arbor: University of Michigan Press.

Measuring development progress in Africa: the denominator problem

Roy Carr-Hill

Institute of Education, London, UK

ABSTRACT   In developing countries, assessments of progress towards development goals are based increasingly on household surveys. Typically, they omit by design: the homeless; those in institutions; and mobile, nomadic or pastoralist populations. Moreover, in practice household surveys typically underrepresent: those in fragile, disjointed households; slum populations and areas posing security risks. Those six subgroups constitute a large fraction of the "poorest of the poor". These "missing" poor are estimated to constitute about 11 per cent of the population of sub-Saharan Africa. Their omission from the sampling frames of household surveys leads to substantial biases in the assessment of progress towards the Millennium Development Goals.

RÉSUMÉ   Dans les pays en voie de développement, l'évaluation des progrès accomplis vers l'atteinte des objectifs du développement repose de plus en plus souvent sur les enquêtes auprès des ménages. Or, elles excluent généralement à la source les sans-abris, les individus placés en établissement et les populations mobiles, nomades ou pastorales. En outre, en pratique, elles sous-représentent les ménages fragiles ou éclatés dans l'espace, les populations des bidonvilles et celles des régions à haut risque pour la sécurité. On estime que ces sous-groupes, qui constituent une large part des plus pauvres parmi les pauvres, comptent pour onze pour cent de la population de l'Afrique subsaharienne. Leur omission dans les plans d'échantillonnage des enquêtes ménages entraine des biais importants dans l'évaluation des progrès accomplis dans la réalisation des Objectifs du Millénaire pour le développement (OMD).

Introduction

The United Nations Development Programme (UNDP 2013) has recently produced estimates showing substantial progress towards the Millenium Development Goals (MDGs) by 2015. Their estimates are based on a combination of official statistics and household surveys, and there is no recognition of the problem of undercounting of the population and especially of the poorest groups (Carr-Hill 2013). The aim of this article is to produce estimates of the "progress" between 1990 (the baseline year) and 2010 (the latest year of data availability for many indicators) corrected for these undercounts for sub-Saharan Africa (SSA).

First, in the remainder of this introduction, we provide a rapid overview of the general problem of undercounts and identify the subgroups most likely to be missing; in the second section, we make estimates for the size of each of these subgroups in 1990 and 2010; in the third section, we make overall estimates of missing populations and their impact on estimating progress towards the MDGs; and in the final section, we draw conclusions and make recommendations.

Censuses are not censuses

It is well recognised that censuses face problems of complete enumeration. Groups of adults have been excluded from censuses in some countries for political or practical reasons (Buettner and Garland 2008). For example, seasonal and temporary internal migrants or other highly mobile economic groups are often excluded from national censuses (Deshingkar 2006), especially when they are not on official household lists. In addition, in many developing countries the census enumerators are often police or other government officials whose incentive is to confirm their own registration work and to catch anyone who has escaped their net.

Moreover, in most middle- and low-income countries, vital registration systems have never been fully functioning (Powell 1981; Chan et al. 2010; Vlahov et al. 2011), and there has been a similar decline in donor interest in censuses and vital registration systems (Setel et al. 2007), as evidenced by the demise of the International Institute for Vital Registration and Statistics, and an increasing reliance on household surveys.

The main sources are often internationally standardised surveys with reasonably large sample sizes (see Table 1), and although now many of these surveys are funded at least in part by national governments, there is in fact very little variation in either content or methodology to respond to national circumstances.[1]

There is the obvious "throwing the baby out with the bathwater" problem with this move away from censuses to relying on surveys, because drawing a sample for a survey depends on having a sampling frame in the first place, which is frequently based on the census. Clearly, any problem with the census, if used as the sampling frame for a national survey, will lead to that sampling frame being biased.

The United Nations has developed guidelines for good census practice (UN 2008), and clear adoption of these UN guidelines has at least made interpretation and comparison easier; the quality of censuses in developing countries has probably improved between 2000 and 2010,

Table 1.   Major international social surveys: sample size, sponsor, focus and coverage.

	Sample size	Sponsor	Focus	Coverage
Demographic and Health Surveys (DHS)	5,000–30,000 households	Macro International funded by USAID	Health, fertility, infant and child mortality, HIV/ STD, domestic violence	90 countries (200 + surveys), ca. every 5 years
Labour Force Surveys (LFS)	"Relatively large-scale"	ILO or national statistical offices	Employment	Countries (200+ surveys), ca. biennial
Living Standards Measurement Surveys (LSMS)	2,000–5,000 households	World Bank	Consumption and expenditure, household activities	34 countries (100 + surveys), ca. every 5 years
Multiple Indicator Cluster Survey (MICS)	5,000–20,000 households	UNICEF	Children and women: education, maternal and infant health	60 countries (200 + surveys), ca. every 5 years

Sources: Information from main website pages of DHS (www.dhsprogram.com), LFS (http://www.ilo.org/dyn/lfsurvey/lfsurvey.home), LSMS (http://econ.worldbank.org/WBSITE/EXTERNAL/EXTDEC/EXTRESEARCH/EXTLSMS/0,,contentMDK:21610833~pagePK:64168427~piPK:64168435~theSitePK:3358997,00.html) and, MICS (http://www.childinfo.org/).

with many more countries carrying out censuses and technological innovation in mapping, enumeration and data capture (UN Statistical Division 2010). However, although the guidelines are clear in principle, there can still be problems in enumeration in practice for the basic concept of housekeeping, for example, poor servants in rich households being left out; with counting mobile populations who are not easily traceable; and with counting *de facto* rather than *de jure* populations, where there are disputes over nationality; those internally displaced either as a result of civil war or because of environmental change (for example, floods, nuclear accidents) that has made their homes uninhabitable. Homelessness is particularly difficult: the basic problem is that "who we define as homeless determines how we count them" (Peressini, Mcdonald, and Hulchanski 2010, 1).

The problems with counting institutional populations (care homes, [some] factory barracks, hospitals, the military, prisons, refugee camps, religious orders and school dormitories) are entirely different: we know where they are (in most cases), but they are not individually identified, and there is still considerable variation over how some of the institutional population groups should be included in the population count (Wagner 2013), whether as special census blocks or special households.

Careful reporting of censuses, as per the UN guidelines, will acknowledge how well these groups have been enumerated and most categories – including the military and prisoners – are included as aggregate numbers in estimated census population counts of developed countries, but not in the census reports of many developing countries. Further, in developing countries, according to the UN Population Division (Buettner and Garland 2008), children are systematically undercounted, mainly because of dramatic underreporting of births, especially in rural areas (Hill and Choi 2006)

Using official census statistics to assess poverty levels

There is a huge literature on how to measure poverty on an international comparative basis[2] spanning several decades (OECD 1975; McGranahan et al. 1972; ILO 1976) and several disciplines. However, in this context – the measurement of development progress over time – for better or for worse, a crude cash measure (US$1 or US$2 a day) – has been adopted by most international organisations as the flagship measure, even though it makes little allowance for non-food needs which are mostly monetised in urban, but not in rural areas (Mitlin and Satterthwaite 2012).

The census documents for the large population countries in sub-Saharan Africa have been examined for any commentary about difficulties or problems encountered. In fact, such internal commentary is rare, and an extensive web search was carried out for other commentary. The sparse results of these efforts are included in Table 2. It is clear that many of the censuses have encountered severe difficulties in implementation, and that some either left out some groups by design, or have been forced to omit certain areas or groups.

Using household surveys to assess poverty

The additional problems with using household surveys to assess the absolute level of poverty or of any related characteristic means, in contrast to the view of Muñoz and Scott (2004), that they are an inappropriate instrument for obtaining information about the poorest of the poor, especially in developing countries. This is because household surveys, with rare exceptions, typically omit by design:

- those not in households because they are homeless;
- those who are in institutions, including refugee camps; and
- mobile, nomadic or pastoralist populations.

Table 2. Known omissions/difficulties and undercounts officially acknowledged in large country censuses in sub-Saharan Africa.

	Omissions	Difficulties	Estimate of undercount
Kenya	Under-representation of north-eastern Kenya	Carrying out census in slums; other interests (famine/hunger, drought, resettlement); insecurity , enumeration of pastoralists	n.a.
Nigeria	Under-representation of minority ethnic and religious groups	2006: national census was met with protests, boycotts, charges of fraud, and at least 15 deaths. Thousands of enumerators walked off the job because they hadn't been paid, and many people said they had not been counted (Lalasz 2006).	n.a.
South Africa	Undercount estimation based on Post Enumeration Survey	High walled area, migration, new settlement	14.6%

Sources: Kenya: Kenyan National Bureau of Statistics; Opiyo (2010); also see "Kibera's Census: Population, Politics, Precision," *MapKibera blog* (Maron 2010); Nigeria: Lalasz (2006); South Africa: http://SANews.gov.za (accessed 30 October 2012).

In addition, in practice, because they are difficult to reach, household surveys will typically under-represent:

- those in fragile, disjointed or multiple occupancy households (because of the difficulty of identifying them);
- those in urban slums (because of the difficulty of identifying and interviewing); and
- may omit certain areas of a country deemed to pose a security risk.

If one wanted an empirical – as distinct from a theoretical – definition of the "poorest of the poor", the above collection of six population subgroups could hardly be bettered. But there is – rather strangely – little recognition of the problems that arise when relying on surveys: for example, Atkinson and Marlier (2010), in their book on measuring social inclusion, dismiss the problem in half a page. The issue is particularly important for children who are the focus of many of the MDGs.

A comprehensive search was carried out of the meta-documentation of the four main standardised household surveys – the DHS, the LFS, the LSMS and the MICS – and a sample of country surveys. None of the meta-documents, including those from the DHS (Vaessen, Thiam, and Le 2005) or the LSMS (Grosh and Glewwe 1998; Scott, Steel, and Temesgen 2005) – which is the most professional and most concerned with quality, justifying its relatively small sample sizes specifically because of its attention to non-sampling errors – had anything to say about the coverage of the homeless, institutional populations, the mobile and/or any special arrangements to cover slum areas.[3]

Comparing the intended coverage of censuses and household surveys

Population censuses are, of course, themselves surveys of a kind and, as we have illustrated above, have faced many of the same problems in the past; but a modern census will intend to include the mobile (because they refer to those present in the household on a specific day or night), will cover those in institutions, will attempt to cover those in urban slums and in less secure areas exhaustively, will (if necessary) carry out special counts of the homeless, and will attempt to estimate the numbers of pastoralists, with varying degrees of success (Misra and Mal-hotra 1982). In other words, a census can potentially solve many of the problems of omitted popu-lations, but this is not possible for household surveys.

Nevertheless, although modern censuses recognise that they have to include these groups in the population counts, they are often reduced to making overall estimates of their size and location, so that individual members of those groups are not included in the sampling frames available for household surveys. In developing countries, these marginalised groups may not be included at all, even in the estimated population counts.

The lack of recognition of these problems has meant that no systematic attempt has been made to estimate the size and distribution of the population groups "missing" from the sampling frames of national household surveys, in addition to those who might be missing from the census. For obvious reasons, it is difficult to estimate numbers in these groups. The following sections docu-ment what is known or can be estimated.

How many are potentially "missing" from population counts and from sampling frames of household surveys?

There are several groups that may be excluded from censuses which are not considered below because they are not necessarily the poorest: for example, those caught up in civil wars or econ-omic and environmental migrants (Myers 1997). In addition, enumeration conventions (excluding temporary immigrants or non-nationals in censuses) leave out groups who may not be the worst off, although these are likely to be small numbers in sub-Saharan Africa. The focus here is on groups for which there are credible sources, and that are normally among the poorest.

This author acknowledges that the estimates for the percentages of the nomads, refugees and urban slum dwellers who are likely to be missing from the sampling frames of household surveys are imprecise, and this imprecision is compounded by making overtime estimates.

Nomads

Researchers (Catley, Lind, and Scoones 2013) agree that agro-pastoralists have increased substan-tially as a proportion of all pastoralists, and for this reason higher and lower estimates of the pro-portions excluded are made for 1990 and 2010 compared to the 1 in 5 observed by Carr-Hill et al. (2005).

Refugees

The numbers of unauthorised immigrants into the United States is estimated to have grown from 3.5 million in 1990 to 11.2 million in 2010 (Passel et al. 2013). Given that there have been similar patterns of mass movement across SSA over the period and that border controls would be much weaker when compared to the US, it seems more than reasonable to assume that there would have been at least a three-fold growth of illegal immigrants in SSA countries. On the other hand, many of those would have been counted in their country of origin; so we have made the conservative assumption that there were as many illegal immigrants as official refugees in both years.

Slum dwellers

No estimate of the global numbers of slum dwellers existed before the millenium. "The first esti-mate by UN Habitat came in 2003 and was close to the billion mark; this meant that Target 11 was not just short on ambition but also based on an arbitrary figure" (UN Habitat 2003a, 49). The range of estimates is used below in order to be consistent with UNICEF's estimates of the numbers of street children.

Detailed justification of each of the following categories is given in Carr-Hill (2013).

Homeless

Rather obviously, household surveys will omit nearly all homeless and many street children. Estimating numbers is fraught with difficulties.

Adults

UN Habitat (2003a) estimated the number of homeless people worldwide to be between 100 million and one billion, depending on how they are counted and the definition used; essentially a distinction between those without any roof at all over their heads (the smaller estimate of 100 million) who will almost certainly be omitted from all household surveys, and the much larger numbers in informal – usually illegal – squatter settlements with no security of tenure and at risk of immediate eviction.

Children

SOS Villages estimates that there are 53.1 million orphans in sub-Saharan Africa, many of whom will be living on the streets. Many of these would be counted in conventional censuses and carefully designed household surveys where informal settlements are included if the children live with their families but work on the streets. But, equally, many will not be included.

There are no comparable estimates over time of numbers missing for either adults or children.

Institutionalised populations

Household surveys, by definition, omit from their sampling frame those in institutions: care homes; (some) factory barracks; hospitals; the military; prisons; refugee camps; religious orders; and school dormitories. Even where the intention is to extend the coverage to some or all of these institutions, the census-based sampling frames may not cover them, either because there was no attempt to enumerate them or because, as mentioned above, aggregate numbers and not names are collected. It would therefore require an additional special survey exercise to construct the sampling frame, and this will only happen on a country specific basis.

Hospitals and care homes

Those in hospitals will on average be poorer because morbidity is associated with poverty (see, for example, Lopez 2002). Hospital populations will typically be included in population censuses, but they are not included in the sampling frames of household surveys. There are estimated to be about 20 million hospital beds worldwide, concentrated in developed countries,[4] and the estimates for sub-Saharan Africa are for an increase from 1.2 to 1.8 million beds which, given the high and increasing levels of overcrowding, probably represents an increase from between 1.5 and 1.8 million missing from household surveys in sub-Saharan Africa in 1990 to between 2.3 and 2.6 million missing in 2010.

Prison

In developing countries, the Thai prime minister acknowledged that "90 percent of convicts in prisons are poor people" (Thai Foreign Office 2003). Walmsley (2003) estimates the total prison population of the world is estimated at about 9.8 million, mostly as pre-trial detainees (remand prisoners) or as sentenced prisoners. The numbers in sub-Saharan Africa were about 700,000 in 2008, but no earlier figures could be found.

Refugees

Refugees will not be routinely counted in annual national population censuses in developing countries because they are not considered as part of any nation's population – nor are they included in the sampling frames of any household survey – so they cannot, of course, make any contribution to survey-based estimates. However, the United Nations High Commissioner for Refugees has published figures annually on numbers of registered refugees, internally displaced persons and stateless persons.[5] The overall totals for sub-Saharan Africa were 6.5 million in 1993 (UNHCR 1994) and 10.2 million in 2010 (UNHCR 2010), but these figures do not include illegal immigrants, which we assume were approximately the same size in both years.

Nomadic and pastoralist groups by world region

Censuses and surveys very rarely include gypsies and nomadic/pastoralist populations who have much less access to services. While it is difficult to assess their income and wealth, and there clearly are some who are rich-in-kind (or rich-in-assets), the majority are usually poor in all senses. There is no reliable information available on the number of nomadic pastoralists (Garcia and de Leiva Moreno 2003) worldwide. Over 25 years ago, it was estimated that there were around 17.3 million pastoralists in Africa, 3.4 million in the Middle East and South Asia and no more than 2 million in Central Asia – a total of 22.7 million (Sandford 1983). More recent estimates, for most countries – with a few exceptions such as Iran and Mongolia – are much larger. Adding up these estimates gives a current overall total of about 66 million – triple the earlier estimate. In particular, in the Horn of Africa (excluding Somalia), the recent estimate was of about 24.2 million (Carr-Hill et al. 2005); that is, a 72 per cent increase over Sandford's estimate for the *whole* of Africa over the last 25 years.

The only internationally comparable source is that compiled by the International Livestock Research Institute (see Thornton et al. 2002), based partly on livestock numbers. Moreover, although these estimates are much larger they have been used because they are consistent in definition across countries and over time; and although there are some substantial discrepancies in specific countries,[6] overall the more recent estimates are in line with the Thornton-based estimates. For sub-Saharan Africa, Thornton's estimate was 61.9 million in 2000 and 147.4 million by 2050. By backward extrapolation and interpolation, we estimate that there were 48.5 million in 1990 and 79 million in 2010.

The surveys carried out by Carr-Hill et al. (2005) in six countries in the Horn of Africa included cross-checking census data with estimates made by local officials. These suggested that about 1 in 5 were not included in censuses. But, given that many of those included in the estimates will be sedentarised agro-pastoralists who would be counted both by censuses and household surveys, a higher range of between 1 in 5 and 1 in 4 for 1990 and a lower range of between 1 in 6 and 1 in 5 for 2010 are used to estimate the "missing" numbers. The estimated numbers missing were between 9.7 and 12.1 million in 1990 and 13.2 and 15.8 million in 2010.

Those who are difficult to reach

Fragile and disjointed households

The task of the census enumerator or survey interviewer is made much more difficult when either identifying the household head and/or counting the numbers in the household are ambiguous. This is particularly an issue in many countries in sub-Saharan Africa because new forms of household are developing as a response to the impact of HIV/AIDS. These will include elderly household heads with young children, grandparent households (Kalipeni et al. 2004, 277), large households with unrelated fostered or orphaned children attached (Foster 2002), child-headed households (Richter and Desmond 2008), and single-parent-, mother- or father-headed households (Zimba and Tembo 2007). While those groups will usually be included in a census and often a survey, those in other types of living arrangements – such as cluster foster care, where a group of children is cared for formally or informally by neighbouring adult households (Gallinetti and Sloth-Nielsen 2010); children in subservient, exploited or abusive fostering relationships; itinerant, displaced or homeless children (Barnett and Whiteside 2006, 203); neglected, displaced children in groups or gangs (Hunter and Fall 1998) – will all often be excluded from both censuses and household surveys. Despite the large number of studies, no systematic way of identifying these different types of household and then counting them has been agreed (Carr-Hill 2013).

Urban slums

Those in slums[7] will be among the poorest in any country (Montgomery 2009). Accurate statistics are difficult to come by, because poor and slum populations are often deliberately and sometimes massively undercounted by officials (Davis 2006).

The most recent estimates from UN Habitat (2011) are that there are more than a billion living in urban slums in developing countries; the same figure has been repeated since 2003, while urban populations have increased from 2.1 to 2.5 billion, with no obvious signs of *extensive* urban redevelopment (of the order of 150 million new homes?) in SSA or elsewhere to cater for the growth in urban populations; in any case:

> Data collection and analysis on urban slums encounters a critical problem. Information is rarely disaggregated according to intra-urban location or socio-economic criteria. Thus, slum populations and the poorest squatters are statistically identical to middle class and wealthy urban dwellers. *Worse, the poorest urban populations are often not included at all in data gathering.* (UN Habitat 2003b, 48; emphasis added)

The subgroups of slum populations missed by household surveys therefore are often completely ignored (Montgomery 2009). Agarwal (2011, 14) shows how official statistics for India "do not include unaccounted for and unrecognised informal settlements and people residing in poor quality housing in inner city areas on construction sites, in urban fringes and on pavements" (see also Sabry 2010).

The few surveys that have been conducted in those slums show sharp gradients of participation in formal education by income quintile within urban populations (UN Habitat 2003b). In the large-scale surveys, slums are not differentiated from other urban areas. Vlahov et al. (2011) discuss at length the limitations of national sample surveys in providing the detail needed by each district or urban locality for planning development interventions.

A substantial minority of households in the slum areas of developing country cities are therefore uncounted in many censuses (and thus not included in the UN Habitat estimates mentioned above). Moreover, even where they are counted in censuses, many would in practice be excluded from the sampling frames of household surveys. For sub-Saharan Africa, the extrapolated estimated numbers living in urban slums was 123 million in 1990 and 200 million in 2010. Based on the preceding discussion (and other literature), conservative estimates has been made, that between 1 in 10 and 1 in 5 of the urban slum populations are uncounted. Those guesstimates suggest that there were between 12.3 and 24.6 million missing in 1990, which had increased to between 20 and 40 million in 2010.

Insecure or isolated areas

Given the security situation – or simply difficulty of transport – in many countries, it can often be difficult for the implementing institutions to carry out a fully representative survey or census. This will obviously be specific to context and country (for example, north-east Kenya, west Nepal, and so on); but there is no systematic evidence as to the numbers involved.

Overall estimates of missing populations and their impact on estimating progress towards the MDGs

The official story about poverty and progress

According to the UNDP, there have been substantial improvements between 1990 and 2010 in sub-Saharan Africa: poverty – defined as the percentage of people living on less than $1.25 a day (2005 purchasing power parity) – has declined from 56.5 per cent to 47.5 per cent; and the proportions with access to improved water and sanitation facilities has improved dramatically, especially in rural areas (see Table 3).

Absolute numbers missing

For sub-Saharan Africa,[8] the totals in the sub-sections above add up to between 39.6 and 52.2 million in 1990 and between 56.6 and 79.5 million in 2010 (Table 4).

Moreover, the estimates do not include the homeless, those in fragile or disjointed households or those in areas where there are security risks. It could be argued that the homeless would mostly be from urban slums so that there would be double counting (and if, as some have argued, the UNICEF estimate of street children is a massive over-estimate, the numbers look plausible), but the other two categories (large, but of unknown size) are definitely additional and have definitely increased (plausibly, at least doubled?) between 1990 and 2010 especially in sub-Saharan Africa. Estimates of between 50 and 65 million in 1990 and between 70 and 105 million in 2010 are not unrealistic.

These latter figures are compared to the estimated population of sub-Saharan Africa of 519.5 million in 1990 and 867.3 million in 2010; in 1990, the estimate of 45–65 million

Table 3. Proportion of population using an improved drinking water source (MDG indicator 7.8) or an improved sanitation facility (MDG indicator 7.9).

	1990			2010		
	Total	Urban	Rural	Total	Urban	Rural
Percentage using an improved drinking water source						
Sub-Saharan Africa	49	83	36	61	83	49
Percentage using an improved sanitation facility						
Sub-Saharan Africa	26	43	19	30	43	23

Source: UNDP (2013).

Table 4. Estimates of population groups missing from sampling frames of household surveys in sub-Saharan Africa (millions).

	1990		2010	
	Minimum	Maximum	Minimum	Maximum
Pastoralists	9.7	12.1	13.2	15.8
Institutionalised				
Refugees	13.0	13.0	20.4	20.4
Hospitals	1.5	1.8	2.3	2.6
Prisons	0.7	0.7	0.7	0.7
Slum populations	12.3	24.6	20.0	40.0
Total	37.2	52.2	56.6	79.5

represent 8.5–12.5 per cent undercounts; and in 2010, the estimates of 70–105 million represent an 8.0–10.0 per cent undercount. Even the latter might be judged acceptable overall, given the known deficiencies in African statistical systems (Jerven 2013); but as a 42.5–62.5 per cent undercount in 1990 or a 40–60 per cent undercount in 2010 of the poorest wealth quintile is scandalous, and it makes a mockery of monitoring development progress because neither the baseline nor the current estimates are secure. Estimates of absolute levels of poverty in different years – and, specifically the estimates for 1990 which are the baseline for MDGs – have to be revised.

Impact of missing numbers on estimates of poverty and progress

The official numbers for those in poverty were 289.7 million in 1990 and 415.9 million in 2010 (UNDP 2013). Making the reasonable assumption that all those missing would also be in poverty, the corrected figures, using the higher estimates, are 35.7 million and 520.9 million. Using the higher estimates in the population estimates, the corrected population figures are similarly inflated to 584.5 million and 972.3 million, so that the percentages in poverty are 60.7 per cent and 53.6 per cent, a 7 per cent fall – from a higher baseline and still above half – rather than a 9 per cent fall to below half according to the official story.

    Looking at an indicator with breakdowns between rural and urban, such as the percentages using improved drinking water, we know that all the missing pastoralists are rural and we assume that all the refugees are rural with all the remainder being urban. In 1990, this translates to about 25 million missing rural and 35 million missing urban; in 2010 about 40 million missing rural and 65 million missing urban.

    The impact of the missing populations is substantial (see Table 5): there has been an improvement, but at a much lower level in both urban and rural areas.

Discussion of findings and existing proposed solutions

It is urgent to understand the extent and nature of the denominator biases both for planning and research on inequalities: while this is less relevant in developed countries (but see Carr-Hill 2014), it is especially important for assessing development progress (for example, towards the MDGs) in developing countries.

    Although there are technical procedures for improving census counts of special groups, these do not solve the sampling frame problems of household surveys, which are the major source of poverty estimates in many developing countries. In developing countries, both problems remain:

Table 5. Official numbers and revised numbers using improved drinking water and sanitation (numbers and percentages).

Official numbers and percentages	1990			2010		
	Total	Urban	Rural	Total	Urban	Rural
Population	512.7	146.6	366.1	856.3	323.55	532.88
Using improved drinking water	251.0	121.0	129.9	531.6	258.8	272.8
With improved sanitation facilities	133.2	63.1	82.2	259.7	131.5	128.2
Percentage using improved drinking water	49.0	82.6	35.5	62.1	80.0	51.2
Percentage with improved sanitation	25.3	43.4	22.2	30.3	40.6	24.1
Corrected population and percentages						
Population	577.7	171.6	401.13	961.3	363.5	597.8
Percentage using improved drinking water	43.4	70.5	32.4	56.2	71.2	45.6
Percentage with improved sanitation	23.1	36.8	20.5	27.4	36.2	21.8

Source: UNDP (2013) and author's calculations.

first, of counting in the census; and second, if one wants to carry out a survey, identifying the location and size of different segments of the population.

Counting displaced and illegal groups

It is easy to count the numbers of formal refugees – even if they are not included in national censuses – because UNHCR manages the camps or national governments keep records of those who have been granted, or are applying for, asylum. It is much more difficult to count "informal" refugees; while preliminary estimates of trends at least into Northern countries could be made from the trends in the numbers applying for asylum in different countries (as a measure of attractiveness), those procedures would not work for South–South illegal migration because those countries do not generally keep those types of records.

Moreover, in many countries there are large groups of internally displaced persons or internal migrants, who are omitted for quasi political reasons; and other groups that are often left out, such as gypsies, homeless and illegal servants in rich households.

Counting and sampling nomads and pastoralists

This is one of the most difficult groups to count simply because they are moving. However, in many cases, the men, women and youth move but the grandmothers and children stay behind, so that there would be possibilities of counting the household populations in their tented settlements, so long as those can be identified (Mayer et al. 2009). Reasonable samples of pastoralists have also been obtained through livestock censuses; for example, through combining local level surveys with remote sensing (Galvin et al. 2001). Documenting change in their human population, however, remains, on the whole, elusive, and will remain so – whether through censuses or surveys – while at least some of nomadic/pastoralist groups remain permanently mobile.

Counting urban slum populations

It is clear that a substantial minority of slum populations are simply uncounted even in the censuses. The numbers missed by typical household surveys will be much larger. But the chaotic nature of some large urban slums makes it difficult to follow a systematic procedure, whether counting for a census or constructing a sampling frame for a survey.

The Bangladesh Bureau of Statistics developed a procedure for constructing a sampling frame for their 2005 census. In the first phase, a basic map was constructed based on satellite images geo-referenced to produce accurate street maps of cities. Suspected slums based on estimated population density and roofing materials were located and delineated on the corrected maps, although a substantial number of slum areas (around 30%) were not identified by the two criteria of density and roofing material. In the second phase, referred to as "ground trothing", settlements identified as slums were assessed or checked on the ground and, after interviewing local residents, a comprehensive description of general conditions in suspected slum settlements, including estimates of population size.[9]

Such procedures should, in principle, produce a reasonably reliable frame for a population census. However, some of the slum communities can be visually obscured even from satellite imagery, and the need to rely on relatively unknown key informants for estimating slum sizes may itself lead to politically local biases (Schurmann 2009); and similar procedures used in the Indonesian and Timor Leste censuses encountered security problems in follow up and verification.

An alternative approach has been to conduct a survey based on one of the standardised surveys using a sample frame specially designed for informal slum settlements. A survey in Kibera and in other slum settlements in Nairobi in 2000 was designed so that its findings could be compared to the DHS (African Population and Health Research Center 2002). Kenya National Bureau of Statistics (KNBS) and UNICEF (2009) carried out a specific survey in Mombasa's informal settlements. However, special surveys like this are just that – special – and are not a common occurrence.

Sampling frame problems for surveys

The fundamental problem of a household survey is precisely that it is a household survey and will therefore not cover those who are not in households. Although special surveys could be, and have been, carried out of those who are in fixed institutions, they tend to be expensive, they often involve proxy respondents (National Centre for Social Research 2003), and the results tend to be difficult to integrate with those from the corresponding household survey.

For those not in fixed institutions, satellite imagery together with verification on the ground is also possible (as mentioned above), but at the moment is still very expensive and will still not solve the problems of identifying the poor. Thus, these circumstances leave us with the following problems to consider:

- Refugees will not be identified through GPS techniques and are unlikely to declare themselves or want to be interviewed when the interviewer arrives;
- Nomads and pastoralists will not be at the GPS location when the interviewer attempts to find them;
- A GPS position in an urban slum can be verified on the ground but, given the high level of mobility, this will not provide a satisfactory sampling frame;
- If censuses are used as the sampling frame, adjustments for new building or demolitions can have a big impact on small areas, with implications for weighting samples, and the logistics of field work.

Therefore, although these may provide technical solutions to the problem of enumerating or at least counting population subgroups currently missing from many censuses, these procedures still do not solve the sampling frame problem of household surveys.

Post-enumeration surveys

The classic method of adjusting for a census undercount involves conducting a sample survey to identify people who were missed by the census and people who were counted twice or counted in the wrong location. It is not clear that these methods have produced valuable corrections to the census count (Breiman 1994). Examination of the procedures for more recent post-enumeration surveys shows that there has not been any improvement (Stark 2004).

International efforts to improve statistical procedures

In 2005, the UN's Department of Economic and Social Affairs produced an edited compilation on the problems of household surveys in developing and transition countries. Yansaneh (2005, 22) recognises that non-coverage of household surveys was a major issue and pointed to the exclusion of homeless people, those in institutions and nomads, because of "practical" difficulties, but did not mention refugees nor many of those in urban slums. He goes on to claim that non-coverage of primary sampling units was a less serious problem than non-coverage of households and of eligible persons, but that is not necessarily the case in slum areas. Lepkowski (2005, 155) adds that living quarters for seasonal and transitional workers are also very difficult to survey, especially when part-time survey staff are employed in the task of listing housing units.

Lepkowski (2005, 157) also suggests that the initial housing list can be augmented by interviewers being trained to use a half-open interval procedure in which an interviewer is given a housing list and instructed to identify any additional housing units between the initial target house and the next house on the list. Finally, he emphasises that survey analytical reports ought to give clear definitions of the target population including any exclusions. The frame should be described in sufficient detail to see how non-coverage might arise and even to make an overall assessment of the size of the potential error.

In addition, several leading donor agencies have become concerned about data quality. The International Monetary Fund (IMF) has developed the General Data Dissemination System (GDSS) and the Special Data Dissemination Standard (SDDS), promoting the standardisation of reporting about the quality of statistical data. These initiatives provide countries with (1) a framework for data quality to identify key problem areas; (2) an economic incentive through facilitating access to international capital markets; (3) a common motivation for advancing data quality discussions in private; and (4) technical support for evaluation and improvement programmes. Their prescriptions seem to have received more attention, however, in developed countries (for example, Laliberté, Grünewald, and Probst 2004).

Recommendations and conclusions

Recommendations for improving the coverage and quality of African censuses

International organisations should revive the International Institute for Vital Statistics and Registration – see also the recommendations in Vlahov et al. (2011) – to support national census organisations in developing these standard procedures and in developing and testing procedures for counting pastoralists (perhaps based on livestock numbers) and other nomads (gypsies, highly mobile workers, long distance truck drivers, travellers), illegal immigrants, slum dwellers, and so forth.

National census organisations in collaboration with international organisations should:

- Eliminate *de jure* definitions in censuses and adopt a *de facto* approach systematically to ensure that all people resident at the time of the census are enumerated, whether or not they have resided for a certain period, or are temporary residents (for example, at a hotel) at that address, or have been included in any form of national registration system;

- Adopt consistent and transparent definitions and procedures for counting the homeless and institutional populations whether fixed (care homes, hospitals, prisons, and so forth) or mobile (for example, the army);
- Use satellite imagery and on-the-ground verification for difficult-to-identify settlements such as slums.

Furthermore, in many African censuses the definition of a household is based on the Western model of a nuclear family, which is simply not applicable in many African contexts. National census organisations should ensure that the basic definition of a household is appropriate to the national context.

Progress can only be made if difficulties are acknowledged. The lack of internal commentary in the census reports of large African states was demonstrated earlier (see Table 2). Not only has the capacity for implementing censuses been weakened by the lack of international interest or support, the capacity for analysis of the coverage and quality of the census returns is almost non-existent.

Counting the total population

In the absence of any immediate solution to the sampling frame problem it is possible, with an assumed pattern of desired outcomes by wealth quintile, to make top-down estimates of the missing populations (Carr-Hill 2014). This was based on the observation that, in several of the DHS datasets, the gradient of desired outcomes is "wrong" or inappropriate. The values of the bottom quintile should be lower than a backwards linear projection from the other four (richer) quintiles because, as severity of poverty deepens, then conditions get relatively worse. However, in many cases, the value in the bottom quintile was higher than the linear projection and these datasets are from countries where numbers "missing" are thought to be large. Crude estimates of the numbers missing can be made by calculating the numbers required to restore linearity or the expected concave gradient on the assumption that all those missing are in the bottom quintile. The problem is that there is little basis for the shape of the "expected" gradient, so that the only real use for this procedure would be to make minimum or maximum estimates.

Ability to collect social statistics on the poorest of the poor

Social statistics in between censuses are collected through large-scale surveys or through administrative records of the service providers.

With regard to surveys, this article has extensively documented the problem of using household surveys to collect statistics on the poorest of the poor. In addition, where international standard surveys (such as DHS, LSMS or MICS) are used, there can be additional problems of poor translation – usually from English – and of appropriateness and interpretation of crucial concepts, for example the variability in the definition of a household (discussed in the previous section).

An obvious approach to correcting household surveys would appear to be to compare the results of the surveys to the census sampling frames upon which those surveys are based. This could give us an idea of the quantitative extent of this problem, and the estimated undercounts in different strata which could be used to provide a range of post-stratification weights. If these estimates were available for several countries, this would allow for sensitivity analysis of the impact of undercounting across a range of countries.

In principle, this is feasible with existing data and marks a clear way forward. For example, if data from a range of countries show that nomadic peoples get undercounted by 10 per cent to 45 per cent, then any household survey could carry out sensitivity analysis on its conclusions by up-weighting the nomads in its sample in accordance with the extremes of this range. Then there would be a fruitful research agenda in explaining the variance in undercounting between countries. The problem currently is that, while micro data are available from several censuses (Integrated Public Use Microdata Series [IPUMS]; https://www.ipums.org/), there are only a small number of contemporaneous household surveys for large countries (such as those in Table 2).

Another possibility would be to carry out a heavily funded census of a diverse region in Africa for which a census exists. Such an intensive census would provide at least one example of more carefully calculated estimates of the various populations. The census should include as an explicit objective the creation of a survey frame, and could then be followed up by a survey in about five years to assess the replicability of the census findings.

With regard to administrative or service data, the lack of registration systems in many developing countries means that there is no common identifier or means of verifying that records can distinguish between multiple users and a frequent single user. Even where there is an identity card system, its coverage tends to be erratic. Further, the increasing involvement of communities, non-governmental organisations and the private sector in the provision of social services makes the task of compiling a complete picture of service coverage much more difficult; and, in most SSA countries education, health care services and water and sanitation services are provided by state and non-state actors.

Conclusions

Population undercounting means that any social programme risks ignoring the poorest of the poor. This blindness is a public scandal affecting an estimate of between 300 and 350 million of the poorest in developing countries, leading to an overestimate of progress towards development goals and a substantial underestimate of inequalities. The estimates of missing populations are acknowledged to be crude estimates; but the impact of missing populations on estimates of progress towards eliminating $1.25-a-day poverty or improving access to drinking water are substantial.

In the absence of a complete solution, two possible general short-to-medium-term approaches have been suggested: one is a top-down statistical approach; and the other involves detailed comparison of household surveys with the census in the same country. The latter is probably the more promising, but it is research that cannot be carried out following a universal protocol – it has to be carried out by locally knowledgeable researchers. A third possibility was to carry out a heavily funded intensive census, for comparison with an existing recent census, and to provide a sampling frame for a subsequent sample survey in order to assess the extent of sample survey undercounts.

The problem should be addressed immediately by international and national organisations, both in terms of developing reliable birth and death registration and promoting more reliable and transparent censuses, and of developing and testing agreed procedures for estimating the impact of missing populations on survey based estimates of progress towards development goals. There is limited value in having goals *per se* and no point in using resources to monitor them if we do not know where we are or from where we started.

Acknowledgements

A version of this paper was presented in Vancouver at the special conference on African Social Economic Development: Measuring Success or Failure, organised by the School for International Studies, Simon

Fraser University and held on 18–20 April 2013. The current version has benefited considerably from the comments of the participants at that conference.

Biographical note

Roy Carr-Hill has degrees in Mathematics and Philosophy, a diploma in Social Policy, a Masters in Criminology and a DPhil in Penology. He has taught at the University of Sussex in the UK and at the Universidade Eduardo Mondlane in Maputo; and researched in developing countries for the last 35 years in the areas of education, health and social planning. He has been interested in the problem of estimating the size of the missing subgroups for over 15 years.

Notes

1. The Centre for Disease Control (CDC) have also carried out a series of reproductive and health surveys http://www.cdc.gov/reproductivehealth/Global/Surveys.htm (accessed 30 November 2012).
2. The measurement and commentary on poverty itself has of course a much longer history: in the UK, obvious examples are Booth (1902–1903) and Rowntree (1901).
3. UNICEF has carried out Wave 4 MICS surveys including Roma Settlements in Macedonia (UNICEF 2011) and Serbia (UNICEF 2010) (MICS, 2010, 2011) and in the Informal Settlements in Mombasa (KNBS and UNICEF 2009), but there is no indication that they used different approaches to identification of households.
4. All developed countries have more than 250 beds per 100,000; while all developing countries had less than 250 per 100,000.
5. All refugees include official refugees and those in refugee-like situations; the category of internally displaced persons (IDPs) included both IDPs and returned IDPs; others includes Asylum Seekers, Returned Refugees and Various.
6. For example, for India the National Convention (2005) estimates that there are 60 million nomads in India and 110 million including de-notified populations, compared to the Thornton-based estimate of about 3.75 million; in contrast, the estimate for Pakistan is "a few million" (Spooner 1984), while the Thornton-based estimate is over 18 million.
7. A community was declared to be a slum if it met 4 of 5 basic conditions: poor housing conditions; high overall population density; very poor sanitation and inadequate water sources; high prevalence of people below poverty level; and insecure land tenure (précised from Angeles et al. 2009).
8. The data in this section are for sub-Saharan Africa as a whole: detailed data for each country in sub-Saharan Africa are available from the author.
9. Both the Bangladeshi and Indian censuses go to considerable pains to locate and enumerate slum dwellers but there are problems (Schurmann 2009).

References

African Population and Health Research Center. 2002. *Population and Health Dynamics in Nairobi's Informal Settlements: Report of the Nairobi Cross-Sectional Slums Survey (NCSS) 2000.* Nairobi: APHRC.

Agarawal, S. 2011. "The State of Urban Health in India: Comparing the Poorest Quartile to the Rest of the Urban Population in Selected States and Cities." *Environment and Urbanization* 23 (1): 13–28.

Angeles, G., P. Lance, J. Barden-O' Fallon, N. Islam, A. Q. M. Mahbub, and N. I. Nazem. 2009. "The 2005 Census and Mapping of Slums in Bangladesh: Design, Select Results and Application." *International Journal of Health Geography* 8: 32.

Atkinson A. B., and E. Marlier. 2010. *Analysing and Measuring Social Inclusion in a Global Context.* New York: United Nations Secretariat, Department of Economic and Social Affairs.

Barnett, T. A., and A. Whiteside. 2006. *AIDS in the 21st Century: Disease and Globalisation.* London and New York: Palgrave Macmillan.

Booth, C. 1902–1903. *Life and Labour of the People in London.* London: Macmillan.

Breiman, L. 1994. "The 1991 Census Adjustment: Undercount of Bad Data?" *Statistical Science* 9 (4): 458–537.

Buettner, T., and P. Garland. 2008. *Preparing Population Estimates for All Countries of the World: Experiences and Challenges.* Rome: Committee for the Coordination of Statistical Activities.

Carr-Hill, R. A., A. Ashete, C. Sedel, and A. de Souza. 2005. *The Education of Nomadic Peoples in East Africa: Synthesis Report: Djibouti, Eritrea, Ethiopia, Kenya, Tanzania and Uganda*. Buenos Aires and Abidjan: United Nations Economical, Scientific and Cultural Organization (UNESCO), International Institute for Economic Planning (IIEP) and African Development Bank.

Carr-Hill, R. A. 2013. "Missing Millions and Measuring Development Progress." *World Development* 46 (June): 30–44.

Carr-Hill, R. A. 2014. "Non-household Populations: Implications for Measurements of Inequality and for Resource Allocation in the UK." *Journal of Social Policy*, forthcoming.

Chan, M., M. Kazatchkine, J. Lob-Levyt, T. Thoraya Obaid, J. Schweizer, M. Sidebes, A. Veneman, and T. Yamada. 2010. "Meeting the Demand for Results and Accountability: A Call for Action on Health Data from Eight Global Health Agencies." *Public Library of Science, Medicine* 7 (1): e1000223.

Catley, A., J. Lind, and I. Scoones. 2013. *Pastoralism and Development in Africa: Dynamic Change at the Margins*. London: Earthscan.

Davis, M. 2006. *Planet of Slums*. London and New York: Verso.

Deshingkar, P. 2006. *Internal Migration, Poverty and Development in Asia*. Brighton: Institute of Development Studies and Overseas Development Institute.

Foster, G. 2000. "The Capacity of the Extended Family for Orphans in Africa." *Psychology, Health & Medicine* 5: 55–62.

Gallinetti, J., and J. Sloth-Nielsen. 2010. "Cluster Foster Care: A Panacea for the Care of Children in the Era of HIV/AIDS or an MCQ?" *Social Work Maatskaplike Werk* 46 (4): 486–495.

Galvin, K. A., R. B. Boone, N. M. Smith, and S. J. Lynn. 2001. "Impacts of Climate Variability on East African Pastoralists: Linking Social Science and Remote Sensing." *Climate Research* 19: 161–172.

Garcia, S. M., and I. de Leiva Moreno. 2003. "Global Overview of Marine Fisheries." In *Responsible Fisheries in the Marine Ecosystem*, edited by M. Sinclair and G. Valdimarsson, 1–24. Rome: FAO and CABI Publishing.

Grosh, M. E., and P. Glewwe. 1998. "Data Watch: The World Bank's Living Standards Measurement Study Household Surveys." *Journal of Economic Perspectives* 12 (1): 187–196.

Hill, K., and Y. Choi. 2006. "Neonatal Mortality in the Developing World." *Demographic Research* 14 (18): 429–452.

Hunter, S., and D. Fall. 1998. *Orphans and HIV/AIDS in Zambia. An Assessment of Orphans in the Context of Children Affected by HIV/AIDS*. Lusaka: UNICEF.

International Labour Organisation. 1976. *Employment, Growth and Basic Needs: A One World Problem*. Geneva: ILO.

Jerven, M. 2013. *Poor Numbers: How We Are Misled by African Development Statistics and What to Do About It*. Ithaca, NY: Cornell University Press.

Kalipeni, E., S. Craddock, J. R. Oppong, and J. Ghosh, eds. 2004. *HIV & AIDS in Africa: Beyond Epidemiology*. Malden, MA: Blackwell.

Kenya National Bureau of Statistics (KNBS). 2009. *2009 Population and Housing Census*. Nairobi: KNBS.

Kenya National Bureau of Statistics (KNBS) and UNICEF. 2009. *Kenya Coast Province Mombasa – Informal Settlements: Monitoring the Situation of Women and Children. Multiple Indicator Cluster Survey*. Nairobi: KNBS.

Lalasz, R. 2006. "In the News: the Nigerian Census." Population Reference Bureau. Accessed November 20, 2012. http://www.statmyweb.com/s/nigeria-census.

Laliberté, L., W. Grünewald , and L. Probst. 2004. *Data Quality: A Comparison of IMF's Data Quality Assessment Framework (DQAF) and Eurostat's Quality Definition*. Luxembourg and Washington, DC: Eurostat and International Monetary Fund.

Lepkowski, J. 2005. "Non-observation Error in Household Surveys in Developing Countries." Chap. 8 *Household Sample Surveys in Developing and Transition Countries*. New York: UN, Department of Economic and Social Affairs, Statistics Division.

Lopez, A. 2002. "Mortality and Morbidity Trends and Poverty Reduction." Chap. 3 in *Selected Papers of the Fifth Asian and Pacific Population Conference*, 73–90. UNESCAP Secretariat. Accessed March 21, 2014. http://ww.unescap.org/esid/psis/population/popseries/apss158/part1_3.pdf.

McGranahan, D. V., C. Richard-Proust, N. V. Sovani, and M. Subramanian. 1972. *Contents and Measurement of Socio-Economic Development*. New York: Praeger for UNRISD.

Mayer, A- M., M. Myatt, M. A. Aissa, and N. Salse. 2009. "New Method for Assessing Acute Malnutrition in Nomadic Pastoralist Populations." *Field Exchange* 35 (March). Accessed November 30, 2013. http://fex.ennonline.net/35/newmethod.aspx.

Misra, P. K., and K. C. Malhotra, eds. 1982. *Nomads in India: Proceedings of the National Seminar*. Calcutta: Anthropological Survey of India.

Mitlin, D., and D. Satterthwaite. 2012. *Urban Poverty in the Global South; Scale and Nature*. Abingdon: Routledge.

Montgomery, M. 2009. "Urban Poverty and Health in Developing Countries." *Population Bulletin*, 64: 2–15.

Muñoz, J., and K. Scott. 2004. "Household Surveys and the Millenium Development Goals." *PARIS 21 Task Force on Improved Statistical Monitoring Development Goals*. http://paris21.org/sites/default/files/monitoringMDG-household-full.pdf.

Myers, N. 1997. "Environmental Refugees." *Population and Environment* 19 (2): 167–182.

National Centre for Social Research. 2003. *Health Survey for England*. London: NCSR.

OECD. 1975. *Measuring Social Well-Being*. Paris: OECD.

Opiyo, C. O. 2010. *Best Practices in Census Implementation: The Case of the 2009 Kenya Population and Housing Census*. Presented at the UN Regional Seminar on Census Data Dissemination and Spatial Analysis in Nairobi, Kenya, September 14–17.

Passel, J. S., D'Vera Cohn, and A. Gonzalez-Barrera. 2013. "Population Decline of Unauthorized Immigrants Stalls, May Have Reversed." September 23. PEW Research Center, Washington.

Peressini, T., L. Mcdonald, and D. J. Hulchanski. 2010. "Towards a Strategy for Counting the Homeless." Chapter 8.3 in *Finding Home: Policy Options for Addressing Homelessness in Canada*, edited by D. J. Hulchanski, P. Campsie, S. B. Y. Chau, S. W. Hwang, and E. Paradis. Toronto: Cities Centre, University of Toronto.

Powell, N. P. 1981. "Major Obstacles to Achieving Satisfactory Registration of Vital Events and the Compilation of Reliable Vital Statistics." In *Technical Papers of the International Institute for Vital Registration and Statistics, No 15*. Bethesda, MD: International Institute for Vital Registration and Statistics.

Richter, L. M., and C. Desmond. 2008. "Targeting AIDS Orphans and Child-headed Households? A Perspective from National Surveys in South Africa, 1995–2005." *AIDS Care* 20 (9): 1019–1028.

Rowntree, B. S. 1901. *Poverty: A Study in Town Life*. London: Macmillan.

Sabry, S. 2010. "How Poverty is Underestimated in Greater Cairo, Egypt." *Environment and Urbanization* 22 (2): 523–541.

Sandford, S. 1983. *Management of Pastoral Development in the Third World*. Chichester: Wiley.

Schurmann, A. 2009. *Bangladesh Urban Health Survey: Methods and Reproductive Health Results*. Paper presented at the International Conference on Urban Health Nairobi, Kenya, October 18–23.

Scott, K., D. Steel, and T. Temesgen. 2005. "Living Standards Measurement Study Surveys." Chap. 23 in *Household Sample Surveys in Developing and Transition Countries*, 523–556. New York: United Nations, Department of Economic and Social Affairs, Statistics Division.

Setel, P. W., S. B. Macfarlane, S. Szreter, L. Mikkelsen, P. Jha, S. Stout, C. AbouZahr (on behalf of the Monitoring of Vital Events writing group). 2007. "A Scandal of Invisibility: Making Everyone Count by Counting Everyone." *The Lancet*, 370 9598: 1569–1577.

SOS Children's Villages USA. 2013. Based on a projection from *UNICEF (2006) Africa's Orphaned and Vulnerable Generations: Children Affected by Aids*. Accessed April 1, 2013. http://www.sos-usa.org/our-impact/childrens-statistics.

Spooner, B. 1984. "Nomads in a Wider Society." *Cultural Survival* 8 (Spring): 23–25.

Stark, P. B. 2004. "Census Adjustment." In *Encyclopedia of Social Science Research, Vol. 1*, edited by M. Beck, A. Bryman, and T.F. Liao, 112–113. Thousand Oaks, CA: Sage Publications.

Thai Foreign Office, Public Relations Department. 2003. *Strategies for Fighting Poverty*. Accessed December 10, 2012. http://thailand.prd.go.th/ebook/review/content.php?chapterID=9.

Thornton, P. K., R. L. Kruska, N. Henninger, P. M. Kristjanson, R. S. Reid, F. Atieno, A. N. Odero, and T. Ndewa. 2002. *Mapping Poverty and Livestock in the Developing World*. Nairobi: International Livestock Research Institute.

United Nations (UN). 2008. *Principles and Recommendations for Population and Housing Censuses, Revision Series M No 67/Revf 2; ST/ESA/STAT/SER.M/67(Rev 2)*. New York: UN, Department of Economic and Social Affairs. http://unstats.un.org/unsd/demographic/standmeth/principles/Series_M67Rev2en.pdf.

UN Habitat. 2003a. *The Challenge of Slums: Global Report on Human Settlements, 2003*. New York: UN.

UN Habitat. 2003b. *Slums of the World: The Face of Urban Poverty in the new Millenium*. New York: UN Habitat.

UN Habitat. 2011. *State of the World's Cities 2010/2011*. New York: UN Habitat.

United Nations Development Programme (UNDP). 2013. *Human Development Report 2013: The Rise of the South: Human Progress in a Diverse World*. New York: UNDP.

UN High Commissioner for Refugees (UNHCR). 1994. *Populations of Concern to UNHCR: A Statistical Overview*. Geneva: Office of the United Nations High Commissioner for Refugees.

UN High Commissioner for Refugees (UNHCR). 2010. *Statistical Online Population Database*. Geneva: Office of the United Nations High Commissioner for Refugees. http://www.unhcr.org/pages/4a013eb06.html. Data extracted December 20, 2010.

UNICEF. 2010. *Multiple Indicator Cluster Survey in Serbia*. New York: UNICEF.

UNICEF. 2011. *Multiple Indicator Cluster Survey in Macedonia*. New York: UNICEF.

UN Statistical Division. 2010. *Report on the Results of a Survey on Census Methods used by Countries in the 2010 Census Round*. 2010 World Population and Housing Census Program, Working Paper: UNSD/DSSB/1, New York.

Vaessen, M., M. Thiam, and T. Le. 2005. "The Demographic and Health Surveys." Chapter 22 in *Household Sample Surveys in Developing and Transition Countries*, 495–522. ST/ESA/STAT/SER.F/96. New York: United Nations, Department of Economic and Social Affairs, Statistics Division.

Vlahov, D., S. R. Agarwal, R. M. Buckley, W. T. Caiaffa, C. F. Corvalan, A. C. Ezeh, R. Finklestein, et al. 2011. "Roundtable on Urban Living Environment Research." *Journal of Urban Health* 88 (5): 793–857.

Wagner, P. 2013. "Staff and Volunteers." Prison Policy Initiative. Accessed November 20, 2013. http://www.prisonpolicy.org/staff.html.

Walmsley, R. 2003. *World Prison Population List*. 4th ed. Home Office, Research Paper Findings no. 188.

Yansaneh, I. S. 2005. "Overview of Sample Design Issues for Household Surveys in Developing and Transition Countries." Chapter 2 in *Household Sample Surveys in Developing and Transition Countries*. ST/ESA/STAT/SER.R/96. New York: UN, Department of Economic and Social Affairs, Statistics Division.

Zimba, J., and B. Tembo. 2007. "Women Have to Cope as AIDS, Economic Woes Afflict Zambia." *ISIS International*, June 4. Accessed November 30, 2013. http://www.isiswomen.org/index.php?option=com_content&task=view&id=713&Itemid=200.

Monitoring performance or performing monitoring? Exploring the power and political dynamics underlying monitoring the MDG for rural water in Ethiopia

Katharina Welle

Science and Technology Policy Research (SPRU), University of Sussex, Brighton, UK

ABSTRACT Performance monitoring, most prominently exemplified in the Millennium Development Goals, is often perceived as providing objective results. Using the case of access to rural water supplies in Ethiopia, this article explores the power and political dynamics inherent in sector performance monitoring. It traces how the framing of access via employing different calculation methods led to divergent portrayals of water access in Ethiopia's Southern Region (23.7%–54%). While acknowledging that powerful actors can choose monitoring results to serve a particular end, such as a positive policy picture of access, this article illuminates the plural character of monitoring processes and their potential for a more reflective practice.

RÉSUMÉ Les données issues de l'évaluation et du suivi des programmes et politiques de développement sont souvent considérées comme objectives, ce qui est particulièrement bien mis en évidence pour les Objectifs du Millénaire pour le développement. Cet article examine les dynamiques politiques et les rapports de pouvoir inhérents au suivi du rendement dans le secteur de l'approvisionnement en eau des régions rurales éthiopiennes. Il démontre comment la formulation des méthodes de calcul explique l'ampleur des variations dans les estimations de l'accès à l'eau dans la région sud du pays. Tout en reconnaissant que les décideurs ont pu manipuler les données pour des fins politiques, l'auteure met en relief les fins multiples des processus d'évaluation pour conclure sur la façon dont ils peuvent inspirer une pratique réflexive.

Introduction

In March 2012, the Joint Monitoring Program (JMP) of the WHO and UNICEF, the United Nations' official mechanism for monitoring the Millennium Development Goal (MDG) 7c on water supply and sanitation, declared that the global target had been reached: in 2010, five years ahead of the 2015 schedule, the world's population without sustainable access to safe drinking water had been halved (WHO 2012). At first glance, this looks like an important achievement. And it is, keeping in mind that in 1990, at the end of the first water decade with the goal to provide water and sanitation to all, sector experts concluded that the sector's efforts had hardly been able to keep up with population growth (Carter, Tyrrel, and Howsam 1993).

The progress in providing water supply infrastructure since 1990, the baseline date for MDG 7c (UNDESA 2012), is illustrated in figures for Ethiopia. The number of water supply schemes increased from a mere 7,000 for the whole country in 1990 (Rahmato 1999) to over 90,000 in 2011 (Debela 2013). But, setting global targets and monitoring performance against these is deeply political and related achievements can be highly contested. Again, Ethiopia lends itself as a case in point. In 2010, the JMP (WHO and UNICEF 2012) reported an increase of water supply access from 14 per cent in 1990 to 44 per cent for Ethiopia, while the Ethiopian Ministry of Water and Energy (MoWE 2011) estimated that the country's water access had reached 68.5 per cent. For rural water supplies the differences in figures are even starker. While the JMP reported that 34 per cent of Ethiopia's population had rural water access in 2010, the figure put forward by the MoWE was 65.8 per cent.

The different results can be explained by the way in which the JMP and the MoWE measured access: while the JMP measured access through water use based on household surveys, the MoWE drew on average user numbers per scheme type-based infrastructure surveys (Butterworth et al. 2013a). The two figures thus tell different stories about the same reality: one about use and one about infrastructure provision.[1]

The observation that in performance monitoring actors choose different methods, which result in such discrepant official access estimates, hints at its political character. A critical examination of performance monitoring is highly pertinent, given that the MDGs, and their currently discussed successors, the Sustainable Development Goals, have made the measurement of performance pervasive on the policy agenda in sub-Saharan African countries and beyond.

Tracking performance is closely linked to aid effectiveness, an agenda that determines donor–recipient relations, particularly in highly aid-dependent countries, many of which are in sub-Saharan Africa. One of the five pillars identified as increasing the effectiveness of aid is "managing resources and decision making for development results" (OECD 2005, 7). The logic underlying results-based mangement (RBM) is that it enables policy makers to measure and reward success (Osborne and Gaebler 1992), which ultimately increases the effectiveness of aid, and its accountability.

Some circles of development analysts and practitioners fundamentally question the RBM model and its underlying logic. For example, the "bigpushforward",[2] an informal network of practitioners, critically engages with the politics of evidence and results-based management in relation to aid development topics. This article builds on this type of engaged scholarship, with the intention of broadening the space for critical engagement with performance monitoring, particularly the way it is often presented in the sector, namely as an objective means for informing robust policy decisions. The strategy for opening up a discussion space is based on the connotations of the word "performance". According to the Oxford English Dictionary, the definition of "performance" has two meanings: First, performance is described as "the process of performing a task or function […] i.e. in terms of how successfully it is performed"; second, it is "the act of presenting a play" (Oxford Dictionaries 2010). In the first meaning of the word, "performance" is the success with which a particular task is executed; in its second meaning, "performance" is the act of showcasing something, an act of stage management. While in the first case, reality is seen as measurable in an objective manner based on performance indicators, in the second case, reality is a subjective act of performance that is presented to an audience. In this article, I approach performance monitoring as a set of multiple processes that are subject to political and power dynamics and I explore the implications for development policy and practice.

The Ethiopian rural water sector lends itself as a case study for a number of reasons: improving performance monitoring has been a key undertaking of sectoral reforms in Ethiopia since 2005; in 2010–2012, the MoWE carried out a National Water Supply, Sanitation and Hygiene (WASH) inventory, with substantial investments into the sector's human and financial resources that further demonstrate the sector's emphasis on improving performance monitoring; the Ethiopian water sector also exhibits complexities typical of development assistance related to large volumes of aid, questions of ownership and parallel systems and procedures (Welle et al. 2009).

The findings in this article are based on a case study of the 2008 regional Water Resources Inventory (WRI) carried out in Ethiopia's Southern Region.[3] The data comprise of document reviews, participant observation, and semi-structured interviews. For data analysis, the process tracing method was employed, a research methodology that traces the micro-steps and links that lead to a specific outcome (Bennett and George 2005a, 2005b).

This article is structured as follows. In the first section I briefly recapture the rise and prevalence of performance monitoring under the aid effectiveness agenda in general and in the water sector in particular. Then I explain the concept of performance monitoring and my approach to exploring the political and power dimensions inherent in such processes and results. The regional WRI in 2008 provides the case study material for my analysis, followed by a discussion and conclusions.

The rise of performance monitoring under aid effectiveness

In development cooperation, some form of performance monitoring has been practised for a long time (Hailey and Sorgenfrei 2004). A popular example is the log frame approach, a planning and management tool originally introduced in the development sector by the United States Agency for International Cooperation (Meier 2003). However, the global declaration of the MDGs in 2000 represents a substantive shift in emphasis: it made the measurement of development results omnipresent in the political agenda at sector, country, and international levels (Black and White 2004).

As a consequence of the global aid effectiveness agenda, performance measurement has become crucial for all water supply, sanitation, and hygiene interventions in countries heavily dependent on aid. This is apparent at various levels. At the national level, many of these countries have embarked on sector reform processes that entail the establishment of performance monitoring systems as a key element of reform. An early example of this is the set of "golden indicators" of performance and annually agreed strategic undertakings developed in Uganda in the early 2000s by the then Ministry of Water, Lands and Environment (Pinfold 2006; Ssozi and Danert 2012). A review by the World Bank's Water and Sanitation Programme (AMCOW 2011) on progress in monitoring performance in the rural water supply subsector across 33 sub-Saharan African countries found that, from 2006 to 2010, 15 countries had reviewed their performance and set new strategic actions, 10 had reviewed their progress but not set new targets, and eight countries had not undertaken any performance monitoring of their rural water supply.

The importance of performance monitoring in the water sector and the reproduction of the model's inherent logic among sector stakeholders are illustrated in Ethiopia. In a recent presentation of preliminary results of the National WASH (water, sanitation and hygiene) Inventory to sector partners, the Ethiopian MoWE states that "government is committed to accurately measure progress towards the achievement of the [...] MDG targets with regard to WSS [Water Supply and Sanitation] – for better quality plan and allocation of resources to accelerate progress" (MoWE 2012). This point was reiterated at a sector meeting in April 2013, in which sector stakeholders came together to discuss the lessons learned and how to maximise the impact of the National WASH Inventory (Welle 2013).

Definition and concepts related to performance monitoring

Performance monitoring refers to the measurement of development results as opposed to the inputs and activities related to an intervention (OECD 2010). Performance monitoring is part of RBM (results-based mangement), a public management model that focuses on the achievement of measurable results. The origins of RBM go back to the early twentieth century, when so called "scientific principles" were introduced in the private sector to factory production processes in order to achieve greater or even output at lower costs (Kanigel 1997, cited in Ramalingam et al. 2009). Based on the premise that a focus on monitoring results would make services more efficient, economical, and effective (Mayne and Zapico-Goni 1997), RBM became popular in the public sector as a means to increase the accountability of public policies to citizens. An early example of using RBM elements to restore trust in the public sector is the introduction of output measures in a New York public bureau in 1912 (Williams 2003). RBM was widely introduced in member countries of the Organisation for Economic Cooperation and Development (OECD) in the 1980s under the term "New Public Management" as a way of managing public services (Hood 2001). From there, it spread to the systems of many development agencies and strongly influenced the MDGs and aid effectiveness agenda (Hulme 2010).

In the field of development cooperation, the OECD *Glossary of Key Terms in Evaluation and Results-Based Management* (OECD 2010) is a commonly cited source. According to the OECD, performance monitoring refers to a "continuous process of collecting and analysing data to compare how well a project, programme or policy is being implemented against expected results" (2010, 33). Performance measurement assumes a direct cause–effect relationship between measuring the results of development interventions and setting new objectives, made explicit in a causal sequence "beginning with the inputs, moving through activities and outputs, and culminating in outcomes, impact and feedback" (OECD 2010, 33), as illustrated in Figure 1.

The role of performance monitoring in this single-stranded cause–effect chain is the feedback loop from results to setting or revising objectives, as displayed in Figure 1. Underlying this management model is the idea that policy processes follow a rational, single-stranded flow, from the setting of objectives in the form of desired results to their achievement, and that performance monitoring functions as a tool to uphold the loop between them. This model is based on the idea that policy results can be achieved by employing "scientific principles" (Rebien 1996).

Criticisms of performance monitoring

Its proponents value RBM for reducing complex reality to a limited set of desired objectives and for suggesting a rational chain of inputs and activities to achieve them. Its critics dispute that, by

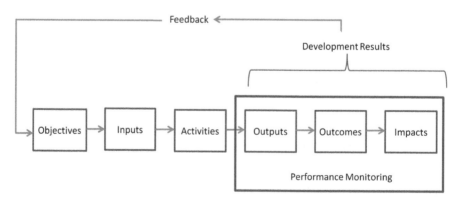

Figure 1.   OECD results chain.
Source: Author, based on OECD (2010).

doing so, the model misrepresents a complex reality. For instance, by its reduction to a few, measurable results represented by a small set of quantitative indicators, performance monitoring may end up disguising rather than informing what is really happening (Perrin 1998). In this context, it is argued that developing indicators is a political process, since indicators will represent only a particular perspective of a more complex reality, but not necessarily a relevant one. Some critics go further and highlight that results-based approaches, via abstract and aggregate numbers, can serve as instruments of control that seem to establish an accountability against narrow, predefined objectives (Eyben 2013). Viewed from this perspective, performance monitoring becomes an act of "image management", thereby creating a truth that mirrors a particular viewpoint (Power 1997).

In the context of the MDGs, critics have questioned their value in assessing international development (White 2003). They caution that the introduction of performance measures in a development cooperation context can lead to an incentive to neglect poor and deprived populations, since it may be more difficult to achieve measurable results when trying to reach these groups (Clements 2005). This point is relevant in relation to MDG 7c, on access to water supply and sanitation, which has been criticised, for instance, for missing out aspects of water quality and sustainability of access (Mehta 2006). Another concern relates to the capacity of statistical offices to adequately measure progress against MDG targets based on data gaps that can seriously affect the quality of statistical analysis (Jerven 2013).

Performance monitoring from the perspective of the politics of knowledge production

The above criticisms suggest that, in reality, performance monitoring can be deeply subjective and political. By bringing in a perspective that focuses on the politics of knowledge production, it is possible to examine the political and power dynamics inherent in monitoring processes in more detail.

One way of bringing the political and power dynamics to the centre of analysis is through an explicit reference to the broader social settings in which appraisal processes, such as performance monitoring, take place. The adjective "social" here refers to the wider systems in which appraisal is embedded and the institutional and governance processes that interact with it (Stirling et al. 2007). Smith and Stirling (2007) highlight that for any type of appraisal its inputs can be broad or narrow. An example for a dimension of breadth is the variety of perspectives – professional, disciplinary, or other – which contribute to the production of knowledge. The authors further hold that, independent of the breadth of inputs, social appraisal outputs "'open up' or 'close down' the formation of discursive and material commitments in wider governance" (Smith and Stirling 2007, 356). An example here is the MoWE's choice of a particular result out of several alternative results, which portrays water access based on average users of a water supply infrastructure.

A monitoring exercise involves many steps, from setting objectives, choosing a strategy, developing questions, choosing monitoring agents, implementing the monitoring exercise, and analysing the data to presenting results. In each step, the actors with existing material interests, and who are involved in discursive practices and constrained by existing structures, will imprint their interpretations and preferences. As a result, the same phenomenon can be appraised in different ways, with contrasting results. This basic observation suggests that appraisal processes are subject to power. Different agents, depending on their relative power positions, are able to influence appraisals, based on their particular interests and constraints. By doing so, they make choices that have the effect of elevating some appraisal areas.

According to Stirling (2005, 2008), one way that agents exercise power is by framing the inputs into appraisals as well as their outputs.

The term "framing" is popular in several different areas of the social science literature (Fisher 1997). In the field of interpretive policy analysis, the authors Martin Rein and Donald Schön are well known for their work on framing as a way to analyse complex policy controversies (Rein and Schön 1993, 1996; Schön and Rein 1994; Rein 2006). According to Rein and Schön (1996, 89), frames are "strong and generic narratives that guide both analysis and action in practical situations. Such narratives are diagnostic / prescriptive stories that tell, within a given issue terrain, what needs fixing and how it might be fixed". The above definition suggests also that framing, as a narrative, establishes a specific cause–effect relationship among different possible explanations of cause and effect through the employment of "generic" and "unifying" metaphors to imply a particular cause of action. The authors give the example of two different portrayals of urban housing in Boston. One story presents the situation as a cycle of disease and decay in need of renewal. The alternative story is of urban housing as constituted by social interaction and informal networks of natural communities that need to be preserved (Schön and Rein 1994). In the same manner as the urban housing example, performance monitoring can be seen as being mediated by actors' framings.

In appraisal, Stirling et al. (2007, 16) refer to framing as "the particular contextual assumptions, methodological variables, procedural attributes or interpretative issues that different groups might bring to a problem, shaping how it is bounded and constituted, and the relative salience of different factors". For example, employing a cost–benefit analysis to assess the construction of a dam will lead to different results from a social and environmental impact analysis. Stirling and colleagues' definition of framing emphasises method. Their reference to methods also fulfils the function of telling a story in a particular way, based on the method used to appraise a particular problem. Methods, therefore, can be seen as constitutive of a story.

Framing has a bearing on the inputs into any form of appraisal exercise, whether participatory or expert-analytic in nature. Framing occurs in the design, implementation and analysis of appraisal through, for instance, choosing the methods for its design, the way the enquiries are carried out, or by selecting among the data collected in the analysis. Independent of the framing of inputs, framing also influences the outputs of appraisals, which often are regarded as no longer part of the appraisal exercise; for example, the prioritising of research agendas in an organisation, or the prioritisation of research results that are communicated to a wider audience (Stirling 2008).

By drawing attention to how actors, through their framings, broaden or narrow performance monitoring processes and how monitoring results are opened up or closed down, it becomes possible to identify how, based on their rationales, actors choose some appraisal methods over others. Stirling (2008, building on Fiorino 1989) differentiates between substantive, normative and instrumental rationales. The substantive and instrumental rationales are relevant here. A substantive rationale refers to a situation in which the intention is "to achieve better ends" (Stirling 2008, 268), for example to better understand a particular phenomenon in question. An instrumental rationale "aims to secure particular ends" (Stirling 2008, 269). With reference to David Collingridge (1980, 1982, 1983), Stirling highlights that an instrumental rationale may bear on appraisals through weak or strong justification. In reference to strong justification, Stirling (2008, 276) refers to a situation in which dominant interests seek to enact favoured social commitments by framing appraisals to justify a very particular decision outcome. For example, an actor may choose narrow parameters to monitor access to water supplies in order to yield a positive picture of policy. Based on their rationales, and by using a position of power, agents are able to elevate some results over alternative appraisal outputs. While power can affect appraisal exercises in many different forms, the focus of this article is the exercise of power through framing appraisal inputs and outputs. I explore these dynamics through the lens of the WRI (Water Resources Inventory) carried out in Ethiopia's Southern Region in 2008.

The Ethiopia Southern Region's Water Resources Inventory of 2008

Ethiopia's Southern Region is located in the southwest of the country. It comprises approximately one-tenth of Ethiopia's territory and, with 16 million inhabitants, about 20 per cent of the country's population (BoFED 2011). Ethiopia's Southern Region is democratically constituted, with elected representatives at the regional, zonal, *woreda* (district), and *kebele* (subdistrict) level (Zewde and Pausewang 2002).

From 2001/2002 until 2007/2008, the regional Bureau of Water Resources (BoWR) reported a continued upward trend in access to rural water supply from 31 per cent to over 64 per cent of the population (BoWR 2009b). However, lower level government sector staff members strongly contested the figures portraying this continual increased water access in quarterly sector review meetings. According to the former BoWR head, this debate escalated in 2007, when the region was experiencing a drought, and over 50 per cent of the population were judged to be in urgent need of water. Emergency reports and response operations that tankered water to communities in need directly contradicted the continued upward trend in water access reported by the Bureau. In response to the precarious situation and related disputes over official access figures, the regional president requested a WRI (Water Resources Inventory) to obtain a more reliable picture of the water supply situation in the region. The president allocated a separate budget to this activity and chaired the inventory process himself, thereby lending it political weight.

The WRI is an inventory of existing improved water supply schemes in the Southern Region and of potential areas and sources for future schemes. Regarding existing schemes, the data collection form contains 17 parameters related to the production and consumption of water from improved sources, designed to calculate access based on the sector's access definitions and parameters, which are explained below.

Measuring rural water access in Ethiopia

In Ethiopia, the Universal Access Programme (UAP) (MoWR 2005, 2009) sets out the sector's targets and strategy for urban and rural water supplies. As indicated in its name, the UAP has the ambitious target of achieving universal access to water supplies (98% in the case of rural areas) by 2015. The 2009 version of the UAP provides official standards for access to rural water supplies. The document refers to rural water supply access as a situation in which every person obtains 15 litres of drinking water per day from an improved source within 1.5 km radius of their home. However, to measure access, the UAP estimates the proportion of the population that potentially can obtain 15 litres per person per day from a functional or temporarily non-functional but repairable water supply scheme.[4] This means that, for calculating access, the UAP refers to an average beneficiary number per scheme type that is divided by the population of the area. For instance, a hand-dug well is estimated to serve 270 people on average (MoWR 2005), regardless of whether or not it is functional. This method not only disregards the functionality status of the scheme when estimating access, but also the two parameters of volume and distance to the source that make up the definition of water access; it also omits other potentially relevant factors such as water quality.

Exploiting access parameters for portraying a specific access situation

Depending on the parameters used for calculating access, and on the calculation method employed, the resulting rural water supply access figures can differ widely. In internal sector review meetings, sector government staff exploited the sector program's ambiguity regarding service levels to achieve universal access. Specifically, they used different types of information as the basis for access figures that best represent their interests. The head of a zonal water department commented on the dynamics in internal sector progress review meetings:

> The problem is that it has been very subjective. The regional office calculates by projecting water coverage using the 2000 inventory. And we [the zonal water department] were using the 2004 inventory. The *woredas* [district water offices] are also using the 2004 inventory but they use actual population figures from their *woredas*. So, we were not using uniform information. (Personal communication)

According to the same official, in 2007, as a result of using different data sources, the regional BoWR reported access for his zone as 69 per cent, the zonal sector department reported it as 27 per cent, while *woreda* sector offices in the zone provided a figure of 12–15 per cent. Investigating the actors' rationales sheds light on the reasons for portraying different figures. Asked about the motives for using different data, the same head of department explained:

> [T]he problem comes when, for the budget allocation, water coverage data is important at the regional level. So, when the region asks for water coverage for a *woreda*, the regional office reports some number. The zonal and *woreda* office will oppose it because the coverage of the regional office is most of the time higher. And this will not help the *woreda* to get a big budget. So the *woredas* and the zone oppose the regional figure. There is always some quarrel in the meeting in this regard. (Personal communication)

His explanation indicates that the regional BoWR is under pressure from the federal ministry to report high figures that support a story of successful progress towards "universal access", the sector's ambitious policy goal. The *woreda* water offices, for their part, also have an instrumental rationale, but towards a different end: they are interested in reporting low figures in the expectation of increasing their chances of receiving capital budget for water supply. In other words, the political and material motives of sector government staff at different administrative levels were important drivers for the contestations of rural water access figures in the Southern Region in 2007. Next, I provide a detailed examination of the process surrounding the data analysis methods employed in the 2008 WRI, which was carried out in order to clarify the water access situation in the region. In that process, the data analysis team broadened out their methods of data analysis.

Broadening appraisal in the WRI by using different calculation methods

After aggregation of the WRI data, the BoWR set up a team of six regional experts from among its staff members to conduct data analysis. The immediate concern was to analyse information responding to access questions, to inform the next regional budgeting round. Based on interviews with three members of the team, consulting two draft versions of the WRI report, and a PowerPoint presentation by the team to the Minister of Water Resources, I identified three main calculation methods, which, along with their results, are presented in Table 1.

The first method intended to determine access along the distance parameter of the UAP. This method involved the team adding up the numbers of users reported as residing within 1.5 km of a functional scheme. Using Method 1, rural access was 21.5 per cent (BoWR 2009b), and urban and rural access combined 23.7 per cent.

In the second method, the data analysis team included scheme users from beyond 1.5 km in the Method 1 calculation. This resulted in 31.8 per cent access for rural areas in the region and 35.5 per cent for rural and urban areas (BoWR 2009b).

In the third method, the team calculated access based on the UAP's formula, which estimates population served based on average beneficiaries per scheme type, regardless of its functionality

Table 1.   Data analysis and results in the Water Resources Inventory (WRI) of 2008.

Calculation method	Rural	Urban	Total
Method 1[a] including all users judged to live within 1.5 km of the scheme	21.5%	43.1%	23.7%
Method 2[a] adding up all reported scheme users	31.8%	68.3%	35.5%
Method 3[b] adding up average users by scheme type	No data	No data	53.9%

Notes: [a]the source for Method 1 and Method 2 is BoWR (2009b); [b]the source for Method 3 is BoWR (2009a).

status, the official access calculation method of the UAP. According to this method, access for the rural and urban population combined is 53.9 per cent (BoWR 2009a).

All three calculation methods use a narrow set of indicators, namely users reported to live within and beyond 1.5 km and average beneficiary numbers by scheme type. Yet, by choosing three different calculation methods, the analysis team exercised agency and thereby broadened the inputs into appraisal, here the WRI. The team's report also shows that the team was reflexive in its approach: the report elaborates on the advantages and disadvantages of each calculation method. In particular, the team highlighted that Method 3, based on the UAP "scheme potential" parameters, has a number of limitations: the analysis is not based on actual user data, the standard population assumed to be served per scheme is not based on the scheme's actual capacity, and volumes consumed and user distances from schemes are not verified (BoWR 2009a). A separate important result in the report is that scheme non-functionality, recorded as 27 per cent in the region, is a major factor reducing regional access but not captured in the UAP access calculation (BoWR 2009b). The report also highlights inequalities between different *woredas* and *kebeles*, an aspect not captured by regional aggregate figures, and that shallow hand-dug wells and small protected springs, although low cost, are not sufficient to satisfy local demand. The team recommended Method 1, which refers to the distance notion of access in the UAP. The reasons given in the report for their recommendation were that this method is based on actual user numbers, and because it most adequately satisfies the UAP's minimum access to water requirement of a distance of less than 1.5 km of the household's dwelling.

The team's analysis demonstrates that performance monitoring involves employing a variety of methods, here weighed up by the analysis team against how well they represent the situation on the ground. The team's assessment of the advantages and disadvantages of the different methods indicates that they pursued a "substantive" rationale: they were interested in capturing, to as great an extent as possible, the water "supply" situation in the region. In their report, the team concludes that non-functionality is a major factor impacting access, a result that responds directly to the original objective of the WRI to uncover why official sector reports show a positive access trend while there continues to be reports of water scarcity in the region.

Furthermore, the wide disparity between figures for water access resulting from the three different calculation methods (23.7% to 53.9%),[5] where the lowest figure represents less than half of the highest figure, suggests that a definitive picture of performance monitoring may be elusive. The presentation of the three calculation methods emphasises that the measuring of a phenomenon (in this case access) depends crucially on different framings to interpret it. The three different methods used help to illustrate that performance monitoring can be seen as representing an abridged story of access. The full stories told by each method convey divergent pictures of rural water access in the Southern Region.

The presentation of the WRI results to the federal minister, examined below, provides further insights into how powerful actors, based on their rationales, can close down appraisal results.

Exercising power to close down the WRI results

When the federal MoWR was made aware of a sharp drop in water access for the Southern Region, based on the results of the regional WRI, it reacted by rejecting these results. A delegation, led by the Minister, travelled to the region to resolve the situation. The Bureau of Water Resources data analysis team mounted a presentation to the Minister, in which they described their calculation methods as explained above. In line with their view of the relative strengths and weaknesses of each method, the team recommended Method 1, relating to the distance parameters of the UAP method (BoWR 2009a). However, the Minister insisted on Method 3, the UAP's method to calculate rural water access based on average beneficiary numbers. According to one of the data analysts present at the meeting, the Minister argued that Method 3 was simpler than the other methods, while another data analyst present at the meeting said that the Minister acknowledged that:

> scheme potential has vast limitations and does not directly address the exact coverage of the area; rather it tells you what is the potential of the scheme whether there is a beneficiary there or not. (Personal communication)

Despite this recognition, the Minister was not willing to accept other data analysis methods proposed by the experts from the BoWR. Instead, he sent the BoWR an official letter confirming the parameters adding beneficiaries by scheme type as the official method to be used in the future. According to the regional experts involved in the data analysis, the official calculation method was "forced on them" by the MoWR and "not that much satisfactory" (personal communication). The regional Cabinet, which originally had commissioned the WRI, did accept its results and allocated an increased maintenance budget to the BoWR. According to the former head of the BoWR, the main issues discussed in the regional government were related to sustainability – that is, keeping schemes functional.

Monitoring performance or performing monitoring?

This analysis of the Minister's intervention shows how a powerful actor, here the Minister, can "close down" appraisal outputs in order to justify "instrumental rationales". I interpret the Minister's insistence on the calculation method as reflecting an "instrumental rationale" behind the push for progress towards the sector goal of "universal access", driven by a desire to show evidence of positive developments in the subsector. The Minister used his positional power to impose a particular – positive – calculation method, an indication that, in the case of this formal performance monitoring exercise, the direction of accountability was upwards in the hierarchy, with the calculation method driven by political pressure from the federal level. The process of "closing down" the WRI results to the parameters based on average beneficiaries per scheme type as a representation of access can be interpreted as an act of stage management. The interpretation of performance as being stage managed is reinforced by the Minister's acknowledgement of the limitations related to the "scheme potential" calculation method.

However, the findings from this case study also show that, despite pressure for closure to this particular result, the same appraisal was also "closed down" to alternative results reflecting more "substantive rationales". In the case of the WRI, the Southern Region Cabinet acted independently of the Federal Minister to use results to serve a more substantive imperative. Rather than simply supporting prior political aims, the objective was to achieve a substantively improved understanding of problems relating to rural water access in the region. That the Cabinet pursued a substantive rationale is further supported by the discussion of the WRI in the regional Cabinet, focusing on the high non-functionality rates across rural water schemes in the region and by the subsequent allocation of a higher maintenance budget to the BoWR and increased repair activities following the WRI.

The case study highlights that outputs from the same appraisal process can be used simultaneously to "close down" different results, presented within wider governance discourse. The case provides evidence that appraisal, that is the WRI, was subject to political pressures that variously accommodated the interests and perspectives of different actors. These may be separate from the formally stated rationale or imperatives driving the exercise as a whole. In the case of the WRI, for the closing down to alternative appraisal results, it was important that the regional government was interested to find ways for improving access across the region.

Conclusions

This article highlighted that monitoring processes can involve contestations over data and calculation methods; for example, the case of regular reporting in the Southern Region, the intervention of the Minister to impose his interpretation on the WRI results, and rows over internationally reported JMP figures versus national figures reported by MoWR. This emphasises the political nature of monitoring processes and the wider governance debates surrounding them. My focus on the instrumental and substantive rationales behind the access framings of different individual actors shows that powerful actors can manipulate appraisals to justify their favoured ends even when these are at odds with official appraisal objectives. This is exemplified by the Minister's closing down of WRI results to obtain a result that portrayed positive progress towards "universal access". The example shows that performance monitoring can be understood as the "performing of monitoring", on a stage where different actors (stakeholders) mount performances of water supply access according to their particular individual objectives and interests.

The instrumental use of data has been well documented and criticised for upholding a seeming accountability in relation with RBM under the aid effectiveness agenda (Hulme 2010; Eyben 2013). The examples in this article echo other cases in which performance monitoring is used in the public sector to overcome crises in governance. Examples include the introduction of performance measurement in a New York public bureau in 1912 (Williams 2003), and the well-known public service reforms introduced across OECD countries since the last quarter of the twentieth century (Hood 2001). Going further back in history, James Scott has documented the politics of measurement in early modern Europe as "an act marked by the play of power relations" (Scott 1998, 27). The insight that "[a]ll too often policy makers use statistics as drunken men use lamp posts – for support rather than illumination" (Picciotto 2003, 228) is therefore hardly a new revelation.

But are we therefore to discard performance monitoring processes altogether? The findings from this case study suggest otherwise. In particular, the fact that the data analysis team employed three different calculation methods highlights the plural and dynamic character of social appraisal processes in which stakeholders are able to broaden out inputs into appraisal. Furthermore, the WRI inventory case indicates that appraisals can be closed down to more than one result, as demonstrated by the regional Cabinet's discussion of the high rate of non-functionality, and the related allocation of a higher maintenance budget for water supply. This perspective brings the plurality of appraisal processes to the forefront of analysis, highlighting that the closing down of specific official performance monitoring results represents just the tip of the iceberg of a larger body of knowledge in relation to rural water access. The findings from the WRI in Ethiopia's Southern Region illuminate that beneath formal monitoring results lie a larger set of plural monitoring processes and related results. When subject to actors' substantive rationales, as was the case for the Southern Region's Cabinet, performance monitoring can usefully inform water supply access decisions in concrete settings.

The findings from Ethiopia's Southern Region's WRI highlight also that agency is not confined to a singular, powerful actor, but that power is situated. Depending on the specific context, different stakeholders are able to shape appraisal processes and related results. The results from Ethiopia's National WASH Inventory show that the acceptability of a particular method can change over time, becoming more politically acceptable. In the National WASH Inventory of 2011, three years after the WRI was implemented, the MoWE used three different calculation methods for defining rural water access:

- water access of users within 1.5 km (Method 1 of the WRI), resulting in 49 per cent access in rural areas;
- water access of users irrespective of their distance from the scheme (Method 2 of the WRI), resulting in 64 per cent access in rural areas; and
- water use based on the results of an ample survey of 12 million households, resulting in 45 per cent access.

The MoWE used the results from Method 1 to refer to water access in Ethiopia. As a result, the latest figures for rural water access of the MoWE and the JMP have come much closer, differing in only six percentage points (45% versus 39%) (Welle 2013).

Implications for policy and practice

What follows from this insight for policy and practice? This article's findings suggest a higher emphasis on supporting plural monitoring processes in concrete settings. Taking the rural water supply subsector as an example, there are a number of possible suggestions that come to mind. For instance, when designing reporting and inventory processes, more attention could be paid to the needs of those who collect and analyse data. Particularly, more care could be given to building the capacity of sector stakeholders at the decentralised levels for building up a body of knowledge about the water supply situation in their areas. As it stands, sector information tends to be handed upwards and analysed with the needs of those at the top of the hierarchy in mind (De Kadt 1994). For instance, in the Ethiopian National WASH Inventory, data analysis started at the regional level, thereby largely ignoring the data needs of zonal and *woreda* (district) water sector offices to use inventory results to inform local water supply infrastructure construction and maintenance decisions. In 2013, some two years after data collection, access to data was still largely confined to the federal level (only 58 of 731 *woredas* in Ethiopia could access their data), while the data itself continued to grow old (Welle 2013). To overcome such bottlenecks, more weight and support should be given to the process of day-to-day reporting of rural water access, and the process of data collection and analysis as part of designing inventories. Of importance here is how to make reporting and sector inventory processes subject to and accessible to a variety of stakeholders at different levels, including water user groups, locally based water officers and local governments. In a nutshell, a critical engagement with performance monitoring should not stop short of redefining water access-related targets and indicators at the national and international level. In addition, there are ample opportunities to encourage further methods of engaging in plural monitoring processes, such as more thorough and systematic analysis of operational data at the local level.

Acknowledgements

I would like to thank Morten Jerven and the independent reviewers for their thoughtful comments on this article, which helped to substantially improve the document. I am grateful to all my interview partners who provided me with rich insights in Ethiopia's water sector monitoring. Furthermore, I would like to acknowledge the financial support of the Economic and Social Research Council to my PhD, on which this article's findings are based.

Biographical note

Katharina Welle specialises in the interface between research, policy and practice of development. Her key expertise is in water and sanitation in the South. Since 2003, she has carried out applied research on water supply, sanitation and hygiene as related to politics and governance, aid relationships in the sector and sector-related monitoring and evaluation. Katharina is currently a Visiting Fellow at the Social Technological and Environmental Pathways to Sustainibility (STEPS) Centre, University of Sussex. She has worked at the Overseas Development Institute and at the Water and Sanitation Program of the World Bank in Kenya, Yemen and Ethiopia.

Notes

1. A detailed discussion of the advantages and disadvantages of the different methods can be found in Butterworth et al. (2013a, 2013b).
2. http://www.bigpushforward.net
3. The full name is Southern Nations, Nationalities and Peoples Regional National State.
4. The UAP distinguishes between three statuses of schemes: functional, non-functional (but repairable) and abandoned. All non-functional, repairable schemes are included in this definition of access.
5. I am using the access figures for rural and urban water combined here, as I did not obtain a disaggregated figure for rural water access for Method 3.

References

African Ministers Council on Water (AMCOW). 2011. *AMCOW Status Country Overviews – Regional Synthesis Report. Pathways to Progress. Transitioning to Country-Led Service Delivery Pathways to Meet Africa's Water Supply and Sanitation Targets.* Washington, DC: World Bank/Water and Sanitation Program.

Bennett, A., and A. L. George. 2005a. *Case Studies and Theory Development in the Social Sciences.* Cambridge, MA: MIT Press.

Bennett, A., and A. L. George. 2005b. "Process-Tracing and Historical Explanation." In *Case Studies and Theory Development in the Social Sciences*, edited by A. Bennett and A. L. George, 205–232. Cambridge, MA: MIT Press.

Black, R., and H. White, eds. 2004. *Targeting Development: Critical Perspectives on the Millennium Development Goals.* London: Routledge.

Bureau of Finance and Economic Development (BoFED). 2011. *Regional Statistical Abstract: 2002 Ethiopian Calendar /2009-10/.* Hawassa: Southern Nations Nationalities and Peoples Regional State.

Bureau of Water Resources (BoWR). 2009a. "Report on Water Access Coverage. (Woreda, Zone and Regional Level 2001 Ethiopian Calendar)." Presentation to Ministry of Water and Energy (MoWR). Hawassa: Southern Nations Nationalities and Peoples Regional State (2001 E.C.).

Bureau of Water Resources (BoWR). 2009b. *Report on Water Supply Access Coverage on Woreda, Zone and Regional Level.* Hawassa: Southern Nations Nationalities and Peoples Regional State.

Bureau of Water Resources (BoWR). 2009c. *Report on Water Supply Access Coverage on Woreda, Zone and Regional Level.* Hawassa: Southern Nations Nationalities and Peoples Regional State.

Butterworth, J., K. Welle, K. Bostoen, and F. Schaefer. 2013a. "WASH Sector Monitoring." In *Achieving Water Security: Lessons from Research in Water Supply, Sanitation and Hygiene in Ethiopia*, edited by R. Calow, E. Ludi and J. Tucker, 49–68. Rugby: Practical Action Publishing.

Butterworth, J., K. Welle, K. Bostoen, and F. Schaefer. 2013b. "Monitoring Access to Rural Water Supplies in Ethiopia." Background paper prepared for the Monitoring Sustainable WASH Service Delivery Symposium, Addis Ababa, Ethiopia, April 8.

Carter, R., S. F. Tyrrel, and P. Howsam. 1993. "Lessons Learned from the UN Water Decade." *Water and Environment Journal* 7 (6): 646–650.

Clements, P. 2005. "Book Review: A Handbook for Development Practitioners: Ten Steps to a Results-Based Monitoring and Evaluation System." *American Journal of Evaluation* 26 (2): 278–280.

Collingridge, D. 1980. *The Social Control of Technology.* London: Frances Pinter.

Collingridge, D. 1982. *Critical Decision Making: A New Theory of Social Choice.* London: Frances Pinter.

Collingridge, D. 1983. *Technology in the Policy Process: Controlling Nuclear Power.* London: Frances Pinter.

De Kadt, E. 1994. "Getting and Using Knowledge about the Poor (with Latin American Case Material)." *IDS bulletin* 24 (2): 100–109.

Debela, T. H. 2013. *Monitoring Water Supplies and Sanitation in Ethiopia.* Addis Ababa: Ethiopian Ministry of Water and Energy.

Eyben, R. 2013. *Uncovering the Politics of 'Evidence' and 'Results'. A Framing Paper for Development Practitioners.* Brighton: Institute of Development Studies.

Fiorino, D. 1989. "Environmental Risk and Democratic Process: A Critical Review." *Columbia Journal of Environmental Law* 14: 501–547.

Fisher, K. 1997. *Locating Frames in the Discursive Universe.* Sociological Research Online.

Hailey, J., and M. Sorgenfrei. 2004. *Measuring Success. Issues in Performance Measurement.* Occasional Paper Series No. 44. Oxford: INTRAC.

Hood, C. 2001. "New Public Management." In *International Encyclopedia of Social and Behavioural Sciences,* edited by N. J. Smelser and P. B. Baltes, 12553–12556. Elsevier Science.

Hulme, D. 2010. "Lessons from the Making of the MDGs: Human Development Meets Results-Based Management in an Unfair World." *IDS Bulletin* 41 (1): 15–25.

Jerven, M. 2013. *Poor Numbers. How We Are Misled by African Development Statistics and What to Do About It.* Ithaca, NY: Cornell University Press.

Mayne, J., and E. Zapico-Goni. 1997. "Effective Performance Monitoring: A Necessary Condition for Public Sector Reform." In *Monitoring Performance in the Public Sector: Future Directions from International Experience,* edited by J. Mayne and E. Zapico-Goni, 3–32. New Brunswick, NJ: Transaction Publishers.

Mehta, L. 2006. *Water and Human Development: Capabilities, Entitlements and Power.* Background Paper for the 2006 Human Development Report "Beyond Scarcity: Power, Poverty and the Global Water Crisis". Brighton: Institute of Development Studies.

Meier, W. 2003. *Results-Based Management: Towards a Common Understanding among Development Cooperation Agencies.* Prepared for the Canadian International Development Agency, Performance Review Branch, for consideration by the DAC Working Party on Aid Effectiveness and Harmonisation. Paris: Organisation for Economic Cooperation and Development (OECD).

Ministry of Water and Energy (MoWE). 2011. *National WASH Implementation Framework.* Addis Ababa: Ministry of Water and Energy.

Ministry of Water and Energy (MoWE). 2012. "National WASH Inventory. Progress and M&E MIS Report." Presentation to development partners, Addis Ababa, Ethiopia, September.

Minstry of Water Resources (MoWR). 2005. *Universal Access Program for Water Supply and Sanitation Services. 2006–2012 International Calendar. 1999–2005 Ethiopian Calendar.* Addis Ababa: Federal Democratic Republic of Ethiopia.

Ministry of Water Resources (MoWR). 2009. *Review of Rural Water Supply UAP Implementation and Reformulation of Plans and Strategies for Accelerated Implementation.* Addis Ababa: Federal Democratic Republic of Ethiopia.

Organisation for Economic Cooperation and Development (OECD). 2005. *The Paris Declaration on Aid Effectiveness and the Accra Agenda for Action.* Paris: Organisation for Economic Cooperation and Development.

Organisation for Economic Cooperation and Development (OECD). 2010. *Glossary of Key Terms in Evaluation and Results-Based Management.* Paris: Development Assistance Committee Working Party on Aid Evaluation.

Osborne, D., and T. Gaebler. 1992. *Reinventing Government: How the Entrepreneurial Spirit is Transforming the Public Sector.* Reading, MA: Addison-Wesley.

Oxford Dictionaries. 2010. *Performance.* Oxford: Oxford University Press.

Perrin, B. 1998. "Effective Use and Misuse of Performance Measurement." *American Journal of Evaluation* 19 (3): 367–379.

Picciotto, R. 2003. "International Trends and Development Evaluation: The Need for Ideas." *American Journal of Evaluation* 24 (2): 227–234.

Pinfold, J. 2006. "Uganda: Assessing Performance of the Water and Sanitation Sector." In *Emerging Good Practice in Managing for Development Results: First Issue, Source Book,* edited by the Organisation of

Cooperation and Economic Development (OECD) and The World Bank, 95–100. Paris: OECD and World Bank.

Power, M. 1997. *The Audit Society: Rituals of Verification*. Oxford: Oxford University Press.

Rahmato, D. 1999. *Water Resource Development in Ethiopia: Issues of Sustainability and Participation*. FSS (Forum for Social Studies) Discussion Paper. Addis Ababa: Forum for Social Studies.

Ramalingam, B., J. Mitchell, J. Borton, and K. Smart. 2009. "Counting what Counts: Performance and Effectiveness in the Humanitarian Sector." In *8th Review of Humanitarian Action: Performance, Impact and Innovation*, edited by ALNAP (Active Learning Network for Accountability and Performance in Humanitarian Action), 1–90. London: ODI.

Rebien, C. R. 1996. *Evaluating Development Assistance in Theory and in Practice*. Aldershot: Avebury.

Rein, M. 2006. "Reframing Problematic Policies." In *The Oxford Handbook of Public Policy*, edited by M. Moral and R. E. Goodin, 389–407. Oxford: Oxford University Press.

Rein, M., and D. Schoen. 1993. "Reframing Policy Discourse." In *The Argumentative Turn in Policy Analysis and Planning*, edited by Durham F. Fischer and J. Forester, 145–166. London: Duke University Press.

Rein, M., and D. Schön. 1996. "Frame-Critical Policy Analysis and Frame-Reflective Policy Practice." *Knowledge and Policy: The International Journal for Knowledge Transfer and Utilization* 9 (1): 85–104.

Schön, D., and M. Rein. 1994. *Frame Reflection: Toward the Solution of Intractable Policy Controversies*. New York: BasicBooks.

Scott, J. C. 1998. *Seeing Like a State: How Certain Schemes to Improve the Human Condition Have Failed*. New Haven, CT: Yale University Press.

Smith, A., and A. Stirling. 2007. "Moving Outside or Inside? Objectification and Reflexivity in the Governance of Socio-Technical Systems." *Journal of Environmental Policy and Planning* 9 (3–4): 251–373.

Ssozi, D., and K. Danert. 2012. *National Monitoring of Rural Water Supplies: How the Government of Uganda did it and Lessons for Other Countries*. St Gallen: Rural Water Supply Network.

Stirling, A. 2005. "Opening Up or Closing Down? Analysis, Participation and Power in the Social Appraisal of Technology." In *Science and Citizens: Globalisation and the Challenge of Engagement*, edited by M. Leach, I. Scoones, and B. Wynne, 15–38. London: Zed.

Stirling, A. 2008. "'Opening Up' and 'Closing Down' Power, Participation and Pluralism in the Social Appraisal of Technology." *Science, Technology and Human Values* 33 (2): 262–294.

Stirling, A., M. Leach, L. Mehta, I. Scoones, A. Smith, S. Stagl, and J. Thompson. 2007. *Empowering Designs: Towards More Progressive Appraisal of Sustainability*. STEPS Working Paper 3. Brighton: Social Technological and Entrepenurial Pathways to Sustainibility (STEPS) Centre, University of Sussex.

United Nations Department of Economic Social Affairs (UNDESA). 2012. "About the Millennium Development Goals Indicators." Millennium Development Goals Indicators: The Official United Nations site for the MDG indicators. Accessed March 20, 2012. http://unstats.un.org/unsd/mdg/Host.aspx?Content=Indicators/About

Welle, K. 2013. *Ethiopia National WASH Inventory: Lessons Learned and Maximising Value. Summary of a Seminar Held on 8th April 2013, Addis Ababa, Ethiopia*. The Hague: IRC International Water and Sanitation Centre.

Welle, K., J. Tucker, A. Nicol, and B. Evans. 2009. "Is the Water Sector Lagging Behind Education and Health on Aid Effectiveness? Lessons from Bangladesh, Ethiopia and Uganda." *Water Alternatives* 2 (3): 287–314.

White, H. 2003. "Using Development Goals and Targets for Donor Agency Performance Measurement." In *Targeting Development: Critical Perspectives on the Millennium Development Goals*, edited by R. Black and H. White, 47–76. New York: Routledge.

World Health Organization (WHO). 2012. "Millennium Development Goal Drinking Water Target Met. Sanitation Target Still Lagging Far Behind." World Health Organization. Accessed March 20, 2012. http://www.who.int/mediacentre/news/releases/2012/drinking_water_20120306/en/

World Health Organization (WHO) and United Nations Children's Education Fund (UNICEF). 2012. *Estimates for the Use of Improved Drinking Water Sources. Ethiopia. Updated March 2012*.

Williams, D. W. 2003. "Measuring Government in the Early Twentieth Century." *Public Administration Review* 63 (6): 643–659.

Zewde, B., and S. Pausewang, eds. 2002. *Ethiopia. The Challenge of Democracy from Below*. Addis Ababa: Nordiska Afrikainstitutet and Forum for Social Studies.

How to do (and how not to do) fieldwork on Fair Trade and rural poverty

Christopher Cramer, Deborah Johnston, Bernd Mueller, Carlos Oya and John Sender

School of Oriental and African Studies (SOAS), University of London, London, UK

ABSTRACT   The Fair Trade, Employment and Poverty Reduction (FTEPR) project investigated poverty dynamics in rural Ethiopia and Uganda. When designing fieldwork to capture poor people often missing from standard surveys, several methodological challenges were identified and, in response, four decisions were made. First, FTEPR focused on wage workers rather than farmers and improved on standard questionnaires when collecting labour market information. Second, researchers adopted contrastive venue-based sampling. Third, sampling was based on clearly identifiable "residential units" rather than unreliable official registers of "households". Fourth, an economic definition of "household" was used rather than the more common definition based on residential criteria.

RÉSUMÉ   Le projet Fair Trade, Employment and Poverty Reduction (FTEPR), qui portait sur la dynamique de la pauvreté dans les régions rurales d'Éthiopie et d'Uganda, a dû relever plusieurs défis pour rejoindre les personnes pauvres échappant aux enquêtes standardisées. Quatre décisions ont été prises à cet égard. Premièrement, le projet a mis l'accent sur les travailleurs salariés plutôt que sur les agriculteurs et il a amélioré les questionnaires habituellement utilisés pour récolter de l'information sur les marchés du travail. Deuxièmement, il a adopté un plan d'échantillonnage raisonné des lieux d'enquête. Troisièmement, l'échantillonnage s'est basé sur des unités résidentielles facilement identifiables plutôt que sur les registres officiels des ménages qui sont peu fiables. Enfin, les ménages ont été définis en termes économiques plutôt qu'en fonction du lieu d'habitation.

Introduction

Policy design and debate often draw on a combination of official or administrative data and on evidence generated by specific or one-off research projects. Bespoke data collection can be a cornerstone for policy: where there is limited official data or where the variables of interest are not routinely collected in official surveys. Further, the findings of microresearch can influence adjustments to the questionnaires used in official surveys. While the limitations of official data on employment and agriculture in Africa have been recognised for many years (Sender and Smith 1986, 100; Sender, Cramer, and Oya 2005; Oya 2013), the quality of project-specific fieldwork evidence is often ignored. Unfortunately, project-specific fieldwork can share many of the weaknesses of official data collection. This article describes the methods adopted for field research in the Fair Trade, Employment and Poverty Reduction in Ethiopia and Uganda project (FTEPR), funded by the UK Department for International Development.[1] Contrasting the FTEPR methods with standard approaches to rural development economics research has broader implications for data use and policy debates.

This paper highlights four methodological contributions. First, in marked contrast to most rural surveys in Africa and to virtually all previous evaluations of Fair Trade schemes, FTEPR methods were designed specifically to collect evidence on *wage workers* rather than producers. It was necessary, therefore, to make an unusually sustained effort to uncover complex, irregular labour market activities, through repeated piloting of re-designed questionnaires and the (re)training of enumerators. Second, the project adopted a form of purposive contrastive venue-based sampling,[2] with clear and transparent site selection criteria. Third, within the selected research sites, sampling procedures, aided by the use of GPS devices and handheld computers, were based on clearly identifiable "residential units" as opposed to "official" household registers. And, fourth, when constructing a household roster the research used an economic definition, discussed below, rather than the more common and often misleading residential criteria. The research method reported in this paper is based on a contrastive case study approach that provides a detailed rationale for the purposive selection of different research sites and that generates comparisons within as well as between sites. The purpose of the research itself was to assess the strength of mechanisms connecting agricultural commodity export production with the lives and prospects of poor rural people, particularly those involved in wage employment. Other publications will report on research findings.[3]

One purpose of discussing the (soft and hard) technology used in this research is to advocate a very simple reform to the way that rural research on poverty is reported, recommending greater openness on how and why particular research sites are chosen and sampling methods adopted. It is suggested that this kind of microresearch may be an important complement to official census or "nationally representative" survey data, in part because it allows for a more precise focus of policy design on areas of specific socioeconomic dynamism and in part because it facilitates greater knowledge about the material conditions of poor people, often missing from official data.

Neglect of wage work in Fair Trade research

A recent review of research on Fair Trade and other ethical labels argues that field studies "lack a convincing and consistent methodology" (International Trade Centre 2011, 25). And Fair Trade is just one among many institutional forms of the broader phenomenon of agricultural exports, where it has been acknowledged that too little is known about the labour market and other transmission mechanisms linking agricultural commodity trade and poverty reduction. Collecting more evidence, specifically on complex rural labour markets, is therefore urgently required.[4] The evidence needed is not available because almost all socioeconomic surveys in developing countries fail to capture data on the most vulnerable, poorly educated, casual and seasonal workers, especially temporary migrant workers (Sender, Cramer, and Oya 2005; Pincus and Sender 2008; Sender and von Uexkull 2009, 64–66).[5]

The key aim of FTEPR research was to provide robust data on wage employment. In contrast, most Fair Trade research has concentrated on producers, idealised as small farm households using family labour to produce certified crops. One systematic review of the certification literature found that "most of the studies reviewed deal with the producer as a self-employed individual and with producer cooperatives" (International Trade Centre 2011, 19). The Fairtrade Foundation commissioned a survey of 33 case studies, which concluded that: "there is limited evidence of the impact on workers of participation in Fairtrade, and more research is required ..." (Nelson and Pound 2009, 35). A recent impact evaluation commissioned by the Fairtrade Foundation of certified smallholder banana organisations failed to obtain any data at all on workers hired by producers or their organisations in two of the three case studies (Smith 2010, 52). Other research on the impact of Fair Trade certification, based on case studies of six rather successful small producer organisations, simply assumes that the landless, women and those with limited education do not benefit from and are "outside the dynamics of Fair Trade labelling" (Laroche and Guittard 2009, 34). The International Initiative for Impact Evaluation (3ie) highlights the problem that "many Fairtrade organisations ... establish a minimum price for producers but do not deal with the conditions of workers that the producers may employ" (3ie 2010, 2).[6] A good and especially relevant example is Jena et al. (2012), whose study of the impact on poverty of coffee certification in Jimma Zone, Ethiopia, fails to examine wage employment and focuses solely on "smallholder farmers".

Thus, the majority of these studies do not even attempt to construct samples of seasonal and permanent wage workers producing Fair Trade certified export commodities. On the rare occasions when wage workers are included in Fair Trade research, information on these workers is often collected from lists of wage workers provided, and sometimes selected, by employers or by officially sanctioned worker representatives (Barrientos and Smith 2006, 4; Omosa, Kimani, and Njiru 2006, 7; Klier and Possinger 2012; Ruben, Fort, and Zuniga n.d., 23). These lists may well be censored and are certainly unlikely to contain all casual workers, let alone recently dismissed or disgruntled workers. The other main information source is focus groups, with group participation guided by employers' advice, or over-representing the leaders of the permanent workforce relative to the numbers of illiterate casual (female) wage workers. A convincing rationale for the selection of members of these focus groups is not usually provided (Pound and Phiri 2009).

The unrepresentative workers who appear on these lists or in these focus groups are, all too frequently, interviewed on their employer's premises (Ewert, Martin, and Nelson 2005, 22–23; Barrientos et al. 2009, 27). Such interviews are unlikely to elicit reliable information; workers who are not interviewed in private and with firm assurances of confidentiality may go to great lengths to avoid the risk of being seen to offend dominant classes. In Nicaragua, for example, some workers for cooperative coffee processing mills were interviewed at their workplace and some while waiting for buses along the roads outside the mills. "Unsurprisingly, workers interviewed outside the mills were more critical of their working place than those interviewed inside. According to these workers, visitors often come to the mill to ask about their working conditions, but they are afraid to say anything negative for fear of losing their job" (Valkila and Nygren 2009, 5).[7]

While rural wage work is commonplace, especially where high value exports are produced, the ideological and practical factors that tend to limit survey coverage of such workers suggest that rural casual wage workers should be regarded as a vulnerable, "hard-to-reach" or "hidden" population, excluded from many official statistical surveys and rural development programmes. Rigorous epidemiological research on similarly hard-to-reach populations, such as illegal migrants, refugees, commercial sex workers and other groups at high risk of HIV, offers valuable lessons for the design of surveys of rural labour markets in Africa. Indeed, the method adopted in FTEPR research shares many features with venue-based sampling, as developed by the US Centers for Disease Control and Prevention (Muhib et al. 2001; Vermund et al. 2010). As Landry and Shen (2005, 1) explain, excluded populations tend not to be missing at random, so that census or survey data is usually biased, "particularly with respect to minorities, immigrant groups, or the homeless". The success of the venue-based method depends on the ability of researchers to triangulate limited quantitative data with ethnographic qualitative work to identify specific geographic areas (or "venues") with a high density of the target population to be sampled (Singh and Clark 2012).

Combined with venue-based sampling, a key decision in this research, given the focus on wage employment, was to invest heavily in enumerator and supervisor training and to develop a more complex questionnaire module on employment than is typical. Instead of using "main" and "secondary" employment categories, an employment matrix containing an exhaustive list of possible activities was developed and enumerators were also required to describe the full array of activities in different sections of the questionnaire, as well as to probe and repeat questions.

Selecting research sites

One unresolved issue in previous Fair Trade research concerns the criteria used in the selection of research sites. Certified or Fair Trade production takes place in very different contexts, with certified schemes varying, among other factors, in terms of the level of external subsidy they have received, the number of producers participating, the number of years of operation and the degree of financial viability. The range of rural areas participating in Fair Trade schemes (and therefore the range of possible research sites within a country) is very wide, but the reasons for deciding to focus fieldwork in a particular rural area, or on one particular group of certified producers, have rarely been explained in any detail.

For example, in one methodologically ambitious "quasi-experimental" study of the welfare impact of Fair Trade programmes, the only rationale for choosing producers is this brief statement: "The selection of FT organisations for the analysis has been conducted in coordination with Solidaridad" (Ruben, Fort, and Zúñiga-Arias 2009; Ruben, Fort, and Zuniga n.d., 17).[8] The study of smallholder banana producer organisations, mentioned above, was carried out in three countries, but provided little discussion of the choice of smallholder organisations or the country context (Smith 2010, 28). Nevertheless, this "Global Assessment of Impact" study did acknowledge that one very important country producing Fair Trade bananas (Colombia) had been excluded for some unstated reason, and that the three banana plantations selected were not at all representative of the majority of Fair Trade certified plantations (Smith 2010, 33). In particular, two of the smallholder case studies involved organisations that were "larger, more sophisticated and/or more supported by external partners" than other Fair Trade organisations. Further, all three banana case studies were also unrepresentative of the majority of Fair Trade producers in that they sold almost their entire output to the Fair Trade market (Smith 2010, 138).

These problems are shared by much economic research in poor rural areas. For example, the most influential rural surveys conducted in Ethiopia in recent decades have made little effort to justify their selection of sample sites. Debates on rural poverty in Ethiopia very often cite the results of the Ethiopian Rural Household Surveys 1989–2004 (ERHS). These surveys selected only 15 (out of more than 20,000) *kebeles* in Ethiopia as the sites for data collection.[9] The rationale provided for the selection of these *kebeles* is confusing: initially some were chosen on the grounds that they were typical (in some undefined sense) of areas affected by the 1984–1985 famine; additional *kebeles* were later selected "to account for the diversity of the farming systems in the country", and it was then claimed that the households in the survey were "broadly representative of households in non-pastoralist farming systems as of 1994" (Dercon and Hoddinott 2009, 6–8).[10] However, 18 agro-ecological zones have been defined for Ethiopia (CSA 2006, 16) and within each of these zones there are many hundreds of *kebeles* that could have been alternatively selected as research sites. The reasons for selecting the 15 particular *kebeles* that continue to be the focus of so much research are not discussed. There were plans to study exactly the same 15 *kebeles* in 2010, not on the old grounds that they are representative of agro-ecological zones, but because they "fall into five main livelihood categories of broad relevance for policy" (Bevan 2009, 14). However, no less than 175 extremely diverse "livelihood zones" have been identified and mapped in Ethiopia (LIU 2011). The 15 *kebeles* selected for the ERHS obviously provide a limited coverage of this wide range of livelihood categories

(LIU 2011, 121). The claimed policy relevance of the selected sites is also questionable; they certainly cannot be useful to illuminate some key economic policy debates – about floriculture, coffee or foreign exchange availability, for example – since they do not represent key areas characterised by agricultural export production.[11] By contrast, a much more transparent discussion of the choice of rural research sites for another longitudinal survey in Ethiopia notes that: "budgeting constraints and concerns regarding the long-term sustainability of the study meant that the rural sites selected were located in relatively better accessible areas. This is likely to have resulted in (surveyed) rural households being located in wealthier sites than the typical Ethiopian rural household" (Outes-Leon and Sanchez 2008, 4).

The choice of fieldwork site may be expedient and more or less defensible. For example, an authoritarian ruling political party or the Fair Trade certifying body or manipulative cooperative union officials may have preselected the area for researchers, discouraging research in other areas; there may be insufficient research funding to travel to more distant research sites; record keeping may be weak at other sites, or production volumes erratic; or local managers and state officials may welcome (or refuse) visits from outsiders. These types of practical consideration will always play a role, but it is difficult to make a judgement about the meaning of research results without a detailed discussion of the reasons for the selection of research sites. It is necessary to weigh up and balance complex information about potential sites, since sampling will have little credibility if it appears to have been ad hoc or arbitrary (Wilson, Huttly, and Fenn 2006). There is, therefore, a strong case for more detailed discussions than are typical of the rationale for and methods of site selection in research projects.

The purposive selection of subsites in the FTEPR was motivated by an aim to understand complex mechanisms and to accumulate new knowledge about rural development processes through old-fashioned theoretically motivated descriptive research. Such methods have been favourably compared to more fashionable "quasi-experimental" methods promoted by "randomistas" – the advocates of randomised control trials (Deaton 2010). Deaton's argument is that it is far more important to achieve an improved understanding of how (through what mechanisms), for whom (which specific population groups) or why the production of export commodities might influence rural poverty, rather than to answer the narrow question of whether or not significant poverty reduction has been achieved on "average" in the "treatment" (the Fair Trade certified) group. Further, a contrastive case study strategy does not have to make over-ambitious claims to establish "control" groups, emphasising rather the complexity and flux within specific rural populations and research sites. A contrastive case study approach can more easily explore and highlight the distributive implications of different institutional arrangements for agricultural export production (for example) than the "randomista" effort to isolate average "treatment" effects.

One principle of site selection – though not the only justifiable one – is that of contrastive case studies. The point of contrastive research is to explore the factors responsible for differences between phenomena in conditions with some common features: first, to establish whether there are contrasts, and what they are (between Fair Trade and non-Fair Trade crop production, or between Fair Trade production and labour in coffee versus flowers, for example); and, second, to try to explain some of these differences (Lawson 2003). FTEPR research adopted a contrastive approach to studying rural employment and poverty dynamics in two very poor sub-Saharan African countries, based on a theoretical interest in the impact of small- and large-scale export crop production certified and non-certified production, and production of different commodities.

A decision was taken to select two commodities in each country, allowing for further contrasts within and – in the case of one commodity – across the two countries. Thus, coffee and flower production in Ethiopia and coffee and tea production in Uganda were chosen for reasons including: the macro-economic importance of at least two of these commodities in Ethiopia and Uganda;

Table 1. Research site[a] selection in Ethiopia and Uganda.

	Ethiopia			
	Floriculture		Coffee	
	Large-scale	Small-scale	Large-scale	Small-scale
Fair Trade	Tefki	n.a.	n.a.	Ferro
Non-Fair Trade	Ziway	Holeta	Limu-Kossa	Kochera
	Uganda			
	Tea		Coffee	
	Large-scale	Small-scale	Large-scale	Small-scale
Fair Trade	n.a.	Mpanga	n.a.	Ishaka
Non-Fair Trade	Ankole	Kabale	Kaweri	Masaka

Note: [a]The names in this table refer to local town and area names.

the labour-intensity and contribution to employment of all these commodities; the relatively long history of Fair Trade and other certification schemes for these commodities; the dramatic contrast between the dynamism of floriculture in Ethiopia and the relative stagnation in the production of both coffee and tea in Uganda and in the production of coffee in Ethiopia; and the opportunity to contrast techniques of *arabica* production (Ethiopia) with those of *robusta* production (Uganda).

Briefly explaining some of the decisions taken in the FTEPR research project helps to illustrate the purposive research site selection method. The contrastive objectives implied that it would be useful to identify several of the most important agricultural commodity exporting sites in each country. As a general rule, within each sample category (certified/non-certified, small-scale/large-scale production) an effort was made to identify cases exemplifying the "best" producing sites in terms of reputation for quality and technological dynamism, in order to achieve consistency in contrastive exploration. Table 1 indicates the degree to which the objective of studying certified and non-certified production on large- and small-scale farms could be combined in each country.[12] As can be seen, it was impossible to identify appropriate research sites to complete all of the cells of the simple matrix in Table 1 because, for example, there are no small-scale Fair Trade certified floricultural enterprises in Ethiopia and no large-scale Fair Trade certified coffee estates in either country. This was one reason for the selection of only six research sites in each country, although the constraints imposed by the FTEPR budget also limited the total number of sites. There are clearly difficulties involved in this approach. It may be difficult, for example, to attribute outcomes to certification as opposed to scale. These challenges may in part be addressed through the detailed evidence and, especially, the qualitative research which was conducted to complement the quantitative survey.

Within the boundaries of each of these 12 research sites, it was possible to achieve additional variation, that is, to identify further contrastive opportunities by careful selection of heterogeneous subsites or "venues", for sampling. For example, some export production subsites are in rural areas of very recent settlement and others in areas where people have been living for many years.[13]

Selecting research subsites and sampling

Beyond the choice of sites, there are important methodological challenges in sampling in order to capture some dynamics of poverty and employment that tend to be disregarded by much socio-economic research. Pragmatic as well as methodological concerns influence sample size.

Sampling procedures may then depend on how important it is to capture *variations* within sites and among subgroups in a population. Some over-sampling may be required to capture people typically ignored in socioeconomic research and to gather evidence on, for example, the heterogeneity of poor rural wage workers. Here over-sampling meant stratified non-proportional sampling. Specific examples of the application of these methodological principles are discussed in more detail below.

For most researchers, practical constraints, including budget limitations, will combine with methodological principles and research objectives to shape samples. The budget for fieldwork was one of the determinants of the overall FTEPR sample size. It was calculated that the first-round quantitative survey could only afford to interview approximately 750 individual respondents, equivalent to about 120 respondents per site, in each country. Since comparisons between sites are an extremely important part of the FTEPR analysis, there were good arguments for achieving a roughly equal sample size in each site, also considering possible variation within sites (Wilson, Huttly, and Fenn 2006, 357–358).

The random sample at each purposively chosen site was large enough to be statistically representative of all female and male adults – aged 14 years or older – resident in the research subsite areas (see Table 2). However, the total sample at each research site was also designed to oversample those adults whose experience has been neglected in previous surveys but is most relevant to FTEPR research – namely, casual wage workers producing the relevant export crop. Qualitative evidence from scoping trips in the preselected sites confirmed that wage workers were a

Table 2.   Summary of FTEPRP[a] sample sizes.

Survey phase	Units measured	ET floriculture	ET coffee	UG tea	UG coffee	Total
Phase 1 Register all RUs in each site, using GPS	Total number of GPS-registered RUs	2280	2813	1350	1906	8349
Phase 2 Create a stratified sample frame using a brief PDA survey across registered RUs (quasi-census)	Number of RUs in quasi-census	1066	1678	890	1380	5014
	Number of individuals living in these RUs	2358	4721	2014	2765	11858
	Sample size of quasi-census (% of total RUs)	46.8%	59.7%	65.9%	72.4%	60.1%
	Average number of adults per RU	2.21	2.81	2.26	2.00	2.4
	Extrapolated number of adults in all sites	5043	7914	3055	3819	19745
Phase 3 Conduct main survey using detailed questionnaires	Total number of individuals interviewed	356	572	343	439	1710
	Estimated % of total population interviewed	7.1%	7.2%	11.2%	11.5%	8.7%

Note: [a]This table uses the following acronyms:
ET: Ethiopia
FTEPRP: Fair Trade, Employment and Poverty Reduction project, supported by the UK Department for International Development
GPS: Global Positioning System
PDA: personal digital assistant (handheld computer)
RU: residential unit
UG: Uganda

heterogeneous group. Thus, it was considered necessary to create a large enough subsample of wage workers to be able to account for variation and allow comparisons. In other words, selective over-sampling reflected the priority given to comparisons among different groups of wage workers. Since the overall site samples were designed to be large enough in absolute terms to be representative of the local adult population, they include and allow for comparisons with both male and female non-wage workers. Moreover, the data from the sampling frame that was constructed in each site also allow for the application of sampling weights whenever inference is designed to apply to the whole population in each site.

In addition, the total sample at each research site was designed to ensure some variation in the characteristics of respondents, mainly through the choice of analytically relevant subsites. Several days of qualitative research and discussions with key informants living in each research site provided sufficient information to identify subsites (venues) where there was a relative concentration of residential units (RUs) housing wage workers. For example, in Ziway two distinctive subsites were selected, both of which contain a large proportion of flower wage workers. The first was in a well-established part of Ziway town, where most residents originated from Ziway or its immediate surroundings. The other subsite was a very new neighbourhood on the border of the rapidly growing town. This is the area where most newly-arriving migrant workers settle, many of them originating from the Southern Nations, Nationalities and People's Region (SNNPR) of Ethiopia. Exclusively sampling in only one of the two venues would have resulted in the virtual exclusion of either group of core respondents.

The point is that each sampling site is likely to contain quite distinct subsites, because rural areas are rarely homogeneous. Through random sampling in several contrasting, purposively selected subsites it was possible to achieve much more heterogeneous samples – samples that included non-wage workers, non-migrant and food crop wage workers, females, more highly paid, and permanent wage workers, for example. The analysis could thus be based on comparisons of data on very different types of local people, leading to a better understanding of the complex determinants of rural welfare.

Official household surveys in Ethiopia and Uganda are based on samples drawn from lists of rural households provided by village-level authorities. Officially maintained registers of "households" are often used as the basis for the distribution of scarce resources such as food aid, or subsidised agricultural inputs and credit; thus rural elites are likely to have good reasons for selective editing of the names appearing on lists of potential beneficiaries.[14] Moreover, fieldwork experience in these two countries, as well as elsewhere in Africa, indicates that these lists are frequently unreliable because, apart from excluding marginalised people who have encroached as squatters and all those living in arrangements that do not correspond to standardised households, the lists are not sufficiently up-to-date to include all newly arrived (or departed) residents.[15]

Handheld computers with global positioning devices allowed FTEPR researchers to obtain sampling lists more accurate than the official registers. The qualitative work discussed above helped identify various subsites. A boundary was drawn around each research subsite with the aid of waypoints defined by the GPS unit.[16] The process of listing residential units started with a complete enumeration (census) by the research officer and a field supervisor of all the RUs observed within the subsite boundaries. An RU was defined as any structure in which at least one person was sleeping. Special care was taken by these senior and experienced members of the research team to record the precise GPS location and to assign an identifier to each RU, including non-conventional RUs such as temporary shacks and the doors of rented rooms where groups of migrants were sleeping. The complete census of a subsite could be accomplished fairly rapidly, since it involved walking up to the door of each RU and entering its position on the handheld computer (personal digital assistant, or PDA).[17] Once the preliminary residential census had been completed, field teams constructed a more detailed and up-to-date sampling frame of all adult potential respondents living in RUs in the research subsite by conducting a PDA-facilitated survey that included a small number of questions, designed to stratify the selection of respondents for the main paper-based interview.

A high proportion of RUs – between 45 and 100 per cent of the total number of RUs identified in the census – were then randomly selected for the next phase of the sampling procedure, using software installed on the PDA.[18] Enumerators were sent to each of the randomly selected RUs (or to all of the RUs[19]) to make contact with any willing adult who had slept in the RU on the previous night. It was usually easy, with the aid of the GPS device and the locations recorded in the census, for enumerators to find these randomly selected RUs and a willing respondent. The interviews were completed electronically, using a short questionnaire installed on the PDA. The PDA survey, equivalent to a quasi-census given the large samples involved, was used to build the final sampling frame for each subsite.

The key information used to define strata for the final sample of adults concerned labour market participation and migration. For example, adults could be classified into the following strata: "never worked for wages"; "currently working for (a named certified or non-certified export crop enterprise)"; "currently working for wages for another farm"; "currently working for wages for an export crop processing factory"; or "recent migrant".[20] It was easy to confirm that the final sample was representative of the large population of adults from which it was drawn – in the sense that the gender, mean age and education of the sample respondents generally closely matched the gender, mean age and education recorded in the population lists. This congruence was expected, since rather high percentages of the individuals in all the strata on the population list were sampled.

Finally, GPS identifiers helped enumerators to locate the individuals selected for the sample and to locate respondents randomly selected as substitutes by the research officer in case the individual originally selected could not be found or did not consent to the interview.[21]

Defining the members of a "household" roster

Official data often import assumptions built into common definitions of "the household". But researchers must decide how to define a household and be clear about the implications of such definitions. Here the FTEPR project eschewed the misleading and narrow criteria used by many other studies, in favour of an approach that allowed the linkages between geographically distant individuals to be better understood. Almost all socioeconomic surveys in developing countries fail to capture data on the most vulnerable, poorly educated, casual and seasonal workers, especially temporary migrant workers.[22] One reason for this failure is that the most influential of these surveys, the Living Standards Measurement-type household surveys (LSMS) promoted and funded by the World Bank throughout the developing world, rely on an *a priori* standardised, narrow and inappropriate definition of "the household" and its "residents". So, in both Ethiopia and Uganda, the Rural Household Surveys and the National Household Surveys fail to collect detailed information from "non-residents" concerning migration episodes in search of wage employment.[23] Important groups of vulnerable wage workers, especially those engaged in seasonal, casual and low-paid jobs outside major urban centres, are frequently not "resident" in households. They live and work for long periods in hostels, labour camps, barracks, construction sites and illegal squatter settlements, or they have been given some space to sleep at their workplace during the harvest season, or while working as domestic servants. These are the "nowhere people", the uncounted flocks of footloose migrants who "drift in and out of temporary worksites" (Breman 2010, 135). Such migrant workers remit part of their wage earnings to other individuals and these remittances are usually recorded in the LSMS Surveys covering the recipients' households. Unfortunately these wage earnings are not classified as wage income in the receiving households, leading to a serious underestimate of the degree to which poor rural households depend on income derived from wage employment.

FTEPR enumerators completed a long, paper-based questionnaire that provided information not only about the selected individual respondent, but also about a large number of other individuals to whom the respondent was "economically linked". The concept of a roster of economically linked individuals replaces the more conventional concept of a "household roster" (based on residential criteria), providing additional and extremely useful information on labour market participation and the other characteristics of individuals usually considered "absent" and therefore irrelevant to an analysis of the welfare of rural populations.[24] The problems and associated "myths" surrounding the use of conventional (residential) definitions of the household in rural surveys in Africa have been subjected to extensive debate and criticism (Guyer and Peters 1987; O'Laughlin 1995; Adato, Lund, and Mhlango 2007; Akresh and Edmonds 2010).[25] Randall, Coast and Leone (2011, 217) point out that, despite widespread international endorsement of the importance of household surveys as providers of data for development planning, "little attention has been paid to the issue of what 'household' means in these surveys: how it is defined for data collection purposes and what the definition implies for the analysis and interpretation of results". There are challenges in using a more realistic definition of economic households, but these are far outweighed by the benefits of not missing relevant linked members and therefore achieving a more solid basis for understanding individual and household welfare.

In selecting the FTEPR respondent, it was not necessary to identify or define a "household head", and the selected respondent was asked many detailed, repeated and probing questions about their own experience in the labour market. The acknowledged unreliability of standard Household Surveys as sources of accurate labour market data stems partly from reliance on proxy respondents (such as the household "head"), partly from insufficient attention to the structure, order and wording of the questions on employment and partly from the brevity of the labour market module in these questionnaires (Bardasi et al. 2011). FTEPR made great efforts to overcome these sources of error, including a protracted effort to train and retrain enumerators to avoid gender stereotypes, the mechanistic application of either the standard international classifications of labour market activities and the assumptions of local urban elites about these activities.[26]

Conclusion

This paper has made it clear how fragile the methodological foundations of many rural socioeconomic studies are, especially perhaps those that study the impact of Fair Trade. Lack of clarity about research site selection and ill-considered sampling methods are often compounded by ideological blind spots. It is to highlight the significance of these methodological weaknesses and to begin to address them that this paper has summarised the fieldwork methods designed for the FTEPR research. Aside from the aim of ensuring that different types of rural wage workers were included along with non-wage workers, three further methodological choices with broad relevance have been highlighted: a site selection protocol allowing for contrastive explanation; the construction of accurate and up-to-date household lists using GPS technology; and an approach to household membership that emphasises economic linkages rather than short-term residence criteria. The hope is that this generates more accurate evidence on the large number of "hidden" wage workers in rural Africa. Jerven (2013) has shown how choice of base year, somewhat arbitrary ideas about rural economies and choices about what economic activity to include and exclude have had profound effects on African national accounts data. Further debate on methods and assumptions underpinning micro-level economic research in Africa can also help to provide new and fuller information about people frequently missing from national statistics and about the complexity of their labour market activities. This, it is hoped, provides a firmer foundation for policy design. Aside from the advantages conferred by new technology, FTEPR has also argued for greater transparency and clarity in presenting the choices made in fieldwork – and this applies as much to project-related data as it does to official data sets.

Biographical notes

Christopher Cramer is Professor of the Political Economy of Development at SOAS. He has worked in and on sub-Saharan Africa for more than 25 years, teaching and conducting research, on rural labour markets, commodity processing and violent conflict.

Deborah Johnston is a Reader in Development Economics at SOAS, London. She has worked on sub-Saharan Africa for over 20 years, researching rural labour markets, poverty, welfare and land. She is co-editor of the *Journal of Agrarian Change*.

Bernd Mueller has been research officer in the FTEPR project, for which he spent extended periods in Ethiopia and Uganda on fieldwork missions. His main research interests include rural labour markets and the political economy of rural development. After his departure from FTEPR, he joined the Decent Rural Employment Team at FAO in Rome, as rural employment specialist.

Carlos Oya is Senior Lecturer in Political Economy of Development in the Development Studies Department, SOAS, London. He has done primary research in Mozambique, Senegal, Mauritania, Uganda and Ethiopia, focusing on the political economy of agrarian change, capitalist accumulation, rural wage labour and poverty. He is also co-editor of the *Journal of Agrarian Change*.

John Sender is Professor Emeritus of Economics at SOAS, London. He has designed surveys and conducted fieldwork in many rural areas of Africa and Asia over a period of almost 40 years, usually focusing on the development of labour markets.

Notes

1. Fair Trade, Employment and Poverty Reduction in Ethiopia and Uganda was a four-year research project (2009–2013) funded by the UK's Department for International Development (DFID); see http://www.ftepr.org/
2. Venue-based sampling is a method developed by the US Centers for Disease Control and Prevention (Muhib et al. 2001; Vermund et al. 2010), among others.
3. See http://www.ftepr.org for information on publications.
4. The *World Development Report 2008* emphasised, for example, that "stunningly little policy attention has been given to the structure, conduct and performance of rural labour markets and how they ease successful transitions out of agriculture" (World Bank 2007, 221).
5. On the poor coverage of rural wage employment in commonly cited Ethiopian surveys, see specifically Rizzo (2011). The more general point has been made that "in much of the development literature on pro-poor growth nowadays, little or no attention is paid to the underlying mechanisms that determine the dynamics of income … specifically, the dynamics of employment growth and of how and to what extent productivity growth translates into the growth in labour earnings is left out of the equation" (Wuyts 2011, 10). Similarly, Amsden (2010, 57) points out: "Despite championing the cause of poor people around the world, and dramatising the human condition, the United Nations' Millennium Development Goals make not the slightest mention of employment generation as a means to battle poverty."
6. Important exceptions to this neglect of wage workers include research by Valkila and Nygren (2009), Luetchford (2008), Maertens and Swinnen (2012) and Maertens, Colen and Swinnen (2011).
7. FTEPR fieldwork highlighted precisely that employers, who have close ties to local officials, are keen to avoid situations where their workers have the freedom to engage independently and privately with researchers. Local security officials and the police in one fieldwork site detained research assistants for several hours and lectured the senior researchers on "proper" research methods, which included asking "the owner" of a large agro-export (multinational) business to select workers and then interviewing only the selected workers at the workplace.

8. A more recent attempt to assess the impact of Fair Trade on poverty reduction also depended upon the Fair Trade organisations funding the research to select the research sites and the producers organisations to be studied (Klier and Possinger 2012, 4).

9. In Ethiopia, the *kebele* is the smallest administrative unit. It is broadly comparable to a ward.

10. A similar claim was made concerning the choice of the 36 villages surveyed in an influential study of poverty in rural Uganda: "The selected villages represent quite well the considerable diversity that exists within the two selected regions." However, the researchers make it clear that the actual choice of villages was heavily influenced by the wishes of district-level bureaucrats; the measures, or the relevance to issues of poverty, of the indicators of "diversity" are not discussed (Krishna et al. 2006). Another study in four districts of rural Uganda (of coffee producers) sampled only those producers appearing in the Uganda National Household Survey (UNHS). Unfortunately, the UNHS was not designed to be representative of coffee producers (or of households in each district), so that the sample cannot be considered representative of *robusta* producers in the districts concerned, let alone of coffee producers in Uganda as a whole. This fundamental problem did not prevent the World Bank-funded researcher from drawing conclusions about "the Ugandan coffee market" and "the majority of coffee grown in Uganda" from unrepresentative data (Hill 2010, 455, 438). The fact that the UNHS specifically excluded larger scale coffee farmers in Uganda from the survey is another important reason for caution in extrapolating its results to the coffee market as a whole (Ssekiboobo 2008, 7).

11. The broader political relevance of the sample is also questionable. The ERHS is not representative of the ethnic and religious composition of the rural Ethiopian population; for example, Oromos are under-represented (Kumar and Quisumbing 2012, 2). Further criticisms of World Bank-funded household surveys in other developing economies, focusing on their failure to provide a robust, transparent record of poverty incidence, has been provided by Walters, Marshall and Nixson (2012).

12. For site selection purposes, large-scale farms were defined as enterprises employing at least 75 wage workers; small-scale farms were defined as enterprises that are members of Fair Trade certified smallholder cooperatives, or as enterprises employing fewer than 75 workers. The Holeta site in Ethiopia was selected not only because it included small-scale flower farms, but also because it was the only area of floricultural production known to have experienced labour disputes and trade union interventions. After site selection these definitions were adjusted in line with sector and geographic norms.

13. A more detailed discussion of the selection of the 12 research sites (including maps), showing how contrastive exploration has been operationalised, can be found in *Methodological Issues*, FTEPR Discussion Paper No.1, "How to do (and how not to do) fieldwork on fair trade and rural poverty" on the project website www.ftepr.org.

14. Ethnographic work in two villages in northeast Ethiopia describes how local officials administering the Productive Safety Net Programme constructed lists of households so as to reserve the benefits of the programme for "the more affluent and economically potent households", excluding "the poorest and chronically food-insecure households", many of which depended on casual agricultural wage labour (Bishop and Hilhorst 2010).

15. For example, fieldwork in Kabale District in Uganda compared the official list of households maintained by one LC1 Chairman with a careful FTEPR village census (the LC1 is the lowest level of local council, usually a village or neighbourhood). The chairman's list was found to be grossly inaccurate. There is also evidence, insufficiently discussed in the relevant survey documentation, that the lists of households at the *kebele* level in Ethiopia, which are regularly used as rural sampling frames, are also unreliable. For example, a choice has to be made between alternative lists of households held by the *kebele* chairman, local health extension workers or development agents; one or more of these lists may well have been amended by the survey team (IFPRI and EEPRI n.d.). It has been admitted that not all villages sampled in the Ethiopian Rural Household Surveys had good lists of registered households (Dercon and Hoddinott 2009, 7). A quantitative survey in the northeastern highlands of Ethiopia, backed up by careful qualitative work, indicated that official *kebele* lists usually excluded households that did not pay tax, as well as some single-person households and people belonging to "socially marginalised groups" (Sharp, Devereux, and Amare 2003, 36).

16. Epidemiologists have pioneered the use of these technologies for surveys in rural Africa; see for example Vanden Eng et al. (2007). FTEPR benefited from advice and training in the use of handheld computers (or personal digital assistants, PDAs) with GPS provided by Anja Terlouw and James Smedley of the Liverpool School of Tropical Medicine.

17. The census of RUs in rural Ethiopia and Uganda was much less problematic than similar exercises listing unregistered urban populations in China with the aid of PDAs (Treiman et al. 2005, 13).

Depending on settlement density and topography, the FTEPR research teams might enumerate between 80 and 150 RUs a day in rural settings, while in the more urban settlements of Ziway the number could rise to more than 300 a day.

18. The software used for GPS navigation and the collection of GPS census data was CDCGPS2, developed by a team of researchers at the Centre for Disease Control (freely available at http://ftp.cdc.gov/pub/gpscs/). The digital questionnaires were designed and programmed using Syware Visual CE (http://www.syware.com/products/visual_ce.php).

19. In some smallholder coffee research subsites in Uganda, all of the RUs identified in the census, as opposed to a random selection of RUs, were revisited to obtain the expanded sampling frame of individuals. This strategy was adopted in research sites where export crop wage workers lived in scattered RUs interspersed with many other RUs containing no such workers. The aim was to ensure that the population list of individuals contained a sufficient number of the scattered wage workers so that a random sample drawn from the list of individuals was likely to capture respondents with and without relevant labour market experience.

20. The list of possible classifications of respondents varied across research sites. The electronic questionnaire included additional questions for some research sites, reflecting the type of variation that FTEPR hoped to achieve in the context of different crops and production conditions.

21. The site selection and sampling methods and GPS technology allow for a follow-up survey of a subsample of the original respondents. FTEPR research also involves qualitative research methods, including life histories of a small sample of those included in the initial survey. The advantages of "nesting" life histories within larger quantitative surveys are described in Schatz (2012) and in Sender, Oya and Cramer (2006).

22. At the other end of the scale, the largest and richest farmers in a rural area may also be excluded from lists of households or farm households because their farms are not defined as being operated by "households" (Choudhry 2008, 11) or simply because surveys of households usually exclude the top end of the wealth/income distribution (Székely and Hilgert 1999; Deaton 2001; Banerjee and Piketty 2003, 4). The domestic and farm servants living with and working for the rural rich are, therefore, also missing from rural household surveys.

23. Some implications of the failure to collect information on young, mobile rural people who are defined as 'non-residents' in conventional household surveys have been quantified using data from Burkina Faso. Their exclusion has a major influence on assessments of rural living standards (Akresh and Edmonds 2010). In Vietnam, assessments of rural and urban living standards have been shown to be unreliable for the same reasons (Pfau and Giang 2008).

24. The definition was designed to include the following four categories of linked individuals: (1) those who live permanently with the principal respondent and who share income and expenditure; (2) those who, even if not sharing residence on a regular basis, make significant economic contributions (in cash or in kind) to the expenses of the household/respondent; (3) those who, even if not sharing residence, regularly depend on economic contributions in cash or in kind from the respondent or others in the RU; and (4) those who, even if not resident at all in the same place as the respondent, either can be relied upon by the respondent, or receive contributions from the respondent.

25. Evidence from different disciplines "shows that the household as defined by survey statisticians may bear little resemblance to the social unit in which people live" (Randall, Coast, and Leone 2011, 217).

26. The innovative FTEPR questionnaire is available at www.ftepr.org.

References

Adato, M., F. Lund, and P. Mhlongo. 2007. "Methodological Innovations in Research on the Dynamics of Poverty: A Longitudinal Study in KwaZulu-Natal, South Africa." *World Development* 35 (2): 247–263.

Akresh, R., and E. Edmonds. 2010. *The Analytical Returns to Measuring a Detailed Household Roster.* Discussion Paper No. 4759. Bonn: Institute for the Study of Labor (IZA).

Amsden, A. H. 2010. "Say's Law, Poverty Persistence, and Employment Neglect." *Journal of Human Development and Capabilities* 11 (1): 57–66.

Banerjee, A. V., and T. Piketty. 2003. *Top Indian Incomes, 1956–2000.* Department of Economics Working Paper Series, Working Paper 03–32. Cambridge, MA: Massachusetts Institute of Technology (MIT).

Bardasi, E., K. Beegle, A. Dillon, and P. M. Serneels. 2011. "Do Labor Statistics Depend on How and to Whom the Questions Are Asked? Results from a Survey Experiment in Tanzania." *The World Bank Economic Review* 25 (3): 418–447.

Barrientos, S., J. Anarfi, N. Lamhauge, A. Castaldo, A. Akua, and N. Akua. 2009. *Social Protection for Migrant Labour in the Ghanaian Pineapple Sector*. Thematic working paper no 30. Brighton: Development Research Centre on Migration, Globalisation and Poverty (DRCMGP), University of Sussex.

Barrientos, S., and S. Smith. 2006. *The ETI Code of Labour Practice: Do Workers Really Benefit?* Brighton: Institute of Development Studies, University of Sussex.

Bevan, P. 2009. *Methodological Approach and Fieldwork Plan*. Oxford: Mokoro Limited.

Bishop, C., and D. Hilhorst. 2010. "From Food Aid to Food Security: The Case of the Safety Net Policy in Ethiopia". *Journal of Modern African Studies* 48 (2): 181–202.

Breman, J. 2010. "A Poor Deal." *Indian Journal of Human Development* 4 (1): 133–142.

Central Statistical Agency (CSA). (2006). *Atlas of the Ethiopian Rural Economy*. Washington, DC and Addis Ababa: Central Statistical Agency with International Food Policy Research Institute.

Choudhry, G. H. 2008. *Consultancy Report on the World Bank Mission to Uganda for Developing a Sample Design for the Uganda Agriculture Census and Surveys*. Washington, DC: World Bank.

Deaton, A. 2001. "Counting the World's Poor: Problems and Possible Solutions." *The World Bank Research Observer* 16 (2): 125–147.

Deaton, A. 2010. "Instruments, Randomization, and Learning about Development." *Journal of Economic Literature* 48 (2): 424–455.

Dercon, S., and J. Hoddinott. 2009. *The Ethiopian Rural Household Surveys 1989–2004: Introduction*. Oxford: University of Oxford Department of Economics and International Food Policy Research Institute.

Ewert, J., A. Martin, and V. Nelson. 2005. *Assessment of the Social Impact of Adoption of Codes of Practice in the South African Wine Industry*. Washington, DC: Natural Resources Institute and DFID.

Guyer, J. I., and P. E. Peters. 1987. "Introduction." *Development and Change* 18 (2): 197–214.

Hill, R. V. 2010. "Liberalisation and Producer Price Risk: Examining Subjective Expectations in the Ugandan Coffee Market." *Journal of African Economies* 19 (4): 433.

International Food Policy Research Institute (IFPRI) and Ethiopian Development Research Institute (EDRI). n.d. *Making Rural Services Work for the Poor and Women: Local Public Investments in Agricultural and Water Services in Ethiopia*. Addis Ababa: IFPRI and EDRI.

International Initiative for Impact Evaluation (3ie). 2010. *Fair and Square: Better Market Share, More Benefits through Fairtrade*. New Delhi: International Initiative for Impact Evaluation.

International Trade Centre. 2011. *The Impacts of Private Standards on Producers in Developing Countries*. Doc. No. MAR-11–201.E. Geneva: International Trade Centre.

Jena, P. R., B. B. Chichaibelu, T. Stellmacher, and U. Grote. 2012. "The Impact of Coffee Certification on Small-scale Producers' Livelihoods: A Case Study from the Jimma Zone, Ethiopia." *Agricultural Economics* 43 (4): 429–440.

Jerven, M. 2013. *Poor Numbers: How We Are Misled by African Development Statistics and What to Do about It*. Ithaca, NY: Cornell University Press.

Klier, S., and S. Possinger. 2012. *Final Report, Fairtrade Impact Study: Assessing the Impact of Fairtrade on Poverty Reduction through Rural Development*. Saarbruecken: Saarland University, Center for Evaluation (CEval).

Krishna, A., D. Lumonya, M. Markiewicz, F. Mugumya, A. Kafuko, and J. Wegoye. 2006. "Escaping Poverty and Becoming Poor in 36 Villages of Central and Western Uganda." *Journal of Development Studies* 42 (2): 346–370.

Kumar, N., and A. R. Quisumbing. 2012. *Policy Reform towards Gender Equality in Ethiopia: Little by Little the Egg Begins to Walk*. International Food Policy Research Institute (IFPRI) Discussion Paper 01226. Washington, DC: IFPRI.

Landry, P. F., and M. Shen. 2005. "Reaching Migrants in Survey Research: The Use of the Global Positioning System to Reduce Coverage Bias in China." *Political Analysis* 13 (1): 1–22.

Laroche, K., and B. Guittard. 2009. *The Impact of Fairtrade Labelling on Small-Scale Producers: Conclusions of the First Studies*. Montreuil: Max Havelaar France.

Lawson, T. 2003. *Reorienting Economics: Economics as Social Theory*. London: Routledge.

Livelihoods Integration Unit (LIU). 2011. *Livelihoods Analysis*. Accessed November 13, 2011. http://www.dppc.gov.et/Livelihoods/livelihoodhome.html

Luetchford, P. 2008. "The Hands That Pick Fair Trade Coffee: Beyond the Charms of the Family Farm." In *Hidden Hands in the Market: Ethnographies of Fair Trade, Ethical Consumption, and Corporate Social Responsibility*, edited by G. De Neve, P. Luetchford, D. Wood, and J. Pratt, 143–169. Bingley: Emerald Group.

Maertens, M., L. Colen, and J. F. M. Swinnen. 2011. "Globalisation and Poverty in Senegal: A Worst Case Scenario?" *European Review of Agricultural Economics* 38 (1): 31–54.

Maertens, M., and J. F. M. Swinnen. 2012. "Gender and Modern Supply Chains in Developing Countries." *Journal of Development Studies* 48 (10): 1412–1430.

Muhib, F. B., L. S. Lin, A. Stueve, R. L. Miller, W. L. Ford, W. D. Johnson, P. J. Smith, and Community Intervention Trial for Youth Study Team. 2001. "A Venue-Based Method for Sampling Hard-to-Reach Populations." *Public Health Reports* 116 (Suppl 1): 216–222.

Nelson, V., and B. Pound. 2009. *The Last Ten Years: A Comprehensive Review of the Literature on the Impact of Fairtrade*. London: Fairtrade Foundation.

O'Laughlin, B. 1995. "The Myth of the African Family in the World of Development." In *Women Wielding the Hoe: Lesson from Rural Africa for Feminist Theory and Development Practice*, edited by D. F. Bryceson, 63–92. Oxford: Berg.

Omosa, M., M. Kimani, and R. Njiru. 2006. *The Social Impact of Codes of Practice in the Cut Flower Industry in Kenya*. London: Natural Resources Institute and DFID.

Outes-Leon, I., and A. Sanchez. 2008. *An Assessment of the Young Lives Sampling Approach in Ethiopia*. Young Lives Technical Note No. 1. Oxford: Department of International Development, Oxford University.

Oya, C. 2013. "Rural Wage Employment in Africa: Methodological Issues and Emerging Evidence." *Review of African Political Economy* 40 (136): 251–273.

Pfau, W. D., and L. T. Giang. 2008. *Groups Excluded from "Representative" Household Surveys: An Analysis Based on Remittances Sent and Received in Vietnam*. GRIPS Discussion Paper 01/2008. Tokyo: National Graduate Institute for Policy Studies (GRIPS).

Pincus, J., and J. Sender. 2008. "Quantifying Poverty in Viet Nam: Who Counts?" *Journal of Vietnamese Studies* 3 (1): 108–150.

Pound, B., and A. Phiri. 2009. *Longitudinal Impact Assessment Study of Fairtrade Certified Tea Producers and Workers in Malawi*. London: Natural Resources Institute and Fairtrade Foundation.

Randall, S., E. Coast, and T. Leone. 2011. "Cultural Constructions of the Concept of Household in Sample Surveys." *Population Studies* 65 (2): 217–229.

Rizzo, M. 2011. *Rural Wage Employment in Rwanda and Ethiopia: A Review of the Current Policy Neglect and a Framework to Begin Addressing It*. Policy Integration Department Working Paper No. 103. Geneva: International Labour Organisation (ILO).

Ruben, R., R. Fort, and G. Zúñiga-Arias. 2009. "Measuring the Impact of Fair Trade on Development." *Development in Practice* 19 (6): 777–788.

Ruben, R., R. Fort, and G. Zuniga. n.d. *Fair Trade Programme Evaluation: Impact Assessment of Fair Trade Programs for Coffee and Bananas in Peru, Costa Rica and Ghana*. Nijmegen: Centre for International Development Issues, Radboud University.

Schatz, E. 2012. "Rationale and Procedures for Nesting Semi-Structured Interviews in Surveys or Censuses." *Population Studies* 66 (2): 183–195.

Sender, J., C. Cramer, and C. Oya. 2005. *Unequal Prospects: Disparities in the Quantity and Quality of Labour Supply in Sub-Saharan Africa*. Washington, DC: World Bank.

Sender, J., C. Oya, and C. Cramer. 2006. "Women Working for Wages: Putting Flesh on the Bones of a Rural Labour Market Survey in Mozambique." *Journal of Southern African Studies* 32 (2): 313–333.

Sender, J., and S. Smith. 1986. *The Development of Capitalism in Africa*. London: Methuen.

Sender, J., and E. von Uexkull. 2009. *A Rapid Impact Assessment of the Global Economic Crisis on Uganda*. Geneva: International Labour Organisation (ILO).

Sharp, K., S. Devereux, and Y. Amare. 2003. *Destitution in Ethiopia's Northeastern Highlands (Amhara National Regional State), Final Report*. Brighton: Institute of Development Studies and Save the Children-UK Ethiopia.

Singh, G., and B. D. Clark. 2012. "Creating a Frame: A Spatial Approach to Random Sampling of Immigrant Households in Inner City Johannesburg." *Journal of Refugee Studies* 26 (1): 126–144.

Smith, S. 2010. *Fairtrade Bananas: A Global Assessment of Impact*. Brighton: Institute of Development Studies, University of Sussex.

Ssekiboobo, A. M. 2008. *Practical Problems in the Estimation of Performance Indicators for the Agricultural Sector in Uganda*. Kampala: Institute of Statistics and Applied Economics, Department of Planning and Applied Statistics, Makerere University.

Székely, M., and Hilgert, M. 1999. *What's Behind the Inequality we Measure? An Investigation using Latin American Data*. Inter-American Development Bank Working Paper No. 340. Washington, DC: World Bank.

Treiman, D. J., W. M. Mason, Y. Lu, Y. Pan, Y. Qi, and S. Song. 2005. *Observations on the Design and Implementation of Sample Surveys in China*. California Center for Population Research Working Papers Series CCPR-006-05. Los Angeles, CA: CCPR.

Valkila, J., and A. Nygren. 2009. "Impacts of Fair Trade Certification on Coffee Farmers, Cooperatives, and Laborers in Nicaragua." *Agriculture and Human Values* 27 (3): 321–333.

Vanden Eng, J. L., A. Wolkon, A. S. Frolov, D. J. Terlouw, M. J. Eliades, K. Morgah, V. Takpa, A. Dare, Y. K. Sodahlon, Y. Doumanou, W. A. Hawley, and A. W. Hightower. 2007. "Use of Handheld Computers with Global Positioning Systems for Probability Sampling and Data Entry in Household Surveys." *American Journal of Tropical Medicine and Hygiene* 77 (2): 393–399.

Vermund, S. H., S. L. Hodder, J. E. Justman, B. A. Koblin, T. D. Mastro, K. H. Mayer, D. P. Wheeler, and W. M. E. Sadr. 2010. "Addressing Research Priorities for Prevention of HIV Infection in the United States." *Clinical Infectious Diseases* 50 (Supplement 3): S149–S155.

Walters, B., R. Marshall, and F. Nixson. 2012. "Consistent and Transparent? The Problem of Longitudinal Poverty Records." *Development and Change* 43 (4): 899–918.

Wilson, I., S. R. A. Huttly, and B. Fenn. 2006. "A Case Study of Sample Design for Longitudinal Research: Young Lives." *International Journal of Social Research Methodology* 9 (5): 351–365.

World Bank. 2007. *World Development Report 2008: Agriculture for Development*. Washington, DC: World Bank.

Wuyts, M. 2011. "Growth, Employment and the Productivity–Wage Gap: Revisiting the Growth–Poverty Nexus." *Development and Change* 42 (1): 437–447.

Collecting high frequency panel data in Africa using mobile phone interviews

Johannes Hoogeveen, Kevin Croke, Andrew Dabalen, Gabriel Demombynes and Marcelo Giugale

The World Bank, Washington, DC, USA

ABSTRACT   As mobile phone ownership rates have risen in Africa, there is increased interest in using mobile telephony as a data collection platform. This paper draws on two pilot projects that use mobile phone interviews for data collection in Tanzania and South Sudan. In both cases, high frequency panel data have been collected on a wide range of topics in a manner that is cost effective, flexible and rapid. Attrition has been problematic in both surveys, but can be explained by the resource and organisational constraints that both surveys faced. We analyse the drivers of attrition to generate ideas for how to improve performance in future mobile phone surveys.

RÉSUMÉ   Le taux de propriété du portable ayant augmenté en Afrique, on manifeste de plus en plus d'intérêt dans l'usage de cette technologie comme moyen de recueillir des données. Cet article présente deux projets pilotes ayant eu recours au portable pour des fins de cueillette de données par entretien, en Tanzanie et au sud de Soudan. Dans les deux cas, des données sur une grande variété de sujets ont été fréquemment collectées auprès d'un panel, de manière flexible et rapide, avec un bon rapport coût/efficacité. Le taux d'abandon a toutefois posé problème dans les deux enquêtes, mais il peut être attribué à des contraintes organisationnelles et au manque de ressources. Les facteurs qui peuvent expliquer ce haut taux d'abandon sont examinés afin de trouver des solutions pour améliorer la performance des futures enquêtes utilisant le portable.

Introduction

Timely, high quality information about well-being, service delivery, income, security, health and many other topics is not readily available in Africa. One reason why this is the case is because in the absence of high quality, comprehensive administrative records, such data are typically collected by nationally representative, face-to-face household surveys. Such surveys are expensive and time consuming and are therefore not implemented very frequently. Furthermore, even where multiple surveys may be available, problems with measurement of variables and comparability over time makes it difficult to learn trends over time. The lack of frequent, comparable and good quality data is problematic for policymakers, since a first step in effective policymaking is a basic understanding of the facts on the ground. As Jerven (2013) has pointed out, the unreliability of national income statistics in much of sub-Saharan Africa makes the process of formulating and evaluating economic policy very difficult. In a different context, Scott (1998) points out that making society "legible" by collecting basic statistics is one of the most fundamental functions of a state.

Yet, there is significant (latent) demand for up-to-date information of the changes in the welfare of the population. What if mobile phone surveys could be used to dramatically increase the frequency and reduce the cost of such data collection? Decision makers need timely data to monitor the situation in their country. How else can they know, for example, whether reports about a looming food crisis are overblown extrapolations based on anecdotal reports, or signs of an emerging disaster? Statisticians, too, could benefit from more frequent information, for example to estimate changes in employment or to validate GDP estimates with farmer-based crop forecasts and price information. Administrators and program managers likewise stand to benefit from rapid feedback on the success of their activities, while civil society could put representative information on service delivery outcomes to good use when framing their demands vis-à-vis government.

The scientific community could also take advantage of high frequency panel surveys whose availability offers opportunities to assess the longer term trajectory of effects in impact evaluations. It also offers opportunities to make impact evaluations more efficient. McKenzie (2012), for instance, argues that when outcome measures are relatively noisy and weakly auto-correlated, such as is the case with business profits, household incomes and expenditures and episodic health outcomes, impact evaluations that use smaller samples and multiple follow-ups are more efficient than the prototypical baseline and follow-up model.

This paper presents an approach to collect a wide range of representative data related to household welfare at high frequency and relatively low cost. The approach combines a standard baseline survey with regular interviews (weekly, every two weeks or monthly) conducted over the mobile phone. A wide range of questions can be asked during the mobile phone interview, including questions that are comparable to those asked in the baseline (to track changes over time) or new questions intended to collect data on emerging issues.

This paper is not the first to suggest that a mobile phone platform can be used to collect high quality panel data in developing countries. For example, Dillon (2009) used mobile phones to carry out 14 rounds of interviews (every three weeks) to track how farmer expectations of their upcoming harvest changed with time in northwestern Tanzania. This paper builds on this literature by documenting lessons learned from two pilot mobile phone panel surveys: one implemented in South Sudan and the other in Dar es Salaam, Tanzania. Of these, the survey in Tanzania has been running longer (33 rounds to date), while the survey in South Sudan operated under more difficult conditions.[1]

Before proceeding, it is worth noting that collecting data using mobile phones is becoming quite a common activity these days in Africa. For example, UNICEF's UREPORT, with over 200,000 participants in Uganda who respond to questions sent by SMS, is a good illustration of approaches that seek feedback from citizens.[2] What distinguishes the model presented in this paper from these other approaches is that the collected data is designed to be representative, as opposed to being based on a sample of people who self-select to be respondents.

The structure of the paper is as follows. In the next section we explain how mobile phone surveys can be made to work in the context of sub-Saharan Africa (SSA). Then we present some results from mobile phone panel surveys in Tanzania and South Sudan. Subsequently we address non-response and attrition. A discussion of the representativeness of the Tanzania survey is followed by a brief overview of other data quality issues that have come up. In the two sections before the paper's conclusion we discuss data dissemination and their use for accountability purposes, drawing particularly from the Tanzania experience and, finally, the costs of carrying out mobile phone surveys.

Why mobile phone surveys?

Conducting surveys by phone is standard practice in developed countries, but has typically not been done in poor countries because phone ownership rates are too low (especially in the pre-mobile phone era). In Tanzania, for example, just 1 per cent of households own a landline phone (DHS 2010). However, the rapid rise of mobile telephony in Africa has changed this. In Tanzania, mobile phone ownership increased from 9 per cent of all households in 2004–2005 to 28 per cent in 2007–2008. By 2010, this number had almost doubled again, to 46 per cent of households, and it reached 61 per cent by 2012.[3] Unsurprisingly phone ownership is particularly high in urban areas: it was 28 per cent in 2004–2005, increased to 61 per cent in 2007–08 and reached 87 per cent by 2012. In the 2010 baseline survey for the mobile phone survey in Dar es Salaam, mobile ownership was found to be as high as 83 per cent.

Mobile phone ownership is widespread, including among poor households. In Tanzania, one in every three households in the poorest wealth quintile owns a mobile phone (Figure 1).

In Kenya, which has one of the highest levels of mobile phone ownership in the region, the Afrobarometer survey of November 2011 shows that households own on average 2.4 mobile phones and that 80 per cent of Kenyan adults have their own mobile phone (Figure 2). Phones are actively used: only 7 per cent report that they never use a mobile phone while 81 per cent make at least one daily call using their mobile phone.[4] This rapid uptake of mobile phone usage is not limited to a few countries. Only 16 per cent of Africans (unweighted mean) now claim to never use a mobile phone. Most either own their own phone (71 per cent) or have access to a phone belonging to someone in or outside the household (Figure 2). Furthermore, the phones are mostly used for making calls, multiple times in a day. Table 1 shows that 66 per cent of Africans use their phone to make or receive a call at least once in a day, while almost half (46%) use it to receive or send an SMS.

With such high rates of mobile phone ownership, representative household surveys using mobile phones become an option. Phone ownership rates above 80 per cent are at or beyond the threshold at which reliable survey research can be conducted: for example, only 80 per cent of US households own a landline, but political polling has typically used landline samples only. The point estimates provided by these surveys are widely considered reliable when corrected by reweighting.[5] This suggests that phone ownership in Kenya or in urban Tanzania is already high enough for reasonable inferences to be made from surveys that exclusively rely on mobile phones. In many rural settings, mobile phone surveys could also be used, provided that

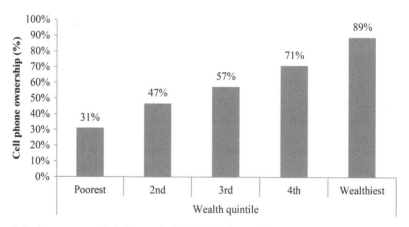

Figure 1.   Cell phone ownership in Tanzania in 2010/11, by wealth quintile.
Source: Tanzania National Panel Survey 2010/11.

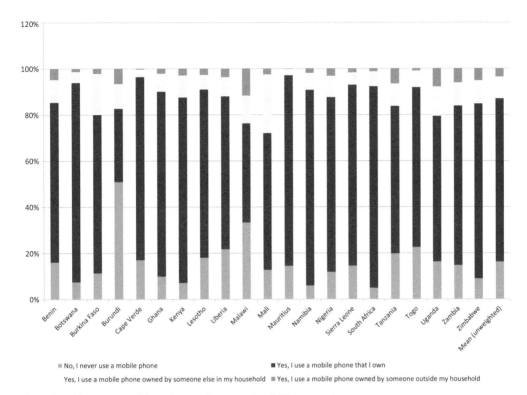

Figure 2.   Phone ownership and usage in a sample of SSA countries.
Source: Authors' own tabulation using Afrobarometer surveys (www.afrobarometer.org). Dates of surveys vary by country from late 2011 to early 2013.

one ensures that a representative sample owns or has access to a mobile phone. This is affordable, as reliable phones can now be bought for $20 or less,[6] meaning that respondents selected for participation in a mobile phone survey and who do not own a phone can be given one. Only respondents living in areas not covered by a mobile phone signal would be left out of such surveys, but even these respondents could be included if use was made of a local enumerator who visits the respondents, collects their responses and then finds a location with a mobile phone signal to relay the responses to the survey administrators.

Furthermore, developing countries in other regions are testing alternative methods of data collection when using mobile phones. For example, pilots in Peru and Honduras tested various methods (call center versus interactive voice response versus SMS) as well as different levels of rewards for participation in a mobile phone surveys.[7] Similarly, the authors of this paper have used mobile phone follow-up surveys in impact evaluations for populations in which the majority of project participants owned mobile phones – for example, in an evaluation of technical training for college graduates in Nigeria. Public health projects in various settings have also used mobile phones for data collection (Tomlinson et al. 2009).

Another reason to consider using mobile phones for household surveys is because mobile phone interviews have been found to produce quality data. Lynn and Kaminska (2013), for example, investigated whether data collected through interviews using mobile phones differs from data collected using landlines. They started by identifying four reasons why the quality of data collected using mobile and fixed phone interviews might differ: line quality, the extent of multi-tasking amongst survey respondents, the extent to which survey respondents are

Table 1. Frequency and manner of phone usage (call and text) from a sample of SSA countries.

	How often do you normally use a phone to make or receive a call?		How often do you normally use a phone to send or receive a text message or SMS?	
	Never	At least once per day	Never	At least once per day
Benin	14%	72%	64%	25%
Botswana	7%	76%	18%	70%
Burkina Faso	12%	63%	69%	22%
Burundi	50%	32%	68%	22%
Cape Verde	19%	61%	30%	46%
Ghana	9%	85%	47%	39%
Kenya	7%	82%	20%	63%
Lesotho	18%	57%	29%	50%
Liberia	22%	60%	43%	43%
Malawi	33%	47%	54%	28%
Mali	13%	53%	65%	24%
Mauritius	14%	79%	32%	58%
Namibia	7%	81%	11%	83%
Nigeria	11%	77%	28%	47%
Sierra Leone	14%	75%	37%	50%
South Africa	6%	77%	14%	66%
Tanzania	18%	63%	32%	50%
Togo	22%	66%	44%	42%
Uganda	19%	55%	43%	31%
Zambia	15%	68%	32%	50%
Zimbabwe	9%	66%	16%	57%
Mean (unweighted)	16%	66%	38%	46%

Source: Authors' own tabulation using Afrobarometer surveys (www.afrobarometer.org). Dates of surveys vary by country from late 2011 to early 2013.

distracted from the task of answering questions, and the extent to which other people are present and able to overhear what the survey respondent is saying. The authors evaluated the extent to which differences in these features affect survey measures via an experiment in which a sample of people who had both mobile and fixed phones were randomly assigned to be interviewed either on their mobile phones or on their fixed phones. They found only small differences in survey measures between mobile phone interviews and fixed phone interviews, and the differences found suggest that data quality may be higher with mobile phone interviews. This they attribute to survey respondents having greater control over whether other people are within earshot and whether others can listen in from another line. When other people can hear the responses being given – which may be more likely when responding on a fixed line – respondents may have a tendency to censor their responses to avoid socially undesirable answers. The surveys discussed in this paper do not offer similar experiments comparing face-to-face and mobile phone interviews. There is, however, some evidence discussed below that answers on "sensitive" issues improved over time, which suggests that the high frequency and long duration of mobile panel surveys may produce data quality improvements over time. For example, reported support for the ruling party – a sensitive issue in Tanzania – has dropped significantly over time. Whether this is due to shifting political winds or increased respondent confidence in the survey is impossible to say.

One aspect to be aware of is that mobile phone panel surveys, which give phones to respondents and that incentivise respondents with call credit after the completion of an interview, are by their very nature an *intervention* as well as a means of data collection. Particularly for respondents that did not own a phone prior to participation on the survey, their ability to access information and to connect with others changes significantly. Moreover, there is some evidence, from Zwane et al. (2011), that simply surveying respondents has the effect of changing their responses. This may be especially problematic in high frequency panels, given that respondents are asked to consider aspects of their lives and state facts or opinions about it at a frequency that is much higher than in ordinary (panel) surveys. In future research we intend to explore whether this "empowers" respondents and changes their behavior. A randomised experiment in which some respondents in the baseline participate in the mobile phone panel and others do not, followed by a second face-to-face interview a year later, would be a good way to assess the impact of participation in a mobile phone panel survey.

There are two ways to set up a representative mobile phone panel survey. One approach exclusively relies on mobile phone interviews and creates a representative sample by calling potential respondents to assess their core characteristics (location, gender, age, education, wealth) and their willingness to participate in the survey. This requires high mobile phone penetration rates and the availability of a database of telephone numbers from which an unbiased sample can be drawn. Another, more conventional approach does not exclusively rely on phone interviews, but rather combines face-to-face interviews during a baseline survey with follow-up mobile phone interviews.

Both approaches are feasible but, given the current penetration rates of mobile phones in sub-Saharan Africa (particularly in rural areas and among poor households), we think the approach that makes use of a baseline survey makes more sense. This baseline will often be a new survey, but it could be that households from an existing survey, such as a national living standard or a poverty survey, are revisited. The latter may seem like a good way to reduce costs. However, given that households will need to be revisited in any case during the baseline survey to select the respondent[8] in order to obtain permission for participation, to familiarise respondents with the mobile interview, and to agree on a good time for phone interviews, the cost advantage of using an existing survey sample is likely to be small. The baseline survey is also the time to distribute phones and, in locations with limited access to electricity, solar chargers. Alternatively, a village kiosk owner who provides phone charging services could be contracted to offer free phone charging to participating households.

Mobile phones offer a multitude of opportunities to gather information. Live interviews carried out by a mobile phone enumerator are one way. SMS (short message service), WAP (wireless application protocol, allowing for web-based mobile phone surveys, suited for high-end phones with internet capability), IVR (interactive voice response) and USSD (unstructured supplementary service data, an approach allowing direct transmission of questions from a phone company server to the respondent's phone) are other approaches.[9] In the current context of sub-Saharan Africa, our suggestion is to collect data using live interviews, whereby enumerators in a call center telephone respondents, ask the relevant questions and enter the responses into a database using a CATI (computer aided telephone interview) system. The decision to rely on call centers for mobile phone data collection is informed by experiences with WAP, IVR and USSD in the early stages of the Dar es Salaam mobile phone survey. Live interviews offer flexibility to conduct interviews in different languages, to vary questions from one round to the next, to ask complex questions which may require explanation, to accommodate illiterate respondents and to reach respondents owning low end phones without internet connectivity. All of these aspects make live interviews the most reliable technology for most of sub-Sahara Africa. Moreover, good enumerators can build rapport with the respondent, supervisors can recall (instead of revisit) respondents for quality control purposes, and live interviews offer the opportunity to ask in-depth, qualitative questions.

Reliance on voice to collect data does not mean that other opportunities offered by mobile phones remain unexploited. Respondents can be alerted that an interview is due through SMS and, following the successful completion of an interview, respondents can receive phone credit that is transferred directly to their mobile phone. Remuneration of the respondent seems likely to be necessary if the aim is to motivate respondents to remain in the sample for a long period of time. The remuneration does not have to be very sizeable, and could largely be seen as a token of appreciation. In Tanzania, for instance, the phone credit that is transferred after every interview varies from 300 to 500 Tanzanian shillings ($0.17 to $0.42), with no discernible impact on response rate (see Table 2). Likewise, the amount of air time compensation was varied experimentally in the South Sudan survey, and a higher level of compensation did not result in a higher response rate.[10] While there is some debate among face-to-face survey practitioners about whether or not to compensate survey respondents for their participation, some form of small compensation seemed clearly appropriate in the case of the Dar es Salaam

Table 2.   OLS regressions on participation in the mobile phone survey.

	(1)	(2)	(3)
D-unreachable in round 1			−9.63266
			−15.5
D-male	−1.176	−0.017	−0.315
	−1.5	0.0	−0.5
D-owns phone	**6.003**	1.468	0.792
	6.3	1.4	0.9
Age	−0.008	−0.017	−0.012
	−0.3	−0.6	−0.6
Years of schooling	0.048	0.031	0.166
	0.4	0.2	1.6
D-rural	−0.640	−1.786	−1.011
	−0.6	−1.7	−1.2
D-house has electricity	−0.074	−0.130	−0.125
	−0.1	−0.3	−0.3
D-poorest quintile	−2.126	−0.815	−0.634
	−1.6	−0.6	−0.6
D-second quintile	**−2.181**	−1.774	−0.650
	−1.8	−1.5	−0.7
D-fourth quintile	0.890	1.164	1.048
	0.7	1.0	1.1
D-wealthiest quintile	−1.086	−0.576	0.097
	−0.8	−0.5	0.1
D-receives Tsh 300	−0.247	0.150	0.639
	−0.3	0.2	0.9
D-receives Tsh 400	−1.144	−0.635	−0.823
	−1.2	−0.7	−1.1
D-Vodacom	**5.755**	**2.016**	0.637
	4.7	1.7	0.7
D-Tigo	**2.580**	−0.907	−0.803
	2.7	−0.9	−1.0
Constant	**9.313**	**17.399**	**19.908**
	4.3	7.5	10.7
Obs	542	450	450
R-squared (adj)	0.18	0.04	0.38

Notes: Dependent variable is the number of times a respondent participated in the last 25 survey rounds. T-values in *italics* underneath the coefficient. Significant coefficients ($p < 0.05$) in **bold**. F test of the wealth quintile variables shows that they are not jointly significant. Tsh, Tanzanian shillings.

survey, which initially called respondents on a weekly basis and which has conducted over 30 rounds of data collection. The sums involved seem small enough that they are unlikely to bias responses in a meaningful way.

Another way to motivate respondents is by keeping them informed about how data they provided is being used. In Tanzania, respondents were notified by SMS when newspapers report stories based on information provided by the respondents. The Dar es Salaam pilot program also released all (anonymised) data within four weeks of its collection.[11]

Selected results from the Tanzania and South Sudan mobile phone panel surveys

The mobile phone survey in South Sudan revisited, late in 2010, 1,000 respondents in 10 urban areas covered in 2009 by the National Baseline Household Survey. During the revisit respondents were identified, mobile phones were handed out (half of them, selected at random, were provided with integrated solar chargers) and agreements were reached about when respondents could best be called. Respondents were provided with and asked to sign a "contract" which prominently displayed the flag of the Government of South Sudan as well as the logos of the South Sudan Bureau of Statistics and the World Bank. The purpose of these documents was to create a sense of commitment on the part of respondents as well as to protect female respondents from over-zealous husbands who might question the intention of the person providing these gifts. Respondents were then called on a monthly basis using a call center operating from Nairobi using interviewers capable of speaking South Sudan's main languages. Respondents who successfully completed an interview were rewarded with an amount varying from approximately $2 to $4.

In August 2010, the survey team in Tanzania visited 550 households in Dar es Salaam, administered a new baseline survey, randomly selected an adult respondent from the household roster to be included in the mobile phone panel, and called respondents on a weekly basis (25 rounds), and then every two weeks (8 rounds). The survey in Dar es Salaam did not distribute phones at baseline. Only later in the survey, when additional budget was secured, were phones distributed to selected respondents. Respondents were rewarded with phone credit varying between $0.17 and $0.42 per successful interview.[12]

The mobile phone survey interview format does not appear to pose major limitations on what can be asked, except that the length of an interview should probably not be more than 20–30 minutes. The interviews for the separate Tanzania survey described in Dillon (2009) lasted 27 minutes on average. Interviews in the Dar es Salaam survey are generally somewhat shorter. This means that an elaborate consumption module or a detailed health module with birth histories are less suited for this type of survey.[13] Mobile phone surveys in South Sudan and Tanzania collect information on a wide variety of issues including health, education, water, security, nutrition, travel times, prices, electricity and governance. The surveys have been used to ask perception questions on topics varying from what respondents considered the most pressing problems to be addressed by the city government to opinions about the constitutional reform process underway at the time in Tanzania. They have been used to collect baseline information for a large scale program on food fortification. They also allow flexible follow up. One of the authors, for example, used the panel to collect additional data when it turned out that the baseline survey lacked some variables needed to answer a particular research question.

Data collected by the mobile phone survey can easily be used to report on a single issue. However, the methodological advantage of panel phone surveys is best illustrated when tracking changes that are very frequent. For example, Figure 3 shows how food security in South Sudan improved between December 2010 and March 2011, something that could have been easily missed by traditional surveys if data collection was conducted, say, in just one of those months.

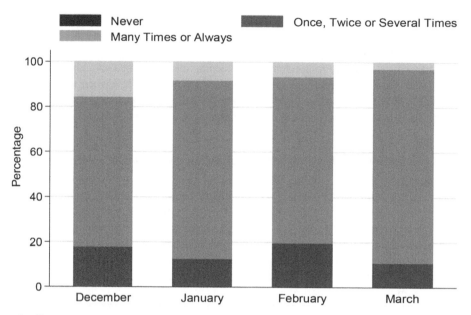

Figure 3. Survey responses to "In the last month, how often if ever, have you or a member of your household gone without enough food to eat?"
Source: South Sudan mobile phone survey, 2010–2011.

Additionally, by combining information collected during mobile phone interviews with the more elaborate information collected in the baseline, more meaningful results are obtained. Results for whether a child received homework or not are disaggregated by wealth quintile (Figure 4), using an indicator that was constructed using asset information collected during the face-to-face interviews of the baseline survey. Such information can be useful to monitor the distributional impact of large scale programs or to track well-being of the poorest in a society during a crisis.

Finally, unlike traditional surveys, mobile phone surveys are methodologically very flexible. Because questions can be changed every round of the survey, it is possible to accommodate new data requests or to respond to emerging issues. After Dar es Salaam was hit by major floods in

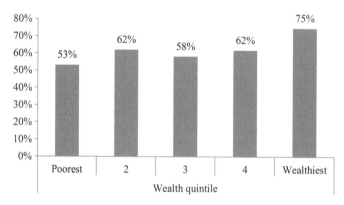

Figure 4. Survey responses to "In the last week, did your child receive any homework?"
Source: Tanzania mobile phone survey, 2012.

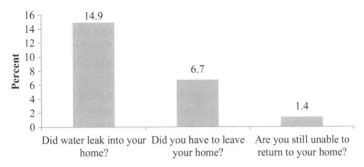

Figure 5.   Questions asked in early January 2012 in response to the December floods in Dar es Salaam.
Source: Tanzania mobile phone survey, 2012.

December 2011, the mobile phone survey asked questions to estimate the fraction of people that had been affected, finding that almost 7 per cent of households had been forced to leave their home (Figure 5). Had the sample size been somewhat larger, it would even have been possible to estimate the percentage of affected households that received assistance from the government, proving real time impact on an important and salient government activity.

A recent innovation that has been successfully tried in the Dar es Salaam survey is to ask the respondent to pass the phone to someone else in the household, for questions that cannot be answered by the respondent. Figure 6 presents responses to questions asked to children attending primary school about the presence of their teacher and the use of books while at school. From these student responses, about 17 per cent of teachers were absent during part of or the whole school day before the interview. These absenteeism rates are consistent with data obtained from school surveys in Tanzania. For example, a study by UWEZO, an NGO that monitors education in East Africa, found that almost 20 per cent of teachers were absent when their school was being assessed.[14]

Other as yet untried approaches can be imagined. For example, mobile phone interviews can be used to ask screening questions to identify respondents who qualify for in-depth interviews. In this way, qualitative and quantitative research methods can be integrated. Selected respondents can be asked to carry out specific monitoring tasks, for instance: What are the prices of certain goods? How much rain fell during the past week? Is the water source in the village functioning? Are specific drugs available at the health facilities? For another example of a program monitoring priority

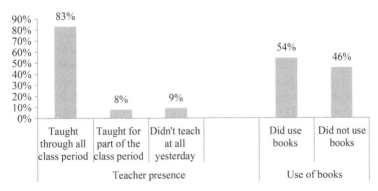

Figure 6.   Questions asked to primary school children about teacher presence and use of books while in school.
Source: Tanzania mobile phone survey, 2012.

that emerged over the course of the survey, in each health-focused round in Tanzania, respondents who had recently purchased malaria medications for themselves or a family member were asked to report on the price of a specific anti-malarial drug (Artemisinin Combination Therapy) for which a large public subsidy was provided, to see whether price reductions were being passed onto consumers. There are many possibilities for this kind of real time public service monitoring.

Apart from accountability, the survey can also provide a platform for randomised experiments to inform the efficacy of a program. Such an experiment could involve designing a randomly assigned encouragement message – such as a message aimed at increasing use of Vitamin A supplementation targeted at all children under five – to some of the families in the sample, to see if this leads to greater participation in the program.[15] In short, such a high frequency panel survey provides a potential platform for low cost survey or information distribution experiments. Of course, such information interventions could influence future responses and therefore "contaminate" the survey, and thus must be weighed against the long term goals of the survey.

Non-response and attrition

A key challenge for high frequency mobile phone panel surveys is non-response (when a respondent participates in some but not all rounds) and attrition (when a respondent drops out of the survey completely). Attrition and non-response are challenges for all panel surveys, but may be particularly an issue for mobile phone panels due to the number of times respondents are invited to participate in an interview.

In this section we rely on data from the Tanzania survey, as this is the longer running of the two surveys. In considering this survey, it is important to take into account that when it was initiated by Twaweza,[16] it was designed as a pilot, to be used to explore which technology would be most suited for a nationally representative mobile phone survey and to identify the systems needed to collect, process, analyse and disseminate survey data on a weekly basis. The focus was on experimenting with the mechanics of high frequency mobile phone surveys rather than on the minimisation of non-response and attrition, which – in addition to budget limitations – is why no mobile phones were distributed at baseline and why households without a mobile phone were allowed to drop out of the mobile part of the survey. The lessons from the pilot have been incorporated into a national mobile phone survey by the same NGO, known as "Sauti za Wananchi" ("The Citizen's Voice").[17] Bearing this in mind, there is still much that can be learned from the Dar es Salaam survey.

During the Tanzania baseline, households were assigned one of four technologies: interactive voice response (IVR), USSD (an approach allowing direct transmission of questions from a phone company server to the respondent's phone; this technology also works on low-end phones), WAP (web-based mobile phone surveys, suited for high-end phones with internet capability) and voice (a call centre).[18] Following the baseline and during the first seven rounds of the mobile phone panel, there were numerous problems with the different technologies: the fraction of respondents owning internet-enabled phones turned out to be very low (eliminating WAP), support from the phone company to run USSD was minimal (especially once mobile banking started to claim the available bandwidth) and IVR turned out to be a clumsy option as questions had to be broken down extensively to avoid too many response options. Voice did not have any of these drawbacks. Hence, after a relatively short period of time, live phone interviews became the technology of choice and all those who were reachable and had access to a mobile phone were put through a basic call centre, which consisted of a group of enumerators who each had multiple phones (one for each phone network, allowing cheaper within network calls) and a computer with a standard data entry screen.

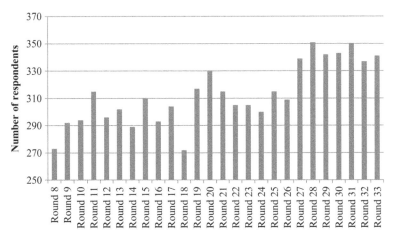

Figure 7.   Number of respondents per round (starting round 8).
Source: Tanzania mobile phone survey, 2012.

Following this decision, the survey ran for another 18 weekly rounds before it was discontinued by Twaweza. Management of the survey was then transferred to the World Bank, which had indicated interest in using the survey to generate feedback for its own programs. After six months of data collection by the World Bank, the survey was again transferred back to Twaweza for an additional six rounds. The implementation model was similar for both organisations: A small survey team was tasked with identifying questions, analysing the data, preparing and publishing reports on the findings and making the anonymised data publicly available. The survey firm that conducted the baseline, DataVision International, was contracted to set up a call center and carry out the mobile phone interviews.[19] Planning is underway, at the time of writing (June 2013), to transfer ultimate responsibility for the Dar es Salaam survey to a local newspaper.

So what does the Tanzania mobile phone survey tell us about attrition and non-response? On the negative side, there was a large initial burst of attrition. This can largely be attributed to the fact that, due to budgetary limitations, the survey team did not hand out phones. When the team initially visited and administered the baseline survey to 550 respondents, it was found that 418 of

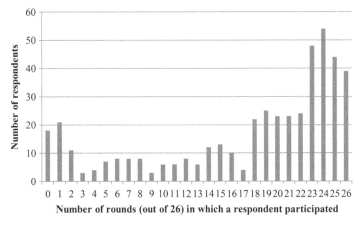

Figure 8.   Respondent participation in the 26 rounds of the Tanzania mobile phone survey.
Source: Tanzania mobile phone survey, 2012.

them owned a phone, 69 had a household member who owned a phone, six could access a phone through a friend and 57 had no phone or access to a phone. Obviously, owning a phone is different from using someone else's phone and when the mobile phone survey switched exclusively to live interviews in round 8, it was assessed that only 458 respondents could realistically be reached.[20]

Between round 8 (when the mobile phone panel began in earnest) and round 26 (before the survey was transferred to the World Bank) an average of 304 respondents, or 66 per cent, participated in the survey (Figure 7). After the survey had been put under World Bank management and oversight was tightened (but after a four months gap in interviews), the number of respondents increased to 343 (75 per cent of the sample).

So after 33 rounds of mobile interviews, the overall non-response rate is 25 per cent of the 458 households in the sample that had access to phones. The rate of attrition, defined as those amongst the 458 who did not respond at all to the mobile phone panel is much lower: only 4 per cent or 18 out of the 458 households never responded to a request for a mobile phone interview.

While we are not aware of comparable cases involving mobile phone panels, the rate of non-response and attrition is far from ideal – yet appears comparable to what has been attained by several non-mobile phone (face-to-face) panel surveys. For example, the Cebu Longitudinal Health and Nutritional survey in Philippines had almost 66 per cent attrition (cited in Baird, Hamory, and Miguel 2008), while Alderman et al. (2001) note that the Bolivian Preschool Program Evaluation Household Survey had 35 per cent attrition. The Kenya Ideational Change survey had 28 per cent attrition for women (and 41 per cent for couples) over a two year interval. In a similar vein, panel surveys that revisit respondents after extended intervals often have relatively high attrition; for example the Kagera Health and Development Survey lost 31 per cent of their respondents between 1994 and 2004. However, specially designed panels such as the Indonesia Family Life Panel or the Kenya Family Life panel, which place high priority on minimisation of attrition (through tracking of migrants, for example), have achieved much lower attrition rates: The Indonesia panel attrition rate was only 9–13 per cent over four separate survey waves (Thomas et al. 2010), while the Kenya Life Panel Survey had 17 per cent attrition over seven years (Baird, Hamory, and Miguel 2008), and the South Africa KIDS survey had 16 per cent attrition over five years. More recently in Tanzania, the National Panel Survey has made significant efforts to minimise attrition. As a result, the first two waves had an attrition rate of just 3 per cent. Low attrition is also possible with mobile phone surveys, as shown by Dillon (2012), who achieved an attrition rate of 2 per cent in a mobile phone survey in northwestern Tanzania. Cole and Fernando (2012) also achieve relatively low attrition (7.5 per cent) in a mobile phone follow up of an impact evaluation in Gujarat, India.

A class of surveys to which these mobile phone panels compare favorably is polling or opinion surveys, which increasingly use phones to collect information from individuals regarding their views or positions on a wide range of topics including elections, policy changes, cultural habits, and so on. According to Keeter et al. (2006), telephone survey researchers are increasingly finding it difficult to reach American households who use sophisticated screening technologies to minimise their participation in random digit dialing (RDD). For instance, between 1997 and 2003, for a sample of 1000 households chosen to participate in a standard five-day survey employing techniques used by most opinion polling organisations, contact rates dropped from 90 per cent to 79 per cent while the response rate declined from an already low rate of 37 per cent to 25 per cent (Keeter et al. 2006, Table 1). Among contacted households, cooperation (those who completed the questionnaire) declined from 43 per cent to 34 per cent. Similarly, in a comprehensive review of over 490 studies published in academic journals between 2000 and 2005 which used surveys, Baruch and Holtom (2008) found that on average, survey non-response rate when data was collected from individuals using phones, web or email was about 47 per cent. Steeh et al. (2001) report that non-response in the 1990s for two well-known random digit dialing surveys – University of Michigan's survey of consumer attitudes and the Georgia State Poll –

were 34 per cent and 63 per cent, respectively. Furthermore, typical telephone polls by media organisations reportedly have a response rate in the neighborhood of 20 per cent.

Thus, the Dar es Salaam survey looks problematic if interpreted as a high attrition panel – but more robust if viewed as a repeated (and reweighted) cross section. But we do not conclude that high frequency mobile phone surveys in similar settings are destined to have high attrition and therefore limited use as panels. As the next section will argue, the rate of non-response and attrition can be explained in large part by the considerable time lag between the baseline survey and the start of the mobile phone interviews, and the additional four-month lag when management of the survey was transferred to the World Bank. Furthermore, this pilot has generated many ideas about where there is room for improvement. Distributing phones and enhanced enumerator and respondent training, for example, would have likely avoided most of the initial reduction in the sample from 550 to 458. Distributing solar chargers to those with limited access to electricity would enhance response rates further: those with access to electricity answered on average in 18.6 rounds versus 16.4 for those without access to electricity. Even the choice of phone provider seems to matter, as those using the premium network (Vodacom) respondent significantly more often (20.1 times) than those using any of the other networks (16.9 times).

Twaweza applied these lessons in its recently launched nationwide mobile phone survey (Sauti za Wananchi) which this pilot was designed to inform, and has achieved less than 10 per cent attrition in its first several rounds. If this performance is maintained, it will be strong evidence that accurate mobile phone data collection at national level in sub-Saharan Africa can be done.[21]

Is the Tanzania mobile phone panel survey representative?

Attrition and non-response are particularly problematic when they occur in a non-random manner, potentially introducing bias into the sample. The most obvious source of bias in a survey like the one implemented in Dar es Salaam is that poorer households are less likely to own phones. This means that any survey reliant on already-owned phones (as the Dar es Salaam survey was) introduces some bias into the initial composition of the sample. Secondly, if poorer or richer households are more likely to drop out over time, then the sample may become more biased as the survey continues. These problems can be addressed. With a bigger budget and with the lessons learned from this pilot, for example, the current Tanzania national survey (Sauti za Wananchi) has distributed phones to all participants, and introduced other measures to reduce attrition such as distribution of solar chargers.[22]

Another set of measures needs to be used to minimise the second problem, which is the gradual bias that is introduced when households do not participate for other reasons. If attrition and non-response are truly random, then the representativeness of the post-attrition sample is comparable to that of the baseline sample, meaning that while sample size has decreased (and standard errors have increased), the point estimates of the follow-up survey are still unbiased estimates of the true population mean. If attrition and non-response are *non-random* and are associated with observable characteristics of respondents which have been recorded in the baseline survey, then it is a manageable problem and can be addressed by reweighting the remaining respondents by the inverse of the probability of attrition.[23] A final possibility is that attrition is non-random but associated with *unobservable* characteristics of respondents. In this case, attrition is quite harmful to the representativeness of the survey: since attrition is based on unobservable characteristics, the survey sample cannot be reweighted according to these (unknown) characteristics.[24] This is certainly possible in our survey, as in any panel survey, but it is essentially an untestable assertion. The question that we address in this section is whether, given the sizeable attrition and non-response in the Tanzania mobile phone survey, the follow-up survey rounds can still be considered representative. Given our detailed baseline survey, we use regression analysis to assess whether attrition is closely linked to observable demographic and behavioral characteristics, or whether it appears to be largely random.

Table 2 presents regression analysis of the determinants of attrition. In the three regressions presented below, the dependent variable is the number of rounds (out of 25) in which the household participated.[25] Column one presents a model including all 550 households visited in the baseline. In this model, economic status is a significant predictor of survey participation. Households without a phone, those using non-premium phone providers and those in the second poorest income quintile are significantly less likely to participate relative to households of median wealth.

In column two, when we restrict the regression to households that reported access to a phone in baseline and were thus kept in the mobile sample, we find that the impact of wealth is reduced. In this regression, location (living in rural Dar es Salaam) and using the premium provider remain significant, while the coefficients on the lower income quintiles are still negative, but are smaller than in the first regression and are no longer statistically significant.

In column 3, finally, the model is altered to include information about whether the respondent could actually be reached at the phone number that he or she had provided at baseline when the mobile survey started to exclusively use live interviews (during round 8).[26] Not being reachable may reflect many factors: a poor phone network, erratic access to electricity for phone charging or a simple mistake by enumerators in recording the phone number at baseline. This specification is included to show that if future mobile phone survey can avoid having "unreachable" respondents at the start (through careful training of enumerators and respondents to confirm phone numbers on the spot, and solutions to the phone charging problem), their follow-up samples are likely to remain representative. We draw this conclusion because once we account for the households which were unreachable from the first round, no other variables show up as statistically significant predicators of attrition.

The message we take from these regressions is that with distribution of mobile phones to non-phone owners and by taking steps to ensure a smooth transition from inclusion in the baseline to inclusion in the mobile survey, non-response can be significantly reduced and representativeness preserved.

Another important conclusion is that, for this survey to remain representative, it is necessary to reweight responses ex-post. Figure 9 illustrates how reweighting is able to largely restore the survey's representativeness by showing how the changing composition of the sample affects

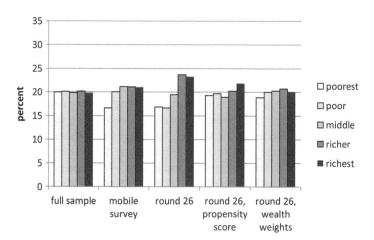

Figure 9. Changing wealth composition of sample.
Source: Tanzania mobile phone survey, 2012.

the per cent of households allocated to different wealth quintiles. The first set of bars presents the survey baseline (550 respondents) with the sample divided (by definition) equally among the five wealth quintiles: each quintile has exactly 20 per cent of the population. When we look at the breakdown across the 458 respondents that were included in the mobile phone survey, poor households are underrepresented. The distribution becomes more skewed towards wealthier households in round 26 (341 respondents). The fourth set of bars shows what the final distribution looks like once the mobile phone sample has been reweighted using a regression that generates a propensity score for participation based on a range of covariates including wealth quintiles, phone ownership, gender, age, urban residence and several other covariates. Reweighting observations by the inverse of the predicted probability of participation, it shows that the original wealth distribution is almost restored. The fifth set of bars show that the original sample wealth breakdown can be recovered completely (within 1 per cent) when the only variables included in the propensity score model are the wealth quintiles.

One conclusion that we draw from this is, that while we can never control for selection based on unobservables, reweighting based on observables should be a standard procedure after every survey round in a mobile phone survey.

Other aspects of data quality

Another concern that one might have about mobile phone interviews is that the respondent could change from one wave to the next. Evidence from the Dar es Salaam survey suggests that this does happen, minimally at first and to a greater degree as the survey progresses. Figure 10 displays data comparing respondents' age four rounds into the survey. It demonstrates that there is a strong correlation between the reported age of people selected at baseline and mobile phone respondents – but that some switching of respondents has also likely begun.

When the same exercise was repeated in round 32, 18 months into the survey, the amount of respondent switching had increased considerably, suggesting a need for more quality control by

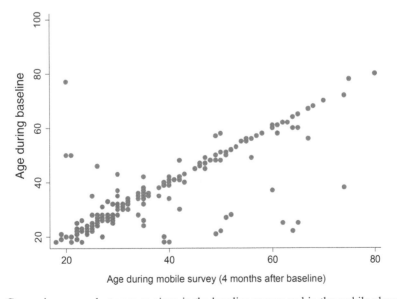

Figure 10. Comparing respondent ages as given in the baseline survey and in the mobile phone survey. Source: Dar es Salaam Baseline Survey and round 4 of the Tanzania mobile phone survey.

the call center to ensure that the respondent selected during the baseline is the one answering the phone (Figure 11). It is a good illustration of how high frequency surveys provide opportunities to identify data quality issues and to correct them in subsequent survey rounds. In this instance, the survey firm has been instructed to ensure that the original respondent answers the phone (when available) or to clearly indicate that the company are dealing with another adult replacing the original household member.

A change of respondents, incidentally, does not necessarily affect the representativeness of the survey if the relevant outcomes are at the household, rather than individual, level. When questions are asked about household characteristics such as access to electricity or water, for example, any adult should be able to answer. Insisting that the same respondent always answers the questions is likely to lead to non-response; there is a trade-off between non-response and insisting that the same respondent always answers. In fact, as long as a change of respondent is captured in the data, it could make sense for a mobile phone survey protocol to allow the original respondent to be replaced by another adult household member.

Finally, it is worth stressing that respondents also make errors. This is illustrated with responses to questions about food fortification in the Tanzania survey. In this round of the survey, baseline information was collected in preparation of a large food fortification program supported by the government and the World Bank. In Dar es Salaam at the time of the survey, almost all salt on sale was fortified (iodised) while wheat flour, maize flour and cooking oil were not. But when asked about whether each of these foods was fortified, significant fractions of responses stated that cooking oil (23%), wheat flour (9%) and maize flour (12%) were fortified, while in fact they were not (Figure 12). In the case of salt, some respondents mistakenly claimed that salt was not fortified (0.3%). Interestingly, no significant differences in errors could be observed between respondents with primary or secondary education, or between respondents who had and had not heard about food fortification. It reaffirms the need to remain vigilant when interpreting survey results.

Similarly, our attempt to update the asset index after 12 rounds met with considerable difficulties. Values for a number of durable consumer goods, such as radios, refrigerators, televisions and video players, were 10–20 percentage points higher when asked over the phone (Figure 13).[27]

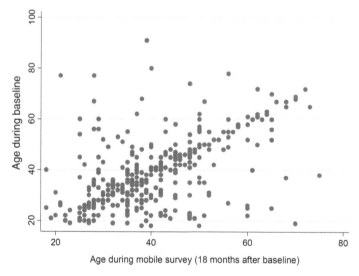

Figure 11.   Comparing respondent ages as given in the baseline survey and in the mobile phone survey. Source: Dar es Salaam Baseline Survey and round 25 of the mobile phone survey.

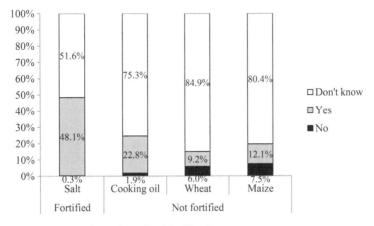

Figure 12. Responses to questions about food fortification.
Source: Tanzania mobile phone survey, 2012.

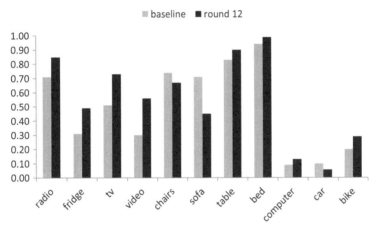

Figure 13. Household ownership of assets, Tanzania baseline survey versus mobile phone survey round 12.

Without a revisit to physically check the presence of these assets, it is impossible to tell whether this increase is due to economic growth and associated asset purchases or because respondents feel freer to put an aspirational spin on their family's wealth status when not observed personally by an enumerator. This suggests that the impact of the technology used when asking different types of survey questions on the responses obtained is an important area for further research.

Uses for the mobile phone survey data

In addition to tracking welfare changes, these mobile phone pilot surveys were intended to inform citizens about key facts about public life and therefore contribute to accountability. In keeping with this idea, substantial effort has been made to disseminate the data widely to ensure that the survey results were used by decision makers or for accountability purposes. Questions were identified with the purpose of making links to high profile government policies and development projects, or for their relevance to ongoing public policy issues and political controversies.

Once the data were collected, easy to understand, factual reports were prepared presenting the findings. These reports were disseminated through a dedicated website from which all survey data could be downloaded (www.listeningtodar.org). The reports were shared by email using a distribution list that includes journalists and other potentially interested parties. A Twitter account broadcasts the main findings (www.twitter.com/darmobilesurvey).

So does it work? The website itself attracts limited traffic and few people download the data available on the site. Attempts to attract media attention have been somewhat more successful. Reports produced have been discussed by NGOs[28] and in academia,[29] they have been disseminated by bloggers[30] and have led to various newspaper articles. It is hard to assess what happens once information is published, but there is an indication that, in some cases, the information is "received" by those responsible for results. For example, the managing director of Tanzania's electricity company felt compelled to explain to the media why so many households connected to electricity are experiencing power cuts and what his company is doing about them.[31]

Once published, information on certain topics travels fast and far. A brief about food price increases was used in a front page article in Tanzania's *The Citizen* newspaper, was picked up by other newspaper such as the *Rwandan Times*[32] and ended up in the World Bank's 2012 *Global Monitoring Report*.

Information also tends to go in unexpected directions. A brief about the limited increase in water connections in Dar es Salaam despite a large scale investment program in the water sector received media attention because of the discrepancy it showed between the data reported by the mobile phone survey and official government statistics.[33]

While the survey briefs have found an audience in some cases, what lessons can we draw from actively disseminating multiple rounds of raw data? One lesson is that providing access to the raw data is far from sufficient. Prepackaged analysis and easily accessible reporting on the data makes dissemination and uptake much easier. As with the discussion of attrition, however, this pilot has generated ideas to be exploited in future iterations of mobile phone surveys in Tanzania and elsewhere. Such ideas include more active social media promotion, institutionalised links to popular and widely accessible venues for public debate such as (for example) popular radio news call-in shows, and relationships with political and bureaucratic actors with interests in the indicators and outcomes being measured. All this is needed if the objective is to ensure that the data, once collected, is utilised by a wide range of people.

Cost effectiveness of mobile phone surveys

How cost effective are mobile phone surveys? Our data give some indication of the marginal cost of a mobile phone survey. The call center contracted to implement 12 survey rounds did so at a rate of $1,400 per round. If one adds the cost for consultants to maintain a website, supervise data collection and to analyse the data, the marginal cost per round increases to $2,500. Given that these rounds averaged 343 respondents, this comes to about $4.10–$7.30 per interview. Dillon (2012) notes a relatively similar marginal cost per survey: $6.98.

In addition to these marginal costs, one needs to include the cost of a baseline, which will often be between $50 and $150 per respondent, depending on the complexity of the survey and the distances that have to be covered.

Whether this is cost effective depends on the purpose of the survey. The ability to carry out an entire survey in Dar es Salaam and to report on its results for $2,500 seems quite cost effective. But if one keeps in mind that the typical round in the Dar es Salaam survey asks 17 questions (with a maximum of 44), then the cost per question is about $0.42. This is relatively high when compared to face-to-face surveys, so if the intention is to ask many questions it may be more cost effective to opt for a face-to-face interview.

Not surprisingly, costs will vary from country to country because the costs of a baseline survey, equipment, utilities, calling rates and labor differ. Our experience with these pilots and other phone surveys in other countries suggest that for about $300,000, it is possible to conduct a baseline and collect 12 rounds of data (monthly panel) for 2,000 households. More specifically, these costs break down as follows: (1) set up costs (baseline and distribution of phones) $150,000; (2) equipment (computers, solar chargers) $60,000; (3) call center staff (12 months) $24,000; and (4) implementation (network calling charges, small compensation to households, phones) $80,000. If the survey goes on for longer than a year, the second year costs become substantially lower.

Conclusion

The evidence presented demonstrates that mobile phone panel surveys have potential to provide rapid feedback and to address existing data gaps at limited expense. Mobile phone panel surveys should not be considered substitutes for household surveys; rather they will often make use of an existing household survey to serve as baseline. Moreover mobile phone surveys are not the right platform for lengthy interviews; when interviews are lengthy, face-to-face interviews are probably more cost effective. But a national statistical system that used a combination of both methods could be a substantial improvement to the status quo.

The evidence from the Tanzania and Sudan surveys suggests that mobile phone surveys can collect quality data in a timely manner. The Tanzania panel survey pointed towards the importance of putting in place mechanisms that avoid attrition right from the implementation of the baseline. Our work suggests that once households are included in the mobile phone survey, they are likely to remain in the survey. The work also suggests that because of their high frequency, quality control of mobile phone surveys is dynamic and issues identified in one round can be corrected in the next.

Finally, the success of mobile phone panels will not only be measured by whether relevant and quality data is being produced in a timely manner, but also by how many people actually use the results from the surveys. Our work suggests that making the data publicly available is not sufficient. Analysis and active, strategic dissemination are needed to ensure that data finds its way into the public domain.

Disclaimer

All authors work for the World Bank. The findings, interpretations and conclusions expressed in this paper are entirely those of the authors. They do not necessarily represent the views of the International Bank for Reconstruction and Development/World Bank and its affiliated organisations, or those of the Executive Directors of the World Bank or the governments they represent.

Acknowledgements

This paper has benefited from support from the PSIA Trust Fund (TF099681), the BNPP Trust Fund, which financed some of the Afrobarometer questions on ownership and uses of mobile phones, and the Demand for Good Governance group.

Notes

1. The lessons learned from these pilots are currently being incorporated into mobile phone panel surveys that are planned in a number of African countries.
2. http://ureport.ug

3. These figures are from the 2004/2005 DHS, the 2007/2008 Tanzania HIV/AIDS and Malaria Indicator Survey; the 2010 DHS, and the 2011/2012 HIV/AIDS and Malaria Indicator Survey.
4. A total of 61 per cent send or receive a text message at least once a day and a remarkable 23 per cent send or receive money or pay a bill via mobile phone at least once a day.
5. Blumberg and Luke (2008). For an example of a reputable survey firm applying these approaches see: http://www.ipsos-na.com/download/pr.aspx?id=11397. Note also that the accuracy of landline only polling may be degrading over time, see http://fivethirtyeight.blogs.nytimes.com/2012/11/10/which-polls-fared-best-and-worst-in-the-2012-presidential-race/.
6. All references to dollars in this paper are to US dollars.
7. Information about this project can be found at http://siteresources.worldbank.org/SOCIAL PROTECTION/Resources/280558-1138289492561/2158434-1332878435565/RSR-L2L-PPT_19March 2012.pdf
8. Since this approach aims to create representative samples of the adult population, it necessitates the random identification of a respondent within the household.
9. Smith et al. (2011) provide an overview of different ways to gather data using mobile phones.
10. Surprisingly, response rates were slightly lower for households that received more compensation.
11. Data and reports from the Tanzania pilot survey are available online and can be downloaded from: www.listeningtodar.org/
12. Remarkably in both Sudan and Tanzania the amount of the reward did not have a discernible impact on response rates (see Table 2 for evidence from Tanzania).
13. This raises another issue for future research: whether it is possible to track changes in consumption by using poverty mapping techniques (Elbers, Lanjouw, and Lanjouw 2003) with a set of correlates that is more sensitive to changes in consumption levels than assets which is currently used in poverty mapping.
14. See http://in2eastafrica.net/tanzania-teacher-absenteeism-fuelling-poor-education-uwezo-study/
15. An example of such an experiment involved a partnership between the Dar es Salaam mobile phone survey, the NGO Helen Keller International (HKI), and the Tanzania Ministry of Health, which tried to maximise the coverage of Vitamin A Supplementation (VAS) days, which are held bi-annually in Dar es Salaam in July 2013. Half of the families in the survey were given an encouragement message about the importance of Vitamin A supplementation and the upcoming event, and the other half a placebo message encouraging other unrelated healthy behaviors.
16. Two of the authors worked at Twaweza at the time.
17. See http://twaweza.org/go/sauti-za-wananchi-english
18. Because of its limitations SMS was not considered.
19. Reports and data produced, including the baseline data, can be obtained from: www.listeningtodar.org
20. Some respondents could not be reached either because their numbers had been captured incorrectly, or because they never seemed to have their phones on.
21. http://twaweza.org/uploads/files/Sauti-za-Wananchi-English.pdf
22. http://twaweza.org/uploads/files/Sauti-za-Wananchi-English.pdf
23. Alderman et al. (2001) suggest that even where attrition is non-random, key parameter estimates are often not affected, using examples from Bolivia, Kenya and South Africa. Fitzgerald, Gottschalk and Moffitt (1998) draw similar conclusions from the US-based Panel Survey on Income Dynamics, as does Falaris (2003) with respect to surveys in Peru, Côte d'Ivoire and Vietnam (cited in Thomas et al. 2010).
24. Beegle, De Weerdt, and Dercon (2011) suggest that attrition in developing country settings is likely to be related to unobservable traits, in part because attrition is often linked to migration.
25. This is not dependent on functional form. For example, the results are not substantially different when the dependent variable is a binary variable which takes a value of one when the respondent has participated in more than half of all survey rounds, or when probit is used instead of the OLS linear probability model.
26. In this regression, round 1 is used to determine persistence in non-response. To avoid autocorrelation, this round is omitted from the sum of rounds in which the household participated.
27. Discrepancies are present both with and without reweighting of results to reflect attrition.
28. http://blog.daraja.org/2012/02/independent-monitoring-of-dars-water.html
29. http://www.viewtz.com/2012/02/13/world-bank-cause-of-economic-hardships/
30. http://godfreynnko.blogspot.com/2012/02/most-citizens-do-not-know-if-their-food.html
31. http://www.ippmedia.com/frontend/index.php?l=39618 and http://www.ippmedia.com/frontend/index.php?l=39551
32. http://www.newtimes.co.rw/news/index.php?i=14892&a=11334
33. http://www.thecitizen.co.tz/sunday-citizen/-/20105-govt-figures-on-access-to-clean-water-inflated

References

Alderman, H., J. Behrman, H.-P. Kohler, J. A. Maluccio, and S. Watkins. 2001. "Attrition in Longitudinal Household Survey Data." *Demographic Research, Max Planck Institute for Demographic Research* 5 (4): 79–124.

Baird, S., J. Hamory, and E. Miguel. 2008. "Tracking, Attrition and Data Quality in the Kenyan Life Panel Survey Round 1." University of California Berkeley: CIDER Working Paper.

Baruch, Y. and B. C. Holtom. 2008. "Survey Response Rate Levels and Trends in Organizational Research." *Human Relations* 61 (8): 1139–1160.

Beegle, K., J. De Weerdt, and S. Dercon. 2011. "Migration and Economic Mobility in Tanzania: Evidence from a Tracking Survey." *The Review of Economics and Statistics*, 93 (3): 1010–1033.

Blumberg, S. J., and J. V. Luke. 2008. *Wireless Substitution: Early Release of Estimates from the National Health Interview Survey, July–December 2008*. Atlanta, GA: Centers for Disease Control.

Cole, S. A. and A. N. Fernando. 2012. "The Value of Advice: Evidence from Mobile Phone-Based Agricultural Extension." Harvard Business School Working Papers 13–047, Harvard Business School.

Dar es Salaam Baseline Survey. n.d. Twaweza, Dar es Salaam, Tanzania.

Demographic and Health Survey (DHS). 2004/2005. United Republic of Tanzania, National Bureau of Statistics, Dar es Salaam, Tanzania.

Demographic and Health Survey (DHS). 2010. United Republic of Tanzania, National Bureau of Statistics, Dar es Salaam, Tanzania.

Dillon, B. 2012. "Using Mobile Phones to Collect Panel Data in Developing Countries." *Journal of International Development*, 24 (4): 518–527.

Elbers, C., J. O. Lanjouw, and P. Lanjouw 2003. "Micro-Level Estimation of Poverty and Inequality." *Econometrica* 71 (1): 355–364.

Falaris, E. M. 2003. "The Effect of Survey Attrition in Longitudinal Surveys: Evidence from Peru, Côte d'Ivoire and Vietnam." *Journal of Development Economics* 70 (1): 133–157.

Fitzgerald, J., P. Gottschalk, and R. Moffitt. 1998. "An Analysis of Sample Attrition in Panel Data: The Michigan Panel Study of Income Dynamics." *Journal of Human Resources* 33 (2): 251–299.

Jerven, M. 2013. *Poor Numbers: How We Are Misled By African Development Statistics and What to Do About It*. Ithaca, NY: Cornell University Press.

Keeter, S., C. Kennedy, M. Dimock, J. Best, and P. Craighill. 2006. "Gauging the Impact of Growing Non-Response on Estimates from a National Random Digit Dial Telephone Survey." *Public Opinion Quarterly* 70 (5): 759–779.

Lynn, Peter, and Olena Kaminska. 2013. "The Impact of Mobile Phones on Survey Measurement Error." *Public Opinion Quarterly* 77 (2): 586–605.

McKenzie, D. 2012. "Beyond Baseline and Follow-up: The Case for More T in Experiments." *Journal of Development Economics*, 99 (2): 210–221.

National Baseline Household Survey. 2009. Republic of South Sudan, National Bureau of Statistics, Juba, South Sudan.

Scott, J. 1998. *Seeing Like a State*. New Haven, CT: Yale University Press.

Smith, G., I. MacAuslan, S. Butters, and M. Tromme. 2011. *New Technology Enhancing Humanitarian Cash and Voucher Programming. Research Report Commissioned by CalP*. New York: CalP (Cash Learning Partnership).

Steeh, C., N. Kirgis, B. Cannon, and J. Dewitt. 2001. "Are They Really as Bad as They Seem? Non-Response Rates at the end of the Twentieth Century." *Journal of Official Statistics* 17 (2): 227–247.

Tanzania National Panel Survey. 2010/11. United Republic of Tanzania, National Bureau of Statistics, Dar es Salaam, Tanzania.

Tanzania HIV/AIDS and Malaria Indicator Survey. 2007/2008. United Republic of Tanzania, National Bureau of Statistics, Dar es Salaam, Tanzania.

Tanzania HIV/AIDS and Malaria Indicator Survey. 2011/2012. United Republic of Tanzania, National Bureau of Statistics, Dar es Salaam, Tanzania.

Thomas, D., F. Witoelar, E. Frankenberg, B. Sikoki, J. Strauss, S. Cecep, and W. Suriastini. 2010. "Cutting the Costs of Attrition: Results from the Indonesian Family Life Survey." BREAD (Bureau for Research and Economic Analysis of Development) Working Paper No 259.

Tomlinson, M., W. Solomon, Y. Singh, T. Doherty, M. Chopra, P. Ijumba, A. C. Tsai, and D. Jackson. 2009. "The Use of Mobile Phones as a Data Collection Tool: A Report from a Household Survey in Peru." *BMC Medical Informatics and Decision Making* 9 (51). doi:10.1186/1472-6947-9-51.

Zwane, A., J. Zinman, E. Van Dusen, W. Pariente, C. Null, E. Miguel, M. Kremer, D. S. Karlan, R. Hornbeck, X. Giné, et al. 2011. "Being Surveyed Can Change Behavior and Related Parameter Estimates." *Proceedings of the National Academy of Sciences* 108 (5): 1821–1826.

Index